# Philosophy and Kafka

# Philosophy and Kafka

Brendan Moran and Carlo Salzani

LEXINGTON BOOKS
*Lanham • Boulder • New York • Toronto • Plymouth, UK*

Published by Lexington Books
A wholly owned subsidiary of The Rowman & Littlefield Publishing Group, Inc.
4501 Forbes Boulevard, Suite 200, Lanham, Maryland 20706
www.rowman.com

10 Thornbury Road, Plymouth PL6 7PP, United Kingdom



British Library Cataloguing in Publication Information Available

**Library of Congress Cataloging-in-Publication Data**
Moran, Brendan.
Philosophy and Kafka / Brendan Moran and Carlo Salzani.
pages cm
Includes index.
ISBN 978-0-7391-8089-1 (cloth : alk. paper) — ISBN 978-0-7391-8090-7 (electronic)
1. Kafka, Franz, 1883–1924—Philosophy. 2. Literature—Philosophy. I. Salzani, Carlo, 1972– II. Title.
PT2621.A26Z7767 2013
833'.912—dc23 2013004768

The paper used in this publication meets the minimum requirements of American National Standard for Information Sciences—Permanence of Paper for Printed Library Materials, ANSI/NISO Z39.48-1992.

Printed in the United States of America

To A. and L. with gratitude

# Contents

# Introduction

*Brendan Moran and Carlo Salzani*

This book on philosophy and Kafka is a beginning. A book on "Philosophy and . . ." is always a beginning, or at least never an end. To an unusual extent, however, Kafka's writings indicate, sometimes even thematize, that we are not going to finish our efforts to interpret them. In this sense, they could seem unusually philosophical: They are openly resisting conclusive readings. More than most subjects that might be studied, Kafka's writings recall for us that we can conceivably always return to them and begin again. This book on philosophy and Kafka is a beginning, then, and must acknowledge that all its topics remain open for discussion.

The book emerged from a group of people interested in writing on the topic, and finding that there had not really been a book on it. The research on Franz Kafka is ever-expanding, and continuously generates interest and new works. "Philosophical" questions and topics are obviously central to Kafka-scholarship, and the literature on the subject abounds, but usually in a dispersed form (journal articles, book chapters), or in book-long studies that focus, however, on particular issues, interpretations, or—as is often the case—on philosophical thinkers such as Heraclitus, Søren Kierkegaard or Friedrich Nietzsche.[1] Although the majority of the publications on Kafka focus on biographical aspects or on literary interpretation that does not presume to be "philosophical," a number of book-length studies have indeed appeared in which the question of the relation between philosophy and Kafka is central. Some of them focus, in one way or another, on theoretical or philosophical aspects of Kafka's work, such as time and history, violence, ethics, and freedom.[2] Other studies confront Kafka's thought and work with a philosophical tradition, or analyze his work through a perspective such as psychoanalysis, phenomenology, deconstruction, or "post-structuralism."[3] Other works focus on particular philosophical readings or on particular readings that might be construed as "philosophical," such as those by Walter Benjamin or Jacques Derrida.[4] Finally, some studies attempt a philosophical take on certain aspects of Kafka's work.[5] The present volume is unique, however, in bringing together a considerable variety of essays that focus on major philosophical readings of, or on philosophical issues present in, Kafka's writings. More specifically, the novelty of the volume is that it focuses specifically on the "philosophical" while bringing together a fairly wide range of such perspectives on Kafka. With no claim to offer more than a beginning, the present volume opens to a multifarious constellation of readings, commentaries, affinities, and themes that may be associated with both philosophy and Kafka's work.

It is surprising perhaps that—to our knowledge at least—there has not yet been a book with this title, *Philosophy and Kafka*. After all, Kafka's writings often evolve into discourses or analyses that could be included in works even very conventionally deemed "philosophical." Perhaps the title *Philosophy and Kafka* has, however, seemed too grandiose—too grand a title for a book possibly to do justice to it. Insofar as conscious decisions played a role in our selection of the title, one reason has been to encourage more consideration of this topic that has already been shown to be so rich in potential. The title was chosen over "Kafka and Philosophy" at least partly to encourage contributors not to make philosophy a mere appendage of their analyses, but rather to give a sense in which something that could be called "philosophy" could be, or perhaps could not be, at work in Kafka's texts.

For this purpose, there has been no wish and no attempt to provide for the volume a definition of philosophy—each contribution implicitly or explicitly works with different conceptions of philosophy. It might seem incumbent on the editors of a book titled *Philosophy and Kafka* that they define Kafka's *literature*, or at least define what they might mean by *philosophy*. We have decided against doing that. The book contains essays that might, in some cases, venture a response to those questions concerning philosophy and Kafka's literature; it does not seem advisable for us to preempt the volume-essays with our own responses to those questions. Nor do we wish to seem to be elevating philosophy in relation to literature. The volume arises from a sense that philosophy emerges from, can be a way into, or a way of considering, much of Kafka's writings. The hope is simply that the contributions might demonstrate or consider this in an interesting way—a way of interest both to those reading Kafka or more broadly concerned with literature, and to many of those who consider themselves to be doing, or to be interested in, philosophy.

After all, something called philosophy has shown interest in, and offered readings of, Kafka's work at least from the time his novels were published posthumously in the mid-1920s by Max Brod (Benjamin's interest was awakened with the much earlier appearance of some of the stories), and the outpouring of such readings continues unabated. The readership of Kafka, insofar as it has been publishing its reflections, has included many who associate Kafka's work with figures or currents of philosophy such as Kierkegaard, Nietzsche, and existentialism, but also many other authors and streams from the tradition of "philosophy." Prominent readers of Kafka include some of the most read authors in twentieth century and contemporary "philosophy": Walter Benjamin, Albert Camus, Theodor W. Adorno, Hannah Arendt, Gilles Deleuze and Félix Guattari, Jacques Derrida, Giorgio Agamben. Not only do Kafka's stories and novels contain excurses that could themselves sit readily in a work more strictly associated with philosophy, but there are also his marvelous aphorisms and various excurses in the *Nachlass* that are so often reminiscent of those by Nietzsche, however different they might be from Nietzsche's own texts. Contributions in the present volume also find comparably important passages in Kafka's letters and diary entries. Kafka's stories and novels have, in any case, always invited association with writings readily identified as philosophy; Kafka himself was fairly preoccupied with Kierkegaard at times, and the reception of his works continued this preoccupation from the early days of Max Brod's studies to today. This association of Kafka and Kierkegaard will occasionally be discussed in the present volume. The reception of Kafka's stories and novels has, in any case, drawn on the philosophical tradition more than is the case for many "literary" writers.

This volume arises very specifically from a workshop held on August 4, 2010, for the twelfth international conference of ISSEI (the International Society for the Study of European Ideas) in Ankara, where about half of the essays were first presented in shorter form as papers. Other contributions were subsequently sought and added in order to enrich and better provide a range of perspectives that have arisen or can arise with regard to Kafka's oeuvre. The volume obviously cannot claim completeness. As editors of the volume, we have sought, however, to provide a varied and manifold indication of readings and issues that could arise under the rubric of *Philosophy and Kafka*.

This priority of variety informs, therefore, the composition of the volume itself. Some essays focus on commentaries on Kafka's work that either demonstrate or claim something about philosophy: commentaries by Benjamin, Adorno, Arendt, Deleuze and Guattari, Derrida, Agamben. In their ensemble, the essays signify some of the perspectives from which Kafka's work has been analyzed by those working in philosophy. Other essays consider the possible relevance of certain philosophical outlooks for examining Kafka's writings: Kafka is considered in relation to Socrates, Spinoza, Kant, Kierkegaard, Nietzsche, Heidegger, Wittgenstein, Blanchot, and Levinas. Finally, yet other essays discuss Kafka's writings in terms of a specific philosophical theme, such as communication and subjectivity, language and meaning, knowledge and truth, the human/animal divide, justice, anxiety, law, the sublime, mimesis. This summary division into "groupings" only aims at presenting a broad picture of the volume; the mentioned themes, motifs, and interpretations obviously mingle to the point that a number of contributions could figure under any such grouping.

We have simply endeavored to present essays for which an implicit, and sometimes explicit, concern is the relationship of literature and philosophy. More precisely, the essays implicitly or explicitly explore the question of the philosophical significance of a literature such as Kafka's. Rather than providing biographical, historical, theological, literary-critical or stylistic accounts, the volume is an attempt to put together a large number of perspectives and expositions in which philosophy figures in the consideration of Kafka. It is hoped that the essays also thereby indicate some ways in which Kafka's writings are a rich nexus for considering various conceptions of the relationship of literature and philosophy. In this regard, the volume has four specific purposes.

One goal of the volume is to present new and original essays focusing on specific philosophical commentaries on Kafka: Brendan Moran's contribution concentrates on aspects of Walter Benjamin's reading; Brian O'Connor's essay provides an overview of the importance of Kafka in Adorno's aesthetics; Isak Winkel Holm's essay compares Kafka's outlook with Hannah Arendt's readings and theories; Ronald Bogue addresses the significance of Kafka in Deleuze's work; Paul Alberts considers Derrida's reading; Carlo Salzani elaborates Kafka's importance for Agamben's philosophy.

A second goal of the volume is to examine ways in which Kafka's oeuvre raises questions that are pertinent to philosophical theories and systems of the past: Andrew Russ relates Kant's system to Kafka's "negative aesthetics"; Peter Schwenger uses Levinas's and Blanchot's theories to approach Kafka's mode of writing; Dimitris Vardoulakis draws on Spinoza's *Theologico-Political Treatise* to examine freedom and law in *The Trial*; Paul Alberts compares Hans Kelsen's positivist theory of law with Kafka's (and Derrida's) rendering of the problem of law; Brendan Moran includes consideration of Kafka's work in relation to Kierkegaardian-Heideggerian anxiety and Levinas's ethics; and Karen Zumhagen-Yekplé compares Kafka's work with Wittgenstein's philosophical outlook and rhetorical modes.

A third goal of the volume is to consider philosophical insights that Kafka's works may themselves offer. A number of essays thus examine Kafka's writings in terms of specific philosophical themes: Kevin Sweeney analyzes the question of personal identity and communication in "The Metamorphosis"; Rainer Nägele discusses the issue of knowledge and truth in "Investigations of a Dog"; Paul Haacke and Chris Danta, in their respective essays, analyze the human/animal divide—and its biopolitical implications—in some short stories; Dimitris Vardoulakis explores the intertwining of freedom and law in *The Trial*; and Karen Zumhagen-Yekplé considers Kafka on the question of what might transcend language and logic.

Finally, a fourth goal of the volume is to explore the relationship of literature or poetry with philosophy. This theme obviously underlies, in various and distinct ways and forms, all of the essays in the volume. It takes, however, a more central position in certain contributions: Rainer Nägele is concerned with a definite "knowledge" that is presented in "Investigations of a Dog"; Andrew Russ discusses Kafka's literature as a uniting of the noumenal and the phenomenal in a sublime that is barely conceivable in a Kantian framework; Dimitris Vardoulakis analyzes Spinozist law and freedom in *The Trial*; Brendan Moran proposes that the heterogeneous physicality in Kafka's writings involves an attentiveness often not possible for religion, ontology, and ethics; Peter Schwenger discusses the undecidable element as the contribution of Kafka's writing to philosophical thinking; and Karen Zumhagen-Yekplé argues for the ethical and philosophical significance of a mode of writing, like that of Kafka and Wittgenstein, which pushes language to its limits and opens up new exegetical spaces for the readers.

The remainder of this introduction will be devoted to providing more detail concerning the essays and the way in which they have been assembled for the volume.

## Philosophical Investigations

The essays under the title "Philosophical Investigations" unite in their exploration of Kafka's texts in relation to a specific idea or figure in the tradition of philosophy. These philosophical ideas or figures are nonetheless very heterogeneous. They span from Socratic ignorance to Spinozist ethic, from the Kantian sublime to Wittgenstein's style, from the question of personal identity to the relation between insomnia and writing.

For Rainer Nägele's "I Don't Want to Know that I Know: The Inversion of Socratic Ignorance in the Knowledge of the Dogs," Western thought is more or less influenced by the Socratic knowledge that we know we do not know. This essential Socratic virtue and ideal of not knowing is the precondition of all knowledge, the virtue and the ideal that drives the determination of provisional certainties. On the basis of the late fragmentary text by Kafka that Max Brod published under the title "Forschungen eines Hundes" ("Investigations of a Dog"), Nägele explores the possibility that this modest proposal, "I know that I do not know," could be a primordial lie of Western knowledge, indeed a denial of an unbearable knowledge. The unbearable knowledge is a truth that we all know and yet somehow deny. Adapting Nietzsche's view that most—if not all—humans want to know anything but the truth, Nägele proposes that Kafka's "Investigations of a Dog" concerns an unbearable knowledge common to all and admitted by none. Kafka's dog barks after that knowledge that all have, yet no one can or will pronounce. In this quest, the dog goes to the limit of life, as do other determined figures—such as students—in various stories by Kafka. Whereas Socrates is after the ideas that we all purportedly have and can at any time be brought to light with the right method, the knowledge enigmatically displacing Kafka's texts—not only the story of this dog—is everywhere present. It is a dislocated secret in all surfaces. Kafka's dog festers on his question about the undisclosed knowledge that is had by all. The story thereby arrives at a great paradox: The knowledge had and borne by all can be touched only by every single individual. The dog's question is each individual's question of life (*Lebensfrage*). If we could accept this Kafkan truth, Nägele proposes, we could better live together.

Also with an emphasis on a known but rarely acknowledged freedom that is the ultimate law, Dimitris Vardoulakis's "Kafka's Empty Law: Laughter and Freedom in *The Trial*" draws on Spinoza in order to consider the law in Kafka's *The Trial*. Like Deleuze, Vardoulakis notes an intellectual affinity between Spinoza and Kafka. Spinoza's *Tractatus Theologico-Politicus* and Kafka's *The Trial* are concerned with a freedom that is an empty law requiring not submissive obedience but rather rebellion against attempts to fill the emptiness. For Spinoza, the law's emptiness signifies its liberatory potential. Vardoulakis adapts this aspect of Spinoza's outlook to suggest that laughter is an expression of freedom in the world of *The Trial.* Humor draws on the freedom that is an omnipotent and omnipresent empty law. Adapting Deleuze and Guattari, Vardoulakis portrays Kafka's humor as *immanent* in Josef K.'s failures. K's failure to live up to ostensibly transcendent claims can be laughable, and—in Kafka's world—such laughter is the conduit to freedom. In Vardoulakis's reading of the priest's story about the gatekeeper and the man from the country (also known as the separate story "Before the Law"), the gatekeeper suspends access to the law so that the law can remain open. The gatekeeper functions as Spinoza's figure of the philosopher, whose role is to resist any stultifying obedience. For Vardoulakis, it is as if the gatekeeper is conveying to the man from the country that it might be best to desist from submissively waiting for an entrance to the law and instead to rebel. Such a rebellion would be in accord with the Spinozan admonition to stop seeing the empty law as a tool that leads to resigned obedience.

In Andrew Russ's "A Kafkan Sublime: Dark Poetics on the Kantian Philosophy," there is a somewhat related reflection on Kafka as a writer who may thaw animosities of literature and philosophy. Russ notes such a thawing in Kierkegaard, Nietzsche, and the elaborate crossovers in literature and philosophy throughout the twentieth century, but he is specifically interested in Kafka's usage of philosophical challenges in his fictions. Russ thus reads Kafka's covert version of the sublime as corresponding to what Jean-François Lyotard calls the sublime as a "spasming" of reason. Kafka's major characters experience this *spasming* in themselves, their institutions, their environments, and their societies. There is a violent oscillation of limitation and limitlessness, the depths and the lofty, servitude and domination, fear and hubris. There is no reconciliation of the eternal and the finite. The incommensurability that characterizes Kant's critical project as an opportunity for humility, but also for a kind of elevation of the human being, is turned by Kafka into a pervasive and unresolved wound. The result—however unwittingly—is a parodying of the Kantian sublime by the Kafkan sublime. According to Russ, this reversal of Kantian elevation into Kafkan devastation is to be found in most of Kafka's narratives. In contrast with Kant's epistemic and moral presumptions, Kafka—Russ proposes—is something like an ontologist of the human situation in which morality and knowledge have been exhausted. The promise of the modern, which Kant tries to prepare in epistemology, ethics, and aesthetics, collapses in Kafka's lampooning of the hopes placed in this promise.

The question of the ethics of writing is also central to Karen Zumhagen-Yekplé's "The Everyday's Fabulous Beyond: Nonsense, Parable, and the Ethics of the Literary in Kafka and Wittgenstein." Through a comparative reading of Kafka's short piece "On Parables" ("*Von den Gleichnissen*") and Wittgenstein's *Tractatus Logico-Philosophicus*, both written in 1922—and with the aid of the latter's "Lecture on Ethics"—Zumhagen-Yekplé pursues the philosophical significance of the two authors' rhetorical modes of riddle, irony, and nonsensical expressions. The two texts, she argues, are marked by absence—that is, their philosophical or ethical point is made through what is *not* in them, rather than through any explicit statement or argumentation. More than "saying" or "teaching" anything, these texts entail an interpretive challenge and leave it up to the readers to figure out how to learn something from that absence. They open thereby a space for continuing the exegetical work, which is also a space for ethics, since, for Wittgenstein, ethics is the "running-up against the limits of language." In a sort of exegetical double movement, Zumhagen-Yekplé interprets Wittgenstein's *Tractatus* through the lens of Kafka's piece in order to illuminate the role that imaginative language plays in the book's overall aim, and reads "On Parables" in relation to Wittgenstein's philosophical method, his views on ethics and nonsense, in order to unfold its hidden ethical potential. Both texts are exemplary of an engagement with literature and philosophy that challenges the readers' attitude toward everyday language and life and points in the direction of a frustrated—but nonetheless essential—yearning for transcendence.

Developing further some of his previous work, Kevin Sweeney—in "'You're nobody 'til somebody loves you': Communication and the Social Destruction of Subjectivity in Kafka's *Metamorphosis*"—examines the way in which Gregor Samsa's transformation into an insect gradually erodes his family's love and emotional support for him, and thereby challenges his status as a person. Sweeney uses the expression, "personal identity," in "the traditional philosophical sense": It pertains to a relationship of sameness or identity between temporally distinct stages of a human being's life whereby one would say that the individual is the same person. Sweeney contends that *The Metamorphosis* could be read as the scene of a clash between competing theories concerning personhood and non-personhood. The first third of the novella especially lends itself to a Lockean-Cartesian theory of personhood whereby personal identity with an earlier self is established; notwithstanding his transformed physical body, Gregor is reflectively conscious not only of his present consciousness but also of his earlier experiences. In the second section of the novella, however, involuntary insect-like behaviors occur more often, and this is where Sweeney detects the prevalence of the Behaviorist perspective that relies on publicly observable behavior to suggest Gregor is ceasing to be a person and has been transformed into an insect being. Sweeney's reading leans, however, toward Social-Constructionism, for which a social group or community has the power to grant or withdraw the status of personhood. Sweeney proposes that a Social-Constructionist reading is especially helpful for interpreting the final third of the novella, where the human beings closest to Gregor—Gregor's family—finally decide that he is not Gregor anymore and can be confiscated. Sweeney concludes, nonetheless, that no theory reigns in any part of the novella, which provides too much ambiguity and confusion to be entirely submitted to any theory of "personal identity."

Such ambiguity and confusion regarding personal identity come to the forefront as Peter Schwenger's "Kafka's Insomnia" examines Kafka's writings by drawing especially on Emmanuel Levinas and Maurice Blanchot but also on others, such as Maurice Merleau-Ponty and E. M. Cioran. Schwenger is concerned with a nocturnal "nowhere" where thought is a restless, interminable movement. In this "night," thought does not "get anywhere" any more than it comes from anywhere; it is without goal, defies control. Insomniac thought is out of control. In Blanchot's terms, we do not think but rather *it*—the night—*thinks*. As Levinas puts it, it is the night itself that watches. These are the sorts of perspectives that Schwenger brings to his readings of diary entries and writings by Kafka. In the liminal space of insomnia, in the space between sleep and wakefulness, the night gives Kafka as writer possibilities that the day cannot. This liminality is apparent in Kafka's writing—for instance, in stories that, like their insomniac author, lie somewhere between sleeping and waking. Blanchot regards *The Castle* as a story of insomnia, for—as Schwenger extrapolates—*The Castle*, like many other works by Kafka, includes endless discussions—speculations, explanations, interpretations that are often at odds with one another and reverse themselves even as they are being put forward. In so many of Kafka's works, there is such interpretative insomnia, which Schwenger—adapting Blanchot—characterizes as a watching over absent meaning. That watching may speak, however strangely, in the writer's words. As writer, Kafka is the insomniac subject that has become anonymous object of the night.

## Philosophical Topics

In the essays assembled under this title, there are attempts to explore Kafka's writings (novels, stories, diaries, letters) for their importance with regard to "philosophical topics." These topics revolve around questions ranging from animality to justice, and it is striking how this range involves discussions that actually overlap while remaining quite distinct.

Chris Danta's "Animal Bachelors and Animal Brides: Fabulous Metamorphosis in Kafka and Garnett" concerns the way in which Kafka's animals horrify us by violating the perceived species identity of the human—violating the human, then, in a manner that could be called "ontological." In *The Metamorphosis*, Gregor Samsa wakes transformed, continues to think and feel as a human being, but his monstrous appearance eventually makes it impossible (as Kevin Sweeney also stresses) for Gregor's family to recognize this. Where *The Metamorphosis* distinguishes itself from David Garnett's 1922 novel *Lady into Fox*, Danta suggests, is in hinting that others in the story, apart from the stricken protagonist, might feel their humanness debased by the animal within them. In this animality, the "human" becomes, in Danta's words, "ontologically isolated." Danta refers to "an ontological martyr" that becomes separate not just from other members of the human species but from the species itself. In "A Report to an Academy," Red Peter further demonstrates the susceptibility of the human to the nonhuman animal; he does so not just by making a transition from ape to man, but also by becoming "an ontological hypocrite": human by day, ape by night. With Red Peter and Gregor, there is performance of an ontological ambivalence between humanness and animality, as is the case too when the bride becomes a fox in Garnett's *Lady into Fox*. For Danta, these works convey not only alienation of modern humans from animality but thereby also—in the disregard of animality—from each other.

Paul Haacke's "Kafka's Political Animals" discusses "Jackals and Arabs" and "A Report to an Academy" as two of the more overtly political stories that Kafka wrote. They are "fabulist critiques of contemporary ideology"—satires of humanism, ethnocentrism, and nationalism but also of what Haacke calls the "biopolitics of catharsis" on which such outlooks often depend. These outlooks tend to presuppose orders that they expect our emotional, moral, and mimetic faculties to reproduce. Considering Aristotle's idea of the "political animal" in relation to Kafka's readings of Nietzsche and Kierkegaard, and in relation to current theories of biopolitics (Foucault, Agamben, Derrida), Haacke argues that Kafka's animals represent a world of confusion for "ideologies" that would presume to eliminate such confusion. This confusion is Kafka's deviation from what Haacke depicts as the biopolitics of catharsis. For the sake of mimetic identification with existing order, the latter biopolitics requires that the human tragically expunge emotions deviating from "the body politic." Correlative to this notion of mimesis in the *Poetics*, Aristotle's *Politics* develops the zoological idea of man as a "political animal." In contrast, Kafka explores more relentlessly the conflict between natural life and human society; he thus presents hybrid human-animal figures in many of his stories. Haacke notes possible influences of Friedrich Nietzsche's theory of *ressentiment* and slave morality on Kafka's parodic portrayal in "Jackals and Arabs" of a naturalist fantasy of purification. Kafka's story emerges as a critique of the biopolitics of catharsis around which discourses of nationalism often turn. "A Report to An Academy" is read by Haacke as Kafka's mocking the Darwinian idea of adaptive survival and the Enlightenment idea of progress through cultural education or *Bildung*. Such is Kafka's politics. Kafka's animals don't speak for human nature in general or any given culture in particular, and they reject cathartic, absolute notions of "the human." As they undermine mimetic and cathartic ideals, these "political animals" remind us how little we let ourselves be political in this way.

Isak Winkel Holm's "The Calamity of the Rightless: Hannah Arendt and Franz Kafka on Monsters and Members" is concerned with Kafka's implicit conception of justice. Whereas Arendt, "as a philosopher," is especially concerned with the legal or quasi-legal norms that should entitle every subject, even a stateless refugee, to appear in political space, Kafka, "as a literary writer," analyzes the norms of "imagination" that determine whether a human being appears to fellow human beings "as a subject at all." Among Kafka's literary texts, Winkel Holm includes Kafka's diary account of his relationship with the employees in the family-owned asbestos factory. Winkel Holm claims that Arendt ultimately circumvents the question of literary form in her essays on Kafka; he contends that she tends to treat literary form as a transparent medium through which we gain access to sociological types. In contrast, literary form is indispensable in Kafka's analysis of social institutions. In the case of the diary entry, literary form is stereoscopic: The women are seen with Kafka's eyes, but from two slightly different perspectives—the managerial and the non-managerial, the dehumanizing and the respectful. In Arendtian terms, Winkel Holm argues, the reader's reflective movement prompted by the stereoscopic literary form can be characterized as political thought. This form does not involve "the abstract medium of philosophical concepts or political opinions" but, rather, "literary images" in which different perspectives on the social world can be opened. Although Kafka's works tend to depict the negotiations of "first-level justice" (negotiations of how to allocate social goods or mete out punishment) as farcical mock trials, he keeps his focus, throughout his entire literary production, on the "second-level" question of who counts as a subject of justice and who does not. The calamity of the rightless in Kafka's works provides a kind of "photo negative of Kafka's implicit conception of justice." This conception of justice, as Winkel Holms elicits it, is a democratic justice in which there is guaranteed coordination of predictability, dignity, equality and political participation.

Paul Alberts's "Knowing Life Before the Law: Kafka, Kelsen, Derrida" is about the interplay between legal and literary construction. He turns, therefore, to the philosophical question of the relation of law to literature. Somewhat like Isak Winkel Holm, Alberts contends Kafka does not simply denigrate law but also indicates hope for law that would not disillusion humans' "epistemic"—their philosophical—capacities. The latter epistemic inclination is, according to Alberts, incorporated in some of Kafka's texts. In these texts, Alberts detects a formal structure, a "critical rhythm," that heightens skepticism about the law. Alberts contrasts this outlook with legal positivism—specifically the positivism that Hans Kelsen hoped to establish with his *Pure Theory of Law*. Whereas Kelsen discusses a transcendental principle that grounds law, Kafka's *The Trial*, for instance, provides parodies of such a notion with its references to "higher" court. Turning to Derrida's treatment of "Before the Law," Alberts suggests an affinity between deconstruction and the Kafkan texts—both the *The Office Writings* and the literary texts—that deflate law's pretensions to order life adequately. There is no *general* rule (or law) of decipherment. Kafka's epistemic insufficiency is an invitation, perhaps not to a "modern sublime" that *breaks* bounds of reason, but to a socially shared experience of the insecure borders of knowledge. Alberts reads Kafka's *Trial*, for instance, as setting out from the dream-like (or nightmare-like) realization that, contrary to the aspirations of modern legal positivism, there is no "Basic Norm" that guarantees the field of normative statements. Experience of a particular instance of law may well stimulate desire for something general that finally orders all law. Alberts notes Derrida's exploration of this regress—this *pursuit* of origin—in Kafka's legend "Before the Law." Like Kelsen, Kafka treats the drive to secure the legal network as a problematic at the heart of law. For Kafka, however, the problematic is worthy of dramatic burlesque. If the legend told to Josef K. is the condensed scene of an epistemic need, Alberts concludes, it also underscores the importance of the interpretive act and relationship, and thereby the intense bonds of being-together (like the man from the country and the gatekeeper), the necessity of the other in the place before the law.

## Philosophical Readings

This final part of the book contains discussions of specific readings of Kafka's works. These specific readings obviously are not all the "philosophical" readings that have been made of Kafka's texts. The analyses offered in this section do, however, propose new perspectives on four of the most celebrated philosophical analyses of Kafka, those by Benjamin, Adorno, Deleuze, and Agamben.

Brendan Moran's "Anxiety and Attention: Benjamin and Others" focuses on the relationship of anxiety with attention in Benjamin's reading of Kafka. Somewhat like Søren Kierkegaard and Martin Heidegger, Benjamin distinguishes anxiety from fear. For Kierkegaard and Heidegger, fear is about something specific that seems threatening. Anxiety might also arise from a threat, but the threat is *ultimately* nothing particular, and is rather the nothing that is the inexpungible, mysterious condition of the possibility of anything. Kierkegaard and Heidegger both present anxiety—anxiety with regard to the nothing—as potentially penultimate to resolute attention to the nothing that is the ground of all beings. Emmanuel Levinas's principal objection to both Kierkegaard and Heidegger is that their views entail a disregard for other humans. For Levinas, other humans are the very possibility for experience of the ultimate Otherness of existence. Accordingly, ethics has primacy over Kierkegaardian religiosity and Heideggerian ontology. Into this controversy, Moran brings writings by Benjamin on Kafka. Whereas Kierkegaardian-Heideggerian anxiety is supposed potentially to open us to an attention that is ultimately free of particulars of sense-experience and of sociality, the anxiety addressed by Benjamin is distinctly attentive to sense-experience, particulars, and indeed sociality. Yet this anxiety is also distinct from the primacy of ethics that is emphasized by Levinas. Benjamin's Kafka-writings concern an anxiety that is distracted by multifarious diversions. This attentive distractedness is discussed by Moran as a physically felt eluding of transcendence—whether the transcendence is religious (Kierkegaard), ontological (Heidegger), or ethical (Levinas). Moran concludes, however, with some remarks on how this physicality of anxiety might require an attention that also resists Benjamin's own views about possibilities for overcoming anxiety.

Brian O'Connor's "On the Mimesis of Reification: Adorno's Critical Theoretical Interpretation of Kafka" concerns Adorno's radical re-conception of the notion of mimesis. O'Connor examines Adorno's focus on the *expression* of reality that modernist artworks show themselves capable of achieving. This expression consists in giving *aesthetic form* to social reality. The form—not content, image, or representation—is the key property of what constitutes the specifically *aesthetic* construction—the aesthetic mimesis—of social reality. So powerful is this mimesis that modern works such as Kafka's attest to the horror of the twentieth century. For Adorno's articulation of modernist mimesis, Kafka qua writer is pivotal by virtue of his aesthetic mimesis of social reality. This mimesis is not a philosophy or a historical narrative that Kafka pumps into his work. Adorno does not try to find an implicit theory, or illustrated examples of philosophical insights, in the texts; Adorno does not "read off" a Kafkaesque philosophy from the literary work. The form of Kafka's texts is that they cannot be unlocked. This form is, however, a confrontation with societal myth—the closures by which a society lets itself be content. The mimesis requires that art cannot be content with closure by historical context: There could be no artistic mimesis if there were an omnipotent societal superego. The artwork performs the falsity of the superego. This performance is Kafka's mimesis of reification. The mimesis is the development of form as a response to societal evolution. Incapable of being translated into purely theoretical terms, this expression qua art—this aesthetic mimesis—is a comportment that is creative precisely in eluding conceptual containment. The latter elusion, O'Conner suggests, is the allure of Kafka's work for Adorno's social criticism.

In endeavoring to show how Kafka's writings, like literature generally, "run parallel to philosophy" for Deleuze, Ronald Bogue's "'In the Penal Colony' in the Philosophy of Gilles Deleuze" indicates many variations in the readings by Deleuze (and Deleuze and Guattari) of "In the Penal Colony" as well as of other texts by Kafka. With regard to "In the Penal Colony," Bogue notes that for Deleuze and Guattari the breakdown of the torture machine reveals a truth beneath the dominant order's view of itself as unified, efficient apparatus. Adapting Deleuze and Guattari and others, Bogue characterizes this aspect of Kafka's work as "bachelor" art—while also stressing that the sex of the desiring "machine," which overcomes the torture machine, is not central. The term "bachelor" serves to highlight an impersonal function, a deterritorialized and deterritorializing force at play. If the artist is such a *machine célibataire*, a bachelor machine, Kafka must keep the writing machine running in order to avoid any premature closure of its deterritorializing force. Bogue shows that the readings by Deleuze (and Deleuze and Guattari) provide quite different—even conflicting—responses to the question of whether the writing machine of "In the Penal Colony" succeeds at deterritorializing. Some readings suggest there is irony and humor that open law to critique. Other readings suggest that "In the Penal Colony" represents a negative critique of the law, whereas *The Trial* provides both a negative critique and a positive assessment of the law's potential for transformation. Yet other readings suggest "In the Penal Colony" is a relatively positive presentation of the law, whereas *The Trial* is more negative. Throughout all this, Bogue demonstrates that "In the Penal Colony"—as a parody of the institutions of law—proves to be as vital an element in Deleuze's thought as *The Trial*. Deleuze's explorations of this parody convey how literature is integral to Deleuze's philosophical work.

Finally, Carlo Salzani's "In a Messianic Gesture: Agamben's Kafka" assesses the importance, influence and significance of Kafka in the work of Giorgio Agamben. As many commentators have noted, Kafka holds a central place in the work of the Italian philosopher: Strongly influenced by Benjamin's readings, Agamben sees in Kafka's oeuvre both an unparalleled critique of modernity and of its political and cultural stalemate, and the traces of a political strategy—messianism—which would allow its overcoming and would open the way to a different human history. Salzani traces Agamben's long career to find in almost all of his works the "long shadow" of Kafka in this dual role. This presence is shown to become central in the still unfinished *Homo Sacer* project, for which Kafka's notion of law constitutes the cornerstone: Kafka's legal world—epitomized by the parable "Before the Law"—unveils the true nature of law, which Agamben—borrowing the expression from Gershom Scholem—defines as *being in force without significance*. Law, that is, affirms itself with the greatest force precisely at the point in which it no longer prescribes anything, like the door of the Kafkan parable which, precisely through its openness, keeps the man from the country in the ban. At the end of the parable, however, Kafka also points to the possibility of a messianic reversal when the door of the law is finally closed. Indeed, the messianic strategy shown by the Kafkan texts consists in such de-activation—even a de-activation of the whole machinery of the Western cultural and political tradition. Salzani adds, however, a further interpretive layer: Kafka, he argues, also influences Agamben with a philosophical "mode" revolving around messianic "gestures." Benjamin identified the "gesture" as the most characteristic trait of Kafka's prose. Agamben takes up Kafka's gestures as an intellectual strategy whereby a poetic, paradoxical prose hardly explains. The prose seeks, rather, a messianic reversal in the paradox itself, in the usage of sense to convey prevailing or preponderant non-sense. Kafka's prose, and Agamben's account of it, thereby push philosophy to its limit.

## Notes

1. See for instance David Schur, *The Way of Oblivion: Heraclitus and Kafka* (Cambridge, MA: Harvard University Press, 1998); Friedrich Balke, Joseph Vogl, Benno Wagner, eds., *Für Alle und Keinen. Lektüre, Schrift und Leben bei Nietzsche und Kafka* (Zurich, Berlin: diaphenes, 2008); Patrick Bridgewater, *Kafka and Nietzsche* (Bonn: Bouvier Verlag, Herbert Grundmann, 1974); William Hubben, *Dostoevsky, Kierkegaard, Nietzsche, and Kafka. Four Prophets of Our Destiny* (New York: Collier Books, 1962); Leena Eilittä, *Approaches to Personal Identity in Kafka's Short Fiction: Freud, Darwin, Kierkegaard* (Helsinki: Academia Scientiarum Fennica, 1999).

2. See, for instance: Beda Allemann, *Zeit und Geschichte im Werk Kafkas* (Göttingen: Wallstein, 1998); Paul DeNicola, *Literature as Pure Mediality: Kafka and the Scene of Writing* (New York and Dresden: Atropos Press, 2009); Rolf J. Goebel, *Constructing China: Kafka's Orientalist Discourse* (Columbia, SC: Camden House, 1997); Arnold Heidsieck, *The Intellectual Contexts of Kafka's Fictions: Philosophy, Law, Religion* (New York: Camden House, 1994); Kiarina Kordela and Dimitris Vardoulakis, eds., *Freedom and Confinement in Modernity: Kafka's Cages* (New York: Palgrave Macmillan, 2011); Elisabeth Kellinghusen, *Wir graben den Tunnel zu Babel: Kritik der Totalität—Eine subversive Vertiefung der Gedanken-Gänge Franz Kafkas* (Vienna: Passagen, 1993); Michael Löwy, *Franz Kafka. Rêveur Insoumis* (Paris: Éditions Stock, 2004); Ferruccio Masini, *Franz Kafka. La metamorfosi del significato* (Turin: Ananke, 2010); Davide Stimilli, *Fisionomia di Kafka* (Turin: Bollati Boringhieri, 2001); Jochen Thermann, *Kafkas Tiere: Fährten, Bahnen und Wege der Sprache* (Marburg: Tectum, 2010); Joseph Vogl, *Ort der Gewalt. Kafkas Literarische Ethik* (Munich: Wilhelm Fink Verlag, 1990).

3. Such works include the following: Neil Allan, *Franz Kafka and the Genealogy of Modern European Philosophy: From Phenomenology to Post-structuralism* (New York: Edwin Mellen Press, 2005); Johanna Bossinade, *Theorie der Sublimation: Ein Schlüssel*

*zur Psychoanalyse und zum Werk Kafkas* (Würzburg: Königshausen & Neumann, 2007); Axel Hecker, *An den Randern des Lesbaren: Dekonstruktive Lekturen zu Franz Kafka: Die Verwandlung, In der Strafkolonie und Das Urteil* (Vienna: Passagen, 1998); James Whitlark, *Behind the Great Wall: A Post-Jungian Approach to Kafkaesque Literature* (Cranbury, NJ: Associated University Presses, 1991).

4. Among the many texts are the following: Sabine I. Gölz, *The Split Scene of Reading: Nietzsche/Derrida/Kafka/Bachmann* (Atlantic Highlands, NJ: Humanities, 1998); Rainer J. Kaus, *Kafka und Freud: Schuld in den Augen des Dichters und des Analytikers* (Heidelberg: Carl Winter Universitätsverlag, 2000); Sven Kramer, *Rätselfragen und wolkige Stellen: Zu Benjamins Kafka-Essay* (Lüneburg: zu Klampen, 1991); Jose E. Milmaniene, *Clinica del Texto: Kafka, Benjamin, Levinas* (Buenos Aires: Biblos, 2002); Bernd Müller, *"Denn es ist noch nichts geschehen": Walter Benjamins Kafka-Deutung* (Vienna: Böhlau, 1996).

5. See, for instance: Remo Cantoni, *Franz Kafka e il disagio dell'uomo contemporaneo* (Milan: Unicopli, 2000); Stanley Corngold, *Lambent Traces: Franz Kafka* (Princeton, NJ: Princeton University Press, 2006); Sonja Dierks, *Es gibt Gespenster: Betrachtungen zu Kafkas Erzählung* (Würzburg: Königshausen & Neumann, 2003); Joachim Hubbert, *Metaphysische Sehnsucht, Gottverlassenheit und die Freiheit des Absurden: Untersuchungen zum Werk von Franz Kafka* (Bochum: Brockmeyer, 1995); Walter H. Sokel, *The Myth of Power and the Self: Essays on Franz Kafka* (Detroit, MI: Wayne State University Press, 2002).

## Works Cited


Allan, Neil. *Franz Kafka and the Genealogy of Modern European Philosophy: From Phenomenology to Post-structuralism*. New York: Edwin Mellen Press, 2005.

Allemann, Beda. *Zeit und Geschichte im Werk Kafkas*. Göttingen: Wallstein, 1998.

Balke, Friedrich, Joseph Vogl, Benno Wagner, eds. *Für Alle und Keinen. Lektüre, Schrift und Leben bei Nietzsche und Kafka*. Zurich, Berlin: diaphenes, 2008.

Bridgewater, Patrick. *Kafka and Nietzsche*. Bonn: Bouvier Verlag, Herbert Grundmann, 1974.

Bossinade, Johanna. *Theorie der Sublimation: Ein Schlüssel zur Psychoanalyse und zum Werk Kafkas*. Würzburg: Königshausen & Neumann, 2007.

Cantoni, Remo. *Franz Kafka e il disagio dell'uomo contemporaneo*. Milan: Unicopli, 2000.

Corngold, Stanley. *Lambent Traces: Franz Kafka*. Princeton, NJ: Princeton University Press, 2006.

DeNicola, Paul. *Literature as Pure Mediality: Kafka and the Scene of Writing*. New York and Dresden: Atropos Press, 2009.

Dierks, Sonja. *Es gibt Gespenster: Betrachtungen zu Kafkas Erzählung*. Würzburg: Königshausen & Neumann, 2003.

Eilittä, Leena. *Approaches to Personal Identity in Kafka's Short Fiction: Freud, Darwin, Kierkegaard*. Helsinki: Academia Scientiarum Fennica, 1999.

Goebel, Rolf J. *Constructing China: Kafka's Orientalist Discourse*. Columbia, SC: Camden House, 1997.

Gölz, Sabine I. *The Split Scene of Reading: Nietzsche/Derrida/Kafka/Bachmann*. Atlantic Highlands, NJ: Humanities, 1998.

Hecker, Axel. *An den Randern des Lesbaren: Dekonstruktive Lekturen zu Franz Kafka: Die Verwandlung, In der Strafkolonie und Das Urteil*. Vienna: Passagen, 1998.

Heidsieck, Arnold. *The Intellectual Contexts of Kafka's Fictions: Philosophy, Law, Religion*. New York: Camden House, 1994.

Hubben. William. *Dostoevsky, Kierkegaard, Nietzsche, and Kafka. Four Prophets of Our Destiny*. New York: Collier Books, 1962.

Hubbert, Joachim. *Metaphysische Sehnsucht, Gottverlassenheit und die Freiheit des Absurden: Untersuchungen zum Werk von Franz Kafka*. Bochum: Brockmeyer, 1995.

Kaus, Rainer J. *Kafka und Freud: Schuld in den Augen des Dichters und des Analytikers*. Heidelberg: Carl Winter Universitätsverlag, 2000.

Kellinghusen, Elisabeth. *Wir graben den Tunnel zu Babel: Kritik der Totalität—Eine subversive Vertiefung der Gedanken-Gänge Franz Kafkas*. Vienna: Passagen, 1993.

Kordela, Kiarina, and Dimitris Vardoulakis, eds. *Freedom and Confinement in Modernity: Kafka's Cages*. New York: Palgrave Macmillan, 2011.

Kramer, Sven. *Rätselfragen und wolkige Stellen: Zu Benjamins Kafka-Essay*. Lüneburg: zu Klampen, 1991.

Löwy, Michael. *Franz Kafka. Rêveur Insoumis*. Paris: Éditions Stock, 2004.

Masini, Ferruccio. *Franz Kafka. La metamorfosi del significato*. Turin: Ananke, 2010.

Milmaniene, Jose E. *Clinica del Texto: Kafka, Benjamin, Levinas*. Buenos Aires: Biblos, 2002.

Müller, Bernd. *"Denn es ist noch nichts geschehen": Walter Benjamins Kafka-Deutung*. Vienna: Böhlau, 1996.

Schur, David. *The Way of Oblivion: Heraclitus and Kafka*. Cambridge, MA: Harvard University Press, 1998.

Sokel, Walter H. *The Myth of Power and the Self: Essays on Franz Kafka*. Detroit, MI: Wayne State University Press, 2002.

Stimilli, Davide. *Fisionomia di Kafka*. Turin: Bollati Boringhieri, 2001.

Thermann, Jochen. *Kafkas Tiere: Fährten, Bahnen und Wege der Sprache*. Marburg: Tectum, 2010.

Vogl, Joseph. *Ort der Gewalt. Kafkas Literarische Ethik*. Munich: Wilhelm Fink Verlag, 1990.

Whitlark, James. *Behind the Great Wall: A Post-Jungian Approach to Kafkaesque Literature*. Cranbury, NJ: Associated University Presses, 1991.

# PART I

# PHILOSOPHICAL INVESTIGATIONS

# CHAPTER 1

# I Don't Want to Know that I Know: The Inversion of Socratic Ignorance in the Knowledge of the Dogs

*Rainer Nägele*

> Knowledge we have. Whoever strives for it with special effort is under suspicion of striving against it.
> —Franz Kafka[1]

"We," if such a collective pronoun is permitted in order to point to a certain characteristic of Western thought, are more or less touched by the Socratic knowledge that we know that we do not know. It has been proposed to us as an ideal. It is the essential Socratic virtue: the virtue of not knowing as the precondition of all knowledge, the reduction of all certainties of knowledge as the condition for possible provisional certainties.

The power of this not knowing has proven itself triumphant in the modern sciences. The pathos of scientific modesty that claims to know nothing, that does not want to know anything that has not been proven in ever renewed experiments and has withstood all tests of falsification may suddenly turn into the arrogance of a knowledge that claims a certain absoluteness for itself: another moment of the "dialectic of Enlightenment."

In view of an accumulated historical experience of such moments, the question arises whether this modest proposal, "I know that I do not know," could possibly be a *proton pseudo*, a primordial lie of Western knowledge: a radical denegation of an unbearable knowledge. The pathos of this formula of modesty goes hand in hand with another pathos proclaiming the human drive for truth. Nietzsche's cynical (i.e. doglike—cynical derived from the Greek *kyon* = dog) gaze was not the first to notice that most humans want to know anything but the truth.

To utter such observations at the present historical moment is not without a certain danger. For what, if not the Socratic knowledge and admission of ignorance, could better oppose all the fundamentalisms that assert themselves more and more shamelessly? They are not limited to one religion. And while religions might be particularly susceptible to murderous fundamentalist temptations, what is called here—with a very problematic term[2]—fundamentalism, exerts its power far beyond the sphere of religion. One might even see it at the core of a scientific authority that excludes any other form of knowledge.

Could there be another form, another way to enter into this whirlpool between knowledge and ignorance, between obsessive denial and hysterical affirmation? A form that neither falls into phobic denial nor terrorizes the world with affirmative certainties? Perhaps a very silent knowledge to which each subject is subjected and exposed in absolute solitude. It would be a knowledge that is not communicable in a Habermasian sphere of communication, and yet it would be the irreducible ground of all communicability.

Such a knowledge, which is common to all and yet which no one wants or is able to pronounce, is the enigmatic core of a late fragmentary text by Franz Kafka. Max Brod published it under the title "Forschungen eines Hundes" ("Investigations of a Dog"). A dog speaks in a curious mixture of a representative voice of the canine community and a voice distanced from it. A similar structure exists in Kafka's last narrative, "Josefine, die Sängerin" ("Josefine, the Singer"): a mouse speaks and wonders about the folk of mice and its ambivalent relationship to the one (perhaps) singing mouse. That animals speak has a long literary tradition in which these speaking creatures present human situations and conditions in a more or less defamiliarized manner. The animal "itself," if such an expression would be possible, is then "actually," "really" already negated, erased through an anthropomorphic sign and figure. Since Kafka's animals necessarily speak a human language, they also cannot escape their annihilation in an anthropomorphic rhetoric.

And yet, something resists. The singularity of this resistance calls for deciphering. Perhaps one could say, in a first step, that if the speaking animal is suspended in its human language, the human form is no less suspended in the animal form. But this is only an approximative and provisional description of what happens. It is valid only if this mutual suspension implies the radical suspension of all our all too familiar concepts of the human and the animal. Kafka's animals are living *Grenzbegriffe*, liminal concepts. This seems now like the all too familiar allegorical reduction to which Kafka's texts often have been exposed. But if the living *Grenzbegriff* is an allegory—and where there is human language, there is allegory—it is an allegory that undoes precisely the conventional allegory, the embodiment of a pre-existing concept, by liquidating any possibility of a pre-existing concept. Kafka's speaking animals signal an extreme limit. Thus Kafka's dog, who incessantly barks after that knowledge that all have, yet no one can or will pronounce, goes to the limit of life in his hunger experiment. He thus resembles in many ways recurring human figures in Kafka's stories, often students, who in a kind of doggish stubbornness pursue indefatigably, and yet to exhaustion, the traits of their scripts to the extreme limit—which of course can always only be their limit, never the real limit.

To speak of an extreme limit, an *äußerste Grenze*, is not without risk. It is precisely the rhetorical place of fundamentalists, founders of religions, and murderous fanatics. Kafka had a sense for this and Walter Benjamin, one of his best readers, noticed the line that Kafka's lucid sobriety had drawn. There is a rather enigmatic and little noticed phrase in Benjamin's Kafka essay, almost a non sequitur. Benjamin's essay is characterized by two specific traits: it refuses, as Benjamin himself notes, any "supernatural," i.e. theological, as well as any "natural," (i.e. in this case any pseudo-psychoanalytic) interpretation. What remains when both the supernatural and the natural are excluded? In one word: language which is neither supernatural nor natural. It is the language of humans, but it is also the language above the heads of humans (*überhaupt* but not *übernatürlich*, rather *außernatürlich*, extra-natural). Language, however, must not be understood in the narrow sense of the language of words (indeed no language is defined simply by its words), but language as a structure that includes the language of motifs and gestures. And this is the first characteristic of Benjamin's Kafka reading: the notation of gestures and motifs (somewhat shamelessly copied without reference at the beginning of Deleuze's and Guattari's essay on Kafka).

The other road, or method, that Benjamin pursues is the narrative mode: he puts Kafka's narratives into constellations with other narratives. Almost every section of the essay begins with *Es wird erzählt* . . . ("It is narrated . . .," "The story goes . . ."). Among other narratives, there is a Talmudic legend of a princess exiled into a foreign village. In what seems at first glance a naive allegorical application of the legend to Kafka's novel *The Castle*, Benjamin comments: "For just as K. lives in the village, at the foot of the Castle mountain, today's man lives in his body; it glides away from him, it is hostile toward him. It can happen, one morning, that the man wakes up and he is transformed into a vermin.[3] The foreignness—his foreignness—has taken over. It is the air of this village that blows in Kafka, and that is why he did not succumb to the temptation to become a founder of a religion."[4]

It is this last phrase that strikes one as curiously strange, coming from somewhere else like a non sequitur: "and that is why he did not succumb to the temptation to become a founder of a religion." Any negation presupposes the possibility of an affirmation—in this case: Kafka could have been tempted to become the founder of a religion. In fact, there is quite a bit of secondary literature on Kafka that, if it does not exactly make him the founder of a religion, nevertheless pushes him very close to that role or at least into the proximity of a prophet. The closer Kafka's writing gropes toward the extreme limits of its possibilities, the more Kafka's lucidity senses precisely this danger. Thus we read in a note of 1922: "'Hunt' is only an image, I can also say 'storm toward the last earthly limit' and that is storm from below, from the side of humans, but since this, too, is only an image, I can substitute for it the image of a storm from above, toward me. // All this literature is storm toward/against a limit, and had Zionism not intervened, it could have easily evolved into a new secret doctrine, a Kabbalah. There are traces for such a possibility."[5] Why it was Zionism that prevented Kafka from developing a secret doctrine, making him the founder of a new religion, would need a separate investigation.

There is another line I would like to pursue: the extreme earthly limit that Kafka invokes is also a limit of (re-)presentation which can never exit from the realm of images and figures. As limit of (re-)presentation, it is also the limit of the human sphere. Kafka noted this already very early on. In a prepared speech to Rudolf Steiner, from whom he seeks some counsel concerning his painful situation between his desire to write and his job, he says: "And here I have experienced mental states (not many) that resemble closely those clairvoyant states that you, doctor, described; in these states I inhabited completely and totally every idea that came to me, but I also completely occupied each idea and I felt myself not only at my own limit, but at the limit of the human sphere itself."[6] The animals that speak and act so frequently in Kafka's texts mark a limit of the human, even if they cannot completely escape the human sphere in so far as they represent and are represented.

In the "Investigations of a Dog," there is a particularly strange phenomenon that marks this liminal situation of the world of the dogs: the human world is completely excluded from the perception of the dogs. This inexistence of the human world in the perception of the dogs is at the same time the kernel and the reason for all the riddles that the investigating dog would like to decipher. One of the central questions, for example: why does the nourishment that, according to the dog scientists, comes from the earth, come for the dogs from above? And even more enigmatically, the dog finds in one of his experiments that the food does not simply fall to the earth when the dog intentionally misses it, but it follows him in the air: "the food pursued the hungry one!" ("Investigations" 479).[7] Or there is the enigmatic phenomenon of *Lufthunde* (air dogs) that seem to hover in the air and only rarely touch the earth; the reader, in contrast to the dogs who perceive nothing of the human world, can easily recognize these air dogs as highbred poodles carried by human hands.

This exclusion of the human world from the perception of the dogs produces paradoxical effects. One might first think that this emphasizes the world of the dogs as a self-enclosed world. Indeed the narrator dog seems to confirm this: "When I asked for example: From where does the earth take this food? was it, as it might seem, the earth that interested me, or the worries of the earth? Not at all, such things were, as I soon recognized, completely outside my interest; my only interest was the dogs, nothing else. What is there, after all, besides the dogs? To whom can one call in the wide empty world? All knowledge, the totality of all questions and answers, is contained in the dogs. If only one could make this knowledge effective, if only one could bring it into bright daylight. But the most garrulous dog is more locked up in his silence than tend to be those places where the best food is stored" ("Investigations" 441).[8] This extreme enclosure in their world excludes precisely that which characterizes the world of the dogs more than most other animals: their close relationship to the human world. We don't know really how dogs perceive the human world, but that they do perceive it in whatever manner is manifest. Thus it is exactly by the exclusion of an essential mark of the dog-world that the latter's coherence and enclosure is broken up.

One can also say, and indeed the dog does say: what is excluded is not simply outside, but rather that which is locked up deeply inside the dog world, the knowledge that all possess and that none can admit to himself and to the others. It is a knowledge which they apparently do not know, a knowledge that belongs to another scene than their manifest knowledge and thus is excluded and foreign: an outside in the innermost intimacy, a kind of "extimicy" to use a word coined by Lacan.

This structure corresponds exactly to the relationship of the narrating dog with the community of the dogs: a dog "in the middle of the community of the dogs . . . a dog among dogs," as he describes himself, and yet excluded from it through "a small fracture" (*Bruchstelle*). As small as this fracture might be, it expels the narrating dog from the other ex- and included scene. Thus, when he speaks, he seems to speak from this other scene, as the representative of the Other, of this other knowledge and of the knowledge of the Other. Yet, this is not quite true. When he asks himself, in the voice of another dog, "Well then, why do you reproach the others for their silence while you are silent yourself," he can only cynically (i.e. as a dog) say: "Easy answer: because I am a dog." A dog among dogs, "not a hair's breadth outside of the essence of the dogs." He is not the Other, and yet he is somewhat other, different, and in his slight otherness and difference not "outside of the essence of the dogs," but rather intimately connected to this essence, a little irritating spot, a symptom ("Investigations" 445).

At this point, correspondences emerge with a figure that, at first glance, seems to be far removed from, and is yet deeply embedded in, Kafka's text: Oedipus, who, in the Sophoclean version, is both a foreigner (ξενος) and citizen, even a native of Thebes.[9] He is the solver of riddles, the one who does not tire of questioning and investigating. To be sure, at least at first, he achieves something that Kafka's dog never comes close to: he liberates the community from the Sphinx (who, by the way, in the Sophoclean play is also called a "dog") and the plague.[10] But then, Oedipus becomes another source of the plague. And while Kafka's dog does not exactly bring the plague, his questioning and his investigations are a continuous irritation in the body of the canine community. There is nothing, or little, that allows us to assume that Kafka intended such correspondences. And yet their effect is there. If such correspondences have a power, it is rarely ever due to "influence"—direct influences are in most cases only superficially effective—but they owe their effects to objective constellations that emerge only from intensive immersion in the material.

Whether intentional or not, the narrative fragment of the "Investigations of a Dog" is preceded by another fragment, that expresses a suspicion in a simile that corresponds strikingly to the prehistory of Oedipus: "From the beginning on, I have had a certain suspicion in regard to me, a suspicion that is similar to the suspicion of a child in regard to his adoptive parents, even when it is carefully kept in the belief that his adoptive parents are his biological parents. There is some kind of suspicion there, no matter how much the adoptive parents love the child as their own and lack nothing in tenderness and patience; it is perhaps a suspicion that emerges only at times, only in long intervals, only at small accidental occasions, but which is nevertheless alive, and it has not disappeared when it rests at times, but it only gathers forces and at an opportune time it can develop, in one leap, from a tiny discomfort into a big wild malignant suspicion that tolerates no fetters and that destroys unscrupulously everything, the suspecting one together with the one who is suspected."[11] The suspicion directed against the narrator becomes in the simile the prehistory of Oedipus. His suspicion about his adoptive parents drives him toward his fate. It is, as a matter of fact, his truth that he wants to know and that, in another scene, he already knows, even if he cannot and will not pronounce it until he is forced to. Seven times the word *Verdacht* (suspicion) and its derivations appear in the fragment quoted. Not *Denken* (thinking), but a *sich verdenken*, a kind of misthinking, a parapraxis in thought, takes shape in the *Verdacht* and produces the catastrophe that, for Oedipus, is both the turn toward his truth and his annihilation.

If we follow further the traces of Oedipus, we are led to ever new strange paths, even if they might be *Holzwege.* In the background is the riddle of the Sphinx: the riddle of the strange creature that walks on four legs in the morning, on two legs at noon and on three legs in the evening. In Kafka's narrative there is something like a primal scene: the encounter with the seven dog musicians that occasions the radical turn with which the narrative begins: "How my life has changed and how it has not changed basically (*im Grunde*)!" The strange music of these dogs that seems not even to be their music, but coming from elsewhere—they themselves, the dogs, "did not speak, they did not sing, they were generally silent with a certain doggedness"—this music is not the only thing that makes its lasting impression on the young dog and drives him into an increasing isolation, although he remains a dog among dogs. He suddenly realizes another strange thing that scandalizes him: "the miserable ones performed both the most ridiculous and the most obscene thing: they walked on their hind legs." The four-legged animals have become two-legged. Insofar as the animal fable represents a human world, it allegorizes itself in this strange event. For the young little dog, this is a moment of panic, the hour of Pan, which for the Greeks was noon, when, in the riddle of the sphinx, the enigmatic creature walks on two legs. And even the three-leggedness of the evening is not lacking in Kafka's story. Having grown old, almost without any more contact with the other dogs, the narrating dog only occasionally meets a neighbor dog in the vain hope he might share his question with him. It is "an old dog, somewhat smaller than I, who am barely of middle size, brown, with short hair, his head bent in tiredness, with limping pace, dragging his left hind leg due to an illness" ("Investigations" 453). He walks more or less only on three legs.

If indeed the riddle of the sphinx is inscribed in Kafka's story, would not then be the answer to the story as to the riddle: Man? The story of the dog and the community of the dogs would then find its solution as a simple animal fable and allegory of the human world. But already in the story of Oedipus, the solution of the riddle is not the end, but the beginning of the real story of Oedipus. To be sure, the sphinx has plunged into the abyss, the plague has disappeared; Oedipus, the solver of riddles, has redeemed the city. But then everything begins again, the plague returns and the questions are more insistent than ever. He who knew the answer to the riddle of the sphinx is confronted with seemingly unanswerable questions and driven to questioning by a knowledge that he has without knowing it. And yet, as Hölderlin comments, "the spirit of Oedipus, knowing everything, utters in wrathful presentiment" what the consciousness of Oedipus does not yet know.[12]

Oedipus, the solver of riddles, solves the riddle with one word. The word of solution is the riddle. When he says "Man," ανθρωπος, he has chased away the doglike sphinx and with her perhaps all the dogs. But then, by condensing that which in the riddle of the sphinx has a temporality—morning, noon, and evening—into what is treated as the word "Man, that suggests a timeless essence," he has erased precisely that which is the essence of Man and of the human: his temporality. Indeed, the Greek texts speak much less of Man and humans (ανθρωπος) than of the mortals (θνητοι or βροτοι). Thus in the Sophoclean version of Oedipus, the solver of the riddle has to pass through the course of the day, from morning to evening until the night falls in which Oedipus truly will have been he who he is. This day, Tiresias says to him, gives birth to you and annihilates you. The doglike sphinx who, in her riddle, articulated the abstract figure "Man" into the temporality of the course of a day has caught up again with Oedipus: he must live her riddle, the riddle of temporality and mortality until at the end, to translate freely a German idiom, he has gone to the dogs (*er ist auf den Hund gekommen*).

The oscillation between the human world and the world of the dogs can be vertiginous. Kafka's dogs speak and they even know something like sinfulness (*Sündhaftigkeit*), both qualities that seem to ascribe them clearly to the human world. But at the same time, they clearly act specifically like dogs. They are liminal creatures, and the narrating dog in his integration in the community of the dogs—a dog among dogs—and his distance from them, that minimal and yet abyssal fracture that separates him from them, is embodied limit. The story that he tells is a simile and is not a simile. It is the transgression of the human in and through the animal world. The opinion that the dogs are a simile for the human world is based on the assumption that the dogs are an image and the human condition that which is actually meant (*das Eigentliche*). But for Kafka (and not only for him) there is nothing but image, presentation and representation, *Vorstellung* and *Darstellung*. That which is thought of as the actual, real meaning, the *Eigentliche*, exists only as a limit against which the (re-)presentation storms. But, of course, this sentence is also only an image.

One consequence of this particular status of the story and its dogs is a recurring mode of speech in which affirmation and negation are equally valid. The very first sentence sets the tone: "How my life has changed and how it has not changed basically (*im Grunde*)!" ("Investigations" 432). The whole community of the dogs is structured by this undecidability of yes and no: intimate community, "all in one pile"; but immediately the opposite is affirmed: "No other creature lives, to my knowledge, so far dispersed like we dogs" ("Investigations" 425-26). And when the dog experiences "something extraordinary," as for example the seven dog musicians, the next sentence declares: "In itself it was nothing extraordinary" ("Investigations" 427).

In this apparently neutral play and counterplay of affirmation and negation, one may occasionally notice, however, a particular accent on the negation. Thus, in the first sentence—"How my life has changed and how it has not changed basically (*im Grunde*)!"—the *im Grunde* is emphatically placed at the end of the sentence. No less emphatic is the initial position of *In itself* (*An sich*) in the sentence, "In itself it was nothing extraordinary." That which, for the dog, means an immense change, what for him is something extraordinary is, perhaps, basically (*im Grunde*) and *In itself* (*An sich*) nothing. This could, however, also mean that *Grund* (ground, basis) and the In-itself are nothing, at least for the dogs and for us, because the world for us exists only in its (re-)presentations.

Yet this nothingness of ground and of the in-itself is not simply nothing. It marks a limit, a border where each statement, each sentence, each "it is" is transformed into an "it is as if." It is as if that knowledge that all possess, and which nobody knows or wants to know, were located there.

At this point, a certain precision is necessary. If so far it has been claimed that we are dealing here with a knowledge that is the opposite of the Socratic "I know that I do not know," one might object that, after all, the Socratic "midwifery" is the art of giving birth to a knowledge that we all already have in a hidden way. In addition, the narrating dog shares several qualities with Socrates. He too, like Socrates, is an ατοπος (*Phaidros* 229c) who is not quite at home or at his place in the community of his species. Above all he shares with Socrates the radical limitation of his research and questioning to the sphere of that species to which he nevertheless belongs: in his case, the dogs. Asked about the status of various mythological stories and beings by Phaidros, Socrates refuses to give it much thought, saying: "I am still not able to know myself as the Delphic oracle commands. Thus I would find it ridiculous to think of other things as long as I am ignorant in this matter" (*Phaidros* 229e-230a). In a similar way, Kafka's dog decidedly has complete disinterest in all *the manifold creatures* outside the community of the dogs in order to concentrate all his research on what he refers to as *die Hundeschaft*, the "dogdom": "my only interest was the dogs, nothing else" ("Investigations" 441).

But precisely in this proximity and similarity to and with Socrates, a radical difference emerges: not so much an opposition but a shift of the unknown knowledge to another scene. The Socratic knowledge which we all purportedly have, can supposedly at any time be brought to light with the right method. It would be something like Freud's preconscious in contrast to the radical otherness of the unconscious or a kind of *mémoire volontaire* in contrast to Proust's *mémoire involontaire*.

The knowledge that displaces so enigmatically Kafka's texts—not only the story of this dog—is of a very different kind. It shares with Freud's unconscious the strange structure that it is atopically displaced and yet everywhere present. It is not in a mysterious "beyond," but the manifest secret in all surfaces. One might say of it what the hunter Gracchus tells of himself in one of the Gracchus-fragments: "All the books are full of it, in all schools, teachers write it on the blackboard." And after a long list (later crossed out by Kafka), that could be infinite, he sums it up as the ubiquity of "these old, old stories."[13]

For us mortals, whether dogs or humans, these are, as the dog says, "things that one would rather not touch," or as the hunter Gracchus says, things for which one simply does not have time in the short human life except perhaps on a deathbed in Hamburg, like the master of the hunter Gracchus in one of the fragments. But when the dog does touch on such things he also touches on very concrete things, such as the fact that the dogs follow "prescriptions that are not those of the dogs but rather directed against them" ("Investigations" 426). One may assume that these are prescriptions coming from the humans that are radically excluded from the perception of the dogs. Just like the air dogs and the food, these prescriptions are free floating in the perception of the dog. This implies that humans in this story are not simply the signified of the signifier "dogs," but that they are the *atopic topos*, the displaced place of the doggish unknown knowledge. The simple allegorical solution of the riddle does not solve the riddle, it poses the riddle.

Of course one can, as the dog says, dissolve the riddle in empty babble (*Verreden*), believing that one knows what one says when one uses terms such as "human" or "humankind," or if one reads the dogs as an allegory of Jewish existence. Certainly there are such traits there: certainly it is difficult to imagine speaking dogs without a reference to the human world. It is also not completely wrong to see trained circus dogs in the mysterious musical dogs. The traits of the description fit almost ridiculously well. And one may say then with the old dog: once the *Verreden*, the babbling, has arrived at this point, the case is closed. But the old dog has not forgotten that there was once a mystery for the young dog in all this, and this mystery and riddle remains: "What is closed and finished for the adults is not finished for the little ones" ("Investigations" 434).

To say, for example, the mysterious musical dogs are simply trained circus dogs, would solve nothing; yet such a "solution" would only point at a scene where not only humans, but all creatures are pushed to the limit of their possibilities (and in the case of the musical dogs perhaps already toward the transgression of that limit). Already the first fragmentary novel of Kafka, *Der Verschollene*, ends (if indeed it is an ending and not an unheard of beginning) in a scene of a theatrical circus. The echoes between the manifest theatrical circus of *Der Verschollene* and the presumed latent circus of the musical dogs are loud enough. For when the musical dogs first appear it is not with music but *unter Hervorbringung eines entsetzlichen Lärms* ("producing a horrible noise"); and when Karl, in *Der Verschollene*, gets off the train, he hears something very similar: "*Als er in Clayton ausstieg, hörte er gleich den Lärm vieler Trompeten. Es war ein wirrer Lärm*" ("When he got off the train, he heard immediately the noise of many trumpets. It was a cacophonic noise").[14]

Horrible noise, cacophonic noise is the one side, silence the other side of music: "*Sie redeten nicht, sie sangen nicht, sie schwiegen im allgemeinen mit einer gewissen Verbissenheit*" ("They didn't speak, they didn't sing, in general they just were silent with a certain doggedness")[15] ("Investigations" 428). Noise and silence are the only possible phenomenalizations of what, in this story, is called music and knowledge. Just as the music seems to emanate from the dogs even though there is no manifest musical production to be seen, the knowledge is in them and somehow emanating from them precisely in their dogged silence: "All knowledge, the totality of all questions and of all answers is contained in the dogs, if only they would not know infinitely more than they admit, than they admit to themselves. Even the most garrulous dog is more locked up in his silence than the places where the best food is stored" ("Investigations" 441). And again, noise here is only another form of silence: "*mein und Dein Heulen mischt sich in eins, alles ist darauf gerichet, im Entzücken Vergessen zu finden*" ("Mine and your howling melt into one, everything has only one intention, to find forgetting in ecstasy") ("Investigations" 441-42).

Knowledge and silence are one in the creaturely life of the dog, above all of the speaking dogs, these *parlêtres*, as Lacan names certain creatures. Everything in Kafka's text indicates that this silence is a form of cowardice and anxiety—*hart aus Angst* ("hard with anxiety"), the narrating dog also remains silent—but it is not up to the decision of any individual to break the silence. And it would be dangerous, it would mean to destroy "the foundations of our lives" and to interrupt "the workers in their somber work" ("Investigations" 443).

At this point, Kafka's text touches on a layer, on a limit, that must not be confused with "humanism" and with complacent compromises. Kafka and his dog are not Serenus Zeitblom of Thomas Mann's *Doktor Faustus*. The limit here delineates another scene. And we find here perhaps at least a hint of why Kafka could become someone exploring the extreme limit without succumbing to the temptation to become a founder of a religion.

Kafka does not succumb to the temptation to pronounce the knowledge that afflicts and presses us all, because he knows all too well that any proclamation would only be a noise without music: an all too familiar murderous noise in our world at this point. If at all, it might be more likely indicated and touch our deaf ears in the ridiculous noise and artificial angel-wings and devil trumpets of the theater of Oklahoma.

This knowledge, namely, has a rather paradoxical status. On the one hand, it seems to exist only collectively, a kind of knowledge of a chorus, present in all of the dogs. Already Hölderlin envisioned something in this direction when he projected the possibility that we could move from the conversation (*Gespräch*) that we are (and not simply perform) to being song. Kafka's story defers infinitely this possibility of becoming song, but guards it as an infinitely receding horizon. He is not the founder of a religion. Thus, the other side of this collective knowledge: the knowledge might be there in the collective community of the dogs, in "dogdom," but certainly not in their science. To bring it to light would, however, mean the annihilation of the community of the dogs. But then, there is again another side, another "on the other hand," that belongs to a logic that undermines any dialectical procedure. For if this knowledge would come to light it would certainly interrupt, perhaps destroy, the community of the dogs, but it would interrupt them in something that the dog calls "their somber work" ("*bei ihrem finsteren Werk*"). If a somber work is interrupted, destroyed, would this not then be a promise of light? But such a promise would already be too close to the foundation of a religion—the temptation that Kafka resisted.

The narrating dog leaves open both possibilities. There is the redeeming possibility of pronouncing the secret knowledge: "If you pronounce it, who will resist you? The big chorus of dogdom will join as if it had waited for this. Then you will have truth, clarity, confession as much as you want. The roof of this low life that you denigrate so much will open up, and we all, dog with dog, will ascend into high freedom." But there is another possible consequence: things could become "worse than now," and the whole truth could "be more unbearable than the half truth" ("Investigations" 442-43); and those who remain silent might be considered as preservers of life. At this point, a motif of Nietzsche can be heard: the affirmation of appearance as protection of life.

Against this one might argue, and indeed the dog does articulate this argument against himself: "if the remote hope that we still harbor would turn into utter hopelessness, the attempt to pronounce the word would still be worth it, since you do not want to live the life that you are allowed to live. So, why then do you reproach the others for their silence, and yet you remain silent yourself?" The answer of the dog, as we have already seen, is as easy as it is cynical: "Because I am a dog" ("Investigations" 443). This is the limit where the explorer of limits stops.

And yet perhaps not quite. This dog, who says to himself, "since you do not want to live the life that you are allowed to live," could very well quote Faust who despairs of the limits of knowledge: "*Es möchte kein Hund so länger leben*" ("Not even a dog would want to live like this"). To be sure, Kafka's dog ultimately seems to acknowledge the limits of dogdom and his belonging to the community of the dogs. Arrived at a certain age, he even gives up questioning the dogs, but all the more he haunts and hunts himself with his question. An ultimate paradox opens up: the knowledge had by all which can be borne only by all, by the community of the dogs, by a chorus, that knowledge can be touched only by every single individual, at his or her own risk. The question, at the end, is "my proper question of life" (*Lebensfrage*); "it is directed only to me and it does not bother anyone else" ("Investigations" 443). With this realization, we could live together, even and especially if one dares to be as radical as Kafka.

## Notes

1. "*Erkenntnis haben wir. Wer sich besonders um sie bemüht, ist verdächtig sich gegen sie zu bemühen,*" Franz Kafka, *Kritische Ausgabe. Nachgelassene Schriften und Fragmente II*, ed. Jost Schillemeit (Frankfurt a.M.: S. Fischer, 1992), 76. All translations, if not otherwise indicated, are my own.

2. Indeed, I am operating here with a very provisional term that would need a much closer and thorough analysis.

3. Benjamin uses correctly Kafka's word: *Ungeziefer*, which does not yet specify at all the species of the creature. *Ungeziefer* (like *Unkraut*) does not exist in nature. It only names something—a creature or a plant—that is unwelcome in the cultivated world.

4. "*Denn so wie K. im Dorf am Schloßberg lebt der heutige Mensch in seinem Körper; er entgleitet ihm, ist ihm feindlich. Es kann geschehen, daß der Mensch eines Morgens erwacht, und er ist in ein Ungeziefer verwandelt. Die Fremde—seine Fremde—ist seiner Herr geworden. Die Luft von diesem Dorf weht bei Kafka, und darum ist er nicht in Versuchung gekommen, Religionsstifter zu werden,*" Walter Benjamin, "Franz Kafka," in *Gesammelte Schriften*, eds. Rolf Tiedemann and Hermann Schweppenhäuser (Frankfurt a.M.: Suhrkamp, 1980), II, 424.

5. "'*Jagd' ist nur ein Bild, ich kann auch sagen 'Ansturm gegen die letzte irdische Grenze' und zwar Ansturm von unten, von den Menschen her und kann, da auch dies nur ein Bild ist, es ersetzen durch das Bild des Ansturms von oben, zu mir herab. // Diese ganze Litteratur ist Ansturm gegen die Grenze und sie hätte sich, wenn nicht der Zionismus dazwischen gekommen wäre, leicht zu einer neuen Geheimlehre, einer Kabbala*

*entwickeln können. Ansätze dazu bestehn,*" Jan. 16, 1922, Franz Kafka, *Tagebücher*, eds. Hans-Gerd Koch, Michael Müller and Malcolm Pasley (Frankfurt a.M.: S. Fischer, 1990), 878.

6. "*Und hier habe ich allerdings Zustände erlebt (nicht viele) die meiner Meinung nach den von Ihnen Herr Doktor beschriebenen hellseherischen Zuständen sehr nahestehen, in welchen ich ganz und gar in jedem Einfall wohnte, aber jeden Einfall auch erfüllte und in welchen ich mich nicht nur an meinen Grenzen fühlte, sondern an den Grenzen des Menschlichen überhaupt,*" Franz Kafka, *Oxforder Quartheft* 1, eds. Roland Reuß and Peter Staengle (Basel / Frankfurt a.M.: Stroemfeld / Roter Stern, 2001), 68/69-70/71.

7. "*die Nahrung verfolgte den Hungrigen,*" Franz Kafka, "Forschungen eines Hundes," *Kritische Ausgabe. Nachgelassene Schriften und Fragmente II*, ed. Jost Schillemeit (Frankfurt a.M.: Fischer Verlag, 1992), 479. This text is hereafter cited as "Investigations."

8. "*Wenn ich z.B. fragte: Woher nimmt die Erde diese Nahrung?, kümmerte mich denn dabei, wie es den Anschein haben konnte, die Erde, kümmerten mich etwa der Erde Sorgen? Nicht im geringsten, das lag mir wie ich bald erkannte, völlig fern, mich kümmerten nur die Hunde, gar nichts sonst. Denn was gibt es außer den Hunden?Wen kann man sonst anrufen in der weiten leeren Welt? Alles Wissen, die Gesamtheit aller Fragen und aller Antworten ist in den Hunden enthalten. Wenn man nur dieses Wissen wirksam, wenn man es nur an den hellen Tag bringen könnte, wenn sie nur nicht so unendlich viel mehr wüssten, als sie zugestehn, als sie sich selbst zugestehn. Noch der redseligste Hund ist verschlossener, als es die Orte zu sein pflegen, wo die besten Speisen sind.*"

9. Verse 452: ξενος λογω μετοικος, ειτα δ'εγγενης—Hölderlin translates: "*der ist hier, als Fremder, nach der Rede, / Wohnt er mit uns, doch bald als Eingeborner,*" Friedrich Hölderlin, *Sämtliche Werke. Frankfurter Ausgabe*, Vol. 16, ed. Michael Franz, Michael Knaupp and D.E. Sattler (Frankfurt a.M.: Stroemfeld / Roter Stern Verlag, 1988), 457-58.

10. η ραψωδης ενθαδ ην κυων (when the singing one, the dog, was there), *Oedipus Tyrannos*, v. 391—And does not a mysterious singing dog, who at the same time is a hunter, enter Kafka's story at the extreme moment when his narrator dog is at the edge of death with his hunger experiment?

11. Kafka, *Nachgelassene Schriften*, II, 422.

12. Hölderlin, *Sämtliche Werke*, vol. 16, 252.

13. Kafka, *Oxforder Oktavheft* 4, eds. Roland Reuß and Peter Staengle (Basel / Frankfurt a.M.: Stroemfeld Verlag, 2008), 64/65.

14. Franz Kafka, *Kritische Ausgabe. Der Verschollene*, ed. Jost Schillemeit (Frankfurt a.M.: S. Fischer, 1983), 389.

15. The pun with the doggedness of the musical dogs is a pure (and happy) product of the English language; the German *Verbissenheit* is based on the image of biting into something and not letting loose.

## Works Cited

Benjamin, Walter. "Franz Kafka." In Walter Benjamin, *Gesammelte Schriften*, edited by Rolf Tiedemann and Hermann Schweppenhäuser, vol. II/2, 409-37. Frankfurt a.M.: Suhrkamp, 1980.

Hölderlin, Friedrich. *Sämtliche Werke. Frankfurter Ausgabe*, Vol. 16. Edited by Michael Franz, Michael Knaupp and D.E. Sattler. Basel / Frankfurt a.M.: Stroemfeld / Roter Stern Verlag, 1988.

Kafka, Franz. "Forschungen eines Hundes." In Franz Kafka, *Kritische Ausgabe. Nachgelassene Schriften und Fragmente II*, edited by Jost Schillemeit, 423-82. Frankfurt a.M.: Fischer Verlag, 1992.

———. *Kritische Ausgabe. Nachgelassene Schriften und Fragmente II.* Edited by Jost Schillemeit. Frankfurt a.M.: S. Fischer, 1992.

———. *Kritische Ausgabe. Der Verschollene.* Edited by Jost Schillemeit. Frankfurt a.M.: S. Fischer, 1983.

———. *Oxforder Quartheft* 1. Edited by Roland Reuß and Peter Staengle. Basel / Frankfurt a.M.: Stroemfeld / Roter Stern, 2001.

———. *Oxforder Oktavheft* 4. Edited by Roland Reuß and Peter Staengle. Basel / Frankfurt a.M.: Stroemfeld Verlag, 2008.

———. *Tagebücher.* Edited by Hans-Gerd Koch, Michael Müller and Malcolm Pasley. Frankfurt a.M.: S. Fischer, 1990.

CHAPTER 2

# Kafka's Empty Law: Laughter and Freedom in *The Trial*

*Dimitris Vardoulakis*

## A Cage without Walls?

Hannah Arendt's re-evaluation of Kafka persistently defines his works in terms of what it does *not* stand for—Kafka is not amenable to religion or psychoanalysis, he is neither a realist nor a surrealist, and so on. In the midst of this "negative exegetics" the following assertive statement suddenly appears: "Kafka's laughter is an immediate expression of the kind of human freedom and serenity that understands man to be more than just his failures."[1] The power of this claim resides in the connection between freedom and laughter. This may, at first blush, appear counter-intuitive. As even a cursory look at Kafka's work will reveal, the figure of imprisonment is paramount—from the Red Peter in "A Report to an Academy" and the "Hunger Artist" who are both confined to a literal cage, to a series of implied cages, such as Gregor Samsa's room in *The Metamorphosis*. However, as Kiarina Kordela and I have argued elsewhere, this need not be taken as a sign of despair and resignation but rather as a critique of the liberal democratic—and capitalist—sense of freedom that developed in Europe since the seventeenth century.[2] Further, as I have also shown, this critique of freedom in Kafka is presented through laughter. Comic elements become the technical means for the presentation of a revamped notion of freedom. Instead of an idealized freedom that can never be reached thereby leading to a sense of human failure, Kafka proposes a sense of mediated freedom that consists, above all, in freeing oneself from that idealized notion of freedom.[3] Hannah Arendt points precisely to the same nexus between laughter and freedom in Kafka's work.

Such a positive articulation of non-idealized freedom through laughter is challenged when we turn to a work like *The Trial*, where Kafka describes a generalized sense of encagement by the law. *The Trial* presents a man, Josef K., ensnared by an all-pervasive law. As the novel famously opens: "Someone must have slandered Josef K., for one morning, without having done anything wrong, he was arrested" (*Trial* 3).[4] This is a similar beginning to the *Metamorphosis*. A man wakes up to find himself completely trapped. Josef K., like Gregor Samsa, is also in his room. There is the image of the narrow street outside the window as well, although here the outside intrudes because the neighbors from across the road spy on Josef K. The main difference with *The Metamorphosis* is telling: whereas Gregor is confined in his room throughout the novella, Josef K.'s entrapment by the law disperses over his entire milieu. Josef K. enjoys freedom of movement, but everywhere he goes everyone seems to have already judged him as guilty for something indistinct, unexpressed, unknown. Josef K. finds himself trapped by an omnipresent and omnipotent law—he finds himself trapped in a cage without walls.

The reason for the law's omnipresence and omnipotence in *The Trial* is that the law is empty. As the lawyer Huld explains to Josef K., "the proceedings are not public. . . . As a result, the court records, and above all the writ of indictment, are not available to the accused and his defense lawyers" (*Trial* 113). Josef K. is accused of something, but he is not allowed to know what the accusation is nor the law upon which the accusation is based. The proceedings of the courts, as well, are never made public: "The final verdicts of the court are not published, and not even the judges have access to them" (*Trial* 154). The impossibility of finding the content of the law takes a humorous twist when Josef K. does manage, after a lot of effort, to get hold of the law books of an abandoned court-room, but they turn out to be nothing but dirty books: "They were dog-eared book. . . . K. opened the book on top, and an indecent picture was revealed. A man and a woman were sitting naked on a divan" (*Trial* 57).[5] The book of statutes turns out to be a pornographic illustrated novel. If the law is understood as a proscription—"you shall not do this or that"—then the pornographic content of these law books seems conversely to preach promiscuity.[6] So, not only is the only law book seen by Josef K. devoid of actual laws, its content is also incompatible with the law as such. Such a law devoid of content is, as Patrick J. Glen avers, an "empty norm."[7] This emptiness is what makes the law all the more omnipresent and omnipotent.

Prior to having a close look at the emptiness of the law in *The Trial* it is necessary to contextualize this figure of the empty law. I will do so with reference to Spinoza for several reasons. First, in the manner in which Deleuze emphasizes the laughter in both Spinoza and Kafka, we can say that there is an intellectual affinity, even kinship, between the two.[8] This consists in the determination to counter any ideals, to undermine any universals, with a trenchant insistence on materiality. Second, the *Tractatus Theologico-Politicus* is concerned with the problematic of freedom and the law is presented therein as empty, as pure obedience.[9] Thus, Spinoza's empty law is related to the problem of freedom, just as in *The Trial.* Third, the law's emptiness in Spinoza signifies its liberatory potential.[10] Hence, the detour via Spinoza will provide us with indications of how to identify, in Arendt's words, the "laughter" as the "expression of freedom" in the world of *The Trial* that is dominated by the omnipotent and omnipresent empty law.

## Spinoza's Ethical Laughter

In order to present the conception of freedom in the *Tractatus Theologico-Politicus*, it is required to look at Spinoza's description of empty law. The reason is that, as already intimated, it is through the redemptive potential of the empty law that a sense of non-idealized freedom arises.

The affirmation of the emptiness of the law is best articulated by Spinoza in chapter 14 of the *Tractatus*. This chapter bridges the analysis of the Bible offered in the previous thirteen chapters and the analysis of power and freedom propounded in the rest of the book. This is done with reference to the law. Spinoza writes that "the aim of Scripture is simply to teach obedience. . . . Moses' aim was . . . to bind [his people] by covenant" (*Tractatus* 515).[11] Spinoza avers that the Mosaic law is purely functional. Its function is solely to instill obedience as a means of securing a "covenant," or the creation of a Jewish state. Articulating Spinoza's conception of the empty law in terms of existence, we can say that law as means toward pure obedience corresponds to the modality of necessity. The law is necessary for the creation of a state and that's the only function that the law performs. "Moses, by his divine power and authority, introduced a state religion . . . to make the people do their duty from devotion," writes Spinoza in chapter 5 (*Tractatus* 439). The discussion of the handing of the Ten Commandments to Moses in chapter 1 of the *Tractatus* may appear curious since it concentrates on the question of whether Moses actually heard the voice of God.[12] But this is thoroughly consistent with Spinoza's aim to describe the law as purely necessary. The content as such of the commandments is irrelevant. All that matters is that the commandments will be binding and this requires that they be perceived as necessary by the people in need for a legal framework in order to form a state. In other words, all that matters is the functionality of the law—the fact that the law is a means. Thus, even though the ten commandments might have been written on stone, their content was secondary compared to the modality of necessity they enabled to be perceived as God's law—a necessity required in order to allow Moses to introduce a "state religion." The voice of God, as described in chapter 1 of the *Tractatus*, is precisely that modality of necessity that leads to unquestioned obedience.[13]

The modality of necessity that characterizes Spinoza's empty law is accompanied by the modality of contingency. This is related to the fact that the law is conceived by Spinoza as constitutive to the building of sociality. In chapter 14 of the *Tractatus*, shortly after arguing that the sole purpose of the Mosaic Law was obedience, Spinoza writes: "the entire Law consists in this alone, to love one's neighbor. . . . Scripture does not require us to believe anything beyond what is necessary for the fulfilling of the said commandment" (*Tractatus* 515). We see here again that the law is conceived as empty. The function of the empty law—its necessity—consists solely in the love of one's neighbor, insists Spinoza. This neighborly love becomes the constitutive element of "state religion." In other words, it is indispensable for the creation of a community. Spinoza refers here to Paul's assertion in *Romans* (13.8-10) that "Thou shalt love thy neighbor as thyself. . . . [L]ove [is] the fulfilling of the law." However, just as in the case of the Mosaic Law and the Ten Commandments, here Spinoza again significantly re-interprets—I am tempted to say, "subverts"—Paul's meaning. In the standard interpretation, the love of one's neighbor is the fulfillment of the law in the sense that it points to a universal sense of justice.[14] Spinoza uses neighborly love to refer to contingency instead. When discussing in chapter 3 the universal importance of the Mosaic Law, Spinoza insists that Moses' law was written in order to suit the specific—that is, contingent—needs to the lawmaker/prophet and the people he was addressing at that particular place and time. Or, if law is understood as means, then the law must be adaptable to the given circumstances in which the law is to function. At that point, Spinoza turns to Paul's *Romans*. He interprets the epistle as arguing that "to all men without exception was revealed the law under which all men lived" (*Tractatus* 423). If there is a "universality" to the law, then that "universality" never belongs to one people and is never expressed in one way. Rather, it is a materialist universality, expressed always in contingent terms, related to the living conditions of the people to whom the law applies. Later, when Spinoza addresses explicitly the command to love one's neighbors in chapter 12, he prefaces that by saying that one cannot expect to find "the same markings, the same letters and the same words" in the laws of different people. The "Divine Law" is empty since its content is changeable and it can only be expressed under the modality of contingency (*Tractatus* 508). Thus, any written laws are nothing but "letters that are dead" since statute depends upon the contingent circumstances of the community (*Tractatus* 521). So, whereas Paul presented love as such in order to identify it with universal or divine justice, Spinoza emphasizes instead a love *for*—a love that requires an object that is only ever transient, aleatory, contingent.

The reconfiguring of both the Mosaic Law and the sense of legality in the New Testament are to be understood together. There is, according to Spinoza, a mutual dependency between necessity—the fact that the law's only purpose is obedience—and contingency—the expression of that obedience according to the given, accidental circumstances. The law is empty because it is both necessary and contingent. Or, as Spinoza puts it, "since obedience to God consists solely in loving one's neighbor . . . it follows that Scripture commands no other kind of knowledge than that which is necessary for all men before they can obey God according to this commandment and without which men are bound to be self-willed, or at least unschooled to obedience" (*Tractatus* 511). The contingent expression of the love toward one's neighbor is the fulfillment of the necessity of the law that consists in nothing else than the fact that the law is to be obeyed. Defining the law in terms of such contingency and necessity makes the law a means—a pure functional element. This co-presence of necessity and contingency denominates "state religion" and the theologico-political in Spinoza.

Further, the co-presence of the modalities of necessity and contingency indicates that the emptiness of the law presupposes something more primary. Or, more precisely, there is an element that arises out of the emptiness of the law that cannot, however, be contained by it. This element is associated with rebellion: "faith requires . . . dogmas [that] move the heart to obedience; and this is so even if many of those beliefs contain not a shadow of truth, provided that he who adheres to them knows not that they are false. If he knew that they were false, he would necessarily be a rebel" (*Tractatus* 516-17). The moment that an excess is perceived in obedience, then it is no longer possible to rest content with its dictates, especially if they are false. This overcoming of falsity introduces an instability in the obedience that characterizes the co-ordination of the necessity and the contingency of the empty law. The emptiness of the law—unquestioned obedience, pure authority—is paradoxically premised on the power of rebellion. "No body politic can exist without being subject to the latent threat of civil war ('sedition'). . . . This is the cause of causes," as Étienne Balibar puts it.[15] Rebellion is excessive of the theologico-political nexus of necessity and contingency but in such a way as to underlie "state religion." Rebellion is more primary than state constitution. But this simply means that the law as means has no end. No matter what specific content the law has, that content is always changeable. There is no telos that defines what a state should look like or what a state should proscribe its citizens.[16]

The rebellious countering of the falsities of obedience is associated by Spinoza with the truth making function of philosophy: "The domain of reason . . . is truth and wisdom, the domain of theology is piety and obedience" (*Tractatus* 523). Truth is excessive of the necessity and contingency that characterize the Mosaic and Pauline laws of "state religion." Or, differently put, truth shows that the means lack an end—there is no teleology in nature, as Spinoza makes clear in the preface to Part IV of the *Ethics*. The introduction of truth leads to the third and last modality of existence, namely, possibility. This is expressed in the *Tractatus* as the theory of power or *potentia* and it is introduced in chapter 16 in terms of a theory of rights.[17] According to Spinoza's conception, rights are the expression of one's possibilities: "each individual thing has the sovereign right to do all that it can do; i.e. the right of the individual is coextensive with its determinate power" (*Tractatus* 527). The search for truth is not an abstract activity but rather embedded in existence. It is linked to the exercise of one's right to realize one's power. The notion of right in Spinoza is incompatible with liberal notions of right, according to which rights point to universal human values. Rather, right for Spinoza is precisely the possibility to rebel when truth interrupts the nexus of necessity and contingency, that is, when truth interrupts the emptiness of the law. Or, differently put, right as power is excessive of, and interrupts, "state religion."

At the same time, it is important to note that Spinoza does not lapse into a utopian vision of a world that could be free from empty law. There is no pure expression of power.[18] Rather, the expression of power requires the presence of the empty law. It is the rebellion against the empty law that allows for the expression of power and hence for freedom. In this sense, freedom for Spinoza is the freedom *from* the empty law.[19] Thus, freedom in Spinoza requires the two modalities of necessity and contingency. Freedom is the breaking of the hold of obedience that they institute—a breaking that is enacted through the introduction of truth. Truth, then, forges the connection with the third modality of existence, possibility, giving rise to Spinoza's theory of power that allows for a conception of freedom not as absolute but rather as mediated.[20]

Spinoza's empty law, then, far from an inescapable encagement, offers rather a redemptive potential. The emptiness of the law relies on the way that the modalities of necessity and contingency are co-present. Within this context, the excessive elements of rebellion and truth point to the modality of possibility. Thus the emptiness of the law indicates that a political being can in fact be conceived otherwise. Freedom in fact consists in retaining this "otherwise"—the possibility of resistance and change. Politics is never finalized. There is no universal determination of the right political value that would determine a telos to the state and its laws. Truth is not an abstract thesis or inference valid for ever. Rather, truth is the enactment of that "otherwise"—the possibility of resisting the current political arrangement. According to Deleuze, this possibility—this power—to arrange human relations "otherwise" constitutes Spinoza's "ethical laughter." Deleuze contrasts that laughter to the irony and mockery that characterize the tyrant, whose purpose or telos is to remain in power. Such mockery is "another way of saying that human nature is miserable," whereas the affirmation of life and materiality makes Spinoza's laughter joyful—a laughter that affirms the possibility of change.[21]

## Empty Law without Truth

The empty law of *The Trial* can be understood in Spinozan terms. Specifically, it is possible to understand the emptiness of the law as the conjunction of necessity and contingency. The best place to examine the description of the law's emptiness in terms of necessity and contingency is the parable "Before the Law" that is contained in the chapter "In the Cathedral."

Josef K. goes to the cathedral to meet a customer of his bank. The customer does not turn up. Nevertheless, Josef K. meets a priest who narrates the parable. It is the story of a "man from the country" who wants to be admitted to the law. A gatekeeper does not so much prohibit him from crossing a first gate on the way to the law, as warn him that there are more gates guarded by increasingly ferocious gatekeepers, so it would be better for him to wait for admittance. The man from the country waits for many years, but to no avail. His pleas with the gatekeeper fall on deaf ears. He grows old, his strength and eyesight weaken and as a matter of fact he is about to expire, when a strange thought crosses his mind: How come no one has striven to reach the law all these years, even though everyone wants to have access to it? The gatekeeper responds: "'No one else could gain admittance here, because this entrance was meant solely for you. I'm going to go and shut it now'" (*Trial* 217). This conclusion to the parable fits perfectly the Spinozan framework of the emptiness of the law. We can identify here the necessity and contingency that characterize empty law. There is no proscription against entering the first gate toward the law—the man from the country is free to do so but he is warned against it because of the ferocious gatekeepers that he is bound to encounter further down the road. He does not enter the gate, then, for functional reasons. This functionality determines necessity. Contingency is also present when the gatekeeper asserts that the entrance to the law "was meant solely for you." From this perspective, the law articulates itself through its contingent relation to the subject. The law is not universal but rather suited to the specific circumstances of the man from the country. The combination of necessity and contingency delineates an empty law in the parable that is amenable to the Spinozan conception of empty law.[22]

The affinity with Spinoza is complicated, however, when at the end of the exchange with the priest the question of truth arises. Josef K. avers that it is not possible to understand everything that the priest is saying as true. The priest objects that the category of truth is inappropriate: "'you don't have to consider everything [the gatekeeper says] true, you just have to consider everything necessary.'" Josef K. can be read as conceding the point to the priest when he says that, when truth is separated from necessity, "'Lies are made into a universal system'" (*Trial* 223)—although I will return to this assertion in the following section to explore a different interpretation that retains a Spinozan possibility of resistance.[23] The gatekeeper's articulations determine the law as both contingent and necessary—they determine the law as empty. The separation or disengagement of truth from the empty law creates a dualism, which entails that, in Spinoza's terms, the possibility of freedom is eliminated. The man from the country is presented as being absolutely obedient. Without recourse to truth, he has no recourse to any methods of resistance to the contingent and yet necessary pronouncements of the gatekeeper. Separating the emptiness of the law from truth leads to a different understanding of truth than what we discovered in Spinoza. Truth no longer resists teleology. Or, differently put, truth no longer points to the possibility that the political can be configured "otherwise." Therefore, the way that the empty law is construed as disengaged from truth has repercussions for how the third modality, possibility, can be understood. Possibility is inscribed here as the impossibility of searching for the truth, and hence the impossibility of resistance. Spinoza's rebellious stance is excluded from this construal of power. The fact that the law is empty means that the law is inaccessible, and therefore the representative of the law speaks with a necessity that has absolute authority. The empty law that relies on a necessity without truth can take three guises: a theological, a biopolitical and a moral one.[24] I will examine these in turn.

The incontestable authority of a law devoid of truth can spawn a theological reading of *The Trial* because such a law in *The Trial* draws its power from the fact that it is both invisible and thoroughly pervasive. The invisibility and all-encompassing nature of the law in the *Trial* has often been given a theological interpretation.[25] Passages like the following do seem to allow for such a reading: "'[Everyone is] in agreement . . . that the court, once it brings a charge, is convinced of the guilt of the accused, and that it is difficult to sway the court from this conviction.' 'Difficult?' asked the painter [Titorelli], throwing one hand in the air. 'The court can never be swayed from it. If I were to paint all the judges in a row on this canvas and you were to plead your case before them, you would have more success than before the actual court'" (*Trial* 149). The judges can be understood as metonymies of the divine that, as Augustine demonstrates in his *Confessions*, never responds despite the appellant's pleads.[26] Or, one can understand the judges' absence in negative theological terms, as the absence that makes the presence of their universal judgment possible.[27] What such readings have in common is the supposition that there is a universal dimension to the law that is visible in the universal ascription of guilt. We have here a fallen world because of an original sin. The law is legitimated through such a universalized guilt. And yet, we have already seen that the law's emptiness requires the contingent. How can the law be both contingent and universalized?

The answer is simple enough and it leads from a theological to a biopolitical construal of authority.[28] It is not the content of the law that is regarded as universal. Rather, the emptiness itself of the law is universalized. For instance, no one knows the content of the law that has Josef K. arrested. In the absence of content, everyone in the novel becomes a guardian of the law.[29] Thus, when Titorelli says that the judges are invisible, this is not because the judges are hidden and their judgments assume a universally true content, but because they are everywhere and their judgments are arbitrary. Everyone is a judge, everyone condemns Josef K. from the very first moment of his arrest without charge. In the absence of any justification or legitimacy based on a sense of legality, their judgments are capricious, contingent upon their mood. And yet, their judgments are simultaneously all the more uniform and universal—they all pronounce Josef K. guilty. The effect of this universalization of contingency is that the law is dispersed and all-encompassing—it is omnipresent and omnipotent. Here, everyone is a proxy to the law, everyone is a legitimate judge. Such a dispersal of the law seeking to take control of the everyday characterizes biopolitics, according to the last lecture of Foucault's *Society Must be Defended*. Foucault expresses this idea in one of his examples: "Ultimately, everyone in the Nazi State had the power of life and death over his or her neighbors, if only because of the practice of informing."[30] The dispersal of an empty law makes judgment legitimate and yet also completely arbitrary and thus an instrument of the exercise of unlimited authority. Law's emptiness—the absence of a content to the law—can become the ultimate trick that authority plays, namely, dissimulating a denial of content only so that everyone is forced to supply arbitrarily content every instant anew, and yet always with the same result—ascription of guilt. The emptiness of the law is universal, but in biopolitics this is understood as the license for everyone to pass an arbitrary judgment—that is, a judgment without concern for truth. In this sense, the prison without walls represented in *The Trial* can be viewed as the perfect depiction of the repressive emptiness of the law. This pure authority of the empty law is only possible because the law is dissociated from truth.

There is a final turn to the mechanism that disengages authority from truth, thereby foreclosing the possibility of freedom. This consists in the introduction of morality as the law beyond or above the legal system.[31] As has already been shown, the universalization of the law's emptiness means that the judgments passed are arbitrary—everyone regards Josef K. as guilty, even though none relies on a definite content of the law. There is no process whereby guilt is tested by evidence—there is no "natural justice"—and hence the very idea of a state law becomes dubious. Maybe, then, we are not dealing here with law as statute but rather with law as an unwritten moral imperative. Immanuel Kant describes such a moral imperative in the *Groundwork of the Metaphysics of Morals.*[32] He defines a categorical imperative that can never be given any steadfast content, but it is rather the principle that should determine action "as if" one knew at any time what that content were. It is this "as if" that gives the empty moral law its universal dimension. In *The Ethics of Reading,* J. Hillis Miller examines this empty law by analyzing one of Kant's examples, namely, the proscription against making empty promises—the proscription against lying.[33] Miller shows that Kant cannot determine whether the proscription articulates this empty law through a contractual agreement between humans or through reference to a transcendent law. Both possibilities are necessary and yet they contradict each other.[34] Or, in the terminology used earlier to describe Spinoza's position, an empty moral law is caught in a double bind that is called to decide between contingency and necessity—and yet, it cannot make that decision without annulling its emptiness. Miller compares this Kantian conundrum to Josef K.'s assertion that "Lies are made into a universal system," and infers that "Whether I intend to lie or do not intend to lie I lie in any case."[35] The separation of truth from the empty law indicates a space of judgment and law beyond the legal system—it signifies morality. Nevertheless, the incapacity of that morality to decide between contingency and necessity articulates itself as a lie, thereby contradicting its own moral proscriptions. In other words, the empty law without truth of morality appears as nothing other than a persistent lying. It would be easy to infer at this point that such lying creates a "world order" that represents a lamentable existential condition.

The theological, the biopolitical and the moral interpretations of Kafka's law all lead to despair and a profound sense of failure. In all these construals, Kafka is presented as the most tortured of tortured authors, the most sublimely tragic figure. Guilt is inescapable, there is no possibility of resistance and everything turns into a lie. There is nothing more foreign to Kafka's laughter than condemning the human to such a fallen world with a dispersed power of control and a moral law that exists only as a lie. Such an existential despair is a direct result of separating empty law from truth, which produces a dualism that can be articulated in different ways—theological, biopolitical, moral—and yet with the same result: absolute imprisonment. Deleuze and Guattari note that *The Trial* presents "the law as pure and empty form without content" (*Kafka* 43). They describe this emptying of content as the law's transcendence that posits "a necessary connection of law and guilt." They continue: "Guilt must in fact be the a priori that corresponds to transcendence. . . . Having no object and being only pure form, the law cannot be a domain of knowledge but is exclusively the domain of an absolute practical necessity." They point out to the priest's separation of necessity from truth as the presentation of such a transcendent law (*Kafka* 44-45). The transcendent law that cannot be known, the law that cannot be related to truth, is absolutely necessary because it ensnares the individual in perpetual guilt.

As opposed to this lamentable condition of humanity Deleuze and Guattari insist on a different possibility. They argue that the discovery of Kafka's laughter leads away from dualism and the ensuing despair—and even leads toward the discovery of a promise of freedom in Kafka's writings.

## The Laughter of Freedom

The possibility of such a promise of freedom through laughter can only be discerned by remaining attentive to how truth is re-figured in *The Trial*. We need to return to the separation of the empty law from truth, as it is expressed at the end of the exchange between the priest and Josef K. Citing the passage in its entirety is required so that an alternative interpretation can emerge that no longer leads to despair:

> "The man has only arrived at the Law, the doorkeeper is already there. He has been appointed to his post by the Law, to doubt his dignity is to doubt the Law itself." "I don't agree with that opinion," said K., shaking his head, "for if you accept it, you have to consider everything that the doorkeeper says as true. But you've already proved conclusively that that's not possible." "No," said the priest, "you don't have to consider everything true, you just have to consider everything necessary." "A depressing opinion," said K. "Lies are made into a universal system [*Die Lüge wird zur Weltordnung gemacht*]." K. said that with finality [*abschließend*] but it was not his final judgment [*Endurteil*]. (*Trial* 223)[36]

As seen in the previous section, truth can be separated from the empty law because truth is understood as something universal, unrelated to the possibility of resistance and of seeing the world "otherwise." A different understanding to truth starts arising by noting that the distinction between "finality" and "final judgment" in Josef K.'s assertion introduces a sense of interruption. Josef K. says that lying is a universal principle in conclusion (*abschließend*) but this is not his final judgment since that would have consisted in an endless guilt of the human who, after shedding the yoke of a repressive content to the law, is now even more repressed than ever. This leads inexorably to a lament for human suffering in the state of lying. But by not articulating his final judgment (*Endurteil*), Josef K. interrupts that ceaseless lament, refuses to see humanity as being in a state of perpetual suffering and hence does not seek consolation by the priest.[37]

This interruption is the first move toward retaining a notion of the truth. In fact, such a notion of truth can be gleaned from what Josef K. says about lying. The crucial move is to resist the interpretation that lying—as it is expressed by Josef K.'s formula that "Lies are made into a universal system"—points to the separation of truth from the empty law. In other words, the notion of lying suggested in Josef K.'s statement should not be seen as an apposition to the priest's assertion that what the gatekeeper says is necessary but has nothing to do with truth. When lying is seen as related to truth then lying leads back to the possibility of resistance and the mediated freedom that we discovered in Spinoza.

So, how does truth re-inscribe itself through the figure of lying so as to assert the possibility of freedom? The first point to note is that Josef K.'s statement can be taken to denote a process. "*Die Lüge wird zur Weltordnung gemacht*" does not simply mean that lies are becoming a universal principle, but the process of lying is such a principle. Understanding lying as a process is important because it opposes the presupposition of the priest's previous statement, according to which the gatekeeper's articulations do not pertain to truth but only to necessity. The priest presupposes—and that is what the rejection of the link between necessity and truth amounts to—that truth is universal, or that truth needs to be understood in terms of an assertion of a universally true content. Josef K. responds that lying, as a process, describes how the world is. Understanding lying as a process amounts to a rejection of the premise that truth is to be defined in relation to a content. Instead, Josef K.'s statement allows for an understanding of truth as that which is allowed—that which is *possible*—in relation to the lying that pervades the world. In other words, lying is understood as the untruths of the contingent expression of empty law—as the falsities against which, as Spinoza insists, rebellion is necessary.

Understanding lying—and hence truth—as a process, affects the way the relation between contingency and necessity is understood. When the gatekeeper tells the man from the country that this entrance to the law is only for him and that he will now shut it, the gatekeeper, as already intimated, affirms the contingency of the law as it is applied to the man from the country. But what exactly does the shutting of the entrance mean? From the perspective that seeks to separate the empty law from truth, the entry to the law is barred because the law is empty and it is this emptiness that is universalized. In other words, even though the entrance is solely for the man from the country, still the shutting of that entrance pertains to the guilt that is ascribed to everyone. That is why, also, there is no process here—Josef K. was judged as guilty from the moment of his arrest because everyone is guilty *ab initio*. Conversely, allowing for a relationship between the lying or untruth of the law's articulation and truth highlights the impossibility of eliminating process. The relation between contingency and necessity is not resolved—or, dissolved—in a universalized state that is separated from truth. Rather, it is a relation that is infinitely negotiable, continuously evolving and transformable. It is a relation pregnant with possibilities. There is an agonistic stance articulated as the opposition to any form of occlusion. In this construal, the gatekeeper does not guard access to the law as such—if such a thing exists—but rather to the solidification of the law. The gatekeeper suspends access to the law so that the law can remain open and transformable in its contingency. He shuts the entrance to the law so as to avoid any misunderstanding that the empty law can be attributed a telos. From this perspective, the gatekeeper functions as Spinoza's figure of the philosopher, whose role is to resist blind obedience to the law. It is as if he is telling the man from the country to stop hanging around the gate, submissively waiting for an entrance to the law, urging him instead to rebel. Such a rebellion should be understood in Spinozan terms, namely, as the admonition to stop seeing the empty law as a tool that leads to absolute obedience.

This agonistic stance can be seen as a rebellion against universality. It will be recalled that the universalization of the emptiness of the law is a defining characteristic of the empty law without truth and it results in arbitrary judgments. According to biopolitics, since the law is empty, then everyone can pass judgments, even though such judgments are completely arbitrary. The shutting of the gate is a different form of judgment. It is a judgment that is no longer arbitrary. Rather, it interrupts the process that makes judgment arbitrary. It does so by severing the link between necessity and universality. Or, it is a judgment that insists that a sense of truth is possible, even only as the process of agonism against untruth, against obedience, and against an empty law whose transcendence creates universal guilt. To express this in yet another way, the judgment here inscribes itself as the interruption of occlusion, and hence as the interruption that allows for process to continue.[38]

The possibility of such a sense of judgment is the form that power takes in its agonistic opposition to empty law without truth. Kafka presents Josef K. as arriving at this sense of power, but also as being unable to recognize it. (I will describe shortly the Kafkaesque laughter arising from Josef K.'s inability to recognize the possibility of such a sense of judgment even though he has already arrived at it.)[39] At the end of the dialogue with the priest, Josef K. asserts that "*Die Lüge wird zur Weltordnung gemacht*." The way that the world is organized consists in lying, avers Josef K. here. The corollary of this assertion is that truth is not universal, or, even more emphatically, that there is no universality as such in the world order. Josef K. says this in conclusion to the conversation (*abschließend*) but not so that he makes it into a final judgment (*Endurteil*). It would be recalled that, according to the interpretation that separates the empty law from truth, this concluding remark does not arrive at a final judgment in the sense of an incessant lament for the ineliminable guilt of a "humanity" faced with a transcendent law. But this concluding to the conversation can be read in a completely different way. It can also be taken as the reiteration of the gatekeeper's gesture of shutting the door in the face of the man from the country. The remark that lying is the order of the world is, literally, a shutting up, an *Abschließen*. Josef K. asserts the possibility of an interruption of this process—this dialogue—so that he is not led to the final conclusion that the possibility of judgment (*Urteil*) has ended and is substituted instead by lament. It is a shutting up that allows for the continuation of the process. This process continues because the shutting up affirms an agonistic stance against a final judgment—a judgment about the universalization of contingent necessity that eliminates truth. At the point that Josef K. stops the process that is intended to suspend all process, at the moment that he interrupts the disempowering gesture that separates truth from necessity in order to universalize arbitrary judgment, Josef K. asserts his potential, assumes his power and responsibility. In Spinozan terms, Josef K.'s observation about the pervasiveness of lying is an assertion of his power (*potentia*), an act of resistance against an empty law devoid of truth. This is not a sense of freedom as the opposite of the imprisonment in guilt that is the outcome of a transcendent law. It is, rather, as Deleuze and Guattari put it, a "line of escape and not freedom" (*Kafka* 35). In other words, it is a sense of freedom that operates in a register that is different from that of a law without truth. In fact, it is a liberation precisely from that false promise of freedom contained in transcendent law. This is not an absolute freedom from imprisonment and guilt, but a freedom that is *mediated* by its agonistic relation to that illusory sense of absolute freedom. Josef K. liberates himself *from* the universalization of empty law. He is free *from* the illusory promise of a universal freedom that the empty law without truth offers.

If such a potential has been reached, if Josef K. has discovered the possibility that he has at his disposal in order to adopt an agonistic stance against the all-pervasive biopolitical power, then how can we explain the fact that Josef K. does not grasp that possibility, does not realize that potential? Why does he not recognize this mediated freedom?[40]

There are two crucial aspects to answering why Kafka does not present Josef K. as aware of being free from the unknown accusation that ensnares him. The first aspect is Kafka's own circumspection. Kafka is cautious to pre-empt any illusion that a sense of freedom is still possible when the empty law is separated from truth. There is no theological sense of enlightenment that discloses a spiritual freedom, nor is there a sense of universalized freedom that adheres toward the biopolitical paradigm, nor, finally, an individual freedom within the confines of a moral law. What all these senses of freedom presuppose is the separation of an empty law from truth. Obedience to the law is always seen as a lack of freedom, as an instance of absolute obedience that curtails the individual. They all presupposed the dualism of absolute freedom versus absolute imprisonment. Presenting Josef K. as liberated from the unknown accusation that an omnipotent and omnipresent law leveled against him would have run the danger of appearing as if a sense of absolute freedom from the empty law can be achieved. That would not have been merely a utopian conclusion. Further, by accepting the presuppositions of the separation of empty law and truth it would have affirmed the primacy of that separation itself—thereby asserting the priest's position, according to which the empty law is separated from truth. Absolute freedom is not the opposite of the absolute imprisonment that characterizes transcendent law. Rather, absolute freedom and absolute imprisonment operate within the same dialectic of transcendence that produces an empty law devoid of truth. Kafka wants to avoid any confusion between such a notion of absolute freedom and the mediate freedom that is the immanent expression of a freeing oneself from the guilt induced by transcendence.

Besides wanting to resist any misconception that such an absolute sense of freedom can be achieved, there is a second aspect as to why Josef K. is not presented as aware of being liberated. As already indicated, Josef K. has already reached a sense of freedom different from the absolute—and thus unreachable—freedom presupposed by the separation of the empty law and truth. We saw the discovery of that sense of freedom in the conclusion to the conversation with the priest. The finality of his conclusion to the exchange, his *Abschließen*, it will be recalled, is a form of interruption, like the gatekeeper's shutting of the door. What this interrupts precisely is the universalizing impulse that requires an understanding of truth, no less than of freedom, as absolutes. Josef K. concludes without a final judgment, resisting occlusion in such absolutes. Such an interruption posits a sense of freedom *from* the discourse that understands both freedom and truth as absolutes. And yet, Josef K. remains unaware of it. Like the man from the country, he appears in this occasion, when he finds himself before the empty law, a bit naive, a bit unsophisticated, a bit too obedient to recognize that authority can always be challenged—indeed, that the possibility inherent in making judgments that stake a claim to truth is precisely the challenging of the necessity of authority. Josef K.'s ignorance of what he has achieved is an expression of Kafka's humor.

Kafka laughs with Josef K. by presenting him as having arrived at the conclusion but without being able to recognize it. The entire novel then appears as a joke at the expense of Josef K. The joke consists in the fact that Josef K. constantly strives toward complete liberation—to be granted "complete acquittal," in the vocabulary of *The Trial*—and yet he never realizes it because such an acquittal is unattainable. But the reason is simply that he was looking for the wrong thing—namely, absolute freedom. Everybody was warning him that "complete acquittal" does not exist. Absolute freedom is the chimera that imprisons the subject. Josef K., the bank manager who dresses up like city dandy—someone who aspires to a high social and economic status—acts like the man from the country, an unkempt buffoon with dark nasal hair.[41] We have, on the one hand, someone who is meant to be "in the know" and, on the other, someone who is meant to be ignorant of the ways of the world. They form a comic pair because they are set up as complete opposites, and yet they ultimately appear not dissimilar. They are not only presented with the same task—the attempt to comprehend their relation to the law—they also both fail to see that their relation to the law points to action and truth. They fail to see that there is no inner sanctum of the law that can be reached. There is no absolute freedom. Rather, it is the enacting of their relation to absolute freedom that is a liberation *from* that sense of freedom. Their task is to liberate themselves *from* the emptiness of the law devoid of truth. They both arrive at this conclusion and yet they both fail to see it—until it is too late. The sentence of Josef K. to die "like a dog" recapitulates the erasure of the distance that separates him from this comic pair—the dandy banker lapses into animality and to country ignorance, he descends from his lofty position and thereby meets the animal or a representative of the most low stratum.[42]

Arendt's assertion discussed at the beginning of the chapter makes perfect sense from this perspective. Arendt noted that Kafka's laughter points to a sense of freedom that "understands man to be more than just his failures." Josef K. has indeed failed to recognize his liberation from transcendent law. But this failure is articulated as laughter. Kafka's humor is *immanent* in Josef K.'s failure. This takes two guises. First, it is immanent in the sense that it points to a sense of being that is not reliant on transcendence. One cannot laugh when one is confronted by transcendent ideals—a heroic endeavor toward something lofty and ideal is never meant to be funny. Indeed, laughter is a physical symptom, a bodily expression, that does not point to anything high, anything transcendent. No wonder that it has always being associated with "low" literature.[43] Kafka embraces that low literature—or what Deleuze and Guattari call "minor literature"—that is meant to provoke laughter in the reader.

The second aspect arises when it is recognized that even if a heroic deed that aspires toward transcendent ideals is not meant to be funny, it still can appear laughable. In other words, the failure to live up to transcendence can be subject of laughter.[44] In fact, as we have already seen, Deleuze calls Spinoza's laughter "ethical" precisely because it is an opposition to forms of transcendence that constitute attempts at imprisonment. Deleuze and Guattari raise an equivalent point when they discuss Kafka. They argue that even though Kafka presents an empty, transcendent law that is absolutely necessary in *The Trial*, still "the humor that he puts into it shows an entirely different intention" (*Kafka* 43). In fact, Deleuze and Guattari argue that the empty law without truth is "a superficial movement" in Kafka's work that is needed because it "indicates points of undoing, of dismantling" (*Kafka* 45). What is being dismantled is the structure of transcendence that separates necessity from truth, thereby leading to absolute authority. Laughter performs such a dismantling, or "even . . . a demolition," as Deleuze and Guattari emphatically put it (*Kafka* 45). In other words, laughter leads to an empty law that is conceived in terms of its immanent relation to whoever is before it. Thus laughter functions as the *means* for the expression of a freedom from the empty law without content. In Kafka's world, laughter is the conduit to freedom. The one who laughs at Josef K.'s perennial guilt is Spinoza's necessary rebel who interrupts the nexus of contingent necessity by recognizing its falsity.[45]

## Notes

I would like to thank Norma Lam-Saw and Aleksandra Ilic for reading and commenting on this chapter.

1. Hannah Arendt, "Franz Kafka, Appreciated Anew," in *Reflections on Literature and Culture*, ed. Susannah Young-ah Gottlieb (Stanford, CA: Stanford University Press, 2007), 106-7.

2. See Kiarina Kordela and Dimitris Vardoulakis, "Kafka's Cages," in *Freedom and Confinement in Modernity: Kafka's Cages*, eds. Kordela and Vardoulakis (New York: Palgrave, 2011), 1-6.

3. Dimitris Vardoulakis, "'The Fall is the proof of our freedom': Mediated Freedom in Kafka," in *Freedom and Confinement in Modernity*, eds. Kordela and Vardoulakis, 87-106.

4. The English translation of the *Trial* referenced in this chapter is Franz Kafka, *The Trial*, trans. Willa and Edwin Muir, rev. trans. E.M. Butler (New York: Schocken, 1995).

5. Walter Benjamin observes that filth and decay are constant characteristics of power in Kafka's worlds. Benjamin, "Franz Kafka: On the Tenth Anniversary of his Death," in *Selected Writings*, ed. Michael W. Jennings et al. (Cambridge, MA: Belknap, 2001), volume 2, 794-818.

6. If the law does indeed elide proscription in *The Trial*, then a relevant point can be raised (that I cannot, however, take up in any detail here) about the concluding remark of

the novel, when Josef K. is executed "like a dog." If the law is an expression of desire, then being a "dog" is not an offensive appellative. Rather, it is a re-iteration of the way that the elusive law of *The Trial* conceives of agency.

7. Patrick J. Glen, "The Deconstruction and Reification of Law in Kafka's 'Before the Law' and *The Trial*," *Southern California Interdisciplinary Law Journal* 17 (2007): 26 and *passim*.

8. For instance, we find the following comment in the transcript of "Power and Classical Natural Right," a lecture by Deleuze delivered on December 9, 1980: "[T]here are some very comical pages in Spinoza's *Ethics*. . . . It is a very particular kind of laughter and Spinoza is one of the most cheerful authors in the world. . . . It is Ethical laughter!" http://www.webdeleuze.com/php/texte.php?cle=20&groupe=Spinoza&langue=2 (accessed October 2006). And of Kafka, Deleuze and Guattari write: "He is an author who laughs with a profound joy, a *joie de vivre*, in spite of, or because of, his clownish declarations that he offers like a trap or a circus." Gilles Deleuze and Félix Guattari, *Kafka: Towards a Minor Literature*, trans. Dana Polan (Minneapolis, MN: University of Minnesota Press, 1986), 41. I will discuss further both of these assertions by Deleuze in due course. All subsequent references to this book will be made in-text parenthetically with the title abbreviated as *Kafka*.

9. That Spinoza's *Treatise* is about freedom is made clear from the subtitle that says that the treatise is about the freedom to philosophize and to judge as necessary for the peace of the state. The subtitle says exactly: "Containing Various Disquisitions, By means of which it is shown not only that Freedom of Philosophizing can be allowed in Preserving Piety and the Peace of the Republic: but also that it is not possible for such Freedom to be upheld except when accompanied by the Peace of the Republic and Piety Themselves."

10. My reading of Spinoza's *Tractatus Theologico-Politicus* here is based on, combines and augments two earlier attempts: Dimitris Vardoulakis, "Spinoza's Empty Law: The Possibility of Political Theology," in *Spinoza Beyond Philosophy*, ed. Beth Lord, (Edinburgh: Edinburgh University Press, 2012), 135-48; and Dimitris Vardoulakis, *Sovereignty and its Other* (New York: Fordham University Press, forthcoming in 2013), chapter 4. Both of these contain more detailed analysis than can be offered here of Spinoza's position.

11. The English translation of the *Tractatus* referenced in this chapter is Spinoza, *Theological-Political Treatise*, in *Complete Works*, trans. Samuel Shirley, ed. Michael L. Morgan (Indianapolis, IN: Hackett, 2002), 383-582.

12. For a discussion of this point, see Arthur Jacobson, "Prophesy without Prophets: Spinoza and Maimonides on Law and the Democracy of Knowledge," in *Spinoza Now*, ed. Dimitris Vardoulakis (Minneapolis, MN: University of Minnesota Press, 2011), 135-59.

13. Spinoza in the *Tractatus* describes this perception of necessity as superstition.

14. Alain Badiou, *Saint Paul: The Foundation of Universalism*, trans. Ray Braissier (Stanford, CA: Stanford University Press, 2003).

15. Étienne Balibar, *Spinoza and Politics*, trans. Peter Snowdon (London: Verso, 1998), 68.

16. The opposition to teleology can be traced throughout Spinoza's work. It can already be found, for instance, in Part I of the *Ethics* where teleology is associated with the anthropomorphic understanding of God. See, e.g. the "Appendix" to *Ethics*, Part I.

17. For the distinction between constituent power or *potentia* and constituted power or *potestas* in Spinoza, see Antonio Negri, *The Savage Anomaly: The Power of Spinoza's*

*Metaphysics and Politics*, trans. Michael Hardt (Minneapolis, MN: University of Minnesota Press, 2002).

18. Despite the great merit of clearly drawing the distinction between constituted and constituent power, Negri's interpretation of constituent power still fails to grasp that this distinction in Spinoza never leads to a separation of the two. I take this issue up in the chapter on Negri in a book that I am writing on *stasis* that is the sequel to *Sovereignty and its Other*.

19. Cf. Vardoulakis, "Spinoza's Empty Law."

20. For the concept of freedom *from* or mediated freedom, see my "'The Fall is the proof of our freedom.'"

21. Deleuze, "Power and Classical Natural Right."

22. Jacques Derrida starts from a different distinction, namely, the universality and the singularity of the law. See Derrida, "Before the Law," in *Acts of Literature*, ed. Derek Attridge, trans. Avital Ronell and Christine Roulston (New York: Routledge, 1992), 181-220. For reasons of space I cannot compare this distinction here (see also note 62). For a powerful discussion of freedom in Derrida and Spinoza, see Alexander Garcia Düttmann, "A Matter of Life and Death: Spinoza and Derrida," in *Spinoza Now*, ed. Dimitris Vardoulakis (Minneapolis, MN: University of Minnesota Press, 2011), 351-62.

23. See a recent discussion in Slavoj Žižek, *Iraq: The Borrowed Kettle* (London: Verso, 2004), 160-61.

24. An implication of the argument of my book *Sovereignty and its Other* is that there are *only* three types of empty law without truth, even though there can be of course an indefinite amount of variation within these three types.

25. For a more detailed discussion of theological readings of Kafka, see my *The Doppelgänger: Literature's Philosophy* (New York: Fordham University Press, 2010), chapter 5.

26. Augustine, *Confessions*, trans. Henry Chadwick (Oxford: Oxford University Press, 1991). See also Jean-François Lyotard's discussion of this non-response in *The Confession of Augustine*, trans. Richard Beardsworth (Stanford, CA: Stanford University Press, 2000).

27. See Theodor Adorno's critique of the negative theological interpretation of Kafka in "Notes on Kafka," *Prisms*, trans. Samuel and Shierry Weber (London: Neville Spearman, 1967), 245-71.

28. I am not suggesting here that the theological and the biopolitical dimensions are separated. On the contrary, the suggestion is that they are intimately connected. For a detailed analysis of this connection see my *Sovereignty and Its Other*.

29. Or, more accurately, *almost* everyone becomes such a guardian, because there are certain ambiguous characters, the foremost being Leni, the attorney's assistant, who seem to escape the law's snare.

30. Michel Foucault, *Society Must be Defended: Lectures at the Collège de France 1975-1976*, trans. David Macey (New York: Picador, 2003), 259.

31. Michael Hardt and Antonio Negri show in *Empire* (Cambridge, MA: Harvard University Press, 2000) that biopolitics does rely on moralizing. I do not mean to suggest here that the theological, the biopolitical and the moral interpretations are separate—I only want to argue that they are distinct. I take this issue up extensively in my *Sovereignty and its Other*.

32. Immanuel Kant, *Groundwork of the Metaphysics of Morals*, trans. Mary Gregor (Cambridge: Cambridge University Press, 2002).

33. The distance that separates Kant from Spinoza can be gleaned by comparing Kant's proscription against lying to the argument in chapter 16 of the *Tractatus* that a promise depends on its utility (see 529).

34. J. Hillis Miller, *The Ethics of Reading: Kant, de Man, Eliot, Trollope, James, and Benjamin* (New York: Columbia University Press, 1987), 36.

35. Miller, *Ethics of Reading*, 38. Cf. Jacques Derrida, "Justices," trans. Peggy Kamuf, in *Critical Inquiry*, 31 (2005): 715.

36. *Der Proceß, Kritische Ausgabe*, eds. Jürgen Born, Gerhard Neumann, Malcolm Pasley and Jost Schillemeit (Frankfurt a.M.: Fischer, 2002), 302-3.

37. For the figures of suffering, priesthood, consolation and nihilism, see Friedrich Nietzsche's third essay of *The Genealogy of Morals*.

38. For a more detailed discussed of judgment as well as arbitrary judgment (or, justification, as it is called there), see my *Sovereignty and its Other*, chapter 1.

39. For a novel articulation of the Kafkaesque, see Kiarina Kordela, "Kafkaesque: (Secular) Kabbalah and Allegory," in *Freedom and Confinement in Modernity*, eds. Kordela and Vardoulakis, 128-58.

40. A complicating factor here is the fact that Kafka never finished *The Trial*. According to Brod's arrangement of the chapters, the novel ends with the execution of Josef K., without him achieving any awareness of liberation. This is not to say, of course, that Kafka would have necessarily concluded the same way, had he been able to finish the novel. In any case, as I am about to show, this lack of awareness by Josef K. is in fact conducive to the Kafkaesque laughter that functions as the means to the attainment of this mediated freedom.

41. For a discussion of the nasal hair, see Jacques Derrida, "Before the Law."

42. I do not have the space here to review here the extensive—and expanding—secondary literature on the animal in Kafka's works. The only point that I am making here is that the expression "like a dog" can be seen, amongst other things, as parts of the structure of the humor directed toward Josef K. in *The Trial*.

43. Cf. Mikhail Bakhtin, *Rabelais and his World*, trans. Hélène Iswolky (Bloomington, IN: Indiana University Press, 1984), chapters 1 and 2.

44. For such a notion of failure in Kafka, see Vardoulakis, *The Doppelgänger*, chapter 5.

45. One important—even crucial—question remains at this point. Namely, does this new conception of freedom through laughter do away completely with transcendence? Or, differently put, is it possible to conceive of the empty law that allows for rebellion and truth as completely independent of the empty law without truth that points to transcendence and absolute imprisonment? And if such a separation is possible, how can one find criteria in the absence of any content to the law? These questions cannot be taken up here because of lack of space. But I intend to return to them through a discussion of Jacques Derrida's "Before the Law" that can be made to resonate within this constellation of thinkers that includes Kafka, Spinoza and Deleuze.

## Works Cited

Adorno, Theodor W. "Notes on Kafka." In Theodor W. Adorno, *Prisms*, translated by Samuel and Shierry Weber, 245-71. London: Neville Spearman, 1967.

Arendt, Hannah. "Franz Kafka, Appreciated Anew." In Hannah Arendt, *Reflections on Literature and Culture*, 94-109. Edited by Susannah Young-ah Gottlieb. Stanford, CA: Stanford University Press, 2007.

Augustine. *Confessions*. Translated by Henry Chadwick. Oxford: Oxford University Press, 1991.

Badiou, Alain. *Saint Paul: The Foundation of Universalism*. Translated by Ray Braissier. Stanford, CA: Stanford University Press, 2003.

Bakhtin, Mikhail. *Rabelais and his World*. Translated by Hélène Iswolky. Bloomington, IN: Indiana University Press, 1984.

Balibar, Étienne. *Spinoza and Politics*. Translated by Peter Snowdon. London: Verso, 1998.

Benjamin, Walter. "Franz Kafka: On the Tenth Anniversary of his Death." In Walter Benjamin, *Selected Writings*, edited by Michael W. Jennings et. al., vol. 2, 794-818. Cambridge, MA: Belknap, 2001.

Deleuze, Gilles. "Power and Classical Natural Right." Lecture delivered at Vincennes, 9 December 1980, translated by Simon Duffy. http://www.webdeleuze.com/php/texte-.php?cle=20&groupe=-Spinoza&langue=2 (accessed October 2006).

Deleuze, Gilles, and Félix Guattari. *Kafka: Towards a Minor Literature*. Translated by Dana Polan. Minneapolis, MN: University of Minnesota Press, 1986.

Derrida, Jacques. "Before the Law." In Jacques Derrida, *Acts of Literature*, edited by Derek Attridge, translated by Avital Ronell and Christine Roulston, 181-220. New York: Routledge, 1992.

———. "Justices." Translated by Peggy Kamuf. *Critical Inquiry* 31 (2005):

Foucault, Michel. *Society Must be Defended: Lectures at the Collège de France 1975-1976*. Translated by David Macey. New York: Picador, 2003.

Garcia Düttmann, Alexander. "A Matter of Life and Death: Spinoza and Derrida." In *Spinoza Now*, edited by Dimitris Vardoulakis, 351-62. Minneapolis, MN: University of Minnesota Press, 2011.

Glen, Patrick J. "The Deconstruction and Reification of Law in Kafka's 'Before the Law' and *The Trial*." *Southern California Interdisciplinary Law Journal* 17 (2007): 23-66.

Hardt, Michael, and Antonio Negri. *Empire*. Cambridge, MA: Harvard University Press, 2000.

Jacobson, Arthur. "Prophesy without Prophets: Spinoza and Maimonides on Law and the Democracy of Knowledge." In *Spinoza Now*, edited by Dimitris Vardoulakis, 135-59. Minneapolis, MN: University of Minnesota Press, 2011.

Kafka, Franz. *Der Proceß. Kritische Ausgabe*. Edited by Jürgen Born, Gerhard Neumann, Malcolm Pasley and Jost Schillemeit. Frankfurt a.M.: Fischer, 2002.

———. *The Trial*. Translated by Willa and Edwin Muir, translation revised by E.M. Butler. New York: Schocken, 1995.

Kant, Immanuel. *Groundwork of the Metaphysics of Morals*. Translated by Mary Gregor. Cambridge: Cambridge University Press, 2002.

Kordela, Kiarina. "Kafkaesque: (Secular) Kabbalah and Allegory." In *Freedom and Confinement in Modernity: Kafka's Cages*, edited by Kiarina Kordela and Dimitris Vardoulakis, 128-58. New York: Palgrave, 2011.

Kordela, Kiarina, and Dimitris Vardoulakis. "Kafka's Cages." In *Freedom and Confinement in Modernity: Kafka's Cages*, edited by Kiarina Kordela and Dimitris Vardoulakis, 1-6. New York: Palgrave, 2011.

Lyotard, Jean-François. *The Confession of Augustine*. Translated by Richard Beardsworth. Stanford, CA: Stanford University Press, 2000.

Miller, J. Hillis. *The Ethics of Reading: Kant, de Man, Eliot, Trollope, James, and Benjamin*. New York: Columbia University Press, 1987.

Negri, Antonio. *The Savage Anomaly: The Power of Spinoza's Metaphysics and Politics*. Translated by Michael Hardt. Minneapolis, MN: University of Minnesota Press, 2002.

Spinoza, Baruch. *Theological-Political Treatise*. In Baruch Spinoza, *Complete Works*, translated by Samuel Shirley, edited by Michael L. Morgan, 383-582. Indianapolis, IN: Hackett, 2002.

Vardoulakis, Dimitris. *The Doppelgänger: Literature's Philosophy*. New York: Fordham University Press, 2010.

———. "'The Fall is the proof of our freedom': Mediated Freedom in Kafka." In *Freedom and Confinement in Modernity: Kafka's Cages*, edited by Kiarina Kordela and Dimitris Vardoulakis, 87-106. New York: Palgrave, 2011.

———. "Spinoza's Empty Law: The Possibility of Political Theology." In *Spinoza Beyond Philosophy*, edited by Beth Lord, 135-48. Edinburgh: Edinburgh University Press, 2012.

Žižek, Slavoj. *Iraq: The Borrowed Kettle*. London: Verso, 2004.

CHAPTER 3

# A Kafkan Sublime: Dark Poetics on the Kantian Philosophy

*Andrew R. Russ*

## Introduction

The opportunity exists to initiate a dialogue between the imaginative universe of Kafka's fiction, and the critical, ethical philosophy of Immanuel Kant. It may just be that the consequences of Kant's achievement in philosophy, namely the critical redirection of knowledge away from justification of truth, to its own self-criticism and conditions of possibility, are aesthetically and imaginatively interrogated by Kafka's fictional worlds. This of course involves a reversal of the usual applications of philosophy to Kafka's art, where a philosophy, idea, or body of ideas is used to shed light upon Kafka's fictional intent. I instead aim to show how Kafka's modern fictional constructs and ambiguous rationales can be seen as a dark poetical elucidation of the effect Kantian critique has had upon the subsequent mental, institutional and psychological landscapes of modern societies. What we have in the comparison of these two thinkers is a positive philosophical vision of modernity being mirrored back to us in negative aesthetic form. Kafka shows us the dissipated and degenerating reality of Kant's vision of an emancipated human universe benevolently governed by critical reason.

Kantian critique always began life as an attempt at the unseating of false, unsustainable or dogmatic philosophical, social, and political beliefs, and was always allied with the enhancement of ethical autonomy and the Enlightenment's attack upon superstition and irrational authority. In attempting to secure the reality of human freedom and the undogmatic purity of science, Kant's solution was to leave us suspended between a noumenal autonomy and a phenomenal determinism, condemning us to a doomed modern challenge to negotiate these severed realms with no assurance of their hidden, actual or eventual communion. To Kafka, I attribute the subtle imaginative comprehension that this supposed Kantian solution was in reality a new existential dilemma, one that would involve us in new appreciations of irrational authority, anonymous servitude and superstition, and leave us with no faculty to judge them accurately. Kant attempted the modern securing of our freedom, the apotheosis of our enlightenment, our "emergence from self-imposed tutelage," the ordering of our intellectual faculties, and Kafka counters in response with a not so absurd vision of a modernity that bafflingly and comically enslaves us to unknown things and leaves us with a confused faculty to grasp them.

And so Kafka's supposed ambiguity and elusive philosophical stance can readily be seen as an existential response to a post-Kantian world. This is a thwarted world desirous of communion between the sundered paths of determined, indifferent, chaotic, sensate phenomena and the free-willing ideal dimension of our immortality and numinousity. A world that feels at once freed and captured by reason, unbearably limited by its presence, but whose presence offers limitless prospects. Kantian dualism in its actual living existential apprehension can only be felt as a dizzying oscillation between the claustrophobia and dispersal we experience before our own rationality. Our reason forces us to limit and sanction ourselves with the one hand, while offering us the unlimited with the other. Under the Kantian firmament we are indentured servants to our own infinite possibility, or as Kafka wittily points out, "A cage went in search of a bird" (*Zürau Aphorisms* 16).[1] Like all dualisms, there is an opacity that obfuscates all possible connection between the two realms. And so we are left to sit in what Walter Benjamin saw in Kafka as the "enigma which beclouds," a space between those realms, composing dark poetics on our fate.[2]

Ultimately, Kafka will be seen to be almost unconsciously reworking the idea of the Kantian sublime in his fictions. Where Kant sees the sublime as the awesome magnitude and power of nature overwhelming our mental faculties, but in the last moment redoubling our sense of reason's inscrutable power, Kafka is instead countering with a more dangerous, less edifying idea of the sublime. The venue for Kafka's sublime is not nature, but society, understood broadly as the combined products of our collective rational activity. And the inscrutable and awful feeling is not reason being surprisingly convinced of its power, but is reason being confronted by its products and realizing that it is incapable of properly grasping them.

## Epistemic Instability and Exuberance in Failure

But how best are we to situate Kant and Kafka upon some initial common plateau of thought? That they are separated historically, temperamentally and professionally bodes awkward and somewhat contentious. Kant is not known for his love or knowledge of arts, nor his capacity for granting them their due portion of expertise or efficacy in the human experience (least of all literature). Almost conversely, Kafka seems to flirt with the conceptual and philosophical almost to the detriment of what might be considered beautiful, pleasing and sonorous with traditional ideas of art. Like so many of his contemporaries, Kafka seemed to pick up the philosophical project precisely where it had floundered, taking up in the arms of art what had been set down by an exhausted philosophical trajectory. Perhaps then the best option is to delve into that great controversy that sundered the path of the philosopher from the poet, and to delve into how the distance between them has increasingly shrunk in our modern era.

For when we speak of the sundered paths of literature and philosophy, in our modern era it is true to say that "we have witnessed a growing acceptance of the mixed habitation of this territory."[3]

Ever since Plato admonished the artists for transacting in falsehoods, or at best toying with irresponsible approximations of the truth, philosophy and art have forged separate paths out of the same earth. Much like Kafka's mole in his story "The Burrow," each has spent lifetimes toiling on their labyrinthine constructions, wondering with both fear and hope at the sounds of the unseen creature furtively burrowing nearby, unsure if its horrible sound announces a friend or enemy. Yet the modern era sees a degree of thawing between these old animosities, with figures such as Kierkegaard and Nietzsche utilizing literary tropes for philosophical questioning, and this volume's subject, Franz Kafka, exploiting the dramatic potential of philosophical conundrums in his fictions. Indeed the whole precarious separation between a fictional fantasy and a truthful certainty seems to have collapsed gradually over our modern era, seen most significantly in the elaborate crossovers in literature and philosophy throughout the twentieth century.

Before we can grasp that crossover, we need only to look at those two nineteenth-century philosophers who registered the worried shudders of the philosophical project more keenly than most. More astute on human psychology than philosophical deduction, they recognized the looming failure of philosophy's noble pursuit of truth, and especially how this played out at the existential-individual level. Kierkegaard would plunge headlong into a fideism, or the "leap of faith," that even he dejectedly recognized as near impossible for modern limbs atrophied by lack of serious religious use. He would counsel to leap over the ethical stage of life (see objective, philosophic, based in rational justification), to the realm of the religious (see subjective, mysterious, based in belief). And though Kierkegaard also disparaged the aesthetic realm as one that should be abandoned in favor of the religious, the comfort with which he toiled in the aesthetic realm of suggestive and speculative literary writing, masks and pseudonyms suggest to us that with the religious leap being so demanding, the aesthetic descent could be more capacious. Failing the religious realm, one could fall back to the aesthetic realm and subsist there in an ironic mode, a move far more suited to the modern. And as in his personal life he thrashed with the religious, unable himself to make cleanly the vaunted leap, he correspondingly fell back and flourished in the aesthetic (ironic) realm. Nietzsche, however, bucked against the philosophers in the opposite direction to Kierkegaard. He was almost a secular fideist, and with passionate rage forced philosophy to see the fictions and falsehoods that were sustaining it, and those who lived daily in these tricks of fancy. But Nietzsche asked not for them to be jettisoned for being disrobed of their truth, but simply pushed for their vital life-giving affirmation in the face of their duplicity:

> The falseness of a judgment is to us not necessarily an objection to a judgment . . . and our fundamental tendency is to assert that the falsest judgments . . . are the most indispensable to us, that without granting as true the fictions of logic, without measuring reality against the purely invented world of the uncondi-

> tional and self-identical, without a continual falsification of the world by numbers, mankind could not live—that to renounce false judgments would be to renounce life, would be to deny life. To recognize untruth as a condition of life.[4]

That both Nietzsche's and Kierkegaard's tone and style turned so much to literary styles was no mere coincidence, as both were seeking to reset the search for truth away from the merely philosophic. With its mouldy abstractions, syllogisms, truncations and infinite regressions, philosophy was no longer a living vessel in which to apprehend what life actually held out for us, so these explorers thought. And it was their perception of this failure that lent to the coming century's literary efforts what could be called a productivity in failure. At the outset of modernism, literature took its cue from the failure of philosophy, deciding to make an uneasy home in the impasses and interstices generated by philosophy. As Werner Hamacher observes:

> Failure is generally considered one of the fundamental figures of modernity and especially of modern literature. Modernity and its literature are said to emerge from the collapse of traditional orders, from the corrosion of conventions, and from the loss of the social and aesthetic codes that were once able to secure a certain coherence and continuity for all forms of behavior and production. Modernity is regarded, however, not only as the result of this disintegration but also as its hero: because it recognizes itself in the collapse of the old, modernity must make failure into a principle. . . . Modernity, which draws all its pathos from the fact that it preserves itself only by outdoing itself again and again, consists entirely in the project of conserving the collapse from which it emerges and which it drives ever onward.[5]

No wonder that this acceptance (or celebration) of failure led to the most self-consciously literary of the twentieth century's schools of philosophical thought, Existentialism (with its godfather phenomenology) and its multi-form and polyglot heirs of post-structuralism and post-modernism (and its preeminent analytical tool of deconstruction). Existentialism, with its renewed interest and emphasis upon lived experience, the individual and structures of consciousness, began to have to borrow some of the innate aptitudes of literature. After this, the post-modernists and deconstructionists of the next generation began a more rigorous denunciation of many of philosophy's treasured tropes, and embarked on the uninhibited mining of the literary for new points of departure.[6] The space between philosophy and literature, and its over two-thousand-year history of segregation, does not just collapse in the twentieth century, it is discovered that perhaps there was no separation at all:

> even as philosophy, in the personage of Parmenides, invents its most potent anti-poetic concept, the concept of Being—a concept whose inauguration hails the most thorough breach with the personalized gods of the poets—it still retains poetic and magical elements at its core. It may well be, as Jacques Derrida has claimed, that philosophy can never free itself from its other, that philosophy without metaphor is impossible.[7]

From the perspective of this chapter, the most momentous step toward this détente between philosophers and poets was provided by the revolution in thought that was Immanuel Kant's critical philosophy. In Kant's example, the waters of truth and illusion were significantly muddied, as metaphysics was meticulously disrobed of its speculative truth claims. In Kantian critique the empirical realities assumed behind metaphysical objects (God, world, soul, unity, freedom, purpose etc.) were totally rejected, and reason's investigative objects were relegated to purely regulative functioning, stripped of their former constitutive status. Echoing the lessons learnt from Hume, Kant pushed for the awareness that we could have true knowledge only of that which is empirically possible. But throughout his project Kant is also keen to point out that the human subject is forever troubled by reason's indestructible desire for that which exists outside of the empirically possible, the unlimited and unconditional. Kant's conception of reason seems mesmerized by that which is empirically disallowed, illegal and dangerous for it to seek. In the "Transcendental Dialectic," Kant even calls the operation of reason, the "logic of illusion," suggesting that reason's demands for the limitless and unconditional will never be satisfied to its ultimate satisfaction. Pure reason is here construed as the misguided effort to reach unattainable metaphysical knowledge that, according to Kant, "even after its illusions have been exposed, does not cease to deceive, and continually to lead reason into momentary errors, which it becomes necessary continually to remove" (*Pure Reason* 211).[8]

However, Kant proclaims that the illusions reason strives for are unavoidable, and necessary for the operation of many of our epistemological and moral enterprises. They become regulative devices for guiding our empirical investigations. Furthermore, the manufacturing of reason's illusions demonstrates to us the effective operation of all of the human subject's mental faculties. Disconcertingly, to seek these illusions is apparently reason's proper province. The deceptive and tempting phantoms of reason demonstrate its power and value. This is a faculty with an aptitude to think beyond all sense, but whose attempts must forever be seen as empirically stillborn. Throughout the *Critique of Pure Reason*, and most specifically in the "Transcendental Dialectic," Kant describes for us a world of claustrophobic reason, prone to flights of illusory fantasy, but always chained to the empirical; tempted insatiably with falsehood, falsehoods it is necessary to embrace in qualified fashion to help order our inquisitive nature. This contradiction ushers in a condition that makes the alliance of illusion and truth possible. When the mental faculty capable of the highest human truth is unveiled as perversely prone to being dazzled by its own fictions, and continually makes practical use of these empirically disallowed figments, the strict division between objective truth seeking and subjective fictive creation collapses.

It is in the subsequent ruins of this collapse (solution?) that Kafka found a fertile source of inspiration. This epistemological condition given to the modern world by Kant is aptly expressed in Kafka's 106th Zürau aphorism: "Can you know anything that is not deception? Once deception was destroyed, you wouldn't be able to look, at the risk of turning into a pillar of salt" (*Zürau Apho-*

*risms* 105). In other words, fictions have been so fundamentally our reality, so much the guidance of our being that for them to be completely obliterated from our mentation would destroy us also. Or take the 55th aphorism, which states blankly: "Everything is deception: the question is whether to seek the least amount of deception, or the mean, or to seek out the highest" (*Zürau Aphorisms* 56). Ultimately, what Kant achieved with his critique of metaphysics was a strange combination of fiction and truth, illusions that we are asked to follow as indubitable standards, or as Kafka even more starkly stated, "a superstition and a principle and an empowerment to live" (*Great Wall* 104).[9] Imagine the relish with which the poets would have greeted their old rebukers, the philosophers, who starting with Kant finally admitted that their beloved faculty of reason could no longer be fully trusted, and was partial to being swayed by its own exaggerations and irresponsibilities. The very same criticism leveled at them, the poets, thousands of years earlier in Ancient Greece. As if prompting the theme for the next few centuries of literary and artistic endeavor, Kant creates a crisis in reason. Under his aegis, our reason becomes disenchanted with itself while also aware of its incredible power, its formerly dearest constructions of God, Soul, Cosmos and Freedom are evaporated from their previous objective and phenomenal realm, but still retained as all-governing presences in an incognito or spectral sense.

Let us put this into perspective with a look at the opening sentence of Kafka's short work "On the Question of the Laws":

> Unfortunately, our laws are not generally known, they are the secret of the small group of nobles who rule us. We are convinced that these ancient laws are being strictly upheld, but it is still an extremely tormenting thing to be ruled by laws that we do not know. (*Selected Stories* 129)[10]

Taken as a secular parable of the metaphysical situation that Kant's philosophy bequeaths to us, some subtle variant of this dissociative mental situation is shot through many of Kafka's most troubling situations. Often his narratives are nothing more then the to-ing and fro-ing of this Kantian dynamic between being forced to acquiesce dutifully to forces and laws, while perpetually questioning them on their dubious reality and legitimacy. The court of the trial that is everywhere but unknowable, the officials of the castle that are absolutely infallible but summon K. mistakenly, the gatekeeper of the law who never says "no" but just "not yet," the Great Wall of China, that piecemeal construction, done in stages that will never be fully experienced in its totality by its makers, the seemingly limitless and unconditioned Nature Theatre of Oklahoma that nevertheless provides a physical home and meaning for everyone; all these ideas indulge in this opaque dance of totality and contingency, limitlessness and our limitation before it. Kafka simply places this very Kantian condition in institutional settings (families, courts, castles), with the effect of intensifying concretely the drama of humanity's existential struggles with the elusive ideas that rule it. Perhaps Kafka's story "The Burrow" comes closest to this Kantian spirit, where a hyperrational creature, never fully defined, creates a structure bordering on the infinite with his head, which he describes as his unique instrument. And yet this zenith, this apotheosis breeds only anxiety and suspicion. The ideal cannot be reached; the "thing in itself" is a fiction always proved by that outside it. Often we say Kafka deals with humankind's endless frustrations with outside-imposed systems, but Kafka's worldview—more accurately considered—seems to postulate that the frustration is radically self-imposed. As Josef K. came to understand he was guilty all along, without at any time having had proper access to the machinery of the courts, perhaps for all of us the systems that haunt us may be essential and inborn. The outside provokers are simply there to remind us of the elaborate innate ways we trap ourselves.

Ultimately, this reduction in the distance between the unraveled truth claims of the philosophic and the rhetorical expertise of the literary, revolves around the shift seen in our modern (Kantian) conception of reason. While in the Kantian schema reason still evokes the highest and most important objects of metaphysical analysis, they are also unveiled as mental inventions lacking empirical verification. This ushers in a state of affairs that allows "a theme that is also the object of philosophical deliberation [to be] given literary interpretation in terms of an imaginative world artistically conceived."[11] But most important is that those aesthetic worlds can extend the critique of philosophy's dearest, reason, beyond what reason itself was capable. And perhaps in appending in fantastic new directions those themes traditionally treated by philosophy, an imaginative and aesthetic approach can challenge the sovereignty of reason upon which philosophy was built. There may be significant historical space between the approaches of Kant and of Kafka, but as Henry Johnson Jr. noted, "in the mid-world of history, halfway between pure autonomy and pure heteronomy, reason and rhetoric are inextricably fused."[12] This is what Kafka has to teach us about Kant.

## The Law Wants a House, the Will Wants a History

If we entertain the possibility that philosophy cannot advance without the aid of metaphor, we might ask what metaphor is implied or embedded within Kant's critique of reason. As reason is prone to exceed its authority, a critique is necessary both to secure its rights and rein in its extremes. Ultimately however, it will be reason itself that will perform this function, shown by the fact that Kant calls this authority "critical reason" and even more suggestively, "judicial reason."[13] Kant seems to explore reason under the metaphorical guidance of a "court," "trial" or "judge." This deployment of legal metaphors by Kant was demonstrated by Hans Saner, who wrote of Kant's conception of reason:

> Reason is the permanent judge, and at the same time the permanent defendant. The trial of reason is its own self-imposed, infinite task of self-enlightenment and self-purification. The peace of reason is thus not a state of trustful rest but one of vigilance and self-examination.[14]

Not only is it the figure of the court that piques our interest with regard to Kafka, but also the figure of permanence. Kafka himself intimated this when he famously suggested that it was only our conception of time that made us view what was a "Court Martial" as the "Last Judgment" (*Zürau Aphorisms* 40). We should also note what is obvious to even the most elementary student of legal matters: a court without divisions in its offices is a highly unstable entity. When the judge, jury, defendant and prosecutor are one and the same faculty, one is presented with a metaphorical figure that succinctly demonstrates the metaphysical and epistemological instabilities of Kantian critique. That Kant operates with a host of dualisms, between theoretical and practical reason, phenomena and noumena, morality and history etc., is made all the more unstable by the fact that they are all ultimately adjudicated by a single entity: reason. An impossible situation ensues where the source of the perpetually generating dualisms is also the ground upon which one seeks their resolution, or at least, negotiation. As Kimberly Hutchins notes, "The dual determination of critique in the acknowledgement of reason's limitation and the assertion of its legislative power implies a set of dichotomies and a series of attempts to overcome them."[15]

And so Kant's metaphysical instability reverberates down throughout the whole critical philosophy, moving from the bedrocks of metaphysics and epistemology to the heights of our moral natures. One key part of the critical philosophy that devotes itself to that limitless and lofty aspect of ourselves, is that which concerns our practical reason. Kant goes to great pains to shelter and protect the purity of our moral selves. Our will (the ground of the moral law) must be purely autonomous, and have no object outside itself directing its end whereby it would become mired in the heterogeneity in the world. The moral law must remain entirely independent of the empirical world, as Kant implores with the question, "Is it not of the utmost necessity to construct a pure moral philosophy which is completely freed from everything which may be only empirical and thus belong to anthropology?" (*Practical Reason* 51-52).[16] The great problem with this highly formalistic account of the law and our autonomous will that upholds it, is that we are left divided from ourselves in our historical being. That plane capable of mediating the claims of the noumenal and the phenomenal, namely history, is almost wholly denied in the Kantian formulation of practical reason. Even when Kant does respond to the charge that he had sundered our moral natures from any empirical confirmation in, and consummation with, history, his dualism is only able to usher in history and its purposes as a regulative idea, supplying no real empirical constitutive status. It thus remains a figment or fiction that our reason supplies us to keep us convinced that the moral kingdom will come. But what point our moral law if it soars interminably never to touch the ground upon which we walk? As Lewis White Beck observed of the moral law, "Each moral act at the time it is done is, as it were, an absolutely new beginning, not determined by history, or by nature. History brings us to each present; but in each future we are on our own."[17] It is no mistake that much of the philosophical thought that has captured the imagination of modernity has attempted to answer Kant's challenge of a wholly unconditional moral law, by providing some history for it in the attempt to cloth its abstractness.[18] Nietzsche's genealogy of morals, Marx's class relations and materialist history, and Freud's exposure of totems and taboos in tribal societies are all species of this challenge.

It should be plain that Kafka's great work, *The Trial*, and even more so its gnomic heart as expressed in "Before the Law," can be viewed as masterful parodies of this moral and historical situation. The law wants to be housed, as it cannot exist purely in the immaterial, just as the will wants its history told and seen, as it needs confirmation of its continuing efforts. Kant's formalistic morality cannot provide this. As Derrida, in his insightful reading of "Before the Law," has recognized:

> It seems that the law as such should never give rise to any story. To be invested with its categorical authority, the law must be without history, genesis, or any possible derivation. . . . [But] [l]ike the man from the country in Kafka's story, narrative accounts would try to approach the law and make it present, to enter into a relation with it, indeed, to enter it and become intrinsic with it, but none of these things can be accomplished.[19]

But what would the story of the law look like if it were to be at all possible? Much of Kafka's work can be seen within this trajectory, especially *The Castle*, "The Judgment" and "In the Penal Colony," but pre-eminent in this trend is "Before the Law." All dualisms have the tendency to divide people and things against themselves, making their unity a constant question and need. Kafka undoubtedly saw the world as divided and dualistic, often comically so. In "Before the Law," he dramatized life's endlessly generated divisions around the figures of law and freedom, and in so doing seems to satirize as dismal that which Kant saw as ennobling. He posits that the human being cannot and will not live with the dualism intact, but does not go as far as to say that the dualism will be defeated. He presents a man seeking entry into the house of the Law, stopped by a man whose sole aim is to guard only that singular man from entry, for, as we discover at its end, the entrance he guards was constructed solely for the man seeking admittance. He roars to the dying man, "No one else could be granted entry here, because this entrance was intended for you alone. I shall now go and shut it" (*Trial* 155).[20] The story positively trembles with interpretive instability, impossible to explore extensively here. But some particular themes seem pertinent, many of them suggested by the very interpretative discussion with which the Priest and Josef K. illuminate the text after its telling. Let us firstly accept that as the two men are linked to the same door, that they can be seen as being a metaphor for the divided person engendered by dualism. Of course they recognize each other as separate and at cross purposes, but more significantly the door was created precisely for these two men to be absolutely linked together and not to recognize their odd kinship. No other guard is enlisted to that particular door, no other man ever seeks entry to it. It is not inconceivable that in a world not so schismatic, they would recognize each other as one and the same.

In the Priest and Josef K.'s discussion, the countryman is first of all considered as having been deceived by the guardsman, in much the same way as the Kantian ideas deceive their holders. But alternatively the guardsman is also considered fearful, naive, presumptuous, whose ideas about the interior of the law are childish. At least the countryman seeks the law; the guardsman cannot even endure its earliest "visage." But the guardsman is first considered as dutiful and stolid in his upholding of the law, and to be admired on that count. From this perspective the countryman is his underling, and must submit to his higher authority for his whole life. The guardsman is benevolent, paternalistic and not a little condescending to the countryman in this knowledge. But then again it is presented from its opposite angle. The guardsman is mistaken in his superiority. The countryman is a free man, the guard a mere "bondsman." Not only this, but as the guard only guards the entrance designed for that individual man from the country, his whole purpose and end is encapsulated in that one man, making the countryman his rightful superior. But still the man from the country acquiesces to the guard. Even on the question of knowledge the story cuts both ways. The guardsman is thought to have knowledge of the law because he is in its employ, but how is this possible when he admits that he cannot even endure the "aspect" of the third guardsman on the infinite journey to its interior. The countryman spends his whole life patiently awaiting entry to the law, only to have the door closed on his death. But even here he is said to witness the radiance coming from the door, where the guardsman must through his duty have his back turned to the light. One feels that the interpretations could replicate and switch indefinitely. But most interestingly the instability revolves around questions of law, freedom, duty, will, determinism (destiny) and history (lifespans), all of them key themes in Kant's philosophical project. Kant's project was aimed at showing rationally the meanings and scopes of these terms, placing our knowledge of ourselves on its firmest possible basis. However, in this Kafkan rendering none enjoy solidity of meaning and understanding as this maelstrom of Kantian thematics jostle for priority in all the ensuing interpretations. In this particular choice of subject matter Kafka quite literally concocts a literary pantomime of the Kantian subject.

Most instructive of all are the last words between both the guardsman and the man from the country in the story, and Josef K. and the priest in the discussion outside it. The guard says to the countryman exasperated, but also admiring, "You are insatiable," to which the man from the country replies "Everyone seeks the Law" (*Trial* 154-55). And as long as the world is divided by the Kantian dualism, there will always be that "insatiable" drive to know the law as more than an eternally unfulfilled insensible promise. Finally the priest wraps up the perplexing series of interpretations on the story with "one does not have to believe everything is true, one only has to believe it is necessary." Josef K. responds that it is a depressing thought, for "It means that the world is founded on untruth" (*Trial* 159). In the Kantian universe we are alienated against ourselves as both guard and seeker, hence making us infinitely insatiable, infinitely frustrated, and beholden to a lie within both the world and us.

## The Sublime of Nature and the Subliminal of Society

When Kant's philosophy became overrun with questions of history, purpose, the concord of mind and experience and the relation between the noumenal and phenomenal, his *Critique of Judgment* was composed to attempt an answer to the various schisms and antinomies generated by the critical philosophy thus far devised. Of particular interest to the literary world has been Kant's elusive and highly suggestive analysis on the concept of the sublime. This fascinating treatment transacts in all of Kant's opacities and paradoxes in his assessment of our mental communion with the outside world. In this it cannot help mimicking Kant's previous attempt to describe that communion in the *Critique of Pure Reason*, with the imagination's dark art of "schematizing" the understanding. In that work Kant has described the schematic operation as "an art, hidden in the depths of the human soul, whose true modes of action we shall only with difficulty discover and unveil" (*Pure Reason* 119). And inasmuch as the operation of the imagination's schematism coincides with the operation of judgment in subsuming particulars under concepts or universals, the Kantian discussion of the sublime can be seen as a coda to that "art hidden in the depths" (*Pure Reason* 119). No wonder then its fascination.

For Kant the sublime is the name we give to that which is "absolutely great," and in being "absolutely great," it is necessarily "beyond all comparison" and "without qualification." For this reason when speaking of the sublime "it is not permissible to seek an appropriate standard outside itself, but merely in itself. It is greatness comparable to itself alone. Hence it comes that the sublime is not to be looked for in the things of nature, but only in our own ideas" (*Judgement* 80).[21] In other words, it is entirely inappropriate, according to Kant, to identify any object of the senses as sublime, for the sublime as an idea must necessarily transcend every standard of sense (*Judgment* 80). But like all Kantian ideas, how can its feeling come about unless pricked and prodded by some object (or objects) available to our senses? It is here that Kant deploys his two concepts of the sublime: the Mathematical and Dynamical. The mathematically sublime is conjured by the experience of great magnitude in nature (*Judgment* 78), while the dynamically sublime is conjured by the experience of great power in nature (*Judgment* 90). In both cases, the sublime is not actually in the natural phenomena, but the great forces or magnitudes in sensible nature awaken the suprasensible and superior power of reason in us. Just as elsewhere in the Kantian philosophy, the idea is impotent without the finite world to summon it, but even in this dependent state reason maintains its preternatural rights over the empirical. So Kant leaves us with the thought that what we really encounter is ourselves before the brute enormity and unruly magnificence of nature:

> This makes it evident that true sublimity must be sought only in the mind of the judging subject, and not in the object of nature that occasions this disposition by the judgment formed of it. Who would apply the term "sublime" even to shapeless mountain masses towering one above the other in wild disorder, with their pyramids of ice, or the dark tempestuous ocean, or such like things? But in the contemplation of them, without any regard to their form, the mind abandons

> itself to the imagination and to a reason placed, though quite apart from any definite end, in conjunction therewith, and merely broadening its view, and it feels itself elevated in its own judgment of itself on finding all the might of imagination still unequal to its ideas. (*Judgment* 87)

So it seems that one simply finds in the dark immensities and disordered tempests of the outside world a mere analogue of the "depths of the human soul" (*Pure Reason* 119). Gripped by a fear of the sheer impossibility tasked to the imagination in adequately grasping the immense physicality of nature, we experience a twin feeling of exhilaration at being convinced of our elevated selves. The feeling of the sublime is then also a strange brew of the monstrous and the noble, the gripping abyss of being dissolved, crushed and conquered by nature, with the knowing pleasure of being convinced of, and attracted to, the appreciation of our own unlimited intellect that recognizes its ultimate dominion over nature. Surely Kant is at his poetic best when discussing the sublime, which explains why it has been such a lightning rod for literary-minded philosophers. But Kant of course emphasizes the positive pole of this oscillation, taking it a step further by connecting the experience we have of our moral selves, and the idea of our freedom, with the sublime. He counsels like a father to frightened children, that we should fear not the abyss of the sublime, for to understand its true relation to us is to face up to our real human dignity.

But perhaps Kant pushes the emphasis upon the unifying/edifying side of the sublime too far. After all, the negative pole of dissipation and disintegration is equally experienced by the subject. Perhaps the more accurate sense of the sublime is experienced in the oscillation. As Kant admits, "This movement, especially in its inception, may be compared with a shaking, i.e., with a rapidly alternating repulsion and attraction produced by one and the same object" (*Judgment* 88). While ultimately Kant countered that the sublime is simply a challenge to see how "that which makes us alive to the feeling of this supersensible side of our being" (*Judgment* 88) is the harmonizing of ourselves with the law of reason, others were not willing to go along with the loftiness and elevation implied in Kant's reading of the sublime. Kafka's art certainly does nothing to suggest this option to us. In many intriguing ways his art seems to imply covertly that position which Lyotard directed explicitly at Kant: that the sublime was more accurately a "spasming" of reason. He writes:

> Imagination at the limits of what it can present does violence to itself in order to present that it can no longer present. Reason, for its part, seeks, unreasonably, to violate the interdict it imposes on itself and which is strictly critical, the interdict that prohibits it from finding objects corresponding to its concepts in sensible intuition. In these two aspects, thinking defies its own finitude, as if fascinated by its own excessiveness. It is this desire for limitlessness that it feels in the sublime "state": happiness and unhappiness. . . . The consequence for thought is a kind of spasm. And the Analytic of the Sublime is a hint of this spasm.[22]

Kafka's major characters all inhabit this *spasming* realm of thought and action with regard to the institutions, environments and societies that house and torment them. All of them seem trapped or suspended permanently in a quivering aesthetic landscape where limitation and limitlessness, the depths and the lofty, servitude and domination, fear and hubris oscillate so violently, that the overall effect is one of fibrillation. The eternal and the finite struggle to bridge each other so desperately and unsuccessfully in Kafka's fiction, that they enact a kind of optical illusion. A bridge between them does not exist, so they—the eternal and the finite—are made to switch rapidly from one to the other, over and over again, in the hope that they will take on each other's features and seem fused. But ultimately it is always an illusion. The incommensurability that characterizes Kant's critical project is by Kafka's time recognized as being part of the very fiber of the modern world. Kafka gives an almost unconscious voice to both the ridiculous humor and the human devastation that this Kantian inheritance heralds; the result is the unwitting but inevitable parodying of the Kantian sublime into a Kafkan sublime. When Kant writes that the feeling of sublimity involves "submission, prostration and a feeling of utter helplessness" that at once reminds us of, while doing violence to, the "sublimity of our own nature" (*Judgment* 93), he comes closest to describing what Kafka takes for his own sublime. Consider the archetypal Kafkan character, Josef K. A haughty, proud, dignified man with an innate sense of entitlement is, throughout the novel of *The Trial*, repeatedly asked, forced, tricked, cajoled, seduced and ultimately convinced to prostrate and submit to the forces that he simply cannot adequately fathom. This narrative effect is the sheer reversal of the Kantian sublime, and some measure of this ingredient is to be found in most of Kafka's narratives.

The word sublime itself means lofty, noble and elevated; to climb above the lintel (*limen*) or the threshold. And for Kant the feeling of the sublime is a raising to the level of consciousness a fleeting awareness of reason's transcendence. The motif is all about uplifting what was hidden. But etymologically the word sublime shares its sense with another word that means its exact opposite; the subliminal, or that which lies beneath the threshold.[23] The Kafkan sublime seems to have some of the downward movement of the subliminal about it. The element that is sublime in us, our reason, will be buried beneath the threshold. This part of us that is towering and transcendent will of necessity be lowered into the bowels of our societies. This is different from the Freudian/psycho-analytic sense of the subliminal, where the dark recesses and drives of the psyche will be revealed. Instead, for Kafka, modern society has the effect of banishing the sublime to the subliminal. And it is an important distinction between Kant and Kafka that makes this possible.

Kant took it as impossible for us to attain the feeling of the sublime from human-made objects. At the very least he thought it disingenuous for us to do so, because a humanly determined end, logically speaking, cannot contain within it the requisite excessive force or magnitude that would seize the human imagination in defeat. A defeat that would force it to turn to admire the ideas of reason for solace. Kant writes: "we must not point to the sublime in works of, e.g buildings, statues and the like, where a human end determines the form as well as the magnitude. . . . A pure judgment upon the sublime must, however, have no end belonging to the object as its determining ground" (*Judgment* 83). Thus Kant sees nature's enormity as the only proper realm for prompting the sublime. But what if the human object was expanded to include the whole of our society, the whole gamut and aggregate of our humanly collated world? We could even be less ambitious and limit it to such mammoth institutions as the state, or the law court, or even the family? Are not our societies, and even some singular institutions, the very reflection and product of the Ideas that Kant says confirm our humanity—our freedom, our moral will concretized and reflected in reality? Could not these humanly made objects of unimaginable force and magnitude summon the sublime in us by directing us back to the "inscrutability of the idea of freedom"? There seems nothing to preclude this, and reading many of Kafka's writings gives one the distinct impression that he looks upon our humanly created societies as precisely the terror-inducing ground of the sublime. If the sublime is "what pleases immediately through its resistance to the interest of the senses," then Kafka's vision of the infinite court in *The Trial*, and its parable counterpart in "Before the Law," are certainly set up as resistances to complete sensory and imaginative apprehension. It can be argued that real-life modern societies also meet these requirements, what with their labyrinthine complexity. How can Kant preclude human products from the sublime? It seems that he does so by his own repressions and sublimations, just as he repressed the question of history from the interplay of the phenomenal and the noumenal. Sanford Bubick also discerns this repression of human culture from the Kantian Sublime:

> What Kant specifically represses, in my view, is that the representations within sublime experience are always specifically cultural representations; and that these are representations which (to use Kant's formulation) show us their inadequacy as representations. . . . When I put together what Kant says and what he represses about cultural dimensions of sublime experience, the working description of the sublime that emerges, in Kantian shorthand, is this: the experience of the sublime is the effect of encountering an effectively endless repetition of cultural representations each of which is partially withdrawn from representation.[24]

What Kant represses from our understanding of the sublime, Kafka seeks to bring to light. But in doing this a peculiar thing occurs. When we look to nature and are overwhelmed by its incomprehensibility and impenetrability, the imagination baulks and is referred to the power of reason's ideas. Kant reminds us that we can think infinity, and thus that we are superior to what we encounter in the natural sensible realm. But with Kafka we often do not look at nature, we look at our cultures/societies. When we look at culture/society, and we are overwhelmed by its infinite complexity and unbounded capacities, our imagination seizes up and we implore our reason and its ideas for guidance. But in this case, reason's ideas cannot show us our superiority, for what we seek superiority over and against is the very material creation of those ideas. It can only send us back to the world that is the imperfect reflection of the ideas. The movement is always and every time a failure. In Kant, nature terrifies, and reason steps in to console. In Kafka, society terrifies, and reason keeps rebuking our entreaties for transcendence, in much the same way as the doorkeeper does to the man from the country. When looking at our collective human enterprise, reason does not provide the escape path of crowning our humanity. This is because in this realm reason must keep us below the threshold of transcendence, forever returning us back to the world made in its image. When we turn from the natural sublime to the cultural sublime, the ideas are no longer edifying or ennobling, for they are recognized as the impetuses and foundations for the thing from which we are recoiling.

Thus Kafka asks the perfectly valid question, why can we not be terrified of our reason when all it can do is sublimate us back into the spasming world created by its ideals? The rational ideals are ours collectively, but when played out in society they simply lord over us as officials to whom we can have no access. Kafka's world of "offices and registries, of musty, shabby, dark rooms" of judges, attics, secretaries and remote castles, is the material reflection of our sublimated need and longing for the ideals of reason.[25] By being completely boundless in the realm of the noumenal, they are in fact boundlessly corruptible in the social arena. And by being eternal, unchanging and absolute in ideality, they are venal, fatuous and decrepit in reality. While the Kantian sublime is almost the self-congratulatory gesture of enlightened reason, the Kafkan sublime is the antidote to that. What becomes of the sublime in a society that has assimilated and structured itself according to reason, in answer to the challenge of Kant and the Enlightenment generally? Kafka's literary achievement is a sustained answer to that question.

And thus my conception of the Kafkan sublime runs somewhat counter to how Stephen Dowden has deployed the term. He writes: "Kafka's fiction as a whole and the aphorisms in particular demonstrate unmistakably that the transcendent remains permanently out of reach. The exception to this rule, as I have been arguing, are the few rifts opened by the scattering of sublime moments of the text."[26] Dowden understands the sublime to be the momentary glimpses in Kafka's works that raise the remote possibility of some rising above the threshold; those fractures and cracks on the surface of Kafka's overall aesthetic worldview that usually steadfastly deny the transcendent. It is through these miniscule cracks in the text that Dowden believes the sublime light shines through. I however propose that the Kafkan sublime is precisely the mechanism that drives Kafka's denial of transcendence, the principle that keeps us forever on the plane of immanence. Rather than the exception to the rule, the Kafkan sublime is the rule itself. By applying the sublime to cultural artifice, Kafka drew the conclusion that it will forever force us back below the threshold of ourselves. The cultural artifice is so perceptually and conceptually overwhelming that in some sense it could seem to overleap its human origins.[27] But in that sublime moment it refers us back to those human origins in reason's ideas, and so we must be plunged back into the grubby world and beneath ourselves. The world seems inhuman, but the Kafkan sublime constantly reminds us that yes . . . we did make it.

In keeping with the drift of this essay, by way of closing (or perhaps rounding off) the discussion, let me present to you Kant at his most unusually poetical. At one point in the "Analytic of the Sublime," Kant waxes lyrical about the tumult, boldness, destruction and might of various natural phenomena. And faced before those fearful sights he imagines the human subject, and he sits there with that subject and coaxes him/her gently from their fear:

> But, provided our own position is secure, their aspect is all the more attractive for its fearfulness; and we readily call these objects sublime, because they raise the forces of the soul above the height of the vulgar commonplace, and discover within us a power of resistance of quite another kind, which gives us courage to be able to measure ourselves against the seeming omnipotence of nature. (*Judgment* 91)

And if I may be allowed the temerity and presumption to respond for Kafka, I would begin by imagining him sitting beside the subject looking on in horror not at nature, but at the tangled, tortuous and obscure society stretching before him. He would not console the human subject, but noticing its shocked muteness, he would decide to speak on that subject's behalf: "So, considering our position is insecure, its aspect is all the more fearful for our attraction to it; and we readily call its objects subliminal, because they set the forces of the soul amongst the vulgar and commonplace, and we discover within us a power of subservience quite unlike us, which makes us cower from measuring ourselves against the seeming omnipotence of our very own creation."

## Conclusion

One might reasonably accuse me of an ungenerous attitude to the illustrious Immanuel Kant, for one should never forget that Kantian critique always began life as an attempt at the unseating of false, unsustainable or dogmatic philosophical, social, and political beliefs. This has undoubtedly had a positive and indispensable legacy in the annals of our continued search for increased human freedom. But I take my cue from Kafka, who says: "We are instructed to do the negative; the positive is already within us" (*Zürau Aphorisms* 27). The legacy of Kant's unstable philosophical juggling act, where illusion and truth are strange bedfellows, provides a unique opportunity for the poets to take satirical revenge on their old foe, philosophy. Kafka is one of the first (and acutest) imaginations to play with the dissipation of modern life, a modern societal dissipation that follows so closely the contours of Kant's volatile philosophical legacy. Kafka does not really pursue the epistemic or morality in his tales. He is more of an ontologist, a theorist of the human situation in a landscape where morality and knowledge have been exhausted. His work seems to mock the truths of epistemology and morality in a fashion that Kant unwittingly prepared with his masterful clarifications on these subjects, but whose inevitable collapse he could not possibly have foreseen originating from his own hand. And to leave with Kafka's own ambivalent words on the wisdom of philosophers, they seem to only ever end up proving that the "inconceivable is inconceivable, and we knew that already" (*Selected Stories* 161).

# Notes

1. Franz Kafka, *The Zürau Aphorisms*, trans. Michael Hofmann (New York: Schocken, 2006), 16.

2. Walter Benjamin, "Franz Kafka: On the Tenth Anniversary of His Death," trans. Harry Zohn, in *Selected Writings*, Vol 2, eds. Michael W. Jennings, Howard Eiling, and Gary Smith, (Cambridge, MA: Harvard University Press, 1999), 795.

3. Ole Martin Skilleas, *Philosophy and Literature: An Introduction* (Edinburgh: Edinburgh University Press, 2001), 151.

4. Friedrich Nietzsche, *Beyond Good and Evil*, trans. R. J. Hollingdale (London: Penguin, 1990), 36.

5. Werner Hamacher, "The Gesture in the Name: On Benjamin and Kafka," in *Premises: Essays on Philosophy and Literature from Kant to Celan*, trans. Peter Fenves (Cambridge, MA: Harvard University Press, 1996), 294-95.

6. See Jonathan Culler, *On Deconstruction: Theory and Criticism after Structuralism* (Ithaca, NY: Cornell University Press, 1982). Culler argues the case that deconstruction's aim was to read philosophy rhetorically and literature philosophically. See especially his chapter "Writing and Logocentrism," 89-110.

7. Wayne Cristaudo, *Power, Love and Evil: Contribution to the Philosophy of the Damaged* (Amsterdam and New York: Rodopi, 2008), 108.

8. Immanuel Kant, *Critique of Pure Reason*, trans. J. M. D. Meiklejohn (London: J. M. Dent and Sons, 1986), 211.

9. Franz Kafka, *The Great Wall of China and Other Works* (London: Penguin, 2002), 104.

10. Franz Kafka, *Selected Stories*, trans. and ed. Stanley Corngold (New York: Norton & Co, 2007), 129.

11. Peter Lamarque and Stein Haugom Olsen, *Truth, Fiction and Literature: A Philosophical Perspective* (Oxford: Clarendon, 1994), 391.

12. Henry W. Johnstone Jr., "From Philosophy to Rhetoric, and Back," in *Rhetoric, Philosophy, and Literature: An Exploration*, ed. Don M. Banks (West Lafayette, IN: Purdue University Press, 1978), 64.

13. Hans Saner, *Kant's Political Thought: Its Origins and Development*, trans. E.B Ashton (Chicago, IL: University of Chicago Press, 1973), 254.

14. Saner, *Kant's Political Thought*, 256.

15. Kimberly Hutchings, *Kant, Critique and Politics* (London and New York: Routledge, 1996), 37.

16. Immanuel Kant, *Critique of Practical Reason* (Chicago, IL: University of Chicago Press, 1949), 51-52.

17. Lewis White Beck, *Kant on History* (Indianapolis and New York: Bobbs-Merrill, 1963), xxvi.

18. Richard Beardsworth, *Derrida and the Political* (London and New York: Routledge, 1996), 28: "Now it is precisely this law that modern thought has wished to narrate, deriving it, therefore, from another instance."

19. Jacques Derrida, "Before the Law," trans. Avital Ronell and Christine Roulston, in *Acts of Literature*, ed. Derek Attridge (London and New York: Routledge, 1992), 191.

20. Franz Kafka, *The Trial*, trans. Mike Mitchell (Oxford: Oxford University Press, 2009), 155.

21. Immanuel Kant, *Critique of Judgment*, trans. James Creed Meredith (Oxford: Oxford University Press, 2007), 80.

22. Jean-François Lyotard, *Lessons on the Analytic of the Sublime,* trans. Elizabeth Rottenberg (Stanford, CA: Stanford University Press, 1994), 55-56.

23. While there is no correspondence between the words "sublime" (*erhaben*) and "subliminal" (*unterschwelling*) in German, the roots of the English word "subliminal" were derived from the English "sublime" in the 1880s as a "direct rendering of the German psychological term *unter der schwelle des bewusstseins*, 'below the threshold of consciousness.'" John Ayto, *Bloomsbury Dictionary of Word Origins* (London: Bloomsbury Publishing, 1990), 508.

24. Sanford Bubick, *The Western Theory of Tradition: Terms and Paradigms of the Cultural Sublime* (New Haven and London: Yale University Press, 2000), xiii.

25. Benjamin, "Franz Kafka," 112.

26. Stephen D. Dowden, *Kafka's Castle and the Critical Imagination* (Rochester, NY: Camden House, 1995), 138. It should be born in mind that while Dowden does very cursorily reference Kant, he is not really working with a Kantian conception of the sublime where an emotional feeling is analytically drawn apart with reference to its relation to subjective mental capacities. Dowden is utilizing the more romantic and general notion of the sublime as anything that combines the feelings of awe and terror, and even more generally as fleeting epiphanic moments of transcendence. They are not then further analyzed for how that speaks to our reason.

27. Paul Crowther, *The Kantian Sublime: From Morality to Art* (Oxford: Clarendon Press, 1989), 153.

## Works Cited

Ayto, John. *Bloomsbury Dictionary of Word Origins*. London: Bloomsbury Publishing, 1990.

Beardsworth, Richard. *Derrida and the Political*. London and New York: Routledge, 1996.

Beck, Lewis White. *Kant on History*. Indianapolis and New York: Bobbs-Merrill, 1963.

Benjamin, Walter. "Franz Kafka: On the Tenth Anniversary of His Death." Translated by Harry Zohn. In Walter Benjamin, *Selected Writings*, edited by Michael W. Jennings, Howard Eiling, and Gary Smith, vol. 2, 794-818. Cambridge, MA: Harvard University Press, 1999.

Bubick, Sanford. *The Western Theory of Tradition: Terms and Paradigms of the Cultural Sublime*. New Haven and London: Yale University Press, 2000.

Cristaudo, Wayne. *Power, Love and Evil: Contribution to the Philosophy of the Damaged*. Amsterdam and New York: Rodopi, 2008.

Crowther, Paul. *The Kantian Sublime: From Morality to Art*. Oxford: Clarendon Press, 1989.

Culler, Jonathan. *On Deconstruction: Theory and Criticism after Structuralism*. Ithaca, NY: Cornell University Press, 1982.

Derrida, Jacques. "Before the Law." Translated by Avital Ronell and Christine Roulston. In Jacques Derrida, *Acts of Literature*, edited by Derek Attridge, 181-220. New York: Routledge, 1992.

Dowden, Stephen D. *Kafka's Castle and the Critical Imagination*. Rochester, NY: Camden House, 1995.

Hamacher, Werner. "The Gesture in the Name: On Benjamin and Kafka." In Werner Hamacher, *Premises: Essays on Philosophy and Literature from Kant to Celan*, translated by Peter Fenves, 294-335. Cambridge, MA: Harvard University Press, 1996.

Hutchings, Kimberly. *Kant, Critique and Politics*. London and New York: Routledge, 1996.

Johnstone, Henry W. Jr. "From Philosophy to Rhetoric, and Back." In *Rhetoric, Philosophy, and Literature: An Exploration*, edited by Don M. Banks, 49-66. West Lafayette, IN: Purdue University Press, 1978.

Kafka, Franz. *The Great Wall of China and Other Works*. London: Penguin, 2002.

———. *Selected Stories*. Translated and edited by Stanley Corngold. New York: Norton & Co, 2007.

———. *The Trial*. Translated by Mike Mitchell. Oxford: Oxford University Press, 2009.

———. *The Zürau Aphorisms*. Translated by Michael Hofmann. New York: Schocken, 2006.

Kant, Immanuel. *Critique of Judgment*. Translated by James Creed Meredith. Oxford: Oxford University Press, 2007.

———. *Critique of Practical Reason*. Translated by Lewis White Beck. Chicago, IL: University of Chicago Press, 1949.

———. *Critique of Pure Reason*. Translated by J. M. D. Meiklejohn. London: J. M. Dent and Sons, 1986.

Lamarque, Peter, and Stein Haugom Olsen. *Truth, Fiction and Literature: A Philosophical Perspective*. Oxford: Clarendon, 1994.

Lyotard, Jean-François. *Lessons on the Analytic of the Sublime*. Translated by Elizabeth Rottenberg. Stanford, CA: Stanford University Press, 1994.

Nietzsche, Friedrich. *Beyond Good and Evil*. Translated by R. J. Hollingdale. London: Penguin, 1990.

Saner, Hans. *Kant's Political Thought: Its Origins and Development*. Translated by E.B. Ashton. Chicago, IL: University of Chicago Press, 1973.

Skilleas. Ole Martin. *Philosophy and Literature: An Introduction*. Edinburgh: Edinburgh University Press, 2001.

# CHAPTER 4

# The Everyday's Fabulous Beyond: Nonsense, Parable, and the Ethics of the Literary in Kafka and Wittgenstein*

*Karen Zumhagen-Yekplé*

> Many complain that the words of the wise, time and again, are only parables, but inapplicable to daily life, which is all we have. When the wise man says, "Cross over," he does not mean that one should cross over to the other side, which one could still manage, after all, if the result of going that way made it worth it; he means some sort of fabulous Beyond, something we do not know, which he cannot designate more precisely either, and which therefore cannot help us here at all. All these parables really intend to say is only that the incomprehensible is incomprehensible, and that we knew already. But all that we have to struggle with everyday: that is a different matter.
> Thereupon someone said: Why all this resistance? If you followed parables, you would become parables yourselves and with that free of your daily cares.
> Another said: "I bet that is also a parable."
> The first said: "You have won."
> The second said: "But unfortunately only in parable."
> The first said: "No, in reality; in parable you have lost."
> —Franz Kafka, "On Parables"[1]

> You won't—I really believe—get too much out of reading it. Because you won't understand it; the content will be strange to you. In reality, it isn't strange to you, for the point of the book is ethical. I once wanted to give a few words in the preface which are actually not in it, but which I'll write to you now because they might be a key for you: I wanted to write that my work consists of two parts: the one presented here plus all that I have *not* written. And it is precisely this second part that is the important one. My book draws limits to this sphere of the ethical only from inside as it were, and I am convinced that this is the ONLY *rigorous* way of drawing those limits. In short, I believe that where *many* others today are just babbling, I have managed in my book to put everything firmly into place by being silent about it.
> —Ludwig Wittgenstein, Letter to Ludwig von Ficker[2]

This essay takes up the significance of Wittgenstein's philosophy for our understanding of literature (and vice versa) through a comparative reading of the

* This essay has previously appeared in *Comparative Literature*, Volume 64, no. 4 (2012), 429-45.

stakes and aims of Kafka's and Wittgenstein's circa-1922 puzzle texts "Von den Gleichnissen" ("On Parables") and the *Tractatus Logico-Philosophicus*. I examine the ethical weight of these two writers' shared investment in the philosophical depth of riddles, irony, and parabolic and nonsensical expression as unorthodox modes of indirect instruction about ordinary language and world, the yearning for transcendence and the failure to achieve it. My central aim in discussing Wittgenstein's *Tractatus* and "Lecture on Ethics" alongside Kafka's parable is to examine some of the ways in which Wittgenstein's philosophical outlook, writing, and method (shaped by his general attraction to the Book and book writing as well as by his reading of certain works of literature) are deeply relevant to studies in literature, and particularly to our understanding of literary modernism.[3]

But aside from Kafka's established position as an exemplary figure in the European modernist canon, why bring him into an effort to say something new about Wittgenstein and the relationship between his thought and literary modernism? Kafka is not known to have read Wittgenstein, nor was he one of the modernist figures Wittgenstein was known to have enjoyed. In fact, Wittgenstein's acquaintance with Kafka's writing was, at best, extremely limited. The more than 20,000 pages of Wittgenstein's unpublished writings contain no mention of Kafka, and the only recorded testimony of his having read Kafka at all survives in the form of a humorous anecdote related by the philosopher Elizabeth Anscombe. While a student of Wittgenstein's, she lent him *The Trial* and a collection of stories in an effort to share with him her enthusiasm about Kafka's writing. Upon returning the books to her in rather short order, Wittgenstein quipped: "This man gives himself a great deal of trouble not writing about his trouble." He recommended that she read instead Otto Weininger, a man who, he assured her, really *did* write about his trouble.[4]

A thorough unpacking of the implications of Wittgenstein's loaded yet rather inscrutable comment so as to understand more fully the relationship of his thought to Weininger's writing (and indeed, troubles) would call for a different discussion entirely.[5] My choice to invoke the reported remark at the outset of this essay is inspired not so much by its undeniable epigrammatic qualities as by a relevance to the current discussion that exceeds the merely ornamental. After all, if Kafka is a man who gives himself troubles not writing about his troubles, what of Wittgenstein, the man who troubles to confront the "problems of philosophy" and to disabuse his readers of their philosophical and personal confusions by simultaneously mesmerizing and perplexing them with an enigmatic book the constituent propositions of which he declares at the end to be "simply nonsense" and which opens and closes with the famous dictum "*Wovon man nicht sprechen kann, darüber muß man schweigen*"—what we cannot speak about we must be silent about (*Tractatus* 3 and §§6.54–7)?[6]

Both Wittgenstein and Kafka are men who go to quite a lot of trouble not writing (at least not directly) about their troubles, the problems they grapple with and prompt their readers to grapple with in turn. Indeed, the poetic and philosophical force of the two texts I examine here ironically *depends* upon the very method that Wittgenstein curmudgeonly criticizes in Kafka's work. "On

Parables" and the *Tractatus* are texts whose philosophical or ethical points are made through what is *not* in them, rather than through anything they say explicitly. In Cora Diamond's terms, both texts are marked by absence. Both leave it up to their readers to figure out how to learn something from that absence (of answers, explanations, resolution, or straightforward teaching) by turning it into something that transforms our understanding of the problems and mysteries of language and life.[7] What Eli Friedlander says of Wittgenstein's *Tractatus* also provides us with an apt description of Kafka's parable, since each of these works "perspicuously represents an empty place" of non-meaning we must come to recognize in the midst of our search for meaning. Each performs the intrinsically contradictory task of succeeding in its aim "only by bringing us close to the failure or disintegration of language in such a way as to illuminate or provide an elucidation."[8]

I opened this essay with two epigraphs. The first is Kafka's short parable, the second an excerpt from a letter Wittgenstein sent to Ludwig von Ficker, publisher of the Austrian literary journal *Der Brenner*, which the philosopher saw as a potential home for the *Tractatus*, a text he described as "strictly philosophical and at the same time literary."[9] Kafka's philosophically demanding meta-parable depicts an exchange between a set of interlocutors who vocalize (in a manner reminiscent of the conversations of the *Philosophical Investigations*) conflicting viewpoints about figurative language and its bearing—or failure to bear—on the realities of everyday life. It is a parable with two parts. The first sets out the problem in question: the apparent incommensurability between the mystical words of the "wise" and the unknown "fabulous Beyond" they profess to address, on the one hand, and the concrete language and "things we struggle with every day," on the other. The second is dedicated to a jousting interpersonal exchange that serves as a Kafkan exegesis (depending in part on the *parody* of exegesis) of the problem outlined in the first. The parable as a whole offers no clearly stated lesson or particular message. As Joshua Landy and Frank Kermode point out, parables (Kafka's included, I would argue) seek to challenge and train us by requiring a certain kind of interpretive philosophical and literary work that we must also incorporate into the way we think and live our lives.[10] What Cora Diamond says, in a similar vein, of Wittgenstein's *Tractatus* also applies to Kafka's parable: "The book doesn't 'teach' one philosophy, in the sense that it has no teachings on offer; and as long as one restricts oneself to looking for teachings, one will be unable to learn anything philosophical from it."[11]

"On Parables" opens up a space for readers to continue the exegetical work performed within it by adding further interpretations to the debate. The impulse to add to the parable's last line our own "I bet that is also a parable" signals the bewildering and possibly unending interpretive task that this layered piece demands of its readers. This same inclination to redeploy that riposte with a greater imaginative insight on a critical meta-level in order thereby to rise to the parable's challenge (by rising *above* the failure of its internal voices to identify and put to rest the questions it raises with something wiser than a wisecrack) also speaks to the important way the parable plays upon the hubris and performance anxiety of readers who long to be "in on" the joke and are eager to follow its parabolic movement toward a deeper understanding we worry may entirely elude us. James Conant and Michael Kremer emphasize an oscillation between arrogance and a fear of failure that readers of the *Tractatus* share with the readers of Kafka's parable.[12] Eager to become part of the apparently select readership that will find pleasure in the *Tractatus* by approaching it "with understanding," as Wittgenstein says in the preface, we wonder whether we are up to the challenge of reading the book in such a way as to successfully understand its author and the transformative experience of elucidation that his work as a whole aspires to bestow upon us.

Seeing Kafka's parable as a two-part piece also helps us to recognize something crucial about the interpretive demands it makes of its readers. Understanding what the parable has to teach us depends upon our ability to pay careful attention to the ways in which the *point* of the parable emerges, unstated, from a gap between the two extremes of experience it depicts: everyday facticity, on the one hand, and a fictive and fantastic pure transcendence (represented by the calls to "cross over" to the fabulous beyond and to "become parables"), on the other. In part, Kafka negotiates the tension between these two extremes by playing on the linguistic and generic conventions of parable, prophetic pronouncement and witty gaming repartee, blurring the modes of communication appropriate to each and exploiting our expectations about tone, timing, delivery, and conclusion. The parable, which culminates in a dual gesture of interpretive fallibility and transformative promise, represents the kind of disquieting "grammatical joke" that Wittgenstein describes as having the character of significance that gets at the very depth of philosophy (*Investigations* § 111).[13]

Wittgenstein's *Tractatus*, for its part, is an elaborate two-part puzzle text that functions as an aesthetic medium for its author's unique brand of indirect instruction. The book turns out not to be the straightforward logical-philosophical tract it first appears to be, but a mock doctrine to be cast aside once it has served what its author claims is its "elucidatory" transformative purpose: getting its readers to "see the world in the right way" (*Tractatus* §6.54). Wittgenstein himself maintained that this purported treatise on philosophical logic (which also deals with "the mystical," value, and transcendence; entails brief first-person confession, prophetic pronouncement, and sudden epiphanic insight; and addresses the "problem of the meaning of life" before culminating in the religious figure of a ladder in a final gesture at closure as illusory as it is profoundly revelatory) is really a book about *ethics*. To complicate things further, Wittgenstein insisted that, although the aim of the book is an ethical one, the ethical "part" of the book—the only part that truly matters—is the part that appears nowhere among its spare aphorisms.

The distinguishing formal features and transformative pedagogy of the *Tractatus* all play a role in the ethical aim of the book. This aim involves leading us out of our philosophical complacency and delivering us from the confusions in which we become entangled while philosophizing (confusions such as the idea that there are limits of language and thought to which we can restrict ourselves or go beyond, the idea that there is such a thing as an external point of view from which to survey language and thought, and so on) by engaging us in a process that culminates (at least ideally) in an enlightened understanding and clear vision of the world, life, philosophy, and language (all of which he sees as interdependent parts of the same endeavor). The *Tractatus* lures us into a mock metaphysical theory in order to explode that theory from within by showing us that the sentences that have seduced us into the illusion that they make sense or that we can do philosophy in a traditional vein amount to nothing more than nonsense.

If a central aim of the *Tractatus* is to disabuse us of our tendency to utter nonsense born of metaphysical confusion, in his "Lecture on Ethics" Wittgenstein explicitly claims that all our attempts to give expression to our ethical or spiritual experience of the world are essentially nonsensical—the product of a yearning to "go beyond the world and . . . significant language" by giving in to the "tendency to . . . write or talk Ethics or Religion" ("Lecture" 44).[14] Yet this tendency to utter nonsense is not something we should work to *overcome* (as we are to do with our tendency to come out with metaphysical propositions according to the "strictly correct" method in philosophy he outlines in *Tractatus* §6.53). Wittgenstein emphasizes instead that there is something deeply important about this tendency: although "Ethics so far as it springs from the desire to say something about the ultimate meaning of life, the absolute good, the absolute valuable . . . does not add to our knowledge in any sense," it nonetheless provides us with "a document of a tendency in the human mind" that he "cannot help respecting deeply" ("Lecture" 44).

In a conversation with members of the Vienna Circle recorded by Friedrich Waismann, Wittgenstein brings both Heideggerian dread and Kierkegaardian paradox to bear on his discussion of attempts to talk about ethical experience, attempts that he describes repeatedly and metaphorically as the "impulse to run up against the limits of language":

> In Ethics one is always making the attempt to say something that does not concern the essence of the matter and Never can concern it. It is a priori certain that whatever one might offer as a definition of the Good, it is always simply a misunderstanding to think that it corresponds in expression to the authentic matter one actually means (Moore). Yet the tendency represented by the runningup-against *points to something.* St. Augustine already knew this when he said: What, you wretch, so you want to avoid talking nonsense? Talk some nonsense, it makes no difference![15]

One important starting point for an account of Wittgenstein's relevance to literary studies (in the absence of any clearly stated Wittgensteinian literary program) is to be found in Wittgenstein's claims that our attempts to give voice to the experience of what we take to be ethically or spiritually significant (a category that would seem to include some, if not all, literary endeavors) will necessarily result in nonsense that arises from a tendency that Wittgenstein says *points to something* and which he confesses to respecting deeply. A second point of departure lies in the *relationship* between his early view about the essential nonsense of "ethical" sentences and his tendency (deliberately demonstrative of our own) to turn repeatedly to figurative language and literary example in his effort to put forth this view.

However, Wittgenstein's use of figurative language in his discussion of nonsense and ethics is complicated by his claim that, although ethical and religious language tends inherently toward metaphor and simile, these are but empty figures that necessarily miss the mark. What we vainly attempt to say when we use such language escapes signification because such attempts endeavor, in Eli Friedlander's words, to "present the transcendence of absolute value by means of something that can be said, a fact."[16] As Wittgenstein puts it:

> Thus in ethical and religious language we seem constantly to be using similes. But a simile must be the simile for *something*. And if I can describe a fact by means of a simile I must also be able to drop the simile and to describe the facts without it. Now in our case as soon as we try to drop the simile and simply to state the facts which stand behind it, we find that there are no such facts. And so, what at first appeared to be a simile now seems to be mere nonsense. ("Lecture" 42-43)

The normal tropological movement between what is said and what is meant does not apply in such cases because there is no literal meaning to which ethical language can correspond. Our sentences about ethics represent a desire to signify that is necessarily bound up with a failure to signify. Saying what we mean to say when we talk about significant experience, then, necessarily depends on saying things that, strictly speaking, make no sense at all.

Diamond and Friedlander both take up the question of the literary dimension of Wittgenstein's philosophy by focusing on Wittgenstein's investment in the Book in his early writing. Wittgenstein mentions two books in the *Tractatus*: the work itself and the imagined *The World as I found It*. In the "Lecture on Ethics" he adds two more books that present a view of a great beyond: the fantastical "big book" that contains "the whole description of the world" written by an "omniscient person," which presents us with the sum total of "facts, facts and facts but no Ethics," and its opposite, the apocalyptic book of pure transcendence:

> if I contemplate what Ethics really would have to be if there were such a science, this result seems to me quite obvious. It seems to me obvious that nothing we could ever think or say would be *the* thing. That we cannot write a scientific book, the subject matter of which could be intrinsically sublime and above all other subject matters. I can only describe my feeling by the metaphor, that, if a man could write a book on Ethics which really was a book on Ethics, this book would, with an explosion, destroy all the other books in the world. ("Lecture" 40)

The *Tractatus*, as Friedlander sees it, is stretched between the opposing temptations these two "impossible" books exemplify: that of pure fact and that of pure transcendence."[17] Giving in to the first temptation leads us to see the book as concerned essentially with the possibility of language to picture facts. Giving in to the second is to see the whole point of the book as a mystical grasp of a transcendent source of value outside the world. The *Tractatus* occupies the gap between both extremes. Its primary aim is to open us to our own experience—as revealed through everyday language—by leading us beyond the dichotomy of facticity and transcendence, away from the urge to transcend the limits of language and toward a recognition that our ordinary dealing with things has a significance that is at once linguistically meaningful and ethically valuable.[18]

Wittgenstein's complex project in the *Tractatus* can thus give us a new critical language for articulating the literary and philosophical stakes of Kafka's parable (in which the dichotomy between facticity and transcendence, struggles with mythical limits of language, and the yearning to find meaning beyond them are also central). Reading "On Parables" in light of Wittgenstein's mock-doctrinal early work, with its therapeutic aim, also prompts us to recognize the mock-parabolic and diagnostic (though never curative) aspects of Kafka's short piece. Likewise, looking at the *Tractatus* with Kafka's parable in mind leads to new ways of understanding the role that Wittgenstein's interest in figurative language plays in the book. More broadly, this suggests that looking at these two circa-1922 works in relation to each other calls upon us to account for their shared and respective contributions to a discursive convergence of early twentieth-century writers responding to the complexity of modern life and the cataclysm of war with an urgent attention to difficulty that brings them back to the very oldest riddles (the meaning of life, problems of the self and other minds, the possibility of redemptive change, the contrast between how things are in the world and their significance from the point of view of the "higher"). Both Kafka's and Wittgenstein's works speak to what I take to be a definitive aspect of secular modernism: an attraction to mystery and transcendent experience manifested in an obsession with the transformative power of puzzles, riddles, unanswered—and often unanswerable—questions, and quests for their solutions. Wittgenstein's and Kafka's explorations of language, text, and meaning are marked by a distinctly modernist preoccupation with a combination of hope, loss, possibility, and failure. They are rooted in the concrete world, trying to make sense of it through literature with a philosophical bent (Kafka) and philosophy (which Wittgenstein claimed really ought to be "poeted") that depicts a straining (*within* ordinary language and life) for an ineffable Beyond.

## *Gleichnis* and Likeness

The "*Gleichnis*" of Kafka's title not only means "parable" and "similarity" but also points to figurative and poetic language in general. Wittgenstein was almost certainly thinking of the broader meaning of "*Gleichnis*" when he used the English word "simile" in his discussion of ethical expressions in the "Lecture on Ethics." Given the importance of "*Gleichnis*" to both writers' thought, it is helpful to examine some further salient likenesses between Wittgenstein's and Kafka's works.

Kafka's depiction of different levels of mundane, spiritual, and literary understanding offers us valuable insights into the kind of interpretive engagement a text like the *Tractatus* demands, since the parable (like the "treatise") deals internally with the decisive difference between a reader's imaginatively "getting" the philosophical import of a story (or riddle, or joke) and *not* getting it, between a reader's ability to engage imaginatively and ethically with a text—to make of it something from which philosophy can be learned—or not.[19] It also points to the difference between the person who tries to see from the perspective of the utterer of nonsense or the teller of parables and the person who sees such a worldview as utterly foreign. Kafka's delineation of this difference, like Wittgenstein's, turns on an examination of the relationship (or lack thereof) between the activities and difficulties of everyday life and those of literary expression and/or spiritual or philosophical teaching. The *Tractatus* and "On parables" both implicitly critique doctrines that would posit an unbridgeable divide between ordinary language and world and what lies beyond their mythical limits.

Wittgenstein's and Kafka's puzzles entail an interpretive challenge that is coincident with the aim Wittgenstein saw as ethical. Each draws upon the power of literature and philosophy in order to lead us to transform our attitude toward everyday language and life and also to shift our views about the kind of work that literature and philosophy can do. Although both texts call for a change in attitude toward language and the world that allows us to see problems more clearly, both are designed to call into question the status, value, and even the hope of our ever arriving at solutions to those problems. Both defy our attempts to sum them up neatly; neither offers us the final answer they seem to strive after and that we crave. Furthermore, each of these works ultimately is dedicated to disabusing us of the misconception that there is any such thing as a single "correct" method for attaining philosophical, personal, or linguistic clarity, just as there is no particular ethical "part" of the *Tractatus* or important something or place that lies beyond sensible language toward which philosophy and literature can gesture ineffectually.

Both Wittgenstein and Kafka repudiate explanation, doctrine, and dogmatic thinking, while simultaneously recalling the structure and prophetic tone of narratives of spiritual instruction and conversion as a way of exploring a human yearning for truth and what Wittgenstein calls "wonder," a yearning that motivates our attempts to account for mystery through the construction of doctrine. Due to their mock-doctrinal aspects, both texts are also characterized by a disjunction between what we thought they were getting at and what they end up leaving us with. Wittgenstein claimed he sought not to teach us new truths but to give us a method for seeing more clearly the language and world we already know. Kafka turned to parables not to clarify any particular Truth, but to explore different ways in which the truths to which modern humanity must submit can be transmitted, turned around, and looked at in different ways.

In the preface to the *Tractatus*, Wittgenstein states that the purpose of his perplexing book would be achieved if it gave pleasure to the person who reads it "with understanding." If Wittgenstein frequently speaks of a division between those who will understand the book and those who will not (in claims that would seem to posit a rift not unlike the one Kafka's speaker sets up in his parable), he also suggests in the letter to von Ficker that, in spite of its difficulty, the *Tractatus* is addressed, as Diamond puts it, to the ordinary person's *understanding* rather than to his ignorance.[20] Wittgenstein assures von Ficker that while the book will surely seem *fremd* (strange, foreign), it has much to say that von Ficker would like to say himself, although he may not immediately notice that it has been said. What is difficult about texts like Wittgenstein's and Kafka's has less to do with their content than with the challenge of getting readers to change their mode of approach to the enigmas the texts present in such a way that they come to see and experience differently.

## Kafka's "On Parables," Wittgenstein's "Lecture on Ethics," Nonsense and Secondary Sense

In "On Parables" Kafka offers a treatment of nonsense, tautology, understanding, and transformative yearning in his own brand of literary-philosophical puzzle. In the first part of the piece Kafka's speaker gestures at (and holds at a narrative distance in a ventriloquizing frame) a vague, complaining "many," who deem the parables of the wise inapplicable to the realities of daily life. In their view, the wise man's command that we cross over into an elusive "fabulous Beyond" offers an unhelpful directive since it fails to designate any (literal) place to which we (literally) should *go*. Although its lofty poetic tone or promise of deliverance may hold an attraction for some, the command hardly amounts to a practical prescription for the problems that plague us "here." What's more, strictly speaking, such parabolic commands make no *sense* at all. All that parables do, according to the point of view Kafka's speaker vocalizes, is resort to figurative language that tells us nothing we do not already know. Attempts to explain the meaning of a parable, then, inevitably lead to tautologies like "the incomprehensible is incomprehensible," the very sort of senseless tautologies Wittgenstein uses in the *Tractatus*. The words of the wise do nothing to explain, let alone offer us salvation from, the difficulties of the human condition.

I emphasize Kafka's phrase "cross over" here because it resonates with what Wittgenstein says in his "Lecture on Ethics" about the inherent nonsensicality of ethical or religious statements. Words that traditionally have been understood to have an ethical import ("good," "right," "valuable"), Wittgenstein tells us there, can be used in either a "relative" or an "ethical" sense. When we use them in a relative sense, we assign to the object they modify value that is always *relative* to some pre-established standard or purpose. For example, in a statement such as "This is the right road to Grantchester," we can explain the use of the word "right" by identifying the facts that led us to make this judgment—stating, perhaps, that a certain route is "the right road" to Grantchester because it is the road that gets us there most efficiently ("Lecture" 39).

But such value words can also be used very differently in sentences that make no reference whatsoever to any fixed purpose or standard. When such words are used in an "ethical" sense, when they are used, as Kafka's sage uses them, in parabolic religious statements and imperatives like "cross over" (i.e., to "the right road"), they are used in a context in which they have no predetermined logico-linguistic role. In Wittgenstein's view, when we say that someone ought to get on "the right road," we cannot explain what it is we want to say by an appeal to facts. "Our words used as we use them in science," he claims, "are vessels capable only of containing and conveying meaning and sense, *natural* meaning and sense. Ethics, if it is anything, is supernatural and our words will only express facts; as a teacup will only hold a teacup full of water even if I were to pour out a gallon over it" ("Lecture" 40). All our attempts to put ethics into words will in the end only be vain attempts to "*go beyond* the world and . . . run against the boundaries of language." As a result, Wittgenstein insists in the "Lecture" that nothing that makes sense could ever manage to get at what he is trying to say in his attempts to give voice to the experiences he takes to be ethical. Imagining attempts to resolve the paradox "that an experience, a fact, should seem to have supernatural value" with the suggestion that "what we mean by saying that an experience has absolute value is just a fact like other facts and that all it comes to is that we have not yet succeeded in finding the correct logical analysis of what we mean by our ethical and religious expressions," he concludes: "Now when this is urged against me I at once see clearly, as it were in a flash of light, not only that no description that I can think of would do to describe what I mean by absolute value, but that I would reject every significant description that anybody could possibly suggest, ab initio, on the ground of its significance" ("Lecture" 44). For Wittgenstein, expressions of ethical experience are nonsensical not because we have not yet found the correct ways of articulating them, but because their nonsensicality is their very essence. And we depend upon this nonsensicality in our attempts to say what it is we want to say when we talk about what we take to be ethically or spiritually significant. Nonsensicality is not only the essence of expressions of ethical and religious experience; it is also a vital force behind the poignancy of what we might call "ethical" expressions in the modes and genres, literary or otherwise, in which we choose to give voice to our sense of it. This point lies at the heart of Wittgenstein's claim that ethics includes "the most essential part of what is generally called Aesthetics" ("Lecture" 38).

The *Tractatus* represents Wittgenstein's attempt to curtail our investment in metaphysical nonsense (as well as our tendency to spout it in philosophical theories and metaphysical propositions). As we have seen, however, Wittgenstein's position on the nonsense of ethical sentences does not mean that he would have us renounce all urges to express in words our ethical, religious, or poetical experience simply because these expressions are nonsense. And there is an important difference for Wittgenstein between the *self-conscious* nonsense—the nonsense of the *Tractatus*—intended to lead someone out of an attachment to unexamined nonsense and that un-examined nonsense itself. The difference is not one of category but of *use*.

In the "Lecture on Ethics," Wittgenstein offers several paradigmatic examples of the kind of experience we feel inclined to describe as having ethical significance. His example par excellence is "wonder at the existence of the world" ("Lecture" 41), an experience that may make us want to utter sentences like "how extraordinary that anything should exist" ("Lecture" 41). Expressions of wonder at the world, he tells us, are not expressions of a desire to know the scientific explanations for the world's existence. They are expressions of our *astonishment* at the world's being "*whatever it is*" ("Lecture" 42). But, as Wittgenstein explains, expressing wonder at the existence of the world is like saying "how wonderful that the world is the world" or—to return to Kafka's parable for a moment—expressing wonder at a tautology like "the incomprehensible is incomprehensible." But to express wonder at a tautology is simply nonsense ("Lecture" 42). We are given to saying such things when the world strikes us as somehow strangely miraculous, for "the scientific way of looking at a fact is not the way to look at it as a miracle" ("Lecture" 43). To regard the experience of wonder at the existence of the world as we would a scientific fact is to fail to grasp what Wittgenstein takes to be the ethical import of such an experience. Inseparable from our experience of the world as miraculous is the recognition that there can be no explanation for such a miracle; indeed, that a miracle cannot be explained is part of what makes it a miracle. Once a miracle has been scientifically explained, Wittgenstein asks, "where would the miracle have got to?" ("Lecture" 43).

Attempts to give verbal expression to experiences that have ethical or religious value for us give rise to what Wittgenstein calls a "characteristic misuse of our language" ("Lecture" 41). When we make ethical or religious use of phrases like Kafka's "cross over," he tells us, we might be tempted to think that we are using them as similes or *Gleichnisse*—as figurative stand-ins for some particular something we want to talk about. However, because there are no worldly facts standing behind them, the ethical use of these words is not *metaphorical* (or it ceases to serve that purpose); it is nonsense expressive of a yearning he takes quite seriously. Wittgenstein's discussion of the inexpressibility of ethics in the *Tractatus* and in the "Lecture on Ethics" is ultimately an attempt to show us something about the odd kind of linguistic intention we have when we feel moved, as he says (once again using nonsense masquerading as metaphor), to "go beyond the world" and utter ethical sentences ("Lecture" 44). Our desire to say what we want to say when we feel so moved would only by thwarted if, in an attempt to refrain from uttering nonsense, we tried to limit all our talk to empirical descriptions. Although such ethical talk is inherently nonsensical, it nevertheless plays an important role in our lives, allowing us to express what no empirically meaningful sentence ever could.

Wittgenstein explores this kind of complex linguistic intention in his remarks on what he calls "secondary sense" in Part 2 of the *Investigations*.[21] Here, Wittgenstein discusses the inclination to describe peculiar experiences by saying things like "for me the vowel *e* is yellow" or "Wednesday is fat and Tuesday lean" (*Investigations*, 202, 216). When a person utters a sentence like "the vowel *e* is yellow," though he may call attention to the oddity of the sentence with qualifying framing remarks, he is not, according to Wittgenstein, using the word "yellow" in a non-literal or extended sense. "The secondary sense is not a 'metaphorical' sense," Wittgenstein writes. "If I say, 'For me the vowel *e* is yellow,' I don't mean: 'yellow' in a metaphorical sense,—for I could not express what I want to say in any other way than by means of the idea 'yellow'" (*Investigations* 216). The sentence could of course be made into a logically meaningful one if we gave a new meaning to "yellow" for all occurrences of the word as an adjective applied to vowels or sounds. But when we want to express ourselves in a certain way by saying things like "*e* is yellow," giving the word a new meaning is precisely what we do *not* want to do: "I want to use *these* words (with their familiar meanings) *here*" (*Investigations* 216). In cases like these, saying just what we want to say demands using words like "yellow" outside the contexts in which they have a fixed meaning. Were we to try to rectify the situation by turning a sentence involving ethical nonsense or secondary sense into a determinate meaningful proposition, that sentence would, by virtue of its very meaningfulness, fail to match the kind of complex linguistic intention it expresses.

If Wittgenstein composed the *Tractatus* in an effort to lead us toward recognizing our tendency to find confused metaphysical positions or sentences attractive, in the "Lecture on Ethics" he states that the impulse to utter patent nonsense to talk about the ethical significance of the world is something he does not want to criticize ("Lecture" 44). In his view, our attraction to ethical sentences is not something that deeper self-understanding can or should make disappear. Nor is ethics a limited sphere of philosophical discourse among others. Like logic, ethics penetrates all thought and language. It is not something that one can meaningfully describe. The ethical, which is at one with aesthetics for Wittgenstein, shows itself in our humor, literature, music, art, and—not least of all—in ordinary language. The *Tractatus* is Wittgenstein's attempt to show that philosophical works also have the capacity to express ethical experience in this way, even though he claims that there is nothing said, strictly speaking, within the body of the text. We will not find an ethical theory in the nonsensical sentences of the *Tractatus*. Its ethics reside in the clarifying activity in which it is engaged and toward which he hopes to point his readers.

## *Gleichnis* and Nonsense

Up to a point, Kafka's parable shares this aim, since it also seeks to engage its readers in the work of adopting different ways of seeing the world through riddling and attention to language that Wittgenstein would call nonsense. As I have argued above, Kafka's and Wittgenstein's works span the tension between the pure facticity and pure transcendence represented by the opposing impossible books of Wittgenstein's thought experiments. But while both authors make it their business to call our attention to the pitfalls of inclining toward either extreme, both nonetheless betray their investment in the power of figurative expressions of our longing for transcendence to give voice to our experience of the extraordinary within the ordinary. I take the thrust of Kafka's "On Parables" to be that parables and literary or otherwise figurative uses of language *are* relevant to daily life (not that their lessons are easily understood) and that "crossing over" (by adopting an attitude that allows us to enter imaginatively) into a "realm" where literary or religious language might enliven our daily lives is indeed worth it. But "On Parables" also complicates this picture, calling into question the effectiveness of such an aim and the promise of the process it seeks to set in motion as well as our ability actually to take it up. "On Parables" also seems to critique the implicit call for transformation we find within Kafka's own work, as well as Wittgenstein's.

When Kafka's wise man says "Cross over," he is making use of the kind of ethical or religious expressions Wittgenstein discusses in order to direct his listeners to the "right" road toward an enriched poetic and spiritual world view. As Kafka's speaker says, the sage certainly doesn't mean that we should cross to some actual place that we can designate ostensively. The "location" he is gesturing at is a place beyond the world and sensical language, as it were. Kafka's framing of the discussion that unfolds through the voices of the speaker from the first part and the sage and two interlocutors from the second part allows him to explore not only the different planes of understanding that are the parable's most obvious issue, but also the more subtle questions of levels of engagement with the unconscious, self-conscious, and ethical nonsense Wittgenstein would have us recognize. The spiritual command of Kafka's sage is nonsense in just the way that Wittgenstein sees all ethical, religious (and by extension, poetic and literary) language to be nonsense.

The lesson Kafka's sage wants to convey with his talk of crossing over to "some sort of Fabulous Beyond," the speaker recognizes, can only be expressed if the sage eschews straightforward meaning and cannot "designate more precisely" what he means and wants to say. Utterances like his reveal a complex linguistic intention that cannot be fulfilled by employing a more "precise" sentence that makes full logical sense. What the sage is saying renders strange the relationship between the literal and figurative and proves resistant to interpretations that seek to reformulate his command in straightforwardly factual terms. What Kafka's sage (and in turn the narrator who quotes him to his own purposes) is saying about everyday reality thus *depends* upon literary language—a language that paradoxically gestures not at reality but at a fabulous space beyond ordinary language and world.

In order to understand lessons imparted through nonsense used as a way of expressing ethical significance, the listener must be able to enter imaginatively into the speaker's particular kind of nonsense.[22] And this is precisely what the complaining "many" of Kafka's parable do not do. They cannot entertain the lessons the "wise men" want to teach about the incomprehensible because they do not adopt the imaginative perspective that a deep understanding of their gist would require. In the exchange that takes place in the second (exegetical) part of "On Parables," Kafka further develops his characterization both of a reader or listener oblivious to the complexities of the indirect moral lessons of parables and a second person who at least tries directly—rather than through instructive indirection—to tell others that they should give themselves over to their instructive sway). The exchange between the two interlocutors is initiated by "a man," who, making a sage pronouncement (or perhaps mocking such a pronouncement), intones: "If you were to follow parables, you would become parables and with that free of all your daily cares."

This injunction to "become parables" represents either a literary platitude or yet another example of a nonsensical sentence expressive of a strange linguistic intention conveyed through the use of the secondary sense of a word, in this case "parable." This first man, having examined the first half of Kafka's parable-within-a-parable, is eager to indulge (in a tongue-in-cheek manner at the very least) the imaginary possibility of giving himself over, so to speak, to a life led parabolically. But the meaning of such a suggestion remains unclear. For in what would "becoming parables" consist? A person imaginatively inclined toward literary, fictive, and figurative modes of describing the world might take such a statement in stride, but such a pronouncement seems unlikely to convince the unconvinced. Thus, the first man's approach will likely fail as a therapeutic curative aimed at getting people to overcome their resistance to seeing the importance of parables to ordinary life. Like the wise man in the first part, whose ethical nonsense is not used in such a way that the "many" can understand *him* (in the way Wittgenstein the utterer of nonsense asks us to understand *him*, rather than his sentences, in the *Tractatus*), the spokesman for parabolic conversion also fails to elicit the understanding of his interlocutors or readers with his ethical nonsense (*Tractatus* §6.54). The man who in the second part of the parable suggests that were we to follow parables we would ourselves become parables and rid of our daily cares either sets up a relation between parable and reality that demands a literal interpretation that leads to paradox (once *Gleichnis* becomes reality, where will the *Gleichnis* have got to?) or urges us parabolically toward a kind of death (literal or figurative) that will free us from our daily troubles. Neither one succeeds in bridging the gap between concrete world and figurative word in order to fulfill the yearning to bring the extraordinary to bear on the ordinary that seems to underlie the parable as a whole.

The first man's interlocutor responds to his suggestion with a gesture of one-upmanship: "I bet that's also a parable," he parries. To this claim, the first man concedes, "You have won." "But unfortunately only in parable," the second retorts. The second man's responses to the words of his interlocutor (and opponent, in what has now become a game) demonstrate both the competitive nature of his particular "A-HA *Erlebnis*" and his expertise in designating the outward linguistic and generic *form* of the first man's utterance. However, if what he says represents a momentary interpretive victory, it also demonstrates a far deeper failure to grasp the hermeneutic value of the lessons Kafka's parable would have us grasp. In parable he has lost. But, then, perhaps so has the first man, who has failed to help the second to see things in a way that would lead him to "win" by grasping the full value of parable.

In spite of the fact that the first man gets the last word in providing the apparent punch line, however, "On Parables" ultimately takes its place in a long history of Jewish parables, conundrums, and jokes without a clear moral or solution. Indeed, the seductive appeal of Kafka's text lies in the way it provokes our engagement in interpretation while at the same time thwarting it. As Walter Sokel has pointed out, Kafka's work lures us toward metaphysics and theology, but frustrates and mocks anyone who allows herself to be swept beyond their apparent call for meaning to an attempt to find one.[23] Similarly, in the *Tractatus*, Wittgenstein makes use of a Kierkegaardian mirroring strategy by contriving a mock-doctrinal work of nonsense that lures readers into taking seriously the illusion that what he is saying makes sense only to explode that illusion from within. Like Kafka, then, he entices us with metaphysics and theology as a way of showing us how attractive such illusions can be, how strong our tendency is to defer to the (illusory) authority of what we take to be meaningful philosophical positions, and, finally, how to avoid their sway.

## Rootedness and Reaching

The complexity of the word "*Gleichnis*" in Kafka's title thus carries over into the treatment of the different problems of outlook and confusions about language (poetic and ordinary) that Kafka offers in his parable. Kafka's play with the range of figurative, literal, instrumental, spiritual, and parabolic understandings and misunderstandings of his inscrutable cast of characters allows him to present his readers not with a single mirror in which to see ourselves and our linguistic and spiritual confusion but with a number of mirrors.[24] The ending with which he leaves us is frayed, inconclusive, and open to continued debate and commentary in spite of its snappy punch line. Part of the joke is, of course, that no one really has the last word here.

Both Wittgenstein and Kafka use nonsense (which, for Wittgenstein, is not *Gleichnis*—not likeness, not simile) and *Gleichnis* (which in Kafka's work is not entirely unlike Wittgenstein's nonsense put to literary use) in their efforts to offer a picture of our everyday struggles with the mysteries of life and language and to depict a modern human condition characterized by deep and inherently frustrated yearning for truth, redemption, and ever-elusive answers. In a letter to his friend Max Brod, Kafka describes himself as a man whose feet are rooted in the world (and Word) of an infertile and conservative religious past from which he yearns to be free. His forelimbs, however, *are* free to reach into the heights above him. Although they find nothing firm to grasp, in their desperate waving about, he finds what he calls "inspiration."[25] Kafka's description of his simultaneous rootedness in the world and yearning for a fabulous Beyond points not only to the rooted "stuckness" that is the cause of his despair, but also to the literary creativity that his despair awakens—the inspiration to tell about something new, something "modern" perhaps, in stories that convey the strangeness, mechanization, pain, and beauty of this world and the longing to be free of it, the longing to give oneself over to another realm in the way one can only give oneself over to literature or death. Kafka finds transformative creative expression in his very pessimism about the possibility of transformation. Against such pessimism, Wittgenstein—who in the *Tractatus* still holds out a measure of hope for the redemptive possibilities of personal changes (whether they be the momentary epiphanic revelations he calls seeing the world *sub specie aeternitatis* or a more enduring conversion to "seeing the world *aright*")—

claims that the coincidence of ethics and aesthetics occasions the transformative value of literature, for it is in literature that the experience of the ethical is expressed most compellingly as narrative enlivened by nonsense.

# Notes

I would like to thank Cora Diamond, Nancy Ruttenburg, Louise Hornby, Lanier Anderson, Bluma Goldstein, and Hent de Vries for their helpful comments on earlier versions of this essay. I am also grateful to the members of the Andrew W. Mellon Fellowship of Scholars in the Humanities at Stanford University for an invaluable discussion of these issues.

1. My translation. Here is Kafka's original text "Von den Gleichnissen," in *Kritische Ausgabe. Nachgelassene Schriften und Fragmente II*, ed. Jost Schillemeit (Frankfurt a.M.: Fischer, 2002), 531-32:

*Viele beklagen sich, daß die Worte der Weisen immer wieder nur Gleichnisse seien, aber unverwendbar im täglichen Leben, und nur dieses allein haben wir. Wenn der Weise sagt: »Gehe hinüber«, so meint er nicht, daß man auf die andere Seite hinübergehen solle, was man immerhin noch leisten könnte, wenn das Ergebnis des Weges wert wäre, sondern er meint irgendein sagenhaftes Drüben, etwas, das wir nicht kennen, das auch von ihm nicht näher zu bezeichnen ist und das uns also hier gar nichts helfen kann. Alle diese Gleichnisse wollen eigentlich nur sagen, daß das Unfaßbare unfaßbar ist, und das haben wir gewußt. Aber das, womit wir uns jeden Tag abmühen, sind andere Dinge.*

*Darauf sagte einer: »Warum wehrt ihr euch? Würdet ihr den Gleichnissen folgen, dann wäret ihr selbst Gleichnisse geworden und damit schon der täglichen Mühe frei.«*

*Ein anderer sagte: »Ich wette, daß auch das ein Gleichnis ist.«*

*Der erste sagte: »Du hast gewonnen.«*

*Der zweite sagte: »Aber leider nur im Gleichnis.«*

*Der erste sagte: »Nein, in Wirklichkeit; im Gleichnis hast du verloren«.*

2. For a quotation of the entire letter in English translation, see G.H. von Wright's "Historical Introduction" in *Prototractatus* 15-16. Here is Wittgenstein's original, excerpted from his *Briefe and Ludwig von Ficker*, ed. G.H. von Wright (Salzburg: Otto Müller Verlag, 1969), 35:

*Von seiner Lektüre werden Sie nämlich—wie ich bestimmt glaube—nicht allzuviel haben. Denn Sie werden es nicht verstehen: der Stoff wird Ihnen ganz fremd erscheinen. In Wirklichkeit ist er Ihnen nicht fremd, denn der Sinn des Buches ist ein Ethischer. Ich wollte einmal in das Vorwort einen Satz geben, der nun tatsächlich nicht darin steht, den ich Ihnen aber jetzt schreibe, weil er Ihnen vielleicht ein Schlüssel sein wird: Ich wollte nämlich schreiben, mein Werk bestehe aus zwei Teilen: aus dem, der hier vorliegt, und aus alledem, was ich* nicht *geschrieben habe. Und gerade dieser zweite Teil ist der Wichtige. Es wird nämlich das Ethische durch mein Buch gleichsam von Innen her begrenzt; und ich bin überzeugt, daß es,* streng *NUR So zu begrenzen ist. Kurz, ich glaube: Alles das, was* viele *heute* schwefeln, *habe ich in meinem Buch festgelegt, in dem ich darüber schweige. Und darum wird das Buch, wenn ich mich nicht sehr irre, vieles sagen, was Sie selbst sagen wollen, aber Sie werden vielleicht nicht sehen, daß es darin gesagt ist. Ich würde Ihnen nun empfehlen, das* Vorwort *und den* Schluß *zu lesen, da diese den Sinn am Unmittelbarsten zum Ausdruck bringen.*

3. For different discussions of the relevance of Wittgenstein's *Tractatus* to our understanding of literature, and literary modernism in particular, see Marjorie Perloff, *Wittgenstein's Ladder: Poetic Language and the Strangeness of the Ordinary* (Chicago, IL, and London: University of Chicago Press, 1996); Michael North, "Translation, Mistranslation and the Tractatus," in Michael North, *Reading 1922: A Return to the Scene of the Modern* (New York: Oxford University Press, 1999), 31-64; Michael Fischer, "Wittgenstein as a Modernist Philosopher," *Philosophy and Literature* 17 (1993): 279-85; Michael LeMahieu, "Nonsense Modernism: The Limits of Modernity and the Feelings of Philosophy in Wittgenstein's *Tractatus*," in *Bad Modernisms*, eds. Douglas Mao and Rebecca L. Walkowitz, (Durham, NC: Duke University Press, 2006), 68-93; Stephen Mulhall, *Wittgenstein's Private Language: Grammar, Nonsense, and Imagination in* Philosophical Investigations *§§243–315* (Oxford: Oxford University Press, 2008); and, especially, the essays collected in John Gibson and Wolfgang Huemer, eds., *The Literary Wittgenstein* (London and New York: Routledge, 2004). For an earlier discussion of the *Tractatus* and Kafka's work, see Jorn K. Bramann, "Kafka and Wittgenstein on Religious Language," *Sophia* 14.3 (1975): 1-9; for a more recent discussion see Rebecca Schuman, "Kafka's *Verwandlung*, Wittgenstein's *Tractatus*, and the Limits of Metaphorical Language," *Modern Austrian Literature* 44.3-4 (2011): 19-32. Both Walter Sokel and Stanley Corngold offer thought-provoking readings of Kafka's late parable in their own treatments of Kafka's unique exploration of Gnostic spiritual yearning in the context of a modernist everyday: cf. Walter Sokel, *The Myth of Power and the Self: Essays on Franz Kafka* (Detroit, MI: Wayne State University Press, 2002), and Stanley Corngold, *Lambent Traces* (Princeton, NJ: Princeton University Press, 2004).

4. Ray Monk, *Ludwig Wittgenstein: The Duty of Genius* (New York: Penguin Books, 1991), 498.

5. See, for example, David Stern and Béla Szabados, eds., *Wittgenstein Reads Weininger* (Cambridge: Cambridge University Press, 2004). My discussion of Wittgenstein's *Tractatus* is indebted to a body of secondary literature that puts forth a "resolute" program of reading the *Tractatus*. Resolute readings offer accounts of how the *Tractatus*'s peculiar method and structure serve its therapeutic ethical aim, locating the instructive force of the book not in its attempt to put forth metaphysical doctrines about the way language relates the world, but in the ethical aim of effecting a shift in its readers' world-view. The resolute program insists that readers take seriously Wittgenstein's claim that the propositions that make up the body of the text amount to nothing more than nonsense to be thrown away once they have served their elucidatory purpose. The body of the *Tractatus*, according to resolute readings, represents an elaborate mock-doctrine Wittgenstein self-consciously employs in an attempt to display to his readers the confusion that plagues them. Although the number of proponents of this general line of interpretation has grown steadily in recent years, for relevance to the specific concerns of this essay, see especially Cora Diamond, *The Realistic Spirit: Wittgenstein, Philosophy and the Mind* (Cambridge, MA: MIT Press, 1991), "Ethics, Imagination and the Method of Wittgenstein's *Tractatus*," in *The New Wittgenstein*, eds. Alice Crary and Rupert Read (London: Routledge, 2000), 149-73, and "Wittgenstein and Religious Belief: The Gulfs Between Us," in *Religion and Wittgenstein's Legacy*, eds. D.Z. Phillips and Mario von der Ruhr (London: Ashgate, 2005), 199-38; James Conant, "Throwing Away the Top of the Ladder," *The Yale Review* 79 (1991): 328-64, "Must We Show What We Cannot Say?," in *The Senses of Stanley Cavell*, eds. R. Fleming and M. Payne (Lewisburg, PA: Bucknell University Press, 1989), 242-83, "Putting Two and Two Together: Wittgenstein, Kierkegaard, and the Point of View for Their Work as Authors," in *The Grammar of Religious Belief*, ed. D.Z. Phillips (London: Macmillan, 1994), 248-331, "What 'Ethics' in the *Tractatus* is Not," in *Religion and Wittgenstein's Legacy*, eds. D.Z.

Phillips and Mario von der Ruhr (London: Ashgate, 2005), 39-88, and "Mild Mono-Wittgensteinianism," in *Wittgenstein and the Moral Life: Essays in Honor of Cora Diamond*, ed. Alice Crary (Cambridge, MA: MIT Press, 2007), 31-142; James Conant and Cora Diamond, "On Reading the *Tractatus* Resolutely: Reply to Meredith Williams and Peter Sullivan," in *Wittgenstein's Lasting Significance*, eds. Max Kölbel and Bernhard Weiss (London: Routledge, 2004), 46-98, and *Rileggere Wittgenstein* (Rome: Carocci editori, 2010), with an introduction by Piergiorgio Donatelli and afterword by Silver Bronzo; Alice Crary and Rupert Read, eds., *The New Wittgenstein* (London: Routledge, 2000); Eli Friedlander, *Signs of Sense: Reading Wittgenstein's* Tractatus (Cambridge, MA: Harvard University Press, 2001); Piergiorgio Donatelli, "The Problem of 'The Higher' in Wittgenstein's *Tractatus*," in *Religion and Wittgenstein's Legacy*, eds. D.Z. Phillips and Mario von der Ruhr (London: Ashgate, 2005), 11-38; Rupert Read and Matthew A. Lavery, eds., *Beyond the* Tractatus *Wars* (New York: Routledge, 2011); and Kevin M. Cahill, *The Fate of Wonder: Wittgenstein's Critique of Metaphysics and Modernity* (New York: Columbia University Press, 2011).

6. Ludwig Wittgenstein, *Tractatus Logico-Philosophicus*, trans. C.K. Ogden (London: Routledge and Kegan Paul Ltd., 1933), 3 and §§6.54–7.

7. Cora Diamond, "Introduction to 'Having a Rough Story About What Moral Philosophy Is," in *The Literary Wittgenstein*, eds. John Gibson and Wolfgang Huemer (London: Routledge, 2004), 127-32.

8. Friedlander, *Signs of Sense*, 152.

9. Wittgenstein, *Briefe and Ludwig von Ficker*, 33.

10. Cf. Joshua Landy, *How to Do Things with Fictions* (New York: Oxford University Press, 2012).

11. Diamond, "Introduction," 128.

12. Cf. Conant, "Must We Show What We Cannot Say?," and Michael Kremer, "The Purpose of *Tractarian* Nonsense" *NOÛS* 35.1 (2001): 39-73.

13. Ludwig Wittgenstein, *Philosophical Investigations*, trans. G.E.M. Anscombe (New York: Macmillan Publishing Co., 1953), § 111.

14. Ludwig Wittgenstein, "A Lecture on Ethics," in *Philosophical Occasions, 1912–1951*, eds. James Klagge and Alfred Nordmann (Indianapolis, IN: Hackett Publishing Company, 1993), 44.

15. Ludwig Wittgenstein, *Ludwig Wittgenstein and the Vienna Circle: Conversations Recorded by Friedrich Waismann*, ed. B.F. McGuinness (Oxford: Blackwell, 1979), 69.

16. Friedlander, *Signs of Sense*, 141.

17. Friedlander, *Signs of Sense*, 12-15.

18. Friedlander, *Signs of Sense*, 17.

19. Diamond, "Introduction," 128; "Ethics and Imagination," 157.

20. Diamond, "Ethics and Imagination," 149.

21. See Cora Diamond, "Secondary Sense," in *The Realistic Spirit: Wittgenstein, Philosophy and the Mind* (Cambridge, MA: MIT Press, 1991), 225-42.

22. Diamond, "Ethics and Imagination," 157.

23. Sokel, *The Myth of Power and the Self*, 95.

24. Conant uses this Kierkegaardian mirror analogy in his discussions of changes, from the *Tractatus* to the *Investigations*, in Wittgenstein's notions about therapeutic solution (see, most recently, "What 'Ethics' in the *Tractatus* Is Not").

25. Franz Kafka, *Briefe 1902–1924* (Frankfurt am Main: S. Fischer Verlag, 1958), 337.

## Works Cited

Adorno, Theodor. "Notes on Kafka." In Theodor W. Adorno, *Prisms*. Translated by Samuel and Shierry Weber, 243-71. Cambridge, MA: MIT Press, 1993.

Alter, Robert. *Necessary Angels: Tradition and Modernity in Kafka, Benjamin, and Scholem*. Cambridge, MA: Harvard University Press, 1991.

Bramann, Jorn K. "Kafka and Wittgenstein on Religious Language." *Sophia* 14.3 (1975): 1-9.

Cahill, Kevin M. *The Fate of Wonder: Wittgenstein's Critique of Metaphysics and Modernity*. New York: Columbia University Press, 2011.

Conant, James. "Elucidation and Nonsense in Frege and the Early Wittgenstein." In *The New Wittgenstein*, edited by Alice Crary and Rupert Read, 174-217. London: Routledge, 2000.

———. "Kierkegaard, Wittgenstein and Nonsense." In *Pursuits of Reason: Essays in Honor of Stanley Cavell*, edited by Ted Cohen, Paul Guyer and Hilary Putnam, 195-224. Lubbock, TX: Texas Tech University Press, 1993.

———. "Mild Mono-Wittgensteinianism." In *Wittgenstein and the Moral Life: Essays in Honor of Cora Diamond*, edited by Alice Crary, 31-142. Cambridge, MA: MIT Press, 2007.

———. "Must We Show What We Cannot Say?" In *The Senses of Stanley Cavell*, edited by R. Fleming and M. Payne, 242-83. Lewisburg, PA: Bucknell University Press, 1989.

———. "Putting Two and Two Together: Wittgenstein, Kierkegaard, and the Point of View for Their Work as Authors." In *The Grammar of Religious Belief*, edited by D.Z. Phillips, 248-331. London: Macmillan, 1994.

———. "Throwing Away the Top of the Ladder." *The Yale Review* 79 (1991): 328-64.

———. "What 'Ethics' in the *Tractatus* Is Not." In *Religion and Wittgenstein's Legacy*, edited by D.Z. Phillips and Mario von der Ruhr, 39-88. London: Ashgate, 2005.

Conant, James, and Cora Diamond. "On Reading the *Tractatus* Resolutely: Reply to Meredith Williams and Peter Sullivan." In *Wittgenstein's Lasting Significance*, edited by Max Kölbel and Bernhard Weiss, 46-98. London: Routledge, 2004.

———. *Rileggere Wittgenstein*. Edited by Piergiorgio Donatelli. Rome: Carocci editori, 2010.

Corngold, Stanley. *Lambent Traces*. Princeton, NJ: Princeton University Press, 2004.

Crary, Alice, ed. *Wittgenstein and the Moral Life: Essays in Honor of Cora Diamond*. Cambridge, MA: MIT Press, 2007.

Crary, Alice, and Rupert Read, eds. *The New Wittgenstein*. London: Routledge, 2000.

Diamond, Cora. "Ethics, Imagination and the Method of Wittgenstein's *Tractatus*." In *The New Wittgenstein*, edited by Alice Crary and Rupert Read, 149-73. London: Routledge, 2000.

———. "Introduction to 'Having a Rough Story About What Moral Philosophy Is." In *The Literary Wittgenstein*, edited by John Gibson and Wolfgang Huemer, 127-32. London: Routledge, 2004.

———. *The Realistic Spirit: Wittgenstein, Philosophy and the Mind*. Cambridge, MA: MIT Press, 1991.

———. "Secondary Sense." In Cora Diamond, *The Realistic Spirit: Wittgenstein, Philosophy and the Mind*, 225-42. Cambridge, MA: MIT Press, 1991.

———. "Wittgenstein on Religious Belief: The Gulfs Between Us." In *Religion and Wittgenstein's Legacy*, edited by D.Z. Phillips and Mario von der Ruhr, 199-38. London: Ashgate, 2005.

Donatelli, Piergiorgio. "The Problem of 'The Higher' in Wittgenstein's *Tractatus*." In *Religion and Wittgenstein's Legacy*, edited by D.Z. Phillips and Mario von der Ruhr, 11-38. London: Ashgate, 2005.

Fischer, Michael. "Wittgenstein as a Modernist Philosopher." *Philosophy and Literature* 17 (1993): 279-85.

Friedlander, Eli. *Signs of Sense: Reading Wittgenstein's* Tractatus. Cambridge, MA: Harvard University Press, 2001.

Gibson, John, and Wolfgang Huemer, eds. *The Literary Wittgenstein*. London and New York: Routledge, 2004.

Kafka, Franz. *Briefe 1902–1924*. Frankfurt am Main: S. Fischer Verlag, 1958.

———. "Von den Gleichnissen." In Franz Kafka, *Kritische Ausgabe. Nachgelassene Schriften und Fragmente II*, edited by Jost Schillemeit, 531-32. Frankfurt a.M.: Fischer, 2002.

Kermode, Frank. *The Genesis of Secrecy: On the Interpretation of Narrative*. Cambridge, MA: Harvard University Press, 1979.

Kremer, Michael. "The Purpose of *Tractarian* Nonsense." *NOÛS* 35.1 (2001): 39-73.

Landy, Joshua. *How to Do Things with Fictions*. New York: Oxford University Press, 2012.

LeMahieu, Michael. "Nonsense Modernism: The Limits of Modernity and the Feelings of Philosophy in Wittgenstein's *Tractatus*." In *Bad Modernisms*, edited by Douglas Mao and Rebecca L.Walkowitz, 68-93. Durham, NC: Duke University Press, 2006.

Monk, Ray. *Ludwig Wittgenstein: The Duty of Genius*. New York: Penguin Books, 1991.

Mulhall, Stephen. "Coda: Wittgenstein's Beetle." In Stephen Mulhall, *Wittgenstein's Private Language: Grammar, Nonsense, and Imagination in* Philosophical Investigations *§§243–315*, 133-43. Oxford: Oxford University Press, 2008.

———. *The Wounded Animal: J.M. Coetzee & the Difficulty of Reality in Literature & Philosophy*. Princeton, NJ, and Oxford: Princeton University Press, 2009.

North, Michael. "Translation, Mistranslation and the Tractatus." In Michael North, *Reading 1922: A Return to the Scene of the Modern*, 31-64. New York: Oxford University Press, 1999.

Perloff, Marjorie. *Wittgenstein's Ladder: Poetic Language and the Strangeness of the Ordinary*. Chicago, IL, and London: University of Chicago Press, 1996.

Read, Rupert, and Matthew A. Lavery, eds. *Beyond the* Tractatus *Wars*. New York: Routledge, 2011.

Ricketts, Thomas. "Pictures, Logic, and the Limits of Sense in Wittgenstein's *Tractatus*." In *The Cambridge Companion to Wittgenstein*, edited by Hans Sluga and David Stern, 59-99. Cambridge: Cambridge University Press, 1996.

Schuman, Rebecca. "Kafka's *Verwandlung*, Wittgenstein's *Tractatus*, and the Limits of Metaphorical Language." *Modern Austrian Literature* 44.3-4 (2011): 19-32.

Sokel, Walter. *The Myth of Power and the Self: Essays on Franz Kafka*. Detroit, MI: Wayne State University Press, 2002.

Stern, David, and Béla Szabados, eds. *Wittgenstein Reads Weininger*. Cambridge: Cambridge University Press, 2004.

Winch, Peter. "Discussion of [Norman] Malcolm's Essay." In *Wittgenstein: A Religious Point of View?*, edited by Peter Winch, 96-136. London: Routledge, 1993.

Wittgenstein, Ludwig. *Briefe an Ludwig von Ficker*. Edited by G.H. von Wright. Salzburg: Otto Müller Verlag, 1969.

———. "A Lecture on Ethics." In Ludwig Wittgenstein, *Philosophical Occasions, 1912–1951*, edited by James Klagge and Alfred Nordmann, 37-44. Indianapolis, IN: Hackett Publishing Company, 1993.

———. "Letters to Ludwig Ficker." In *Wittgenstein: Sources and Perspectives*, edited by

C.G. Luckhardt, 82-98. Ithaca, NY: Cornell University Press, 1979.
———. *Ludwig Wittgenstein and the Vienna Circle: Conversations Recorded by Friedrich Waismann*. Edited by B.F. McGuinness. Oxford: Blackwell, 1979.
———. *Philosophical Investigations*. Translated by G.E.M. Anscombe. New York: Macmillan Publishing Co., 1953.
———. *Tractatus Logico-Philosophicus*. Translated by C.K. Ogden. London: Routledge and Kegan Paul Ltd., 1933.

CHAPTER 5

# "You're nobody 'til somebody loves you": Communication and the Social Destruction of Subjectivity in Kafka's *Metamorphosis*

*Kevin W. Sweeney*

The popular ballad, "You're nobody 'til somebody loves you," encourages listeners to find fulfillment as a person with a romantic partner.[1] In Kafka's *Metamorphosis*, Gregor Samsa's physical transformation gradually erodes his family's love and emotional support for him (*Metamorphosis* 3).[2] Their withdrawal of support eventually has the devastating effect of challenging his status as a person and turning him into a nobody. In the final third of the novella, the family's attitude toward Gregor conforms to a Social-Constructionist account of what makes a human being a person. According to this view, a social group or community has the power to grant personhood to an individual or to recognize that individual as a person. The group or human community also has the authority to withdraw from an individual her or his standing as a person. Failure to maintain the appropriate ties to such a social group is grounds for withdrawal of such standing. Or, it puts an individual in jeopardy of having her or his standing as a person revoked or abolished by that social group.[3]

One of the most basic social groups which recognizes individuals as persons is the family. Thus, as a child grows from infancy to adulthood, the family increasingly comes to recognize that individual as a person. Or, the family may adopt someone into the family and come to recognize that individual as a person because of the relationships that individual has established within the family. This person-granting power exercised by a social group such as the family can be abused. In unusual circumstances families or households might come to consider their pets as having almost the status of a person, strange as that may sound. Or, what is especially frightening, a social group might reject the claims of an individual to be recognized as a person because that individual is perceived as not satisfying what that group claims are necessary conditions for being a person. Some social groups have denied that some human beings are persons because they belonged to a particular religion, race, or ethnic group, or because they were of a particular gender or had certain mental or physical disabilities. Of course, there are competing theories that challenge the Social-Constructionist account about what are the necessary conditions for being a person. These theories claim that there are certain natural mental or behavioral requirements for being a person, and they reject the Social Constructionists' view that social groups have the right to grant, reject or withdraw the status of personhood from individuals who otherwise exhibit the natural features of a person.

This competition between different theories about what constitutes a person and what allows an individual to continue being a person is exhibited throughout Kafka's *Metamorphosis*. By having the narrative show the clash between these competing theories, Kafka creates considerable ambiguity about whether Gregor retains his status as a person throughout the narrative or whether he slips gradually into non-personhood. This ambiguity surfaces in the opening sentences of the novella when Gregor's physical transformation is revealed. In reading and discussing Kafka's *Metamorphosis*, readers often want to know: "What kind of insect was Gregor Samsa transformed into? Was he turned into a cockroach or some other kind of beetle?" However, in the novella Kafka does not give a direct answer to that question. He says only that Gregor was changed into a "monstrous vermin" (*Metamorphosis* 3). This is Corngold's translation of Kafka's original German "*ungeheueres Ungeziefer.*" Certainly, no such entomological species exists. In his "Introduction" to another edition of his translation of *The Metamorphosis*, Corngold writes:

> Kafka was an amateur of etymology and very likely aware of the original sense of those haunting "*un-*" words, "*ungeheueres Ungeziefer*" (monstrous vermin), into which Gregor is transformed. "*Ungeheuer*" connotes the creature who has no place in the family; "*Ungeziefer*," the unclean animal unsuited for sacrifice, the creature without a place in God's order.[4]

While the expression that Corngold has translated as "monstrous vermin" establishes an ambiguity about the biological nature of Gregor's transformation, there is still the deep-seated sense that Gregor is now an un-natural being, a corrupted being outside the ordinary classification of life forms, and cut off from any biological connection to the family, or at least his continuing status as a family member is in jeopardy.

In order to preserve the ambiguity and counter any realistic interpretation of Gregor's metamorphosis, Kafka describes the creature as breathing—insects, of course, have a very different system of respiration—and as having several human anatomical features and characteristics, such as a neck and eyes that tear. There is thus no natural biological niche into which one could fit this creature. If one sets aside the view that Kafka introduced these entomological "mistakes" because he was woefully ignorant about insect anatomy, one must conclude that Kafka wanted to maintain some ambiguity about Gregor's physical transformation.

Support for Kafka's wanting to preserve this ambiguity can be found in the following incident. When Kafka's original publisher wanted to show a picture of the "monstrous" creature on the book's title page in order to appeal to fans of horror fiction, Kafka refused to allow any pictures showing what Gregor had been transformed into. Hartmut Binder writes that "Kafka had learned that the illustrator Ottomar Starke had been commissioned to draw a title-page illustration. For this reason on October 25, 1915, he wrote to his publisher:

> It struck me that Starke, as an illustrator, might want to draw the insect itself. Not that, please not that! I do not want to restrict him, but only to make this plea out of my deepest knowledge of the story. The insect cannot be depicted. It cannot even be shown from a distance. Perhaps there is no such intention and my plea can be dismissed with a smile—so much the better. But I would be very grateful if you would pass along my request and make it more emphatic. If I were to offer suggestions for an illustration, I would choose such scenes as the following: the parents and the head clerk in front of the locked door, or even better, the parents and the sister in the lighted room, with the door open upon the adjoining room that lies in darkness."[5]

Kafka's request not to have a pictorial representation of the creature on the title page was made so emphatically because he wished to maintain an ambiguity about Gregor's physical transformation which in turn would support an ambiguity about his psychological transformation.

An ambiguity about the nature of Gregor's physical transformation is also shared by Gregor's parents. Up until the last third of the novella, the family appear to be of two minds about Gregor's remarkable change. On the one hand, the sight of the creature produces revulsion. The mother faints at the first sight of the creature, and the father reacts to the creature not as if it were someone in need of assistance but as a loathsome insect to be driven out of sight. Nevertheless, before they see the creature emerge from his locked bedroom, they believe that Gregor is ill and send for a doctor, and for a locksmith to open the locked door. In response, Gregor "felt integrated into human society once again and hoped for marvelous, amazing feats from both the doctor and the locksmith, without really distinguishing sharply between them" (*Metamorphosis* 11). Even for some time after his first horrific appearance, the parents still think that their son might recover. They ask their daughter, Grete, who now has responsibility for feeding the creature, "whether he [Gregor] had perhaps shown a little improvement" (*Metamorphosis* 23). Their solicitous concern points up their ambivalence. For if Gregor is ill and incapacitated, even if he is repulsive to look at, there is still some hope that he might be restored to health and resume being a valued family member. At the same time, they find him loathsome, an alien being that they do not try to communicate with. Only Grete speaks to him, and she never converses with him. She only talks at him.

Along with the ambiguity about Gregor's physical transformation, one also finds an ambiguity about Gregor's psychological "metamorphosis." Because of this latter ambiguity, major questions arise about Gregor's *personal identity*, about whether or not throughout the narrative he continues to be the same person, or even a person at all. (I am using the expression "personal identity" in the traditional philosophical sense of a relationship of sameness or identity between two temporally distinct stages of a human being's life such that one would say that the individual was one and the same person.) That is, from the time he awoke after "unsettling dreams" until "from his nostrils streamed his last weak breath" (*Metamorphosis* 3, 39) does this creature continue to be the same psychological being? Or, has a psychological metamorphosis occurred during the course of the narrative that gradually transforms Gregor into some other being? Kafka, I believe, creates a psychological ambiguity comparable to the physical ambiguity in order to prevent the reader from being able to reach a definite decision about Gregor's continued personal identity.

The Social-Constructionist theory holds that social groups have the power to abolish an individual's standing as a person, and in doing so can prevent an individual from continuing to be what earlier had been a particular person. In *The Metamorphosis* two other theories of personal identity compete with the Social-Constructionist account as providing the authoritative account of whether Gregor continues to be the same person throughout the novella. These two other theories of personal identity are a Lockean-Cartesian account and a Behaviorist account.[6] Each of the novella's three major sections highlights one of these accounts, although all three theories can be found throughout the novella. By the clash of their opposed philosophical positions, Kafka renders ambiguous Gregor's continued personal identity. Because of the ambiguity about Gregor's continued personal identity, I will refer to this transformed being as either "Gregor" or "the creature" or another neutral identifying term depending on the context of my remarks. I do not take a position on which of the three theories is the correct philosophical position from which to settle the question of Gregor's personal identity. In fact, I claim that, due to the ambiguity and the competing theories, one cannot settle that question.[7]

According to the Social-Constructionist account of personal identity, an individual that has been recognized as a person continues to maintain that status by preserving the social roles and relationships previously established with other persons. On this account, a person is a social entity and in a reflexive way identifies her or himself with the roles and relationships established with other persons in the social group. Gregor would be identified as a brother, a son, and the family bread winner. Personal identity is maintained by continued adherence to these social connections. If these roles and relationships were to be dissolved, an individual would either become selfless or, because of entering into new relationships, become a different self. One of the most important ways that social ties are maintained is through communication. In the novella's third section, the family's discussion about whether or not the creature is still the son and brother that they knew before the fateful morning brings to the foreground the Social Constructionist emphasis on communication. A major concern that the family has is that the creature in Gregor's bedroom has failed to communicate with them. For all that they know, the creature lacks the cognitive capacity both to form intelligible thought that could be linguistically expressed and the ability to understand what family members are saying. The Social Constructionist theory is not alone in thinking that communication is crucial in maintaining and supporting an individual's standing as a person. The other two theories also emphasize the major role played by communication in establishing that an individual is a person.

Communication is a central component in the Lockean-Cartesian theory of personhood. Locke begins his account of personal identity with a definition of a person and the grounds for establishing personal identity. A person, he claims,

> is a thinking, intelligent being that has reason and reflection, and can consider itself as itself, the same thinking thing, in different times and places; which it does only by that consciousness which is inseparable from thinking, as it seems to me essential to it. . . . [A]nd as far as this consciousness can be extended backwards to any past action or thought, so far reaches the identity of that person. . . . [I]t is the same self now it was then; and it is the same self with this present one that now reflects on it.[8]

Locke's view is that one establishes personal identity with an earlier self by one's present self being reflectively conscious of one's present consciousness and being able to be conscious of earlier experiences. One establishes ties to an earlier self through one's memory.

Having awakened from unsettling dreams, the being in Gregor's bed repeatedly confirms his existence as the same conscious subject or self that went to sleep in the room the night before. Through an act of reflective consciousness, he becomes aware of his present transformed condition, and through further reflection establishes his identity as Gregor Samsa. He remembers that the room he is in is his, Gregor's, room and recalls several personal associations with the furnishings. He also remembers that he must catch the early morning train and that if he misses that train, the office manager will learn about it, and his job will be in jeopardy. Thus, in accordance with Locke's account of personal identity, there is good reason to believe that the creature in the bed is personally identical with Gregor Samsa.[9]

The opening scene of the narrative presents Gregor Samsa's consciousness in an alien body, and one might say that Kafka has created a bizarre version of Locke's example of the consciousness of a prince who wakes up in the body of a cobbler.[10] This strange conjunction of a consciousness trying to exert control over an alien body coincides with Descartes' dualist account of human existence. Descartes holds that a person is essentially a private non-physical mind distinct from, but connected in some way to, a physical body. Descartes also believes that the mind is indivisible and despite changes to the body maintains its integrity.[11] This position allows one to believe that despite the physical transformation, Gregor's private mind still remains intact.

In the *Discourse on Method*, Descartes sets out two requirements for being a person, which mechanical automata and other animals lack.[12] A person, he claims, has the power to act from reason and knowledge, rather than just from instinct or mechanical stimulus. A person also has the power to communicate ideas, rather than to just vocally react. According to a Cartesian perspective, the creature who awakens in Gregor's bedroom exhibits both of these features. Hearing his anxious family outside his door, and then hearing that the office manager has arrived, Gregor realizes that he faces a set of practical problems that he must solve. He must exercise his reason and figure out how to get out of bed, unlock the door, reassure his family, and convince the office manager that he is still a conscientious employee.

In addition to these rational tasks, Gregor, at least initially, seems to have the power of speech. He carries on an inner monologue about his predicament that shows articulated thinking taking place. Responding to his parents' frantic pleas, he verbally tries to reassure them, or so he believes, saying, "Yes, yes, thanks, Mother, I'm just getting up." Nevertheless, when he does utter his thoughts, he is shocked at the sound of his voice, "unmistakably his own voice, true, but in which, as if from below, an insistent distressed chirping intruded" (*Metamorphosis* 5). When the office manager asks him to explain his unusual behavior, Gregor blurts out a long plea for understanding and seems to believe that he is speaking intelligibly. However, the office manager's response is to say, "That was the voice of an animal" (*Metamorphosis* 10).

Thus, from the interior conscious perspective of the Lockean-Cartesian position, Gregor believes himself to be exercising the capacity to communicate and thus fulfills a crucial requirement of being a person. Nevertheless, doubts are raised in his own mind that he is in fact uttering meaningful sounds. Prior to the office manager's arrival, the mother seems to take the sounds coming from Gregor's bedroom as meaningful speech. Yet, after the office manager's arrival, there is no indication that the family accepts the vocalizations that the creature utters as intelligible. Having opened the locked door to the bedroom, Gregor approaches his mother: "'Mother, Mother' said Gregor softly" (*Metamorphosis* 14). However, this utterance is not taken for meaningful speech. In the general panic caused by the creature's gruesome appearance, the father brandishes a cane, stamps his feet, hisses, and attempts to drive the creature, as one would attempt to drive a loathsome insect or animal, out of the room and back from whence he came. While the father is stamping his foot and hissing, there is the suggestion that Gregor would like to communicate with his father. However, the narrator informs: "No plea of Gregor's helped, no plea was even understood" (*Metamorphosis* 14).

Gregor's appearance is loathsome to the family, rendering them incapable of trying to communicate with this creature. Communication is also inhibited by Gregor's involuntary reaction to his father's hissing—"If only his father did not keep making this intolerable hissing sound!" In this same section, Gregor also exhibits another involuntary reaction: Approaching his mother and seeing the coffee spilling on the breakfast table, "he could not resist snapping his jaws several times in the air" (*Metamorphosis* 14). The involuntary jaw snapping seems like an insect's reaction to something to eat. Thus, there seem to be competing motivations for Gregor's actions. He appears to be motivated by rational desires to deal with his predicament, assuage the office manager, and verbally reassure his family; however, the chirping sounds he makes, his jaw snapping at the sight of coffee, and his reaction to the father's hissing appear to be exhibitions of insect-like involuntary behavior.

In the second section of the novella, these involuntary insect-like behaviors occur more often, and another theory of what constitutes a person challenges the Lockean-Cartesian theory so prevalent in the novella's first section. This is the Behaviorist perspective which relies on publically observable behavior to settle the question of whether Gregor persists as a person or whether he has been transformed into an alien insect being. The crucial issue is to notice what kind of behavior the creature displays. Persons exhibit one kind of behavior; insects exhibit a very different kind of behavior. The Behaviorist would urge that what might have appeared to be the rational behavior of a person in the first section is now being replaced by insect-like behavior. Examples of such insect behavior would include the creature's tastes in food, which are quite different from Gregor's, and the insect-like crawling around on the walls and ceiling. The creature also hides under the couch when a family member enters, a behavior that one could attribute to insect motivation. However, the narrator reveals that Gregor believes he hides under the couch out of consideration for his family (*Metamorphosis* 17).

In explaining the creature's behavior, one encounters an apparent inconsistency between the consciously asserted motivations and the insect-based ones. Is the creature hiding under the couch out of consideration for the family? Or, is the creature hiding under the couch because that is a behavior that insects display? This ambiguity about motivation raises a question about the reliability of the narration of Gregor's intentions, indicating that he may not know why he is behaving as he does. For example, we are told that "the empty high-ceilinged room . . . made him nervous, without his being able to tell why" (*Metamorphosis* 17). This lack of knowledge about his behavior calls into question the reliability of the way in which his other motivations are identified. Or, it suggests that there are competing motivations. For a Behaviorist, subjectively felt intentions do not carry the evidential weight that publicly observable behavior does. Behaviorists give greater credence to patterns or groupings of observable behavior, such as are collected in the ensemble of insect-like behaviors. The Lockean-Cartesian view asserts that a person's mental states are transparent. One can reflectively tell what mental state one is in.

At this point speech or communication plays a crucial role in trying to decide whether or not the creature maintains a personal identity with Gregor. For Gregor claims to understand what members of his family are saying, such as in the family discussion about finances, but the family never tries to communicate directly with him. We learn that "not a soul had addressed a word directly to him" (*Metamorphosis* 24). He does not appear to them to be capable of communication, and this assumption counts against him as far as maintaining his standing as a person. Although he can understand their speech, he makes no effort to try to converse with them. This lack of effort is remarkable, given his earlier frantic attempts to communicate with his mother and calm the office manager. On the assumption that he is still a Cartesian consciousness, it is puzzling why in the later sections of the novella he does not make a similar attempt to communicate with and reassure his family.[13]

However, there is one faint attempt at communicating his desires to his family. In the novella's second section when the sister and mother attempt to clear furniture from Gregor's room, he does act in a way that can be interpreted as indicating an intention to communicate. Placing his body over a picture on the wall, he intends by this action to express his desire that Grete and his mother should not remove furniture from the room. Nevertheless, when sister and mother see him on the picture, once again, this "plea" to his family is not understood or even accepted as an attempt to communicate. Instead, it is taken to be animal-like behavior; and in his subsequent rushing around, Grete tells her father that "Gregor's broken out" (*Metamorphosis* 27). From a Behaviorist perspective, there is some basis for this interpretation. The creature's agitated behavior can be considered an insect response caused by disturbing the furniture in the room and the commotion resulting from the mother's fainting. Thus, for a Behaviorist there is no indication that the creature is exhibiting the communicative behavior that would be distinctive of a person.

There is another scene later on in the third section that might be construed as illustrating an attempt by the creature to communicate. Grete has usually been the one to take care of Gregor's room; however, on one occasion the mother, without Grete's permission, has attempted to clean the room. On finding out that the mother has usurped her responsibility, Grete angrily complains to her father, and a family shouting match ensues. On hearing this loud emotional scene, the narrator informs that "Gregor hissed loudly with rage because it did not occur to any of them to close the door and spare him such a scene and a row" (*Metamorphosis* 32). One might take Gregor to be participating in the family's emotional outburst. Grete, the father, and the mother express their emotions with tears, shouting and gestures; Gregor expresses his emotional reaction by hissing. Yet, there is a difference between the parents' and Grete's outburst and Gregor's hissing. The shouting, tears and gestures of the three family members are expressed to each other and become heightened by seeing the other members' emotional response. Gregor is alone in his room and seems to be reacting to the loudness of the scene. Although there is some ambiguity about Gregor's response, a Behaviorist, I believe, could interpret the hissing not as an attempt to communicate with the rest of the family but as an insect-like reaction to the agitation in the next room.

For the Cartesian position, if an individual is disabled and unable to speak, establishing an alternative means of communication with others is a necessary endeavor in order to maintain that individual's status as a person. In the *Discourse on Method*, Descartes claims that human beings, who for some reason are "destitute of the organs which serve . . . others for talking[,] . . . are in the habit of themselves inventing certain signs by which they make themselves understood."[14] Gregor's not developing such an alternative means of communication runs counter to what for the Cartesian is an essential feature of personhood. Indeed, when someone has suffered a severe stroke or other incapacitating illness so that the individual is unable to communicate in the usual ways, one of the first things medical attendants try to do is establish another means of communication. Although the family is solicitous about whether Gregor is showing a "little improvement" (*Metamorphosis* 23), they do not attempt to provide a means for him to communicate with them.

In the novella's third section, the Social-Constructionist account achieves prominence. Communication plays a crucial role in that theory; it is one of the main ways that relationships with other social beings are maintained. Gregor's not establishing and maintaining a line of communication with his family, and the family's refusal to believe that such a link is possible, puts Gregor's position as a person in jeopardy. At first the family thinks that the creature in Gregor's bedroom is still a family member although suffering from an incapacitating illness. This prevents them from completely rejecting him as a person. Yet, the father's repeated efforts to force the creature back into the bedroom, and his throwing apples at Gregor and finally wounding him with one, have taken their toll on the family's acceptance of the creature as a person and family member. The result is the following sense of how the father thinks of the relationship between Gregor and the family:

> Gregor's serious wound . . . seemed to have reminded even his father that Gregor was a member of the family, in spite of his present pathetic and repulsive shape, who could not be treated as an enemy; that, on the contrary, it was the commandment of family duty to swallow their disgust and endure him, endure him and nothing more. (*Metamorphosis* 29)

This conviction that the family must "swallow their disgust and endure him" shows that the family has reached a limit in their willingness to accept the creature as a family member. Yet, instead of keeping Gregor's bedroom door locked, the family now leaves it ajar as recognition that the being in Gregor's bedroom is still a member of the family circle and should not be excluded from their conversation. However, no attempt is made by either Gregor or other family members to initiate an inclusive conversation.

Nevertheless, Gregor does not always keep to his room. One might take his coming out of the bedroom on hearing Grete's playing her violin for the roomers as a gesture of emotional support for Grete. The roomers do not find her playing interesting, and he wants to show that as a family member he does approve of her playing. Gregor had planned to send Grete to the Conservatory to study violin (*Metamorphosis* 36). One might also suppose that he wants to leave the private space of the bedroom and enter the public space in which the family assembles. However, once again, there is an alternative motivation for the creature's entrance into the dining room. We know that before the transformation, Gregor did not like his sister's violin playing, but now when she plays for the roomers he finds himself drawn toward her. He asks himself, "Was he an animal that music could move him so?" (*Metamorphosis* 36). Adopting a Behaviorist perspective, one might say that the creature's being drawn toward the music is an insect-like behavioral response described by the Orphic myth that credits music as having a powerful effect on animal behavior.[15]

However, from the family's perspective, the behavior is disruptive. The startling appearance of the creature prompts Grete during the consequent family discussion to argue that they must sever all family ties to the creature. Yet, the father at first seems reluctant to do so and sees no easy way out of their predicament. "If he could understand us," the father says, "then maybe we could come to an agreement with him" (*Metamorphosis* 38). But Grete, articulating the Social-Constructionist position, counters that such an agreement is only possible between persons. She insists:

> You just have to try to get rid of the idea that it's Gregor. Believing it for so long, that is our real misfortune. But how can it be Gregor? If it were Gregor, he would have realized long ago that it isn't possible for human beings to live

> with such a creature, and he would have gone away of his own free will. Then we wouldn't have a brother, but we'd be able to go on living and honor his memory. But as things are, this animal persecutes us, drives the roomers away, obviously wants to occupy the whole apartment and for us to sleep in the gutter. (*Metamorphosis* 38)

Grete argues that the creature is not her brother and the parents' son. He is an animal; she calls him a "monster" (*Metamorphosis* 37). He cannot be a family member because she believes that he has acted in a way that shows he does not value and respect the family. Her brother, as a person, would have exercised his free will and acted out of consideration for the family. The being in Gregor's bedroom is an animal who acts only according to instinct. If the creature were their son/brother, he would have left the family of his own accord. They would then be able to recognize that he was a person and valued family member; however, since he has not acted as a family member, they have to dissolve any family or human ties to the creature. She is emphatic about this. "I won't pronounce the name of my brother," she insists, "in front of this monster, and so all I say is: we have to try to get rid of it" (*Metamorphosis* 37).[16]

While this emotionally charged family discussion has been going on, Gregor has still remained out in the public space of the dining room. Grete now notices that he is there, close by them, and shrieks out a warning. Yet, Gregor's only response is to slowly turn and withdraw into his room. No sooner has he entered the bedroom than the narrator informs that

> the door was hurriedly slammed shut, firmly bolted, and locked . . . . [Grete] had been standing up straight, ready and waiting, then she had leaped forward nimbly, Gregor had not even heard her coming, and she cried "Finally!" to her parents as she turned the key in the lock. (*Metamorphosis* 39)

Locking the creature in the room is the active counterpart to her urging that they must break all family ties to the creature. By ensuring that he cannot come into the family space of the dining room, she has separated him from the family and broken the ties of family membership that according to the Social-Constructionist account have constituted who he is as a person.

Nevertheless, one might see the creature's death as Gregor's sacrificing his own life out of consideration for his family. On this view he is still the rational Cartesian consciousness he was at the beginning of the narrative who continues to act in a morally sensitive way. Yet there is another interpretation of the death: insects do not live very long and in the last half of the narrative the creature has been in decline. The death is just the final event in that insect's short lifespan. However, there are some ambiguities that remain with both of these interpretations, as a close reading of the description of the final moments reveals. The final moment is described in the following way: "Then, without his consent, his head sank down to the floor, and from his nostrils streamed his last weak breath" (*Metamorphosis* 39). The profusion of human anatomical details in the sentence seems to counter a realistic insect interpretation. This seems to take away some of authority from the Behaviorist interpretation. In addition, the phrase "without his consent" takes away some of the voluntary, consciously initiated aspects of the death and undercuts the Cartesian view that Gregor is acting out of consideration for his family.

This ambiguity about whether or not Gregor's death is a meaningful action also raises some questions about the nature of Grete's Social-Constructionist severing of ties between the family and Gregor. Is Gregor fulfilling Grete's claim that if the creature were her brother he would have voluntarily left them? However, if Gregor's death is his voluntarily removing himself from the family, why has he not acted in other ways to respect his relationship with the family? Although the creature claims to understand what the Samsa family members say, he has not initiated a communicative relationship with them. He is "hungry," he says, "but not for these things" that the roomers are eating. If he is emotionally in need of the relationships he used to have with his family, why the silence on his part?

In an article on *The Metamorphosis*, Robert Weninger presents an insightful analysis on the relationship of Gregor's silence to the family's verbally expressed thoughts. He claims that Gregor is silent because "his new insect-like body cannot form human sounds, at best he can produce senseless brutish screeches."[17] Instead, through something like what Weninger labels a "ventriloquist method," Gregor

> succeeds in relegating his subdued voice to his counterparts, thereby forcing them to speak his mind. To be sure, his shell symbolizes his withdrawal, his isolation, and his alienation, but it also forces others to pronounce his unspeakable thoughts, to make his motives known to those who wish to hear. Through ventriloquy, Gregor compensates for his loss of language.[18]

Weninger makes a plausible case that the family articulates what Gregor would have liked to have said about his life and his employment before his transformation. Yet, Weninger holds to a realistic account of Gregor's physical transformation as an explanation about why Gregor remains silent and does not communicate his thoughts to his family. As I have argued, however, the very ambiguity of Gregor's physical transformation and the resulting mental metamorphosis raise questions and create ambiguities about the nature of Gregor's behavior and actions. Each of the three theories challenges the other theories about the nature of Gregor's motivations.

Gregor's lack of trying to communicate with his family after he first attempts to do so on the morning following his transformation clashes with his having interior thoughts that are not expressed. He hears that his family thinks he is a monstrous animal, and yet he does not explain his actions. Thus, it is not enough, as the father says, that the creature needs to understand what the family is saying in order to preserve his personhood; he must also communicate with them in order to hold his place as a family member (*Metamorphosis* 38). Without an articulate appeal from Gregor, the family encounters little resistance in their decision to dissolve his standing as a family member.

In the novella's first section, realizing that something is wrong in Gregor's locked bedroom, the family implore him to open the door to his bedroom. The locked door of his room, referred to as "a regular human room" (*Metamorphosis* 3), signifies the separation between a private mental space and a public space. The locked room is a metonymy for his inaccessible interior mental state. Not only is he cut off physically from the world outside his room, but he is socially removed from his family and the rest of the human community. As Gregor realizes in the opening section, communicating with his family and the office manager through the locked door is crucial if he wants to preserve both his personal identity and his ties to his family. Yet, as the narrative unfolds he falters in his efforts at coming out into the public space and revealing his interior thoughts. The clash among Cartesian, Behaviorist, and Social-Constructionist perspectives renders ambiguous not only his behavior but also his status as a psychological subject. Finally, locked in his room by Grete, Gregor exists unrealized as either a Cartesian subject, a being transformed into an insect, or as a being having a recognized status as family member and person.

## Notes

1. "You're nobody 'til somebody loves you" was written and composed in 1944 by Russ Morgan, Larry Stock, and James Cavanaugh. The song has been recorded many times. Perhaps the most well-known recording is Dean Martin's 1965 version for Reprise Records.

2. Franz Kafka, *The Metamorphosis: Translation, Background and Contexts, Criticism*, trans. and ed. Stanley Corngold (New York: Norton Critical Edition, 1996), 3. Future quotations from *The Metamorphosis* in the body of the chapter will be to this edition and will appear parenthetically in the body of the chapter.

3. An early version of a Social-Constuctionist account can be found in Plato's *Republic* in which citizens of the *polis* are identified in terms of the social roles they perform. In the nineteenth century, a Social-Constructionist account can be discerned in Hegel's view that a person's self-consciousness exists only because it is recognized by other persons (Georg Wilhelm Friedrich Hegel, *The Phenomenology of Spirit*, trans. A.V. Miller [Oxford: Oxford University Press, 1977], 111). Marx also holds the view that a person exists and occupies a particular position with a social formation or class (Karl Marx, "Theses on Feuerbach," *Writings of the Young Marx on Philosophy and Society*, trans. and ed. L. D. Easton and K. H. Guddat [Garden City, NY: Doubleday, 1967], 400-2). For further discussion of the Social-Constructionist account, see Sweeney, "Competing Theories of Identity in Kafka's *The Metamorphosis*," in Kafka, *The Metamorphosis*, Norton Critical Edition, 147-48.

4. Stanley Corngold, "Introduction," in Franz Kafka, *The Metamorphosis*, trans. and ed. Stanley Corngold (New York: Bantam Books, 1972), xix.

5. Hartmut Binder, "*The Metamorphosis*: The Long Journey into Print," trans. Stanley Corngold, in Kafka, *The Metamorphosis*, Norton Critical Edition, 185. Binder quotes from Franz Kafka, *Letters to Friends, Family, and Editors*, eds. B. Colman, N. Glatzer, C. Kuppig, W. Sauerlander, trans. Richard and Clara Winston (New York: Schocken, 1977), 114-15.

6. Behaviorism, as a theory about the nature of a person, derives from materialist theories of mind such as the account proposed by Thomas Hobbes. In the nineteenth century with the rise of Positivism, there is the desire to conduct psychological research on the same basis as research conducted in other sciences. Research should be based

solely on public observation. One should recognize as objective data only that which records an individual's publicly observable behavior. In the twentieth century, Behaviorism is codified as a theory by J. B. Watson (*Behaviorism* [London: Kegan Paul, 1925]). For further elucidation of this and the Lockean-Cartesian account, see Sweeney, "Competing Theories of Identity in Kafka's *The Metamorphosis.*"

7. In my earlier article on *The Metamorphosis*, "Competing Theories of Identity in Kafka's *The Metamorphosis*," I argued that there was an irresolvable tension among the three competing theories of personal identity in the novella. In the present essay, I extend that analysis by focusing on the role of communication, particularly Gregor's lack of initiating any verbal communication with his family, as a crucial factor for all three theories for determining Gregor's continuity as a person.

8. John Locke, "Of Identity and Diversity," *An Essay Concerning Human Understanding* (1690), vol. 1, ed. A.C. Fraser (New York: Dover, 1959), 448-49.

9. In his short story "A Report to an Academy," Kafka uses memory in a Lockean way to mark the change in the narrator from his former existence as an ape to his present life "in the human world." The narrator remarks that as he has made the change "my memories have become more and more closed off from me" (Franz Kafka, *Kafka's Selected Stories*, trans. and ed. Stanley Corngold [New York: Norton Critical Edition, 2007], 77).

10. Locke, "Of Identity and Diversity," 457.

11. René Descartes, "Meditations on First Philosophy" (1641), *The Philosophical Works of Descartes*, vol. 1, trans. Elizabeth Haldane and G.R.T. Ross (New York: Cambridge University Press, 1969), 196.

12. René Descartes, "Discourse on the Method of Rightly Conducting the Reason" (1637), *The Philosophical Works of Descartes*, 116.

13. As I have argued in my earlier article on *The Metamorphosis*, attributing a motivation or a conscious intention to Gregor in the later parts of the novella will be challenged by the competing accounts of his subjectivity.

14. Descartes, "Discourse on the Method," 117.

15. See Sweeney, "Competing Theories of Identity in Kafka's *The Metamorphosis*," 150.

16. For further discussion of Greta's argument, see Sweeney, "Competing Theories of Identity in Kafka's *The Metamorphosis*," 150-51.

17. Robert Weninger, "Sounding Out the Silence of Gregor Samsa: Kafka's Rhetoric of Dys-Communication," *Twentieth Century Literature*, 17.2 (Summer 1993), 102; reprinted in *Franz Kafka's The Metamorphosis*, new edition, ed. Harold Bloom (New York: Bloom's Literary Criticism, 2008), 95-115.

18. Weninger, "Sounding Out the Silence of Gregor Samsa," 111.

## Works cited

Binder, Hartmut. "*The Metamorphosis*: The Long Journey into Print." In Kafka, *The Metamorphosis: Translation, Background and Contexts, Criticism*. Translated and edited by Stanley Corngold, 172-94. New York: Norton Critical Edition, 1996.

Corngold, Stanley. "Introduction." In Franz Kafka, *The Metamorphosis*, translated and edited by Stanley Corngold, xi-xxi. New York: Bantam Books, 1972.

Descartes, René. "Discourse on the Method of Rightly Conducting the Reason" (1637). In *The Philosophical Works of Descartes*, vol. 1, translated by Elizabeth Haldane and G.R.T. Ross, 79-130. New York: Cambridge University Press, 1969.

———. "Meditations on First Philosophy" (1641). In *The Philosophical Works of Descartes*, vol. 1, translated by Elizabeth Haldane and G.R.T. Ross, 131-99. New York: Cambridge University Press, 1969.

Hegel, Georg Wilhelm Friedrich. *The Phenomenology of Spirit*. Translated by A.V. Miller. Oxford: Oxford University Press, 1977.

Kafka, Franz. *Kafka's Selected Stories*. Translated and edited by Stanley Corngold. New York: Norton Critical Edition, 2007.

———. *Letters to Friends, Family, and Editors*. Edited by B. Colman, N. Glatzer, C. Kuppig, W. Sauerlander, translated by Richard and Clara Winston. New York: Schocken, 1977.

———. *The Metamorphosis: Translation, Background and Contexts, Criticism*. Translated and edited by Stanley Corngold. New York: Norton Critical Edition, 1996.

Locke, John. "Of Identity and Diversity." In *An Essay Concerning Human Understanding* (1690), vol.1, edited by A.C. Fraser, 439-70. New York: Dover, 1959.

Marx, Karl. "Theses on Feuerbach." In *Writings of the Young Marx on Philosophy and Society*, translated and edited by L. D. Easton and K. H. Guddat, 400-2. Garden City, NY: Doubleday, 1967.

Sweeney, Kevin W. "Competing Theories of Identity in Kafka's *The Metamorphosis*." In Franz Kafka, *The Metamorphosis: Translation, Background and Contexts, Criticism*, translated and edited by Stanley Corngold, 140-54. New York: Norton Critical Edition, 1996.

Watson, J. B. *Behaviorism*. London: Kegan Paul, 1925.

Weninger, Robert. "Sounding Out the Silence of Gregor Samsa: Kafka's Rhetoric of Dys-Communication." *Twentieth Century Literature* 17.2 (Summer 1993): 263-86. Reprinted in *Franz Kafka's The Metamorphosis*, new edition, edited by Harold Bloom, 95-115. New York: Bloom's Literary Criticism, 2008.

CHAPTER 6

# Kafka's Insomnia*

*Peter Schwenger*

"If it were not for these horrible sleepless nights," Kafka once told his friend Gustav Janouch, "I would never write at all."[1] Nor is he alone in this sentiment. "My trouble is insomnia," Céline declared. "If I had always slept properly, I'd have never written a line."[2] And E. M. Cioran—a "career insomniac" according to Willis Regier—said, "I have never been able to write except in the melancholy of insomniac nights."[3] How, then, are we to understand this intimate relation between insomnia and writing?

There are, according to Cioran, "two kinds of mind: daylight and nocturnal. They have neither the same method nor the same morality" (*Trouble* 17).[4] After the insomniac has fully experienced the revelation of the night, he says a bit later, "the day seems useless, light pernicious, even more oppressive than the darkness" (*Trouble* 31). The night's most profound revelation, then, may be the nature of the day, of what we think of as being awake,[5] of a light that claims to illuminate the world in more senses than one. In his book *Existence and Existents* Levinas asserts that light is what allows the world to be ordered; it "makes possible . . . [an] enveloping of the exterior by the inward, which is the very structure of the cogito, and of sense" (*Existence* 41).[6] So light provides a panoply of metaphors for the ordering activity of the mind, for thought itself: I see your point, it is clear, it is illuminating, brilliant even, you are a bright boy. Night takes all this illumination away along with the shapes of objects, the defined spaces in which both they and their observer are positioned. And so night, Maurice Merleau-Ponty argues in *The Phenomenology of Perception*, has consequences for both the things of the world and those who observe them:

> Night is not an object before me; it enwraps me and infiltrates through all my senses, stifling my recollections and almost destroying my personal identity. I am no longer withdrawn into my perceptual look-out from which I watch the outlines of objects moving by at a distance. Night has no outlines; . . . it is pure depth without foreground or background, without surfaces and without any dis-

* A somewhat different version of this essay has appeared in Peter Schwenger, *At the Borders of Sleep: On Liminal Literature* (Minneapolis, MN: University of Minnesota Press, 2012).

> tance separating it from me. All space for the reflecting mind is sustained by thinking which relates its parts to each other, but in this case the thinking starts from nowhere.[7]

If the *order* of thought is now dissipated in a nocturnal "nowhere," the same can be said of its *origin*, the place from which it starts: thinking cannot be said to "start" at all, simply because it is revealed as always already in progress. This is thought, of course, that cannot be said to be structured in Levinas's sense, or indeed *as* sense. It is a restless, interminable movement of the mind that reveals itself to us in the night. It does not "get anywhere" any more than it comes from anywhere; it is without goal, defies control, makes no progress while always progressing.

For the "nowhere" of the night is not nothing—which might in its own way bring rest, the nirvana striven for in meditative practice. As Levinas describes it, night brings with it something altogether more disconcerting:

> There is a nocturnal space, but it is no longer empty space, the transparency which both separates us from things and gives us access to them, by which they are given. Darkness fills it like a content; it is full, but full of the nothingness of everything. Can one speak of its continuity? It is surely uninterrupted. But the points of nocturnal space do not refer to each other as in illuminated space; there is no perspective, they are not situated. There is a swarming of points. (*Existence* 53)

With this last sentence Levinas moves, briefly, from the metaphysical to the physical. The phenomenon that he is referring to was described by the Czech scientist Jan Evangelista Purkinje as early as 1819. Purkinje described how, on entering a darkened room, one can "see" numerous small points of moving light, which he compared to the swirling of dust particles in a sunbeam.[8] This is one of the effects that can be generated by a *ganzfeld*, a homogenous undifferentiated field of vision; a uniformly cloudy sky is another example. At its extreme, a ganzfeld can produce full-blown hallucinations. The suggestion has been made that these hallucinations can be related to the phenomenon of hypnagogia: images that sometimes appear before the closed eyes just before going over into sleep, but while one is still awake.[9] This suggestion, however, has been disproven by comparing EEG records of both phenomena.[10] The swarming points of light, then, are self-reflective manifestations of the eye's activity, as it seeks to see *something*.[11] Levinas is using this phenomenon as the counterpart of another restless motion, that of the mind cast free from its moorings in the daylight world.

To be "cast free" in this sense is not liberating but disorienting: losing situatedness, one loses self. In the dark there is no boundary, there is no center, there is no way to connect the swarm of points, whether spatial or mental. What there is, is "there is"—the *il y a*, as Levinas calls it—the impersonal fact of existence without regard to a coherent existent, the awareness of Being detached from one's own particular being. And this awareness is something like a waking nightmare: "Being," Levinas writes, "is essentially alien and strikes against us.

We undergo its suffocating embrace like the night, but it does not respond to us" (*Existence* 9). If it is essentially alien, then Being is other than us, even if it is through participation in Being that our own being comes to be. To say we participate in Being is only to say that we exist—not that we are equivalent to existence, which is something beyond our particular version of it. In the formlessness of night, we experience something of what it is like to be without a self, and yet to sense the pervasive presence of existence.

This is the experience that Maurice Blanchot calls "the other night"—other in a number of ways. To begin with, this night is other than the day's conception of it, where night is a time of rest and recuperation, "down time" that is seconded for the day's purposes. Moreover, Blanchot's night is other than the physical fact of darkness—even though darkness, as we have seen, has psychological and philosophical consequences. These consequences, finally, are where the otherness of the "other night" manifests itself. As Blanchot says, "There is no exact moment at which one would pass from night to the *other* night, no limit at which to stop and come back in the other direction" (*Space* 169).[12] Perhaps these notions of passing and limitlessness are the most disconcerting characteristics of the other night where, he says, "the incessant and the uninterrupted reign" (*Space* 119). Motion without end, existence without form, are what one senses in the other night: "Here the invisible is what one cannot cease to see; it is the incessant making itself seen" (*Space* 163). This may recall Levinas's "swarming of points"—and not surprisingly, given the fact that Levinas and Blanchot repeatedly cross-reference each other on this matter of what happens in the night. Along with the incessant movement of the invisible are other forms of the night's restlessness: "In the night, silence is speech, and there is no repose, for there is no position" (*Space* 119). If there is no position, there is also no sleep; for Levinas and Blanchot both view sleep as fundamentally associated with a security of position. Levinas:

> In lying down, in curling up in a corner to sleep, we abandon ourselves to a place; qua base it becomes our refuge. Then all our work of being consists in resting. Sleep is like entering into contact with the protective forces of a place. (*Existence* 67)

Blanchot:

> Where I sleep I fix myself and I fix the world. My person is there, prevented from erring, no longer unstable, scattered and distracted, but concentrated in the narrowness of this place. (*Space* 266)

It is this concentration that we seek when we toss and turn in bed, unable to find exactly the right place that will put a stop to our restlessness.

But in contrast to these "protective forces of place," the other night is non-place: continual distancing, restless movement (in any number of versions) within the incessant, impersonal time that is existence when it is not structured as "our" existence. This is the restless revelation that comes to us in the other night, when we have either left our daylight concerns behind or (more likely) are inundated with them in versions beyond our control: interminable, incessant, uninterrupted. The horror of such moments is that they transform daylight's meaningful agendas into endless meaningless chatter, movement without resolution. There is the suspicion as well that this is the real nature of our existence, which day tries to cover over.

So the affliction of insomnia has to do above all with what happens to thoughts in the dark. To lie awake in the "other night," Blanchot warns, "leaves thought outside of any secret, deprives it of all intimacy, and turns it into the body of its absence. For it lays thought bare to the lack of thought."[13] This seems, on the face of it, an outright contradiction, resolvable only by second thoughts about "thoughts." Certainly, one often-noted characteristic of insomnia is the inability to shut down the mind, the compulsive and unwished-for proliferation of thoughts that keep one from relaxing into sleep. For in the night one reaches no resting point, no conclusion or illuminated "secret" that is not immediately eroded by the continuing flow of thought; and with all the structures of daylight thinking dissolved in the night, the strangest adumbrations are free to appear. Their strangeness means that they cannot be owned or intimate: we do not think, *it thinks*. This "it" should not be given the wrong kind of weight: it is not a malign usurper but merely the adjunct to an action, as William James puts it in his *Psychology:* "If we could say in English 'it thinks,' as we say 'it rains' or 'it blows,' we should be stating the fact most simply and with the minimum of assumption. As we cannot, we must simply say that *thought goes on*."[14] It goes on willfully in the night, dissolving the cogito and the self with it. It is this ruthless, restless destruction that Blanchot gestures toward when he writes that insomnia "lays thought bare to the lack of thought."

Such revelations of the night are never to be known either by those whose consciousness is laid to rest in sleep or by those who merely lie awake, which is something different from true insomnia. For insomnia is a liminal state, uneasily situated between sleeping and waking. The element of waking, though, is not merely a matter of open eyes, since, as Blanchot has suggested, dream is a kind of waking *within* sleep—a suggestion that has recently been corroborated by cognitive researchers who find that the brain functions exactly the same in the dream state as it does in the waking state, even if it's reacting to different sorts of stimuli. So it is that in the liminal space of insomnia, dreams can take place on the hither side of sleep. Consider this diary entry by Kafka for October 2, 1911:

> Sleepless night. The third in a row. I fall asleep soundly, but after an hour I wake up, as though I had laid my head in the wrong hole. I am completely awake, have the feeling that I have not slept at all or only under a thin skin, have before me anew the labor of falling asleep and feel myself rejected by sleep. And for the rest of the night, until about five, thus it remains, so that indeed I sleep but at the same time vivid dreams keep me awake. I sleep alongside myself, so to speak, while I myself must struggle with dreams. About five the last trace of sleep is exhausted, I just dream, which is more exhausting than wakefulness. In short, I spend the whole night in that state in which a healthy person finds himself for a short time before really falling asleep. When I awaken, all the dreams are gathered about me, but I am careful not to reflect on

> them. Toward morning I sigh into the pillow, because for this night all hope is gone. (*Diaries* 73-74)[15]

To linger a bit on the contradictions here: he is "completely awake" and "thus it remains, so that indeed I sleep." But then he cannot have remained awake, especially since at the same time he is having "vivid dreams"—except that these, he says, "keep me awake." Of course one can dream with eyes wide open, in daydreams or reveries, but these are generally indulged in with the dreamer's consent, and Kafka is clearly struggling with his nocturnal visions. One may also dream with eyes shut and still be awake; that is the nature of hypnagogia, which is indeed a "state in which a healthy person finds himself for a short time before really falling asleep," bringing with it a plethora of involuntary images. In fact, just after this passage, Kafka describes a disturbing "apparition" (*Erscheinung*), a blind girl wearing eyeglasses: one eye is "milky-gray and bulbous," the other recedes and is "covered by a lens lying close to it"; the eyeglasses are secured to the girl's face by a support that pierces the flesh and rests on the cheekbone. But the image's personal specificity and psychological charge move it away from hypnagogia (whose images are generally impersonal) and toward dream: Kafka is able to identify a number of sources for this image—his mother's eyeglasses, an acquaintance's daughter—in the manner of Freud, with whose work Kafka was of course familiar.[16] This supports Kafka's designation of these images as "vivid dreams."

The dreams that haunt the insomniac Kafka, then, are not the product of sleep but of a psychological night: as Oates has observed, "We experience Night but are also Night."[17] The insomniac becomes aware of an incessant inner turbulence that dreams tap into but which can also surge forward without the intermediary stage of sleep. So in another diary entry (July 21, 1913) Kafka writes, "I cannot sleep. Only dreams, no sleep" (*Diaries* 291). The dreamer, however, is other than the "I" who cannot sleep, for "I sleep alongside myself." This "other" continually accompanies one, thinking in a manner quite different from that of the day, though it does not cease during the day. It is the very fact that this inner turbulence does not cease, is incessant, that causes Kafka to write, "I just dream, which is more exhausting than wakefulness." Dream, as Blanchot has described it, is indeed an endless restless series of resemblances and associations (*Space* 268). If we are not completely exhausted by our dreams, that is because we follow passively where the dream leads, accepting without question elements and episodes that will baffle us in the morning, when we try to make sense of our dreams. At that point, however, we are already looking at them with what Cioran would call a daylight mind in contrast to a nocturnal one. Cioran's "nocturnal mind," of course, is not that of dream, but of insomnia—an insomnia that is stripped of the acquiescence that carries us through our dreams, but is at the same time impelled by a kind of dream logic. The collision between these two mental modes produces the insomniac's incessant, and incessantly self-destroying, thoughts. For the writer, these can become the errant path of "inspiration," a term that we will return to in a moment. So it is that Kafka repeatedly connects his sleeplessness to his writing—although, appropriately enough, he never decides which precedes the other. In another part of the October 2 entry he says:

> I believe this sleeplessness comes only because I write. For no matter how little and how badly I write, I am still made sensitive by these minor shocks, feel, especially toward evening and even more in the morning, the approaching, the imminent possibility of great moments which would tear me open, which could make me capable of anything, and in the general uproar that is within me and which I have no time to command, find no rest. (*Diaries* 74-75)

But if sleeplessness comes with writing, writing also *demands* sleeplessness. For, Kafka writes Felice Bauer (Jan. 15, 1913), "writing means revealing oneself to excess. . . . That is why one can never be alone enough when one writes, why there can never be enough silence around one when one writes, why even night is not night enough."[18] It's not that night provides a "cover" for one's excesses, but that night is the very milieu of excess, of a continual passing beyond limits. The riskiest revelations of the day, Kafka says in the same letter, still fall short of what is required for writing; only the night gives the writer what he needs; and even the "great moments" of the night, as he says, may not be enough.

How does this nocturnal instruction find its way into Kafka's writing? For however much he may write of insomnia in diaries or letters, it does not figure in his work. Nevertheless, one senses its presence. To begin with, it is there in the sheer liminality of his stories, which like their insomniac author lie somewhere between sleeping and waking. Elements that seem dreamlike are presented with a scrupulously realistic detail that resists any such classification as "dream narratives." This resistance can sometimes be explicit, as it is in "The Metamorphosis." The story begins as Gregor Samsa awakes from "unsettling dreams." For Kafka, waking is always a dangerous transition, and a doubtful one in the sense that we cannot be entirely sure that the transition has been made completely. In this case, because of the powerful pull of the dreamlike premise, the reader may remain unsure, even though Gregor himself quickly decides that what has happened to him "was no dream," and even though the dreamlike premise is developed in a fully detailed realism.

Another kind of undecidability characterizes any work by Kafka, and that is the question of what it "means"—a daylight question, to be sure, and one that in the work is given a nocturnal answer, which is to say no answer. This "no answer" is not a simple denial or recalcitrant silence; it is a prolongation, perhaps even a multiplication, of the question. The work gives rise to what Lois Nesbitt has called "critical insomnia"—by which she does not mean being kept awake by problematical texts. It is rather a model of thought, which she is both investigating and recommending. The insomniac, she writes,

> circles around his obsession, viewing it from different perspectives and arriving at different interpretations of its significance. The process is infinite: the insomniac may return to and reconsider earlier interpretations, but he is never able to commit himself to any one reading of the facts. His mental journey may reveal characteristics of logical thought: fixity of object, systematic analysis of that object, linear or sequential enumeration of ideas. But this logic is at best tempo-

> rary; in the long run his path is as irrational as it is rational, for the links between one idea and the next are often rather the leaps of associative thinking, metonymic slides from one track to another.
>
> What distinguishes insomniac thinking from idle contemplation, however, is the constancy of its object. One motion leads to another and another, but the insomniac's path is circular and not linear; his attention remains focused on the center of that circle.[19]

This description of insomniac thinking becomes that of critical thinking, Nesbitt asserts, in the case of "texts whose very structures and textures force us to become insomniac readers."[20]

Kafka's *The Castle* is one such text. If insomniac thought is circular, as Nesbitt suggests, here the center of the circle, the focus of attention, is the castle itself. Not that the focus is clear enough to repay that attention: "There was no sign of the Castle hill, fog and darkness surrounded it, not even the faintest gleam of light suggested the large Castle. K. stood a long time on the wooden bridge that leads from the main road to the village, gazing upward into the seeming emptiness" (*Castle* 1).[21] With these words both K. and Kafka enter the world of the novel, and we enter it with them. The transition to literature, Blanchot intimates while citing this passage, is also the transition *of* literature, its continual doubling not so much of "life" as of every literary work that has preceded the one we are reading, with no ground other than that provided by such a repetition. This sort of transition is also K.'s since, "in an incomprehensible manner, he decides to break with his own familiarity, as though pulled ahead toward these sites nonetheless without allure by an exigency he is unable to account for. From this perspective," Blanchot concludes, "one would almost be tempted to say that the entire meaning of the book is already borne by the *wooden bridge*," a liminal zone to be sure.[22] When the Castle becomes visible in the next day's light, it first meets K.'s expectations and then disappoints them: "It was only a rather miserable little town, pieced together from village houses, distinctive only because everything was perhaps built of stone, but the paint had long since flaked off, and the stone seemed to be crumbling" (*Castle* 8). As with the "seeming emptiness," there is a good deal of the merely ostensible here, and the promise of a meaningful center deteriorates into the messiness of ordinary life. Similarly, as K. continues to seek the Castle, his focus branches out into numerous digressions, reversals, and blind alleys—a psychology that is expressed by a certain topography. "The vicious circularity of Kafka's spaces has often been noted," Dorrit Cohn writes, and goes on to quote from the beginning of the novel:

> So he set off again, but it was a long way. The street he had taken, the main street in the village, did not lead to the Castle hill, it only went close by, then veered off as if on purpose, and though it didn't lead any farther from the Castle, it didn't get any closer either. K. kept expecting the street to turn at last toward the Castle and it was only in this expectation that he kept going.[23]

This literalizes Nesbitt's notion of "the insomniac's path"; but of course the topography here reflects a certain movement of thought.

Blanchot has described that movement in rather different terms: "In the night," he says, "insomnia is dis-cussion: not the work of arguments bumping against other arguments, but the extreme shuddering of no thoughts, percussive stillness (the exegeses that come and go in *The Castle*, story of insomnia)."[24] *The Castle*, like many other works of Kafka, does indeed include endless discussion: speculations, explanations, interpretations. These are often at odds with one another, and reverse themselves even as they are being put forward—as does the reasoning of the animal in "The Burrow," who seeks to secure another version of the Castle, the core of his branching burrow, which he calls his "Castle Keep." Blanchot expresses this movement through an ingenious deconstructive etymology, breaking *discussion* in two (the word is the same in French or English). The last half, "-cussion," is related to the "bumping," that is more clearly evident in words like *concussion* and *percussion*; it is ultimately derived from the Latin *quatere*, to shake. The negating prefix "dis" turns conflicting thoughts into no-thoughts, a turn that they make all too readily in the insomniac state. The more the insomniac pursues problems in the night, the more they lead inevitably to a final dis-solution, which is not a resting point—rather, "percussive stillness." Yet that combination of movement and stillness can become, in the case of writers like Kafka, their *inspiration.*

Mystical, but perhaps also a mystification, the word "inspiration" covers over peculiarities that Blanchot uncovers again in his musings. Inspiration is for him "a nocturnal state," within which the writer lingers "in search of an errant word" (*Space* 182). Errancy itself is the wandering essence of something that has no center and no conclusion, just as it is the essence, or non-essence, of insomnia. Thus Blanchot can write: "Inspiration, that errant word which cannot come to an end, is *the long night of insomnia*" (*Space* 184). And in both inspiration and insomnia there is a dissolution of identity, a going-beyond the self that is not willed by the self: "The purer the inspiration," Blanchot writes, "the more dispossessed is he who enters the space where it draws him" (*Space* 182). Dispossessed, among other things, of all possibility for rest: "Inspiration pushes us gently or impetuously out of the world, and in this outside there is no sleep, any more than there is rest" (*Space* 185). While there is a sense in which one writes in order to lay to rest the errant word, to fix it on the page and thus to earn the right to sleep, one who has truly understood the night's revelations will resist this drive to a final and fixed production. The writer's words will continue to be errant, will draw the reader—as the author has been drawn before this—into the restless outside that provided the author's inspiration, and now must provide the reader's. The writer, Blanchot says, will seek "*to make of the work a road toward inspiration . . . and not of inspiration a road toward the work*" (*Space* 186; emphasis in original). The aim of such a work, that is, is to reproduce in the reader the state of mind in which it came to be, to induce a "critical insomnia" even in those who are not critics.

This is something quite different from determining the "meaning" of a text. "*Keep watch over absent meaning*": this is, in its entirety, one of Blanchot's axioms from *The Writing of the Disaster* (42). It is unclear to whom it is addressed: to himself, to the reader, to the disaster that *is* to a great degree absent meaning? To all of these, perhaps, and to the writer above all. For if the insomniac writer, keeping watch in the night, has the terrible privilege of access to a knowledge that is fundamentally other, along with that comes an equally terrible responsibility: to write it. This is perhaps the real subject of an enigmatic short piece by Kafka:

> At Night
>
> Deeply lost in the night. Just as one sometimes lowers one's head to reflect, thus to be utterly lost in the night. All around people are asleep. It's just play acting, an innocent self-deception, that they sleep in houses, in safe beds, under a safe roof, stretched out or curled up on mattresses, in sheets, under blankets; in reality they have flocked together as they had once upon a time and again later in a deserted region, a camp in the open, a countless number of men, an army, a people, under a cold sky on cold earth, collapsed where once they had stood, forehead pressed on the arm, face to the ground, breathing quietly. And you are watching, are one of the watchmen, you find the next one by brandishing a burning stick from the brushwood pile beside you. Why are you watching? Someone must watch, it is said. Someone must be there.[25]

The security that is a precondition of sleep—a security of *place*, as has already been noted—is here dissolved. We have, instead, the vision of a place that is the closest thing to a non-place: "a deserted region" that is nevertheless filled with "a countless number"; that is to say, there is *only* this countless number in a vaguely denominated "region" that is deserted by everything else: a desert. It is "open"—too open, since there is nothing to close one's gaze, and nothing to shield people from exposure to an elemental landscape, cold sky and cold earth. This is Blanchot's "nocturnal region" (*Space* 267), with all that we have seen it to imply. The sleepers that we find here are not comfortably resting in order to recoup their energies for the following day: they have collapsed. If they are an "army," they are *in extremis*, worn out by their battles. Their unnamed antagonist may well be the night itself, in which they are "deeply lost"—as are we, at the piece's opening, for it is not specified who is lost. A comparison that implicitly claims to clarify things only obscures them further: "Just as one sometimes lowers one's head to reflect, thus to be utterly lost in the night."[26] The sentence's structure is askew, for the comparison is not about lowering the head but about reflection. And when we understand this, we have still not understood; for how is reflection, with its connotations of conscious and responsible thinking, like being lost in the night? Only, perhaps, in the way that thoughts, when pursued far enough, become non-thoughts, branch out into an interminable region where we find no secure home. This homelessness is our primal condition, which we try to cover over by fixing ourselves in various ways: within actual houses, within constructed identities, within structured systems of ideas. Uncovering all this as "an innocent self-deception," Kafka expresses the state that underlies this deception through a vaguely delineated primitiveness. And here too there is a "watch" within the night. It seems at first that this is a watch undertaken to keep danger away, in order that the sleepers may remain secure. But of course it is never Kafka's project to reassure us of our security, to shore up that self-deception, however innocent it may be. The question is still open—"Why are you watching?"—and the answer retreats into an unknown authority: "Someone must watch, it is said." Yet by *whom* it is said is not specified. The impersonality of "it is said" carries over into the last sentence: "Someone must be there." Since no reason is given for being there, the force of "must" may apply to the being-there itself: a version, perhaps, of Levinas's *il y a*. A state of pure existence demands that one sense its remorselessness—unless one subscribes to that innocent self-deception, as most of us do, bowing to an equally urgent "must." Only in the watches of the night, when anodyne sleep has failed us, do we glimpse something of the impersonal existence that bears up what we like to think of as "our" existence. This nocturnal revelation comes notably to the writer—or writers, since the speaker here is only one of a number of watchmen, scattered at distant intervals in the dark. For Kafka, his fellow watchmen would have been authors such as Hugo von Hofmannsthal or Robert Walser. Their lights are few and far between, and are unheeded by the sleepers. There is a sense of compassion for these oblivious ones, and yet one cannot watch *over* them, one can only watch. And to the degree that one's *being-there* is not one's own, this statement too must be corrected. Levinas writes: "It is not that there is *my* vigilance in the night; in insomnia it is the night itself that watches. It watches" (*Existence* 63). But that watching may speak, however strangely, through the writer's words. After all, Kafka tells us that someone, rather than something, watches. That someone is the writer, the insomniac of inspiration, the subject become anonymous object of the other night.

## Notes

1. Gustav Janouch, *Conversations with Kafka*, trans. Goronwy Rees (New York: New Directions, 1971), 14.

2. Louis-Ferdinand Céline, *Death on the Installment Plan*, trans. Ralph Manheim (New York: New Directions, 1971), 39.

3. Willis Regier, "Cioran's Insomnia." *MLN* 119 (2004): 994.

4. Emil Cioran, *The Trouble with Being Born*, trans. Richard Howard (Chicago, IL: Quadrangle, 1976), 17; qtd. Regier 1004.

5. Joyce Carol Oates, another writer who links her productivity to her insomnia, has stated: "Unable to sleep, one suddenly grasps the profound meaning of *being awake*: a revelation that shades subtly into horror, or into instruction" (*Night Walks* xiii).

6. Emmanuel Levinas, *Existence and Existents*, trans. Alphonso Lingis (Pittsburgh, PA: Dusquene University Press, 2001), 41.

7. Maurice Merleau-Ponty, *Phenomenology of Perception*, trans. Colin Smith (London: Routledge, 2001), 283.

8. Nicholas J. Wade and Josef Brozek, *Purkinje's Vision: The Dawning of Neuroscience* (London: Erlbaum, 2001), 81.

9. For more on hypnagogia, see Andreas Mavromatis, *Hypnagogia: The Unique State of Consciousness between Wakefulness and Sleep* (London: Routledge, 1991). For hypnagogia's relation to literary production, see my "Writing Hypnagogia," *Critical Inquiry* 34.3 (Spring 2008): 423-39.

10. Jirí Wakermann, Peter Pütz and Carsten Allefeld, "Ganzfeld-induced hallucinatory experience, its phenomenology and cerebral electrophysiology," *Cortex* 44 (2008): 1370.

11. On the effects and implications of the ganzfeld, see Brian Massumi, "Chaos in the 'Total Field' of Vision" 144-61 in his *Parables for the Virtual: Movement, Affect, Sensation* (Durham, NC: Duke University Press, 2002).

12. Maurice Blanchot, *The Space of Literature*, trans. Ann Smock (Lincoln, NE: University of Nebraska Press, 1982), 169.

13. Maurice Blanchot, *The Writing of the Disaster*, trans. Ann Smock (Lincoln, NE: University of Nebraska Press, 1995), 52.

14. William James, *Principles of Psychology* (New York: Dover, 1950), 224-25.

15. *The Diaries of Franz Kafka 1910-1913*, ed. Max Brod, trans. Joseph Kresh (New York: Schocken, 1949), 73-74.

16. In his diary entry for September 23, 1912, recording his intense overnight composition of "The Judgment," Kafka admitted to "thoughts of Freud, of course." And speaking of the applicability of Freudianism to Kafka's works on the whole, Max Brod wrote that his friend "was thoroughly familiar with these theories" even if "he never regarded them as anything more than a very approximate, rough picture of things" ("Kafka, Father and Son," *Partisan Review* 4.6 May 1938, 21-22).

17. Joyce Carol Oates, *Night Walks: A Bedside Companion* (Princeton, NJ: Ontario Review Press, 1982), xiii.

18. Franz Kafka, *Letters to Felice*, trans. James Stern and Elisabeth Duckworth (New York: Schocken, 1973), 156.

19. Lois Ellen Nesbitt, "Critical Insomnia: Reading and Rereading Joyce, Proust, and Beckett" (Diss. Princeton, 1988), 3.

20. Nesbitt, "Critical Insomnia," 2.

21. Franz Kafka, *The Castle*, trans. Mark Harman (New York: Schocken, 1998), 1.

22. Maurice Blanchot, "The Wooden Bridge (repetition, the neutral)" in *The Infinite Conversation*, trans. Susan Hanson (Minneapolis, MN: University of Minnesota Press, 1993), 463, n. 3.

23. Dorrit Cohn, "Castles and Anti-Castles, or Kafka and Robbe-Grillet," *Novel* 5.1 (Fall 1971): 22. I have substituted Mark Harman's translation for the Muir translation that Cohn uses.

24. Blanchot, *The Writing of the Disaster*, 49.

25. Franz Kafka, *The Complete Stories*, ed. Nahum N. Glatzer (New York: Schocken, 1971), 436.

26. In the German: "*So wie man manchmal den Kopf senkt, um nachzudenken, so ganz versunken sein in die Nacht.*" Kafka, *Nachgelassene Schriften und Fragmente II*, ed. Jost Schillemeit, *Kritische Ausgabe* (Frankfurt a.M.: Fischer Verlag, 2002), 260.

## Works Cited

Blanchot, Maurice. *The Infinite Conversation*. Translated by Susan Hanson. Minneapolis, MN: University of Minnesota Press, 1993.

———. *The Space of Literature*. Translated by Ann Smock. Lincoln, NE: University of Nebraska Press, 1982.

———. *The Writing of the Disaster*. Translated by Ann Smock. Lincoln, NE: University of Nebraska Press, 1995.

Brod, Max. "Kafka, Father and Son." *Partisan Review* 4.6 (May 1938): 19-29.

Céline, Louis-Ferdinand. *Death on the Installment Plan*. Translated by Ralph Manheim. New York: New Directions, 1971.
Cioran, Emil. *The Trouble with Being Born*. Translated by Richard Howard. Chicago, IL: Quadrangle, 1976.
Cohn, Dorrit. "Castles and Anti-Castles, or Kafka and Robbe-Grillet." *Novel* 5.1 (Fall 1971): 19-31.
Janouch, Gustav. *Conversations with Kafka*. Translated by Goronwy Rees. New York: New Directions, 1971.
James, William. *Principles of Psychology*. New York: Dover, 1950.
Kafka, Franz. *The Castle*. Translated by Mark Harman. New York: Schocken, 1998.
———. *The Complete Stories*. Edited by Nahum N. Glatzer. New York: Schocken, 1971.
———. *The Diaries of Franz Kafka 1910-1913*. Edited by Max Brod, translated by Joseph Kresh. New York: Schocken, 1949.
———. *Kritische Ausgabe. Nachgelassene Schriften und Fragmente II*. Edited by Jost Schillemeit. Frankfurt a.M.: Fischer Verlag, 2002.
———. *Letters to Felice*. Translated by James Stern and Elisabeth Duckworth. New York: Schocken, 1973.
Levinas, Emmanuel. *Existence and Existents*. Translated by Alphonso Lingis. Pittsburgh, PA: Dusquene University Press, 2001.
Massumi, Brian. *Parables for the Virtual: Movement, Affect, Sensation*. Durham, NC: Duke University Press, 2002
Mavromatis, Andreas. *Hypnagogia: The Unique State of Consciousness between Wakefulness and Sleep*. London: Routledge, 1991.
Merleau-Ponty, Maurice. *Phenomenology of Perception*. Translated by Colin Smith. London: Routledge, 2001.
Nesbitt, Lois Ellen. "Critical Insomnia: Reading and Rereading Joyce, Proust, and Beckett." Dissertation, Princeton University, 1988.
Oates, Joyce Carol. *Night Walks: A Bedside Companion*. Princeton, NJ: Ontario Review Press, 1982.
Regier, Willis. "Cioran's Insomnia." *MLN* 119 (2004): 994-1012.
Schwenger, Peter. "Writing Hypnagogia." *Critical Inquiry* 34.3 (Spring 2008): 423-39.
Wade, Nicholas J., and Josef Brozek. *Purkinje's Vision: The Dawning of Neuroscience*. London: Erlbaum, 2001.
Wakermann, Jirí, Peter Pütz and Carsten Allefeld. "Ganzfeld-induced hallucinatory experience, its phenomenology and cerebral electrophysiology." *Cortex* 44 (2008): 1364-78.

# PART II

# PHILOSOPHICAL TOPICS

# CHAPTER 7

# Animal Bachelors and Animal Brides: Fabulous Metamorphosis in Kafka and Garnett

*Chris Danta*

## Perforating the Human

One of the principal ways in which Kafka evokes a sense of anxiety and claustrophobia in his writing is by rendering permeable things we normally think of as impermeable. The reason Kafka's literary universe is such an anxiety-ridden and claustrophobic place is that the integrity of anything cannot be guaranteed—because every thing is susceptible to being penetrated, corrupted or violated by something else. It is perhaps this aspect of Kafka that Milan Kundera had uppermost in his mind when he commented in *The Art of the Novel*, "Not the curse of solitude but the *violation of solitude* is Kafka's obsession!"[1] Think of the opening of *The Trial*, in which a strange man wearing a close-fitting black suit suddenly knocks and enters unannounced into Josef K.'s bedroom. Stranger still is the opening of *The Metamorphosis*, where Kafka presents Gregor Samsa's human solitude being violated: "When Gregor Samsa awoke one morning from troubled dreams, he found himself changed into a monstrous cockroach in his bed" (*Metamorphosis* 87).[2] Whereas in *The Trial* it is Josef K.'s bedroom that is invaded, in *The Metamorphosis* it is Gregor's body. What both these famous openings show—the one more realistically, the other more fantastically—is that in Kafka there is no place for any being to secrete itself so as to become inviolable.

To illustrate Kafka's obsession with the violation of solitude, Kundera discusses the predicaments of the three human protagonists of Kafka's unfinished novels. "The Land-Surveyor K.," he writes:

> must renounce his solitude. And this is his hell: he is never alone, the two assistants sent by the Castle follow him always. When he first makes love with Frieda, the two men are there, sitting on the café counter over the lovers, and from then on they are never absent from their bed. . . . Karl Rossmann is constantly being harassed by everybody: his clothes are sold; his only photo of his parents is taken away; in the dormitory, beside his bed, boys box and now and again fall on top of him. . . . Joseph K.'s story also begins with the rape of privacy: two unknown men come to arrest him in bed. From that day on, he never feels alone: the Court follows him, watches him, talks to him; his private life

> disappears bit by bit, swallowed up by the mysterious organization on his heels.[3]

In this chapter, I want to extend Kundera's analysis in two ways: firstly, by suggesting that what holds for humans in Kafka's writings also holds for other animals. "If I closely examine what is my ultimate aim," writes Kafka in his *Diaries* on 1 October 1917, "it turns out that I am not really striving to be good and to fulfill the demands of a Supreme Judgment, but rather very much the contrary: I strive to know the whole human and animal community, to recognize their basic predilections, desires, moral ideas." (*Diaries* 387).[4] Few authors could lay claim to a worldview as genuinely creaturely as this—and Kafka is rightly seen as a modern fabulist. But what I also want to suggest here is that Kafka's animals horrify us by coming to violate human solitude. *The Metamorphosis* shows Gregor's solitude being violated at the level of his species identity—ontologically, if you like. When Gregor wakes transformed he continues to think and feel as a human being, but his monstrous appearance eventually makes it impossible for his family to recognize this fact. One of the turning points in the story is when Gregor's loving sister Grete strips the last vestige of humanity from her brother by referring to him as "it" rather than "he": "'We must get rid of it,' cried the sister again, 'that's the only thing for it, Father. You have to put from your mind any thought that it's Gregor. Our continuing to think that it was, for such a long time, therein lies the source of our misfortune'" (*Metamorphosis* 139).[5] *The Metamorphosis* is exemplary in showing Kafka's obsession with the violability of the human. What continues to horrify us about Gregor's transformation is that the misfortune that ensues from it might not cease with his death or might not be containable within his body. Where *The Metamorphosis* distinguishes itself from a comparable modern transformation tale such as David Garnett's 1922 novel *Lady into Fox*, I will suggest in the final section of the essay, is in hinting that other characters apart from the stricken protagonist might become the subject of a monstrous transformation by having their humanity violated by the animal.

In Kafka, it is possible to speak about the reverse colonization of the human by the animal—for what the animal does in Kafka is to invade, displace and decontextualize the human. Consider the following example from *The Zürau Aphorisms*, which Kafka wrote while he was convalescing from tuberculosis at his sister Ottla's house in Zürau between September 1917 and April 1918: "Leopards break into the temple and drink all the sacrificial vessels dry; it keeps happening; in the end, it can be calculated in advance and is incorporated into the ritual."[6] In a letter he wrote to his friend Felix Weltsch from Zürau in mid-November 1917, Kafka provides an even more graphic image of the animal invading the human:

> Dear Felix, the first great flaw of Zürau: a night of mice, a frightening experience. I am unscathed and my hair is no whiter than yesterday, but it was the most horrifying thing in the world. For some time I've heard them here and there (my writing is continually interrupted, you'll soon see why), every now and then at night I've been hearing a soft nibbling, once I even got out of bed,

> trembling, to take a look, and then it stopped at once—but this time it was an uproar. What a dreadful, mute, and noisy race. At two I was awakened by a rustling near my bed and it didn't let up from then until morning. Up the coal box, down the coal box, crossing the room diagonally, running in circles, nibbling the woodwork, whistling softly when not moving, and all the while the sensation of silence, of the clandestine labor of an oppressed proletarian race to whom the night belongs.[7]

The mice that compete with Kafka for ownership of the night in Zürau will one day become the subject of his last completed story, "Josefine, the Singer, or the Mouse People," written in March-April 1924. Of more interest to me here, however, is how the mice unsettle Kafka through their ability to enter the human realm unannounced. As Roberto Calasso notes, quoting a bit more of the letter, Kafka's "anxiety was brought on more than anything else by the sensation that those multitudes [of mice] had 'already perforated all the surrounding walls a hundred times, and were lying in wait there.'"[8]

In Kafka, it is as if the human is a permeable surface, already perforated by the animal. It is significant in this regard that Kafka referred to his tubercular cough as "'the animal.'"[9] Rather than the temple or the house, here it is the human body into which the animal enters unannounced. The example of the "animal" cough helps us to understand one of Kafka's signature dramatic gestures—a gesture he performs in all modes of his writing. This is the gesture by which he allows the nonhuman animal suddenly and unexpectedly to take the place of the human. Sometimes this substitution of animal for human in Kafka happens fantastically and forms the starting point for an entire narrative. Here I am thinking once again of *The Metamorphosis*, but also of the dramatic monologue, "A Report to an Academy," in which the ape Red Peter addresses a group of human scientists about his remarkable transformation into a human being. By contrast, some of Kafka's stories not involving any fabulous metamorphosis end with the image of the animal supplanting the human. At the close of "A Hunger-Artist," a lively young panther replaces the hunger-artist, who has finally starved to death in his cage because (as he says to the overseer) he "'couldn't find any food [he] liked.'"[10] When Josef K. is being executed in the final scene of *The Trial*, he pronounces "Like a dog!"[11] to accentuate the ignominy of his demise.

One of the ways in which Kafka generates dramatic tension in his narratives is by making the animal and the human interchangeable. Thus, Gregor wakes up one morning transformed into a monstrous vermin, the ape Red Peter reports to the academy, the hunger-artist ends up in an animal cage and Josef K. compares himself at the point of death to a dog. What makes these situations dramatic is the fact that animal and human cannot coexist in the same place: the survival of the one entails the extinguishment of the other. Gregor's transformation constitutes a death sentence for him, since it causes his family to neglect him to the point of death. Red Peter begins his report to the academy by confessing to its members that he can no longer tell them what it is like to be an ape: "Whatever memories I might have had closed themselves off from me more and more. To speak plainly . . . your apehood, gentlemen, inasmuch as you have something of the sort behind you, cannot be any remoter from you than mine is from me"

("Report" 225-26).[12] The sheer liveliness of the young panther in the cage accentuates the suicidal tendency of the hunger-artist. Josef K. consecrates his gruesome fate at the end of *The Trial* by figuratively evacuating his species identity.

It is not just in his fiction that Kafka makes animal and human interchangeable yet mutually exclusive identities. In an April 1913 letter to his soon-to-be-fiancée Felice Bauer, he expresses his feelings of separation from her by deploying the same animal metaphor he will at the end of *The Trial*: "My one fear—surely nothing worse can either be said or listened to—is that I shall never be able to possess you. At best I would be confined, like an unthinkingly faithful dog, to kissing your casually proffered hand, which would not be a sign of love, but of the despair of the animal condemned to silence and eternal separation."[13] Kafka here momentarily transforms himself into "an unthinkingly faithful dog" in order to present the act of kissing his beloved's casually proffered hand not as a sign of inter-human intimacy, but rather of the animal's alienation from the human. He exploits the ontological discrepancy between human and dog to accentuate his distance from Felice, to condemn himself to "silence and eternal separation"—to the muteness, one might say, of the Zürau mice.

In a characteristic way, Kafka expresses his fear of being unable to possess Felice: by withdrawing power from himself, by transforming himself into something supposedly less significant than a human being—a dog. As Elias Canetti explains in his classic psychological study, *Kafka's Other Trial: The Letters to Felice*:

> Confronted as he was with power on all sides, [Kafka's] obduracy sometimes offered him a reprieve. But if it was insufficient, or if it failed him, he trained himself to disappear; here the helpful aspect of his physical thinness is revealed, though often, as we know, he despised it. By means of physical diminution, he withdrew power *from himself*, and thus had less part in it; this asceticism, too, was directed against power. . . . Most astounding of all is another method he practices, with a sovereign skill matched only by the Chinese: transformation into something small. Since he abominated violence, but did not credit himself with the strength to combat it, he enlarged the distance between the stronger entity and himself by becoming smaller and smaller in relation to it. Through this shrinkage he gained two advantages: he evaded the threat by becoming too diminutive for it, and he freed himself from all exceptionable means of violence; the small animals into which he liked to transform himself were harmless ones.[14]

The act of projecting himself out of the human community and into the community of animals allowed Kafka to dramatize discrepancies of power by allowing him to adopt the position of the animal victim—the harmless animal that is more acted upon by others than acting in and for itself. As Reiner Stach points out in his biography, after composing *The Metamorphosis* late in 1912, Kafka described himself as an animal to Felice a number of times in 1913. He wrote to her a few months after the letter I have just been analyzing: "Often—and in my innermost self possibly all the time—I doubt that I am a human being." And soon after that: "Haven't I been squirming in front of you like something poisonous for months?" Finally, on 16 September 1913: "It is rather that I am lying flat on the ground like an animal that one (not even I) can get hold of, either by coaxing or by persuading."[15]

In Kafka, the animal violates human solitude. It interrupts the inter-human communication by introducing into that communication the somewhat fabulous figure of the animal-in-the-place-of-the-human. Kafka once remarked to the young Czech poet Gustav Janouch, "I am as lonely as—as Franz Kafka."[16] In the letters to Felice I've just been quoting, he is no longer alone like Franz Kafka. He is not even alone like a human being. Rather, he is alone like an animal. He is ontologically isolated. As Stach notes:

> In Kafka's works, "The Metamorphosis" marks the beginning of a series of thinking, speaking, and suffering animals, of learned dogs and voracious jackals, psychotic moles, worldly-wise apes, and vainglorious mice. . . . This metaphor [of the human-as-animal] was particularly enticing, because an animal looks at a person from without—the only conceivable animate without in a world devoid of transcendence. An animal does not "take sides," as Kafka later put it; it is a mute witness, living side by side but not together with man. It is indifferent to what people are saying. Closest to animals are their bodies, the form and vulnerability of which utterly determine their existence. Animals regard the enormous superiority of man as nothing more than a source of constraint and fear; they have no understanding of its origin.[17]

Kafka's animals are guided by the same sense of primordial bodily anxiety as Kafka himself experienced in Zürau when those noisy mice kept crisscrossing his room in the middle of the night. As Walter Benjamin comments in his 1934 essay commemorating the tenth anniversary of Kafka's death: "This much is certain: of all Kafka's creatures, the animals have the greatest opportunity for reflection. What corruption is in the law, anxiety is in their thinking. It messes a situation up, yet it is the only hopeful thing about it."[18]

To become an animal in Kafka is to become a special kind of victim: an ontological martyr. It is to become separate not just from the other members of one's species but also from the species itself. Kafka presents himself as an ontological martyr to Felice when he writes to her, "Often—and in my innermost self possibly all the time—I doubt that I am a human being."[19] But it is important to recognize the theatricality of this gesture. Kafka is not just avowing his solitude here. He is also violating it by turning it into a spectacle for the other. This proves to be a law of Kafka's writing: the violation—or the theatricalization—of solitude is a precondition for the transformation of identity.

"A Report to an Academy" is a case in point. In this story, Kafka theatricalizes the ontological martyrdom of Red Peter. It is particularly fitting that, after several false starts, Kafka eventually decided to cast this story in the form of a dramatic monologue, since this form produces, in keeping with the thematic concerns of the work, the theatre of one.[20] Red Peter tells the members of the academy of how his ontological solitude was violated one day in the Gold Coast when he was attacked and captured by a hunting expedition from the company of the famous German animal trader Carl Hagenbeck: "A hunting expedition by the Hagenbeck company . . . was lying in wait in the scrub by the river bank one evening, just as my companions and I were coming down to drink. Shots were fired; I was the only one hit; and was hit twice" ("Report" 226). When he comes around, Red Peter finds himself in a cage in the steerage of the Hagenbeck steamship, heading back to Germany to be exhibited in the Animal Park in Hamburg. At this point, he realizes that only the most drastic form of action can save him:

> I had in my previous life so many ways out, and now I had none. I was run to a standstill. If I'd been nailed down, my liberty could not have been more attenuated. . . . I had no way out, but I had to find one, for without it I wouldn't be able to live. Pressed against the wall of that crate—it would inevitably have been the end for me. But at Hagenbeck's, the place for apes is against crate walls—well, and so I quite simply ceased being an ape. ("Report" 227, 228-29)

Red Peter is slightly mistaken in saying that, "at Hagenbeck's, the place for apes is against crate walls." Carl Hagenbeck (1844-1913) is the father of the modern, bar-less zoo. In 1907, Hagenbeck pioneered a technique, which became the model for zoos for the remainder of the twentieth century, of exhibiting animals in open enclosures surrounded by carefully hidden moats.[21] But we still take Red Peter's point that the zoo remains for him a kind of cage. To be a victim in Kafka is to lose the freedom of movement—to be nailed down, so to speak, like someone being crucified by others. Red Peter realizes that to acquire more freedom of movement—not as much as he had as an ape, but more than he would have as an ape being exhibited in the Animal Park in Hamburg—he must sacrifice his identity as an ape and become human. He does so by learning to speak and by imitating certain defining cultural practices of Western Europeans such as shaking hands, drinking schnapps and smoking cigars.

As a result of his violent encounter with humans, Red Peter's identity becomes irreducibly ambivalent. He appears before the academy not only as a victim of human violence whose act of becoming human constitutes an act of ontological apostasy, but also as an animal whose sheer vitality threatens the human by threatening to take the place of the human. His report forcefully demonstrates how the birth of the human depends upon the victimization of the animal. Rhetorically, it turns on a popular misconception of Darwin's theory of evolution that humans have evolved from apes. Rather than evolving from apes, Tom Tyler reminds us, "In fact, humans are African apes and are more closely related to chimpanzees and gorillas than either of those two species are to orangutans."[22] "What I have to say will not be anything substantially new to you, gentlemen," states Kafka's ape, "and it will fall far short of what you look to me for, and what, with the best will in the world, I am unable to provide—still, let it be an adumbration of the course on which a onetime ape entered the human world and established himself within it" ("Report" 226). Red Peter presents his metamorphosis as a total change from a so-called lower form of life (the ape) to a so-called higher form of life (the human): "By an exertion without parallel in the history of the world, I have reached the level of cultivation of the average European" ("Report" 234). As W. R. Irwin notes: "In stories of total metamorphosis there is, despite some variation, a marked uniformity. Usually the change is from a higher form of life to a lower, though the second form often has some self-evident relationship, physical or moral, to the first."[23] By moving in the opposite direction—that is, up rather than down the ladder of being—Red Peter makes the physical and moral relationship between humans and apes even more self-evident.

What allows Red Peter to become human is not the fact that humans once were apes but rather the fact that they still are apes. The sharp distinction he sets up between human and ape collapses at the end of the story when he tells his audience about the female chimpanzee his captors have provided for him as a mate: "When I come home at night, after banquets, from learned societies, from cozy get-togethers, I have a little semi-trained lady chimp waiting for me, and I let her show me a good time, ape-fashion. By day I have no desire to see her; she has the perplexity of the trained wild animal in her eye; I alone recognize that, and it is unbearable to me" ("Report" 235). What does Red Peter find so unsettling about the look in his mate's eye? What disturbs him about this look, I would suggest, is that it violates his human solitude by revealing to him the animality of human being. Red Peter demonstrates the susceptibility of the human to the nonhuman animal not just by making an unprecedented transition from ape to man, but also by becoming, in the act, an ontological hypocrite: human by day, ape by night.

## Animal Bachelor

In foregrounding Red Peter's hypocritical attitude and conduct toward his female mate, "A Report to an Academy" recalls a type of fable or folktale known as the animal bride or the animal groom story. As Wendy Doniger notes in her article, "The Mythology of Masquerading Animals, or, Bestiality": "Cultures throughout the world represent our deceptive relationships with animals as masquerades, which operate in both directions: in our rituals, humans often masquerade as animals, but in our myths we imagine that animals masquerade as humans. The most intense version of this universal theme is the tale of bestial deception, the masquerade of an animal as a human in the most intimate of all relationships."[24] What encourages us to see Red Peter in this way—as an animal masquerading as a human being in his most intimate relationship—is the contrast he draws in his report between his daytime and his nighttime identity. Doniger continues:

> Throughout these stories [of animal lovers], we encounter the contrast between day and night. "My night is your day," says the Beast in Jean Cocteau's film of *Beauty and the Beast*. There is an hour of twilight that the French call "*entre chien et loup*" ("between dog and wolf"). That is where these stories take place, for the transitional, marginal, liminal animal transgresses this most basic of all boundaries. Indeed, in Latin (and in many of the Romance languages derived from it), the very words for twilight or dawn (*lux*) and wolf (*luc*) are etymologically related; the wolf is the twilight animal, or, if you prefer, twilight is the hour of the wolf.

> But there is a significant difference between stories in which the primary allegiance of the creature is animal and those in which it is human (or divine). Stories about animal lovers present two variants of a single truth: a human being is really an animal. But the weight of reality is placed differently in different variants, so that when the story is over, either there is a human, or there is an animal. It does matter. Generally speaking, the forms are distributed as in Stith Thompson's motif (B 640.1): "marriage to beast by day, man by night."[25]

The crucial difference between "A Report to an Academy" and a classic animal groom story like "Beauty and the Beast" is this: for Red Peter, the irreconcilability of his daytime and his nighttime identity is not a problem but rather the solution to a problem. It suits Red Peter—it helps him to survive—that others cannot really decide whether his primary allegiance is to the human or to the animal. Rather than as an animal groom, I am suggesting that we think of him as an animal bachelor, which is to say, as someone whose social and sexual identity is single or solitary. Rather than the curse of solitude, what Kafka's animals convey is a sense of proximate estrangement. They are close to us and yet also strange to us. They are ontologically ambivalent—at once animal and human. And the figure that perhaps best captures this sense of ontological ambivalence is that of the animal bachelor.

Kafka's bachelorhood and the theme of bachelorhood in Kafka have been much discussed by critics. As Stach observes: "Franz Kafka is the bachelor of world literature. No one, not even the most open-minded reader, can imagine him at the side of a Frau Doktor Kafka, and the image of a white-haired family man surrounded by grandchildren at play is irreconcilable with the gaunt figure and self-conscious smile of the man we know as Kafka, who blossomed and wilted at an early age."[26] But if Kafka is the bachelor of world literature, then he is perhaps also the animal bachelor of world literature. In animal bride stories, a female animal takes on human shape in order to marry a human groom, but is then exposed on her wedding night or shortly thereafter for the animal she really is. Rather than the desire of the bride, in Kafka it is the desire of the bachelor that provides the inter-special transformation with its potency. Kafkan metamorphosis serves to perpetuate the male protagonist's bachelorhood by removing him from membership in his species. Gregor Samsa and Red Peter are not just bachelors; they are eternal bachelors, perpetual sons. As J.M. Coetzee's character Elizabeth Costello observes in the novel of that name: "It is as hard to imagine the child of Red Peter as to imagine the child of Franz Kafka himself."[27]

In contrast to the animal bride or the animal groom story, the transformation of the human into the animal in Kafka does not pivot on the sexual union of husband and wife, but rather on the moment that perpetually precedes it: the bachelor's frustrated social desire (or, as Kafka might put it, the bachelor's ill luck). In the entry in his *Diaries* for 19 January 1922, Kafka puts the anxiety of bachelorhood in the following heartrending terms:

> The infinite, deep, warm, saving happiness of sitting beside the cradle of one's child opposite its mother.

> There is in it also something of this feeling: matters no longer rest with you, unless you wish it so. In contrast, this feeling of those who have no children: it perpetually rests with you, whether you will or no, every moment to the end, every nerve-racking moment, it perpetually rests with you, and with no result. Sisyphus was a bachelor. (*Diaries* 401)

Gilles Deleuze and Félix Guattari relate becoming-animal in Kafka to his bachelorhood in their influential study *Kafka: Toward a Minor Literature*: "What Kafka does in his room is to become animal," they write, "and this is the essential object of the stories. The first sort of creation is the metamorphosis. A wife's eyes shouldn't see that above all else, nor should the eyes of a father or mother."[28] In this schema, Gregor's situation in *The Metamorphosis* resembles the situation of the writer—for to be a writer is to be proximately separate from other people, to be near to them and yet far away from them, to be a bachelor—even an animal bachelor. "No one knew better than Kafka to define art or expression without any sort of reference to the aesthetic," conclude Deleuze and Guattari. "If we try to sum up the nature of the artistic machine for Kafka, it is a bachelor machine, the only bachelor machine, and, as such, plugged all the more into a social field with multiple connections."[29]

Deleuze and Guattari stress that bachelorhood is a hyper-social rather than an antisocial state. "With no family, no conjugality," they write, "the bachelor is all the more social, social-dangerous, social-traitor, a collective in himself. . . . A machine that is all the more social and collective insofar as it is solitary, a bachelor, and that tracing the line of escape, is equivalent in itself to a community whose conditions haven't yet been established."[30] But if the bachelor founds a community that hasn't yet been established, then I think we have to say that this is a community of one or, in what amounts to the same thing, a community of the scapegoat. According to Michel Carrouges, who coined the term *machines célibataires* in the mid-twentieth century, "A bachelor machine is a fantastic image that transforms love into a mechanics of death."[31] One of the examples Carrouges gives of the bachelor machine is the torture device in Kafka's story "In the Penal Colony," which gruesomely inscribes the criminal sentence upon the body of the accused.[32] But we might also see Kafka's entire body of work as a bachelor machine in the sense that it uses fantastic images to transform love into a mechanics of death. On 21 August 1913, almost a year after he had completed *The Metamorphosis*, Kafka wrote to Felice's father Carl Bauer: "Well, I live in my family, among the best and most lovable people, more strange than a stranger" (*Diaries* 231). Kafka's feelings of estrangement from his family become, in the more exaggerated fictional context of *The Metamorphosis*, Gregor's ostracization from his family and eventual death.

In a 1922 letter to Max Brod, Kafka hits upon the ultimate way to describe himself as an animal victim: "The definition of a writer, of such a writer," he writes to Brod, "and the explanation of his effectiveness, to the extent that he has any: He is the scapegoat of mankind. He makes it possible for men to enjoy sin without guilt, almost without guilt."[33] The scapegoat is the animal victim *par excellence*: it is the animal that is fatally acted upon by the human community—that dies in the act of bearing away the sins of humanity. As I have argued elsewhere in more detail, to see the writer as the scapegoat of humankind is to see the act of writing as traversing a space opened up by the experience of animal victimhood.[34] As David Spurr notes, "The image of the artist as scapegoat belongs to the recurring motif of martyrdom in Kafka."[35] The point I want to underscore here is that it is not just martyrdom that is a motif in Kafka, but also ontological martyrdom—or martyrdom that takes place at the level of species identity.

## Kafka and Garnett

"You can read Kafka's animal stories for quite a while," remarks Benjamin, "without realizing that they are not about human beings at all. When you finally come upon the name of the creature—monkey, dog, mole—you look up in fright and realize that you are already far away from the continent of man."[36] Likewise, in his 1953 essay "Notes on Kafka," Theodor W. Adorno asserts that "The flight through man and beyond into the non-human—that is Kafka's epic course."[37] According to Margot Norris in her contribution to the 2010 collection *Kafka's Creatures: Animals, Hybrids, and Other Fantastic Beings*:

> Kafka's historical and intellectual context readily supports an argument for, rather than against, the contention that his animal stories use the figure of the animal autoreferentially, to gesture towards its creatural ontology, rather than as a displacement for the cultural or ontological human. Such a reading of Kafka makes him a prophetic precursor of contemporary critics of speciesism and what Cary Wolfe calls the "linguacentrism" that afflicts even the most progressive cultural criticism.

Norris supports her claim that Kafka's animal stories are animal stories rather than fables of the human by noting that Kafka read Charles Darwin, Thomas Huxley and Ernst Haeckel and that students and intellectuals of his time discussed the evolutionary continuity between primates and humans "if not as established principle then nonetheless as increasingly respectable theory."[38]

But I think it is a mistake to read Kafka's animals too autoreferentially, as gesturing entirely toward the ontology of the nonhuman. The epic course that Kafka charts in his fiction is not just from the human to the nonhuman but also from the nonhuman back to the human. As I have been arguing, one of the ways in which Kafka uses animals is to figure the separation of human beings from one another. An anecdote from Janouch's book *Conversations with Kafka* helps to confirm this point. Janouch here recounts how he brought a copy of the English writer David Garnett's 1922 novel *Lady into Fox* along to Kafka's house in order to accuse Garnett of copying the original methods of *The Metamorphosis*. *Lady into Fox* is in fact an animal bride story of sorts: the novel begins with the sudden and miraculous transformation of the newly married Mrs. Tebrick, *née* Sylvia Fox, into a vixen and then tells of her gradual loss of humanity—her becoming-fox. The resemblance between *Lady into Fox* and *The Metamorphosis* becomes uncannier still when we consider that the first working title of

Garnett's novel was *The Metamorphosis of Mrs. Tebrick*. But when confronted with Garnett's text, Kafka rejects the idea of plagiarism: "He didn't get that from me," Kafka says. "It's a matter of the age. We both copied from that. Animals are closer to us than human beings. That's where our prison bars lie. We find relations with animals easier than with men." Two weeks later, Kafka reiterated this sentiment to Janouch: "Every man lives behind bars, which he carries within him. That is why people write so much about animals now. It's a longing for a free natural life. But for human beings the natural life is a human life."[39] For Kafka, to depict our proximity to other animals is at the same time to figure our alienation from each other.

Rather than accusing Garnett of copying Kafka, we might more productively think of *The Metamorphosis* and *Lady into Fox* as modern revisions of the animal bride story. Animal bride stories recall a mythic or prehistoric time in which the physical and metaphysical boundaries between human and animal were thought to be permeable, when animals could become human and humans could become animal. But the experience of the modern, industrialized society has inured us to this theriomorphic way of thinking by estranging us from other animals. We now dismiss animal bride stories as mere fairy tales or children's entertainment. As Georges Bataille remarks in his essay "The Passage from Animal to Man and the Birth of Art":

> An animal world does exist, wherein men were formerly integrated. It was populated with animals that man loved. This world did not extend to all animals: it did not include roaches or lice. It also excluded monkeys. It is the poetic animality found in the caves [of Lascaux]. It undoubtedly endures for us, yet we have separated ourselves from it. Humanity was born from it. It was born from it by founding its superiority on the forgetting of this poetic animality and on a contempt for animals—deprived of the poetry of the wild, reduced to the level of things, enslaved, slaughtered, butchered.[40]

*The Metamorphosis* and *Lady into Fox* utilize the mythic permeability of animal and human identity to convey the alienation of modern humans, not just from other animals, but also from each other. Both texts make the point that "We find relations with animals easier than with men."

They do so by playing the human off against the nonhuman animal. While Kafka and Garnett encourage us to identify with Gregor and Mrs. Tebrick in their transformed states, they also stigmatize their animal protagonists by making it the case that those who continue to love them become ostracized from human society. As we have seen, Grete's change of heart toward Gregor has to do with the negative social impact she feels he is having on the family. As Clayton Koelb notes: "The plot of [Kafka's] tale follows a classical crossing or 'chiastic' pattern, in which the fortunes of one character or set of characters improve while the fortunes of others decline. In this case it is Gregor who declines and his parents and sister who improve, and because of that improvement the story does not (and cannot) conclude with Gregor's death."[41] *The Metamorphosis* concerns the inability of the Samsa family to adjust to Gregor's sudden transformation or to be happy when they are with him in his changed state. Metamorphosed, Gregor "excites loathing in those whom he loves."[42] His tragic reduction to the status of a loathsome thing is made complete when the charwoman duly informs the family after his death: "'you don't need to worry about how to get rid of the thing next door. I'll take care of it'" (*Metamorphosis* 145). *The Metamorphosis* thus neatly illustrates Bataille's point that not all animals accede to a state of poetic animality.

By having his protagonist transform into a fox rather than a roach, Garnett expresses an altogether different attitude toward poetic animality than Kafka. "Sir Charles Darwin has recently published the comforting discovery that man is a wild animal," writes Garnett in the second volume of his memoirs, *The Flowers of the Forest*. "I have always known it as regards myself and I have seldom wished to mate with a woman who was not one also."[43] Rather than loathing, what Mrs. Tebrick excites in her husband after she transforms into a fox is an even more ardent love for her. Immediately after her transformation, the couple tries somewhat comically to carry on as if nothing untoward had happened. Mrs. Tebrick continues for a time to wear her old clothes and even maintain her old diet. Her husband is terrified that hunting dogs will attack her and so shoots all his own dogs and tries desperately to keep her indoors. But gradually and inevitably Sylvia becomes more and more foxlike in her behavior and less and less willing to remain domesticated. Eventually Mr. Tebrick is forced to let her go outside, where she mates with a wild fox and produces a litter of cubs. Remarkably, Mr. Tebrick refuses to give up on his wife. Out of love for her in whatever form she takes, he follows her into the wild and even tries to be a sort of father to her cubs. As the novelist John Burnside notes in his "Foreword" to the recent Hesperus edition of Garnett's novel, Mr. Tebrick becomes himself "a half wild creature, able to get down on all fours and play with his wife's cubs."[44] But conquering the apparently abyssal divide between the species, becoming an animal-lover in this way, causes Mr. Tebrick to become isolated from human society and misanthropic:

> But living as he did at this time, Mr. Tebrick grew more and more to be a true misanthrope. He denied admittance to any that came to visit him, and rarely showed himself to his fellows, but went out chiefly in the early mornings before people were about, in the hope of seeing his beloved fox. . . . Yet this all proceeded one may say from a passion, and a true conjugal fidelity, which it would be hard to find matched in this world. . . . How different indeed was he from those who, if their wives go mad, shut them in madhouses and give them up to concubinage, and nay, what is more, there are many who extenuate such conduct too. But Mr. Tebrick was of a very different temper, and though his wife was now nothing but a hunted beast, cared for no one in the world but her. (*Lady* 50-51)

While the Samsas prove incapable of loving Gregor after he transforms into a monstrous vermin, Mr. Tebrick continues to love his wife "though she was now nothing but a hunted beast." But this animal-love comes at a huge personal cost to him: "this devouring love ate into him like a consumption, so that by sleepless nights, and not caring for his person, in a few months he was worn to the shadow of himself. His cheeks were sunk in, his eyes hollow but excessively brilliant, and his whole body had lost flesh, so that looking at him the wonder was that he was still alive" (*Lady* 51). Mr. Tebrick only recovers his health after his animal wife dies in his arms, while desperately seeking to escape from a marauding pack of hounds.

While Mr. Tebrick's physical health deteriorates as a result of loving his animal wife, Grete's physical health blooms after she disconnects herself emotionally from Gregor. *The Metamorphosis* ends with her parents taking note of her metamorphosis into a vivacious young woman:

> While they were talking in these terms, almost at one and the same time Mr. and Mrs. Samsa noticed their increasingly lively daughter, the way that of late, in spite of the trouble that had made her cheeks pale, she had blossomed into an attractive and well-built girl. Falling silent, and communicating almost unconsciously through glances, they thought it was about time to find a suitable husband for her. And it felt like confirmation of their new dreams and their fond intentions when, as they reached their destination, their daughter was the first to get up, and stretched her nubile young body. (*Metamorphosis* 146)

Kafka never liked the ending of *The Metamorphosis*, commenting in his *Diaries* in January 1914: "Great antipathy to 'Metamorphosis.' Unreadable ending. Imperfect almost to its marrow. It would have been better if I had not been interrupted at the time by the business trip [to Kratzau]" (*Diaries* 253). But I think the ending works by hinting at the possible monstrosity of Grete's transformation. Kafka writes in a diary entry from early 1910: "I write this very decidedly out of despair over my body and over a future with this body" (*Diaries* 10). The ambivalence that hangs over the conclusion of *The Metamorphosis* is the potential for despair to determine the future of the body and the narrative. The problem is that Grete's apparently natural transformation into a vivacious young woman might not eclipse the monstrosity of Gregor's because it might not in fact be of a different order to Gregor's. The ending disturbs because it is an utterly unconvincing attempt at catharsis.

Despite superficial resemblances, *The Metamorphosis* and *Lady into Fox* are actually quite different texts with quite different visions of the human-animal relation. Where Garnett gives us an animal bride story and the poetry of the wild, Kafka gives us an animal bachelor story and a human society founded on contempt for other animals. Where Garnett uses the interaction between human and fox to promote the idea of a free natural life, in Kafka there is only (as he puts it to Janouch) "a longing for a free natural life." The contrasting deaths of the animal protagonists in these two texts reveal the contrasting attitudes of their authors to the possibilities of human freedom. Mrs. Tebrick dies outside her home in a frenzy of movement that has the cathartic effect of momentarily reuniting the human lovers:

> His vixen had at once sprung into Mr. Tebrick's arms, and before he could turn back the hounds were upon them and had pulled them down. Then at that moment there was a scream of despair heard by all the field that had come up, which they declared afterwards was more like a woman's voice than a man's.

> But yet there was no clear proof whether it was Mr. Tebrick or his wife who had suddenly regained her voice. (*Lady* 73)

Gregor, by contrast, is as if nailed to the spot in his apartment when he dies alone, in the middle of the night, as his family sleeps:

> He thought back on his family with devotion and love. His conviction that he needed to disappear was, if anything, still firmer than his sister's. He remained in this condition of empty and peaceful reflection until the church clock struck 3 a.m. The last thing he saw was the sky gradually lightening outside the window. Then his head involuntarily dropped, and his final breath passed feebly from his nostrils. (*Metamorphosis* 141)

What makes *The Metamorphosis* such a disturbing text, I would suggest, is that Gregor's ontological solitude continues to perforate human being—a bit like the rotten apple in his back—even after his death. If we think of Gregor as an animal bachelor, then isn't one way to put the horror of this story that Grete will become—in its untold future—an unhappy animal bride?

## Notes

1. Milan Kundera, *The Art of the Novel*, translated from the French by Linda Asher (London: Faber and Faber, 2005), 111, original emphasis.
2. Franz Kafka, "The Metamorphosis," in *The Metamorphosis and Other Stories*, trans. Michael Hoffmann (London: Penguin, 2007), 87. While Kafka's German word *Ungeziefer* is usually translated into English as "vermin," Hoffmann here renders it more specifically as "cockroach." Hoffmann's translation suits my argument insofar as it reinforces a point I make later in the essay that roaches and lice are for us un-poetic animals.
3. Kundera, *The Art of the Novel*, 111.
4. Franz Kafka, *Diaries 1910-23*, ed. Max Brod (London: Vintage, 1999), 387.
5. As Reiner Stach points out in his biography, Kafka initially wrote "We must get rid of him" before replacing it with the more inhuman "We must get rid of it." Reiner Stach, *Kafka: The Decisive Years*, trans. Shelley Frisch (Orlando, FL: Harcourt, 2005), 199.
6. Franz Kafka, *The Zürau Aphorisms*, with an Introduction and Afterword by Roberto Calasso, trans. Michael Hofmann (London: Harvill Secker, 2008), 20.
7. Cited in Roberto Calasso, "Veiled Splendor," in Kafka, *The Zürau Aphorisms*, 113-14.
8. Calasso, "Veiled Spendor," 114.
9. Walter Benjamin, "Franz Kafka: On the Tenth Anniversary of His Death," trans. Harry Zohn, in *Selected Writings Volume 2, 1927-1934*, ed. Michael W. Jennings, Howard Eiland and Gary Smith (Cambridge and London: The Belknap Press of Harvard University Press, 1999), 810.
10. Franz Kafka, "A Hunger-Artist," in *Metamorphosis and Other Stories*, 262.
11. Franz Kafka, *The Trial*, trans. Mike Mitchell, Introduction and Notes by Ritchie Robertson (Oxford: Oxford University Press, 2009), 165.

12. Franz Kafka, "A Report to an Academy," in *Metamorphosis and Other Stories*, 225-26.

13. Franz Kafka, *Letters to Felice*, ed. Erich Heller and Jürgen Born, trans. James Stern and Elizabeth Duckworth (New York: Schocken Books, 1973), 233.

14. Elias Canetti, *Kafka's Other Trial: The Letters to Felice*, trans. Christopher Middleton (London: Caldar and Boyars, 1974), 89-90, original emphasis.

15. Cited in Stach, *Kafka*, 197.

16. Gustav Janouch, *Conversations with Kafka*, trans. Goronwy Rees (London, Melbourne, New York: Quartet Books, 1985), 70.

17. Stach, *Kafka*, 195-96.

18. Benjamin, "Franz Kafka," 810.

19. Cited in Stach, *Kafka*, 197.

20. Kafka began writing the story with a first person narrator who interviewed Red Peter. See "A Report to an Academy: Two Fragments," in Franz Kafka, *The Complete Short Stories*, ed. Nahum N. Glatzer (London: Vintage Books, 2005): 259-62.

21. Something else that makes Hagenbeck a suggestive historical figure for Kafka to allude to in "A Report to an Academy" is the fact that he also exhibited indigenous people alongside animals in his Animal Park in Hamburg. For a good discussion of Hagenbeck's role in the development of the modern zoo and his exhibitions of humans see Nigel Rothfels, *Savages and Beasts: The Birth of the Modern Zoo* (Baltimore, MD: Johns Hopkins University Press, 2002).

22. Tom Tyler, "Four Hands Good, Two Hands Bad," in *Kafka's Creatures: Animals, Hybrids, and Other Fantastic Beings*, ed. Marc Lucht and Donna Yarri (Lanham, MD: Rowman & Littlefield, 2010), 178.

23. W.R. Irwin, "The Metamorphoses of David Garnett," *PMLA* 73.4 (1958): 386.

24. Wendy Doniger, "The Mythology of Masquerading Animals, or, Bestiality," *Social Research* 71.3 (2004): 711.

25. Doniger, "The Mythology of Masquerading Animals, or, Bestiality," 720.

26. Stach, *Kafka*, 42.

27. J.M. Coetzee, *Elizabeth Costello: Eight Lessons* (Sydney: Vintage, 2003), 75.

28. Gilles Deleuze and Félix Guattari, *Kafka: Toward a Minor Literature*, trans. Dana Polan (Minneapolis and London: University of Minnesota Press, 1986), 35.

29. Deleuze and Guattari, *Kafka*, 70.

30. Deleuze and Guattari, *Kafka*, 71.

31. Cited in Allen S. Weiss, *Breathless: Sound Recording, Disembodiment, and the Transformation of Lyrical Nostalgia* (Middletown, CT: Wesleyan University Press, 2002), 97.

32. For an interesting and wide-ranging discussion of the bachelor machine see Michel de Certeau, "The Arts of Dying: Celibatory Machines," in *Heterologies: Discourse of the Other* (Minneapolis, MN: University of Minnesota Press, 1986), 156-67.

33. Franz Kafka, *The Basic Kafka*, ed. Erich Heller (New York: Washington Square Press, 1979), 295.

34. See my essay "'Like a dog … like a lamb': Becoming Sacrificial Animal in Kafka and Coetzee," *New Literary History* 38.4 (2007): 723-39.

35. David Spurr, "Paranoid Modernism in Joyce and Kafka," *Journal of Modern Literature* 34.2 (2011): 183-84.

36. Benjamin, "Franz Kafka," 802.

37. Theodor W. Adorno, "Notes on Kafka," in *Prisms*, trans. Samuel and Shierry Weber (Cambridge, MA: The MIT Press, 1967), 252.

38. Margot Norris, "Kafka's Hybrids: Thinking Animals and Mirrored Humans," in Lucht and Yarri, *Kafka's Creatures*, 19. See also Margot Norris, *Beasts of the Modern*

*Imagination: Darwin, Nietzsche, Kafka, Ernst, & Lawrence* (Baltimore, MD: Johns Hopkins University Press, 1985), 65.

39. Janouch, *Conversations with Kafka*, 22, 22-23.

40. Georges Bataille, *The Cradle of Humanity: Prehistoric Art and Culture*, ed. Stuart Kendall, trans. Michelle Kendall and Stuart Kendall (New York: Zone Books, 2005), 75-76.

41. Clayton Koelb, *Kafka: A Guide for the Perplexed* (London and New York: Continuum, 2010), 117-18.

42. Irwin, "The Metamorphoses of David Garnett," 390.

43. David Garnett, *The Flowers of the Forest* (London: Chatto & Windus, 1955), 19-20.

44. John Burnside, "Foreword" to David Garnett, *Lady into Fox* (London: Hesperus Press, 2008), ix.

## Works Cited

Adorno, Theodor W. "Notes on Kafka." In Theodor W. Adorno, *Prisms*, translated by Samuel and Shierry Weber, 245-71. Cambridge, MA: The MIT Press, 1967.

Bataille, Georges. *The Cradle of Humanity: Prehistoric Art and Culture*. Edited by Stuart Kendall, translated by Michelle Kendall and Stuart Kendall. New York: Zone Books, 2005.

Benjamin, Walter. "Franz Kafka: On the Tenth Anniversary of His Death." In Walter Benjamin, *Selected Writings Volume 2, 1927-1934*, edited by Michael W. Jennings, Howard Eiland and Gary Smith, 794-818. Cambridge and London: The Belknap Press of Harvard University Press, 1999.

Burnside, John. "Foreword." In David Garnett, *Lady into Fox*, viii-xv. London: Hesperus Press, 2008.

Calasso, Roberto. "Veiled Splendor." In Franz Kafka, *The Zürau Aphorisms*, introduction and Afterword by Roberto Calasso, translated by Michael Hofmann, 109-34. London: Harvill Secker, 2008.

Canetti, Elias. *Kafka's Other Trial: The Letters to Felice*. Translated by Christopher Middleton. London: Caldar and Boyars, 1974.

Certeau, Michel de. *Heterologies: Discourse of the Other*. Minneapolis, MN: University of Minnesota Press, 1986.

Coetzee, J.M. *Elizabeth Costello: Eight Lessons*. Sydney: Vintage, 2003.

Danta, Chris. "'Like a dog . . . like a lamb': Becoming Sacrificial Animal in Kafka and Coetzee." *New Literary History* 38.4 (2007): 723-39.

Deleuze, Gilles, and Félix Guattari. *Kafka: Toward a Minor Literature*. Translated by Dana Polan. Minneapolis and London: University of Minnesota Press, 1986.

Doniger, Wendy. "The Mythology of Masquerading Animals, or, Bestiality." *Social Research* 71.3 (2004): 711-32.

Garnett, David. *The Flowers of the Forest*. London: Chatto & Windus, 1955.

———. *Lady into Fox*. London: Hesperus Press, 2008.

Irwin, W.R. "The Metamorphoses of David Garnett." *PMLA* 73.4 (1958): 386-92.

Janouch, Gustav. *Conversations with Kafka*. Translated by Goronwy Rees. London, Melbourne, New York: Quartet Books, 1985.

Kafka, Franz. *The Basic Kafka*. Edited by Erich Heller. New York: Washington Square Press, 1979.

———. *The Complete Short Stories*. Edited by Nahum N. Glatzer. London: Vintage Books, 2005.

———. *Diaries 1910-23*. Edited by Max Brod. London: Vintage, 1999.

———. *Letters to Felice*. Edited by Erich Heller and Jürgen Born, translated by James Stern and Elizabeth Duckworth. New York: Schocken Books, 1973.

———. *The Metamorphosis and Other Stories*. Translated by Michael Hoffmann. London: Penguin, 2007.

———. *The Trial*. Translated by Mike Mitchell, Introduction and Notes by Ritchie Robertson. Oxford: Oxford University Press, 2009.

———. *The Zürau Aphorisms*. Introduction and Afterword by Roberto Calasso, translated by Michael Hofmann. London: Harvill Secker, 2008.

Koelb, Clayton. *Kafka: A Guide for the Perplexed*. London and New York: Continuum, 2010.

Kundera, Milan. *The Art of the Novel*. Translated by Linda Asher. London: Faber and Faber, 2005.

Norris, Margot. *Beasts of the Modern Imagination: Darwin, Nietzsche, Kafka, Ernst, & Lawrence*. Baltimore, MD: Johns Hopkins University Press, 1985.

———. "Kafka's Hybrids: Thinking Animals and Mirrored Humans." In *Kafka's Creatures: Animals, Hybrids, and Other Fantastic Beings*, edited by Marc Lucht and Donna Yarri, 17-32. Lanham, MD: Rowman & Littlefield, 2010.

Rothfels, Nigel. *Savages and Beasts: The Birth of the Modern Zoo*. Baltimore, MD: Johns Hopkins University Press, 2002.

Spurr, David. "Paranoid Modernism in Joyce and Kafka." *Journal of Modern Literature* 34.2 (2011): 178-91.

Stach, Reiner. *Kafka: The Decisive Years*. Translated by Shelley Frisch. Orlando, FL: Harcourt, 2005.

Tyler, Tom. "Four Hands Good, Two Hands Bad." In *Kafka's Creatures: Animals, Hybrids, and Other Fantastic Beings*, edited by Marc Lucht and Donna Yarri, 175-90. Lanham, MD: Rowman & Littlefield, 2010.

Weiss, Allen S. *Breathless: Sound Recording, Disembodiment, and the Transformation of Lyrical Nostalgia*. Middletown, CT: Wesleyan University Press, 2002.

CHAPTER 8

# Kafka's Political Animals

*Paul Haacke*

Bugs, mice, moles, jackals, dogs, cats, horses, apes, and more: animals abound in Franz Kafka's fiction, and what makes so many of them so remarkable is their strangely human qualities. Most seem able to speak, reason, and fantasize by nature, others develop their arts and politics through practice or imitation, and still others end up losing their humanity or animality without any apparent cause. That said, they all resist identification according to an overarching *scala naturae* or "great chain of being." For rather than being mere creatures, or in the process of becoming other creatures, Kafka's animals are to a large extent hybrids—not just literally, in the sense that the creature in "A Crossbreed" is a mix between a cat and a lamb, but more generally, in that they cannot be identified as pure, distinct or exemplary types in a taxonomical or hierarchical system of differentiation. Similarly, unlike typical fables or parables, Kafka's animal stories do not belong to a particular folk tradition or serve a definitive instructional purpose, and thus they also resist adhering to any single ideological doctrine of truth, ethics or politics. As I hope to show here, this is especially evident in "Jackals and Arabs" and "A Report to an Academy," two of the more overtly political stories that Kafka wrote, and in fact the only ones that he specifically called "animal stories."[1] As neo-fabulist critiques of contemporary ideology—whether European, anti-Semitic, or Zionist—Kafka's "Zwei Tiergeschichten" may be read as satires of humanism, ethnocentrism, nationalism, and what I shall call *the biopolitics of catharsis* on which these discourses so often depend. By reconsidering Aristotle's idea of the "political animal" in relation to Kafka's readings of Nietzsche and Kierkegaard, and in relation to current theories of biopolitics from Foucault to Agamben and Derrida, I shall argue that Kafka's animals represent the extent to which political life confounds social divisions instead of overcoming them.

## The Question of Biography

Before focusing on the political implications of Kafka's animal stories, let us first consider his ideas about animality, humanity, and life in general. An increasingly common starting point for Kafka scholars, especially those adopting historicist or new historicist approaches, is to investigate his biography (a term that derives, it should be noted, from the Greek *bios*, meaning way of life, as opposed to *zōē*, meaning life itself).[2] For instance, one intriguing though somewhat facile biographical explanation that has been offered for Kafka's interest in animals is the similarity between his surname and the Czech word for jackdaw or crow, *kavka*, or between his Hebrew name, Amshel, and the German word for blackbird, *Amsel.*[3] More compelling, at least for philosophically minded critics like Walter Benjamin, is the fact that Kafka actually gave the name "the animal" to his persistent cough, a symptom of the tuberculosis that ultimately took his life.[4] This seems to get us a little further, since it connects Kafka's understanding of animality to his anxieties about the body, survival, and Kierkegaard's philosophy of religious faith in the face of "sickness unto death." For Benjamin, Kafka's work represents "the sickness of tradition," and so he imagines that Kafka was writing in earnest when, in one of his early pieces, he conceptualized experience (*Erfahrung*) as "seasickness on dry land (*Seekrankheit auf festem Lande*)."[5] However, Kafka's more ironic attitude is perhaps better represented by a quip he made in the voice of the undead Hunter Gracchus: "The thought of wanting to help me is a sickness and requires bed rest (*Der Gedanke mir helfen zu wollen ist eine Krankheit und muß im Bett geheilt werden*)."[6] Well aware of the oscillation between degeneration and revitalization in his work as well as in life, Kafka may have seen them as inseparable. For just as Bruno Latour argues that the hybrid nature of life renders purification an impossible fantasy,[7] Kafka has left us with the sense that there is no possibility for understanding without the acknowledgment of confusion. Instead of allowing for simplistic answers, he keeps us asking questions: Is death a symptom of life rather than its conclusion? Is the belief in a cure actually a cause of the illness?

If indeed "man is a fatal disease of the animal," as Alexandre Kojève once wrote, then Kafka knew its symptoms all too well. Giorgio Agamben quotes this enigmatic line in his book *The Open: Man and Animal*, and for him, it means that our humanity puts our animality to death. "Man," he explains, "can only be human to the degree that he transcends and transforms the anthropophorous animal which supports him, and only because, through the action of negation, he is capable of mastering and, eventually, destroying his own animality."[8] While this argument is compelling, one could also argue the inverse. Perhaps, like Kafka's cough, it is in fact the animal that persists in plaguing the human? Or, as I want to consider here, perhaps the survival of our humanity depends on the recognition of our hybrid social ecology rather than its violent destruction or shameful disavowal?

According to Benjamin, Kafka's animals appear to represent the shame of being human: "For him, to be an animal doubtless means having forgone human form and human wisdom out of a kind of shame. The way a distinguished gentleman who finds himself in a cheap tavern refrains, out of shame, from rinsing out his glass (*Tiersein hieß ihm wohl nur, aus einer Art von Scham auf die Menschengestalt und—weisheit verzichtet haben. So wie ein vornehmer*

*Herr, der in eine niedere Kneipe great, aus Scham darauf verzichtet, sein Glas aufzuwischen*)."[9] The final lines of *The Trial* would seem to evince this best; as Josef K.'s throat is about to be cut by his captors, he exclaims, "Like a dog!" and then, in what appears to be free indirect discourse, we read: "it was as if the shame would live on after him ("*Wie ein Hund!" sagte er, es war, als sollte die Scham ihn überleben*)."[10] The point of these lines is presumably not that K. actually feels like a dog as he is about to die, but rather that he feels like a human who is being treated like a dog (and an abject one at that). The larger implication here appears to be that it is only humans who are ashamed to be reminded of their animality, or who fear what follows after death as opposed to the fact of death itself. And so, given that Benjamin also defines Kafka's animals as "the receptacles for the forgotten,"[11] we may further argue that they not only represent relics from the past or abjection from the present, but that they remind us of the shame we realize, and try to forget, in the name of being human.

Overall, it might be tempting to conceptualize animalization in Kafka's fiction as a fearful process of dehumanization and decline, especially given the preeminent example of *The Metamorphosis*, except that Kafka also considers animal nature as a form of freedom from fear. This is particularly evident in a letter he wrote to his fiancée, Felice Bauer: "Had you not been lying on the ground among the animals (*unter das Getier gelegt*), you wouldn't have been able to see the sky and the stars wouldn't have been set free. Perhaps you wouldn't have survived the terror of standing upright (*Angst des Aufrechtstehens*)."[12] Here Kafka suggests that it is the upright-walking world of humans that is terrifying rather than the ground level of animals, which is instead what actually allows for the possibility of freedom and survival in the first place.

This belief in animal freedom should help us better understand why the ape in "A Report to An Academy" considers "human freedom" to be a mockery of nature and instead seeks what he calls "a way out" (*ein Ausweg*). In their study of Kafka, Deleuze and Guattari interpret this idea as a "line of flight" or "line of escape," which they associate with their somewhat romanticized ideas of "nomadism" and "deterritorialization."[13] One problem with their understanding of the "becoming-animal" and "becoming-human" in Kafka's oeuvre, however, is that many of his creatures continue to live on as hybrid beings instead of becoming something else. This is especially the case for such unique creatures as the cat-lamb in "A Crossbreed" and Odradek in "Cares of a Family Man," in which combination is far more important than transformation or displacement. For in Kafka's fictions, survival is often less a question of being one thing or becoming something else than of being able to live on in an ecology of hybrids. And when this hybrid ecology is fraught with social division, survival often becomes a question for politics.

## What Is a Political Animal?

Kafka's imagined political ecologies bear the traces of theology as well as philosophy. For instance, in a letter to Max Brod, dated July 5, 1922, he defined a certain kind of writer as "the scapegoat (*der Sündenbock*) of mankind," one who "makes it possible for men to enjoy sin (*eine Sünde*) without guilt, almost without guilt."[14] Although Kafka claimed to have dreaded becoming such a writer, most of us would probably agree that his works make us confront questions of guilt rather than allowing us to feel relieved of it. His tragic-comic style is too ironic to allow for either religious purification, aesthetic catharsis, or logical resolution, but it is also what allows him to expose the potential affinity between them.

The idea of the "scapegoat" or "*Sündenbock*" can be traced back to the ancient religious practice, described in Leviticus 16, in which two goats were sacrificed on Yom Kippur, the Day of Atonement; while one was a gift "for the Lord," the other, "for Azazel," was meant to carry away the sins of humanity to the devil. The aesthetic concept of "catharsis," on the other hand, comes from Aristotle, who derived it from ancient Greek medical discourse not only to describe the purging of emotions in response to a tragedy, but also in order to justify the benefits of the mimetic arts for healing the body politic. Aristotle's argument was not only that catharsis and mimesis made for a successful tragic drama, but also that both are necessary for the maintenance of the polis. Although he avoided discussing the politics of ritual performance itself in his *Poetics*, his arguments could also have been taken to justify the ceremonial murder of the *pharmakoi*, the people who were actually sacrificed as scapegoats for the sake of social purification at the Thargelia festival in fifth-century Athens.[15]

Of course Kafka does not discuss the politics of scapegoating directly either, and his resistance to tragic form—and to what I shall call the *biopolitics of catharsis*—is palpable. While Aristotle depends on the biological metaphor of the body politic in order to defend his concepts of mimesis and catharsis in his *Poetics*, and in turn develops the zoological idea of man as a "political animal" in order to explain his theory of society in the *Politics*, Kafka represents the conflict between natural life and human society by representing hybrid human-animal figures in many of his stories. But what does it mean to say that Kafka's animals are political, let alone *biopolitical*? Aside from offering the catch-all response that everything is political, we might say that there is something in the very genealogy of political philosophy that Kafka's animals seem to inherit. Indeed, Foucault turned to Aristotle early on when he pioneered his theory of biopower and biopolitics in the first volume of his *History of Sexuality*. Writing under the sub-heading "The Right to Death and the Power over Life," Foucault argues that, "For millennia, man remained what he was for Aristotle: a living animal with the additional capacity for a political existence." By contrast, he goes on, "modern man is an animal whose politics places his existence as a living being in question."[16]

Aristotle's classic definition, ἄνθρωπος φύσει πολιτικὸν ζῷον, or *anthrōpos physei politikon zōon*, is generally rendered in English as: "Man is by nature a political animal."[17] Alternative translations may be more accurate, such as "the human being is a social creature" or even "a creature that lives in a city," since all living beings may be referred to by the idea of *zōē*. But since Aristotle's passage goes on to compare human beings to other social or "gregarious" creatures like bees, ants and cranes, there seems to be some reason to keep the phrase "political animal." In any case, Aristotle's point is not that political sociability makes humans unique among animals, but rather that humans are simply *more political* than other animals. As he explains, this is thanks to our ability to speak or think with reason or *logos*, a natural gift that enables us to develop a city-state or *polis*:[18]

> Hence it is evident that the state is a creation of nature, and that man is by nature a political animal. And he who by nature and not by mere accident is without a state, is either a bad man or above humanity; he is like the "Tribeless, lawless, heartless one," whom Homer denounced—the natural outcast is forthwith a lover of war; he may be compared to an isolated piece at draughts.
>
> Now, that man is more of a political animal than bees or any other gregarious animals is evident. Nature, as we often say, makes nothing in vain, and man is the only animal whom she has endowed with the gift of speech.[19]

Since Aristotle defines political life here in terms of *zōē* rather than *bios*, there may be some reason to be cautious about the otherwise compelling theory of biopolitics developed by Agamben, who maintains that Aristotelian philosophy depends on a basic opposition between *zōē* and *bios*, and that these terms may be translated into the theoretical terms of Benjamin, Arendt and Foucault as "bare life" and "political life," respectively.[20] As for Aristotle's quotation from Homer's *Iliad* about the isolated outlaw or outcast,[21] it is arguably related to his distinction elsewhere between animals that are social or political and those that are scattered or dispersed,[22] as well as his extended discussion of human development later on in the *Politics*: "But he who is unable to live in society, or who has no need because he is sufficient for himself, must be either a beast or a god: he is no part of a state. . . . For man, when perfected, is the best of animals, but, when separated from law and justice, he is the worst of all."[23]

As we shall see, these are major concerns for the scattered society of jackals in Kafka's "Jackals and Arabs," who pray for a kind of sovereign biopower of their own, and for the isolated ape in "A Report to an Academy," who manages to transform himself from a beastly, neo-picaresque rascal into a mimetic creature of humanistic *Bildung*. Originally written in early 1917,[24] these two pieces of short fiction were first published consecutively under the title "Two Animal Stories" (*Zwei Tiergeschichten*) in the October and November issues of *Der Jude*, the monthly magazine for Jewish and Zionist discourse that was founded and edited by Martin Buber.[25] After Kafka submitted a portfolio of stories to Buber at the insistence of Max Brod, and these two were selected for publication, he made the specific request that they not be called "parables," and for this reason suggested the title "Two Animal Stories" instead.[26]

Although many of Kafka's writings have been described as parables or fables[27] since then, he evidently resisted these labels himself; even his cat-and-mouse tale "A Little Fable" was given that name by Brod for posthumous publication. For unlike the fables of Aesop or La Fontaine, Kafka's stories do not communicate an explanatory message in the voice of a didactic authority, and they are not presented in the form of teleological narratives that lead to a resolute moral, maxim or conclusion. Instead of providing examples for the purpose of instruction or guidance, they remain ambiguous, paradoxical, and open to multiple or conflicting interpretations.[28] "Jackals and Arabs" and "A Report to an Academy" are especially open to interpretation, along with the animal story "Researches of a Dog" (*Forshungen eines Hundes*), since they are narrated in the first person rather than the omniscient third person. Unlike religious parables and popular fables, these stories do not uphold any definitive values or folk wisdom, but instead work to satirize the very principles of tradition and authority that such wisdom has come to represent.

## The Fantasy of Purification

"Jackals and Arabs" is narrated in the voice of a European man recounting his travels with an Arab caravan in an unnamed desert. While camping out for the night, he is surrounded by a pack of jackals[29] who, lucky for him, turn out to be resolutely pro-European and anti-Arab. When he notices the eldest jackal coming closer, he imagines to himself that it is "as if he needed my warmth," but it turns out that he in fact wants much more. "You have come from the North," the jackal explains, "that is just what we base our hopes on. There is a rationality there that cannot be found here among the Arabs" ("Jackals" 69/271). He then goes on to explain that, although the jackals hate the Arabs, whom they blame for their exile, they do not fear them: "We're supposed to be afraid of them? Isn't it enough of a misfortune to have been banished among such a people (*daß wir unter solches Volk vertsoßen sind*)?" ("Jackals" 70/271). The European remains confused and withholds judgment, wondering whether the conflict may be based on the nature of their "blood" rather than something that could be resolved more politically: "Matters so far outside my province I am not competent to judge; it seems to me a very old quarrel; I suppose it's in the blood, and perhaps will only end with it." The jackal agrees wholeheartedly, replying, "What you have just said agrees with our old tradition (*alten Lehre*). So we shall draw blood from them and the quarrel will be over" ("Jackals" 70/271).

Soon it becomes clear that the jackals' prophecy of a savior from the North involves a violent fantasy of biopolitical catharsis, which they describe several times throughout the story in terms of "cleansing," "purifying" or "purging." This idea of *Reinheit* first appears when they suggest that it may actually be impossible to become pure: "All the water in the Nile couldn't cleanse us of them (*So viel Wasser hätte der Nil nicht, um uns rein zu waschen*). Why, the mere sight of their living flesh makes us turn tail and flee into cleaner air (*in reinere Luft*), into the desert, which for that very reason is our home" ("Jackals" 70/271). When they return to this idea of purification again later, however, they express a bit more hope:

> We must have peace from the Arabs; air we can breathe; a view of the horizon cleansed of them (*gereinigt von ihnen den Ausblick rund am Horizont*); no bleated lament from a ram slaughtered by an Arab; all creatures must perish quietly; undisturbed, they must be drunk dry by us and purified right down to the bone (*bis auf die Knochen gereinigt werden*). Purity, nothing but purity is what we want (*Reinheit, nichts als Reinheit wollen wir*). ("Jackals" 71/273)

At this point, the jackals offer the European a pair of sewing scissors and ask him to cut the throats of the Arabs in the middle of the night. The weapon they happen to have is a strange one, and the reason is left unexplained; perhaps they need the helping hand of a human since they lack fingers? In any case, after he refuses, and one of the Arabs awakens and approaches to inquire what's going on, they scatter. The Arab man explains:

> Of course, Master, it is common knowledge; for as long as there are Arabs, this pair of scissors will go wandering through the desert, and it will wander with us until the end of time. It is offered to every European so he will execute his great work; every European is just the man who seems to them to have been chosen. These creatures possess an absurd hope; fools, true fools they are. That is why we love them; they are our dogs; more beautiful than yours. ("Jackals" 71/273)

Eventually the jackals scatter again when the Arab offers them a dead camel to feast on, and as their muzzles become more and more bloody, he concludes: "Wonderful animals, aren't they? And how they hate us!" ("Jackals" 72/275).

The Messianic rhetoric in Kafka's story is overt, but there is much debate about how it might actually reflect on either Jews or Judaism. Since the story was first published in Buber's journal *Der Jude*, which advocated spiritual renewal among European Jews in response to Theodor Herzl's call for the establishment of a Jewish state in Palestine, some have suggested in varying ways that it represents Kafka's growing interest in Zionism.[30] For instance, Ritchie Robertson has argued that, "as parasitic animals who rely on others to provide their food," the jackals "typify the lack of self-reliance ascribed by Zionists to Western Jews." However, since the story satirizes the jackals' desperate fantasies of purity and sovereignty rather than their impoverished predicament, and since it takes place in a desert populated by Arabs, it would make at least as much sense to argue that it critiques Zionist fantasies of nationalist independence instead of advocating them. Thus there is no reason to accept Robertson's basic assumption that "the story supports the Zionist programme of active self-improvement through developing one's Jewish consciousness and helping in the colonization of Palestine which was favored by the readers of *The Jew*."[31] For in fact Kafka remained conflicted about both Judaism and Zionism for much of his life; while maintaining a critical distance from the religious faith of Buber, Brod, and his lovers Felice Bauer and Dora Diamant, he also developed an affinity for the more atheistic and socialist leanings of his intimate friend Milena Jesenská, with whom he developed an intense personal relationship in 1920.[32] He declared his position especially pointedly in a journal entry dated February 25, 1918: "I have not been guided into life by the hand of

Christianity—admittedly now slack and failing—as Kierkegaard was, and have not caught the hem of the Jewish prayer shawl—now flying away from us—as the Zionists have. I am an end or a beginning."[33]

Another important though less obvious source for "Jackals and Arabs" is Friedrich Nietzsche. As Walter Sokel has observed, the way in which Kafka "links the parasitic with the religious" in representing the jackals' "admission of helplessness"[34] suggests that the story may be read as a parody of Nietzsche's ideas of *ressentiment* and slave morality, especially since it bears remarkable resemblance to an animal story that appears in the pages of *On the Genealogy of Morals*. Obviously drawing from Aesop's fables, perhaps especially one known in English as "The Jackdaw and the Eagle," Nietzsche developed his story about weak lambs and strong birds of prey in order to explain his argument that humans are the only animals that believe in good and evil. Given that Kafka's surname means "jackdaw" in Czech, it's tempting to speculate that he may have turned to "The Jackdaw and the Eagle" as well. Here is Aesop's fable in a recent translation by Laura Gibbs:

> When an eagle seized a sleek and glossy lamb from the flock and carried it off in his talons as a feast for his chicks, the jackdaw decided to do the same thing. Accordingly, he swooped down and clutched at a lamb but his claws got tangled in the wool on the lamb's back and he could not escape. The jackdaw said, "It serves me right for being such a fool! Why should I, who am only a jackdaw, try to imitate eagles?"[35]

And here is what Nietzsche wrote:

> That lambs bear ill-will toward large birds of prey is hardly strange: but is in itself no reason to blame large birds of prey for making off with little lambs. And if the lambs say among themselves: "These birds of prey are evil; and whoever is as little of a bird of prey as possible, indeed, rather the opposite, a lamb—should he not be said to be good?," then there can be no objection to setting up an ideal like this, even if the birds of prey might look down on it a little contemptuously and perhaps say to themselves: "We bear them no ill-will at all, these good lambs—indeed, we love them: there is nothing tastier than a tender lamb." To demand of strength that it should not express itself as strength, that it should not be a will to overcome, overthrow, dominate, a thirst for enemies and resistance and triumph, makes as little sense as to demand of weakness that it should express itself as strength.[36]

Like Kafka's "Jackals and Arabs," both tales represent a biological difference between the weak and the strong, but while Aesop gives voice to the weak jackdaw who fails to imitate the strong eagle, Nietzsche emphasizes the dominance of the birds of prey over the lambs. Just as Nietzsche's birds of prey say to themselves, "We bear them no ill-will at all, these good lambs—indeed, we love them," Kafka's Arab says contemptuously of the jackals. "That's why we like them; they are now our dogs; finer dogs than any of yours." Similarly, both Nietzsche's lambs and Kafka's jackals do indeed express ill-will toward their perceived oppressors, and both are mocked for falling prey to this *ressentiment* as opposed to recognizing or overcoming their weaknesses on their own. In turn, just as Nietzsche adapted Aesop's fable about the strong and the weak to parody the belief that good and evil are ordained by nature or God, Kafka appears to have adapted Nietzsche's mock fable in order to caricature his critiques of *ressentiment* and slave morality, as well as related anti-Semitic fantasies of social parasitism, ritual bloodlust, and vengeful envy. In this way, Kafka may well have been satirizing Zionism as a Nietzchean will to power based on a naturalist fantasy of purification. And so in more ways than one, we may read his story as a critique of the biopolitics of catharsis around which discourses of nationalism so often turn.

## The Irony of Freedom

"A Report To An Academy" is a rather more enigmatic story, and perhaps this is why it has gained greater recognition. Many have also interpreted it as a fabulist or satirical representation of Jewish experience, given its narrative of slavery, conversion, and assimilation and its ideas of escape, freedom, and hope. Furthermore, as Margot Norris has argued, it may also be read as a response to Nietzsche's theory of mimesis, as well as a "pointed illustration of the Darwinian political teleology of the mimetic performance," which in turn paved the way for Kafka's story of reverse evolution a few years later, "The Metamorphosis." According to Nietzsche, Norris argues, "The intellect, as a means for the preservation of the individual, develops its chief power in dissimulation."[37] Similarly, in Kafka's story, the ape's survival in human society is based on a mimetic method of performance and representation that evinces his remarkable intellect as well as what Norris calls "the ultimate, if degrading, effectiveness of adaptive behavior."[38] With further consideration of nineteenth-century ideas about ontogeny recapitulating phylogeny, she argues that Kafka represents Rotpeter's mimetic adaptation as symbolic of human evolution, and that he in turn "rejects Aristotle's autotelic motive (imitation as intrinsically pleasurable) on the one hand, and such anthropomorphic motives as idolatry and *ressentiment*, on the other."[39]

While Aristotle defines man as a political animal in his *Politics*, he also proposes another conception of man as a mimetic animal in his *Poetics*: "Imitation is natural to man from childhood, one of his advantages over the lower animals being this, that he is the most imitative creature in the world, and learns at first by imitation."[40] Kafka's ape appears to excel at such imitation in "A Report to an Academy," but he also tells us directly that he derives no pleasure from it: "I repeat: I was not attracted to the idea of imitating men; I imitated because I was looking for a way out, for no other reason" ("Report" 82/311). As he explains, his idea of "a way out" (*ein Ausweg*) is different from "the great feeling of freedom on all sides," which he gave up on after being captured. In this way, his search is markedly different from the jackals' fantasy of purification in Kafka's other animal story. For instead of hoping for total freedom or "purification" from the power of humans, Rotpeter pursues a mimetic method of adaptive assimilation into their order. His self-described attempt "to slip off into the bushes" (*sich in die Büsche schlagen*) ("Report" 83/312) is especially ironic, since cutting a path through a thicket is generally understood as a natural method of surviving in the wild rather than as a rational strategy for self-preservation in civilized society. In this way, Kafka mocks the Darwinian idea of the adaptive survival at the same time that he mocks the Enlightenment idea of progress through cultural education or *Bildung*.

Instead of valorizing *Bildung*, Rotpeter considers it as merely a means of cultural adaptation, and thus strives no higher than the average: "Through an effort that has hitherto never been repeated on this planet, I have reached the average cultural level of a European (*Durch eine Anstrengung, die sich bisher auf der Erde nicht wiederholt hat, habe ich die Durchschnittsbildung eines Europäers erreicht*)" ("Report" 83/312). While recognizing his education as an achievement of great effort, he evidently takes little pride in it: "When I review my evolution (*Entwicklung*) and its goal so far, I can't complain, but neither am I satisfied" ("Report" 83/312-13). As he explains early on, *Bildung* only became available to him once he let go of his stubborn attachment to his past: "This achievement would have been impossible had I wanted to cling obstinately to my origin, to the memories of my youth. In fact, to give up all such obstinacy was the supreme commandment that I had imposed on myself; I, a free ape, accepted this yoke" ("Report" 77/299).

Although calling himself a "free ape" by nature at the beginning of his report, Rotpeter goes on to explain not only how he was enslaved by his captors, but also how he came to view "human freedom" as a mockery of true nature. For the most part this is because he believes it is based on mimetic self-control rather than instinctive mobility. As he explains, when he first glimpsed acrobats performing their stunts, he realized that they were simply acting for the sake of entertainment rather than truly being free by nature: "'That, too, is human freedom,' I would think, 'high-handed movement.' You mockery of holy Nature! No building could stand up to apedom's laughter at such a sight" (*"Auch das ist Menschenfreiheit," dachte ich, "selbstherrliche Bewegung." Du Verspottung der heiligen Natur! Kein Bau würde standhalten vor dem Gelächter des Affentums bei diesem Anblick*) ("Report" 79-80/305).

The fine line between mimicry and mockery is also a key element of Kafka's narrative discourse. For Rotpeter's account of his life story is not simply a report, it is also a performance that uses the tools of mimesis and logos to mock both the obscure authority of "the academy" as well as the hypocrisy of humanity in general. In turn, by adopting the voice of the subject rather than the authority of the judges, Kafka's story distances itself from the pedagogical forms of the fable and parable, if not even reverses them. Instead of providing a model for instruction, it represents a critique of instruction itself. For while the promise of education is often based on the assumption that knowledge is power, Rotpeter exposes the extent to which power is also constitutive of knowledge. And this is the irony of freedom that Kafka recognized so well.

According to Kierkegaard, irony is a "negatively liberating activity" because it "cuts the bonds that restrain speculation, helps to shove off from the purely empirical sandbanks and to venture out upon the ocean."[41] In many ways, Kafka seems to have indulged in just this sense of philosophical irony in his fictions, perhaps even to the point of what he called "seasickness on dry land." Indeed, as Jean Wahl has demonstrated, Kafka studied Kierkegaard perhaps more than any other philosopher. Yet despite Wahl's otherwise acute observations about Kafka's critiques of Kierkegaard and theology, he concludes his essay on the two by suggesting that we should nonetheless try to read Kafka in the name of absolute faith:

> If we keep up our courage in spite of the horrors which Kafka showed us, if we always think: tomorrow I shall be freed; then we shall be purified; then the unjust punishment will turn into justice and purification. Today more than ever we are ready for such a conviction. There will be a catharsis through our fear for ourselves and through our pity for ourselves. There will be something indestructible which will be the result only of our indestructible faith in the indestructible.[42]

Unfortunately, Wahl's idea of faith in this passage is based on the very principles of absolute justice, purification and catharsis that, as I have argued here, Kafka implicitly rejected. And so, although Kafka did indeed maintain a kind of existential hope in the possibility of freedom, we should not forget that it was always tinged with a taste of irony.

It is this irony that Kafka's animals remind us of above all. They do not represent humanity's struggle for freedom any more than they represent animal instinct; as Benjamin observed, the problem with anthropomorphizing them is that it allows us to forget their creaturely nature: "You can read Kafka's animal stories for quite a while without realizing that they are not about human beings at all. When you finally come upon the name of the creature—monkey, dog, mole—you look up in fright and realize that you are already far away from the continent of man."[43] That said, while Kafka's animals do not speak for human nature in general, or any given culture in particular, they do help us interrogate what it means to be human in the first place. In turn, by understanding them as political animals, we may better recognize how much we are still in the process of becoming political ourselves.

## Notes

1. I will be quoting Kafka's "Jackals and Arabs" (*Schakale und Araber*) and "A Report to an Academy" (*Ein Bericht für eine Akademie*) in English from *Kafka's Selected Stories*, ed. Stanley Corngold (New York: Norton, 2007), 69-72 and 76-84, and when appropriate in German from the *Kritische Ausgabe: Drucke zu Lebzeiten* (Frankfurt a.M: Fischer, 1994), 270-75 and 299-313. References to the two stories will be given parenthetically in the text.

2. I am deriving these definitions of *bios* and *zōē* from Henry George Liddell and Robert Scott's *Greek-English Lexicon* (Oxford: Oxford University Press, 1996). I return to them later in my discussion of Agamben's theory of biopolitics in note 20, although the distinctions between the two are far more subtle than I can do justice to here.

3. See Richard T. Gray, ed. *A Franz Kafka Encyclopedia* (Santa Barbara, CA: Greenwood, 2005), 15.

4. Benjamin refers to this at the end of a particularly rich passage on Kafka's animals: "This much is certain: of all of Kafka's creatures, the animals have the greatest opportunity for reflection. What corruption is in the law, anxiety is in their thinking. It messes a situation up, yet it is the only hopeful thing about it. But because the most forgotten source of strangeness is our body—one's own body—one can understand why Kafka called the cough that erupted from within him 'the animal.' It was the vanguard of the great herd." See Walter Benjamin, "Franz Kafka: On the Tenth Anniversary of His Death," trans. Harry Zohn in *Selected Writings*, vol. 2., eds. Michael W. Jennings, Howard Eiland and Gary Smith (Cambridge, MA: Harvard University Press, 1999), 810.

5. See Benjamin, "Franz Kafka," 809. This line is quoted from "Conversation With the Supplicant" (*Gespräch mit dem Beter*), which Kafka excerpted from his story "Description of a Struggle" and published in the March-April issue of the bimonthly *Hyperion* in 1909. See *Kritische Ausgabe: Drucke zu Lebzeiten*, 389. See also "Beschreibung eines Kampfes: Fassung A" and "Beschreibung eines Kampfes: Fassung B" in *Kritische Ausgabe: Nachgelassene Schriften und Fragmente I*, 89; 157.

6. Kafka, "The Hunter Gracchus" in *Selected Stories*, 112; "Der Jäger Gracchus" in *Kritische Ausgabe: Nachgelassene Schriften und Fragmente I*, 311. Also quoted in Benjamin, "Franz Kafka," 813.

7. See especially Bruno Latour, *We Have Never Been Modern*, trans. Catherine Porter (Cambridge, MA: Harvard University Press, 1993), 3, 10-11.

8. Giorgio Agamben, *The Open: Man and Animal*, trans. Kevin Attell (Stanford, CA: Stanford University Press, 2004), 12.

9. Benjamin, "Letter to Gershom Scholem on Franz Kafka," trans. Edmund Jephcott in *Selected Writings*, vol. 3, 327; *Gesammelte Briefe*, Bd. VI (Frankfurt a.M: Suhrkamp Verlag, 2000), 113.

10. Kafka, *Kritische Ausgabe: Der Proceß*, 312.

11. Benjamin, "Franz Kafka," 810.

12. Elias Canetti interprets this passage as follows: "One must lie down with the beasts in order to be set free, or redeemed. Standing upright signifies the power of man over beasts; but precisely in the most obvious attitude man is exposed, visible, vulnerable. For this power is also guilt, and only on the ground, lying among the animals, can one see the stars, which frees one from this terrifying power of man." See Elias Canetti, *Kafka's Other Trial*, trans. Christopher Middleton (New York: Schocken, 1974), 88. See also Paola Gambarota's discussion of this passage in relation to Umberto Saba's "L'insonnia" and the book of Genesis in "Beyond Revealed Religions: Saba, the Creatures and the Political Animal" in *MLN* 120 (2005): 137-60.

13. See especially Gilles Deleuze and Félix Guattari, *Kafka: Toward a Minor Literature*, trans. Dana Polan (Minneapolis, MN: University of Minnesota Press, 1986), 34-36.

14. Quoted in Franz Kafka, *The Basic Kafka*, ed. Erich Heller (New York: Washington Square Press, 1979), 295. For a more extensive discussion, see Chris Danta, "'Like a dog . . . like a lamb': Becoming Sacrificial Animal in Kafka and Coetzee," in *New Literary History* 38.4 (Autumn 2007): 721-37.

15. My understanding of this practice is based on the account of Jean-Pierre Vernant and Pierre Vidal-Naquet in *Myth and Tragedy in Ancient Greece*, trans. Janet Lloyd (New York: Zone Books, 1988). Their historical evidence offers a compelling alternative to the more theoretical studies of René Girard, whose speculations on sacrifice and mimesis they explicitly put into question.

16. Michel Foucault, *The History of Sexuality I: The Will to Knowledge*, trans. Robert Hurley (New York: Vintage, 1978), 143. Foucault discusses the ideas of biopower

and biopolitics further in his lectures at the College de France in the late 1970s, translated and collected under the title *Society Must Be Defended*, trans. David Macey (New York: Picador, 2002), and in his seminar "The Birth of Biopolitics" in *Ethics: Subjectivity and Truth*, ed. Paul Rabinow (New York: The New Press, 2006). One important fact about Foucault's theory is that he distinguishes *anato-politics*, which revolves around power over the individual body, from *bio-politics*, which refers instead to power over the collective lives of a general population or group of people. It is only the latter that he believes came to the foreground of politics with the rise of the modern liberal state.

17. See for instance the translations of Benjamin Jowett and Stephen Everson.

18. Thus Aristotle also argues in the *Nicomachean Ethics* (I.13) that man is a rational, speaking animal, that is, one who has or takes account of *logos*. Derrida alludes to this when he writes that "man as political animal is indissociable from the definition of man having the logos, logon ekhon," in *The Beast and the Sovereign*, vol. 1, trans. Geoffrey Bennington, eds. Michel Lisse, Marie-Louise Mallet and Ginette Michaud (Chicago, IL: University of Chicago Press, 2009), 347. This harks back to his earlier claim that "*Logos* is a *zōon*" in *Dissemination*, trans. Barbara Johnson (New York: Continuum, 2004), 84.

19. Aristotle, *Politics*, 1253a, l.1-10. See Richard McKeon, ed. *The Basic Works of Aristotle* (New York: Modern Library, 2001), 1129. For an extended discussion of this passage, see R.G. Mulgan, "Aristotle's Doctrine That Man is a Political Animal," in *Hermes*, 102.3 (1974): 438-45.

20. For pointed critiques of Agamben on this point, see Derrida, *The Beast and the Sovereign*, vol. 1, 314-16 and 325-333, and Paul Rabinow and Nikolas Rose, "Biopower Today" in *BioSocieties* 1 (2006): 195-217. See also Laurent Dubreuil, "Leaving Politics: Bios, Zōē, Life," in *Diacritics* 36.2 (2006): 83-98, and James Gordon Finlayson, "'Bare Life' and Politics in Agamben's Reading of Aristotle," in *The Review of Politics* 72 (2010): 97-126.

21. In Robert Fagles' translation, this line from *The Iliad* IX, l.73 reads as follows: "Lost to the clan, / lost to the hearth, lost to the old ways, that one / who lusts for all the horrors of war with his own people," *The Iliad* (New York: Penguin, 1990), 253.

22. *History of Animals*, I.1 488a. See *Aristotle IX: History of Animals*, trans. A.L. Peck (Cambridge, MA: Harvard University Press, 1965), 15. For more on this point, see John M. Cooper, "Political Animals and Civic Friendship," in *Aristotle's Politics: Critical Essays*, ed. Richard Kraut and Steven Skultety (Lanham, MA: Rowman & Littlefield, 2005), 65-90.

23. Aristotle, *Politics*, 1253a, l.31; quoted in McKeon, ed. *The Basic Works of Aristotle*, 1130.

24. An early draft of "Jackals and Arabs" appears in notebook "B" of Kafka's *Octavhefte*, which he worked on between December 1916 and April 1917. After the story was published in *Der Jude* in October 1917, it was republished in December 1917 without Kafka's authorization in *Österreichische Morgenzeitung*, and again later in Julius Sandmeier's *Neue deutsche Erzähler* in the summer of 1918. "A Report to an Academy" was written in April 1917 and published in the November 1917 issue of *Der Jude* as the sequel to "Jackals and Arabs." Both stories were later included in Kafka's collection *A Country Doctor* (*Ein Landarzt*), first published in 1919.

25. While Max Brod had written to Buber suggesting Kafka as a contributor, Kafka initially declined the invitation in a letter to Buber dated 29 November 1915, saying he was "far too burdened" at the time. Evidently he had already become wary of Buber, for in a letter to Felice Bauer dated 16 January, he wrote that he found Buber "dreary" and that he would not think of leaving his room to attend the scholar's lecture on Jewish

myth. Apparently he later acknowledged that he found Buber "remarkable," but also called his writings "tepid." See Gray, ed. *A Franz Kafka Encyclopedia*, 57-58.

26. See Gray, ed. *A Franz Kafka Encyclopedia*, 244.

27. The word "parable" derives from the Greek *parabole*, meaning "to set beside one another" or "to compare," and generally refers to an example story that employs a fictional narrative to illuminate, by way of analogy, a particular circumstance or problem of human behavior. By contrast, the word "fable" derives from the Latin *fabula*, meaning narrative or account, from the root *fari*, to speak, and the Greek *phanai*, to speak or to say. According to Susan Suleiman in her study *Authoritarian Fictions*, Jesus' parables in the New Testament tend to provide a clear didactic meaning, whereas the parables of the Old Testament tend to suggest possible meanings without offering any unequivocal lessons, thereby stressing the process of interpretation rather than the message itself. Fables, according to Suleiman, may be more clearly defined with reference to the exemplary works of Aesop and La Fontaine, which all feature an omniscient narrator speaking for the authority of the "Truth" directly to a reader or listener outside of the story. For Suleiman, "The function of the fable, then, is to allow us to live vicariously—to provide us with experiences lived by others, but whose 'lessons' will affect us as if we had lived them ourselves." Susan Suleiman, *Authoritarian Fictions: The Ideological Novel as a Literary Genre* (New York: Columbia University Press, 1983), 53.

28. According to Gerhard Neumann, Kafka's "gliding" form of paradoxical writing combines the "reversal" typical of traditional paradox along with a unique method of deflection or diversion that moves concepts away from the logic of rational thinking without ending up in total undecidability. See Gerhard Neumann, "Umkehrung und Ablenkung: Franz Kafkas 'Gleitendes Paradox'" in *Franz Kafka*, ed. Heinz Politzer (Darmstadt: Wissenschaftliche Buchgesellschaft, 1973), 459-515.

29. The English word "jackal" and the German *Schakale* derive from the Turkish *çakal*, which may in turn be traced back to Persian and Sanskrit, according to the Oxford English Dictionary. As parasitic scavengers of the desert, they may be compared to the lowly creature with which Josef K. identifies at the end of *The Trial*, although their social behavior as pack animals also suggests an affinity to the rather more proud canines in "Researches of a Dog."

30. One major study of Kafka's relationship to Zionism is Iris Bruce's *Kafka and Cultural Zionism: Dates in Palestine* (Madison, WI: University of Wisconsin Press, 2007). For a critique of Zionist claims to Kafka's work, see Judith Butler, "Who Owns Kafka?" in *London Review of Books* 33.5 (March 3, 2011): 3-8.

31. Ritchie Roberston, ed., *The German-Jewish Dialogue* (Oxford: Oxford University Press, 1999), 196.

32. For a study of Kafka's socialist leanings, see Michael Löwy, "Franz Kafka and Libertarian Socialism," trans. Patrick Flaherty, in *New Politics* 6.3 (Summer 1997): 120-31.

33. Franz Kafka, *The Blue Octavo Notebooks*, trans. Ernst Kaiser and Eithne Wilkins (Cambridge, MA: Exact Change, 1991), 52; *Kritische Ausgabe: Nachgelassene Schriften und Fragmente II*, 98: "Ich bin nicht von der allerdings schon schwer sinkenden Hand des Christentums ins Leben geführt worden wie Kierkegaard und habe nicht den letzten Zipfel des davonfliegenden jüdischen Gebetsmantels noch gefangen wie die Zionisten. Ich bin Ende oder Anfang."

34. Walter Herbert Sokel, *The Myth of Power and the Self: Essays on Franz Kafka* (Detroit, MI: Wayne State University Press, 2002), 129.

35. See "Fable 341: The Jackdaw and the Eagle" in *Aesop's Fables*, trans. Laura Gibbs (Oxford: Oxford University Press, 2002), 163-64. According to Gibbs' editorial commentary, "For the Greeks, the jackdaw was a bird who was supposed to stick to his

own flock. The equivalent of the English proverb 'birds of a feather flock together' was *koloios poti koloion*, 'the jackdaw (stands) next to the jackdaw' (e.g. Aristotle, *Nicomachean Ethics* 1144)." See *Aesop's Fables*, 157.

36. This follows shortly after Nietzsche's conception of man as an animal that promises: "To breed an animal which can promise—is this not the paradoxical task that nature has set itself in the case of man? . . . To be able to stand security for his own future (*für sich als Zukunft gutsagen*) is what a promiser does. . . . This is precisely the long story of how responsibility came to be." See Friedrich Nietzsche, *On the Genealogy of Morals*, trans. Douglas Smith (Oxford: Oxford University Press, 1990), 29. For an extended reading of Nietzsche's mock fable in relation to Aesop, see Thomas Keenan, "Fables of Responsibility," in *Unruly Examples: On the Rhetoric of Exemplarity*, ed. Alexander Gelley (Stanford, CA: Stanford University Press, 1994), 133-140.

37. Margot Norris, "Darwin, Nietzsche, Kafka, and the Problem of Mimesis," in *MLN* 95.5 (December 1980): 1243-44.

38. Norris, 1245.

39. Norris, 1247.

40. Aristotle, *Poetics*, I.4, I.5-9. See McKeon, ed. *The Basic Works of Aristotle*, 1457.

41. Søren Kierkegaard, *The Concept of Irony: With Continual Reference to Socrates/ Notes on Schelling's Lecture Notes*, trans. Howard V. Hong and Edna H. Hong (Princeton, NJ: Princeton University Press, 1992), 123.

42. Jean Wahl, "Kierkegaard and Kafka," trans. Liehhard Bergel in *The Kafka Problem*, ed. Angel Flores (New York: New Directions, 1946), 275.

43. Benjamin, "Franz Kafka," 802.

# Works Cited

Aesop. *Aesop's Fables*. Translated by Laura Gibbs. Oxford: Oxford University Press, 2002.

Agamben, Giorgio. *The Open: Man and Animal*. Translated by Kevin Attell. Stanford, CA: Stanford University Press, 2004.

Aristotle. *Aristotle IX: History of Animals*. Translated by A.L. Peck. Cambridge, MA: Harvard University Press, 1965.

———. *The Basic Works of Aristotle*. Edited by Richard McKeon. New York: Modern Library, 2001.

Benjamin, Walter. "Franz Kafka: On the Tenth Anniversary of His Death." Translated by Harry Zohn in Walter Benjamin, *Selected Writings*, edited by Michael W. Jennings, Howard Eiland and Gary Smith, vol. 2, 794-818. Cambridge, MA: Harvard University Press, 1999.

———. *Gesammelte Briefe*, 6 vol. Frankfurt a.M: Suhrkamp Verlag, 2000.

———. "Letter to Gershom Scholem on Franz Kafka." Translated by Edmund Jephcott in Walter Benjamin, *Selected Writings*, edited by Michael W. Jennings, Howard Eiland and Gary Smith, vol. 3, 322-29. Cambridge, MA: Harvard University Press, 2002.

Bruce, Iris. *Kafka and Cultural Zionism: Dates in Palestine*. Madison, WI: University of Wisconsin Press, 2007.

Butler, Judith. "Who Owns Kafka?" *London Review of Books* 33.5 (March 3, 2011): 3-8.

Canetti, Elias. *Kafka's Other Trial*. Translated by Christopher Middleton. New York: Schocken, 1974.

Cooper, John M. "Political Animals and Civic Friendship." In *Aristotle's Politics: Critical Essays*, edited by Richard Kraut and Steven Skultety, 65-90. Lanham, MA: Rowman & Littlefield, 2005.

Danta, Chris. "'Like a dog . . . like a lamb': Becoming Sacrificial Animal in Kafka and Coetzee." *New Literary History* 38.4 (Autumn 2007): 721-37.

Deleuze, Gilles, and Félix Guattari. *Kafka: Toward a Minor Literature*. Translated by Dana Polan. Minneapolis, MN: University of Minnesota Press, 1986.

Derrida, Jacques. *The Beast and the Sovereign*. Vol. 1. Translated by Geoffrey Bennington. Edited by Michel Lisse, Marie-Louise Mallet, and Ginette Michaud. Chicago, IL: University of Chicago Press, 2009.

———. *Dissemination*. Translated by Barbara Johnson. New York: Continuum, 2004.

Dubreuil, Laurent. "Leaving Politics: Bios, Zōē, Life." *Diacritics* 36.2 (2006): 83-98.

Finlayson, James Gordon. "'Bare Life' and Politics in Agamben's Reading of Aristotle." *The Review of Politics* 72 (2010): 97-126.

Foucault, Michel. *Ethics: Subjectivity and Truth*. Edited by Paul Rabinow. New York: The New Press, 2006.

———. *The History of Sexuality I: The Will to Knowledge*. Translated by Robert Hurley. New York: Vintage, 1978.

———. *Society Must Be Defended*. Translated by David Macey. New York: Picador, 2002.

Gambarota, Paola. "Beyond Revealed Religions: Saba, the Creatures and the Political Animal." *MLN* 120 (2005): 137-60.

Gray, Richard T., ed. *A Franz Kafka Encyclopedia*. Santa Barbara, CA: Greenwood, 2005.

Homer. *The Iliad*. Translated by Robert Fagles. New York: Penguin, 1990.

Kafka, Franz. *The Basic Kafka*. Edited by Erich Heller. New York: Washington Square Press, 1979.

———. *The Blue Octavo Notebooks*. Edited by Max Brod, translated by Ernst Kaiser and Eithne Wilkins. Cambridge, MA: Exact Change, 1991.

———. *Kritische Ausgabe. Drucke zu Lebzeiten*. Edited by Wolf Kittler, Hans-Gerd Koch and Gerhard Neumann. Frankfurt a.M.: Fischer, 1994.

———. *Kritische Ausgabe. Nachgelassene Schriften und Fragmente I*. Edited by Malcom Pasley. Frankfurt a.M.: Fischer, 1993.

———. *Kritische Ausgabe. Nachgelassene Schriften und Fragmente II*. Edited by Jost Schillemeit. Frankfurt a.M.: Fischer, 1992.

———. *Kritische Ausgabe. Der Proceß*. Edited by Malcom Pasley. Frankfurt a.M.: Fischer, 1990.

———. *Kafka's Selected Stories*. Edited by Stanley Corngold. New York: Norton, 2007.

Keenan, Thomas. "Fables of Responsibility." In *Unruly Examples: On the Rhetoric of Exemplarity*, edited by Alexander Gelley, 133-140. Stanford, CA: Stanford University Press, 1994.

Kierkegaard, Søren. *The Concept of Irony: With Continual Reference to Socrates/Notes on Schelling's Lecture Notes*. Translated by Howard V. Hong and Edna H. Hong. Princeton, NJ: Princeton University Press, 1992.

Latour, Bruno. *We Have Never Been Modern*. Translated by Catherine Porter. Cambridge, MA: Harvard University Press, 1993.

Liddell, Henry George, and Robert Scott. *Greek-English Lexicon*. Oxford: Oxford University Press, 1996.

Löwy, Michael. "Franz Kafka and Libertarian Socialism." Translated by Patrick Flaherty. *New Politics* 6.3 (Summer 1997): 120-31.

Mulgan, R.G. "Aristotle's Doctrine That Man is a Political Animal." *Hermes* 102.3 (1974): 438-45.
Neumann, Gerhard. "Umkehrung und Ablenkung: Franz Kafkas 'Gleitendes Paradox'." In *Franz Kafka*, edited by Heinz Politzer, 459-515. Darmstadt: Wissenschaftliche Buchgesellschaft, 1973.
Nietzsche, Friedrich. *On the Genealogy of Morals*. Translated by Douglas Smith. Oxford: Oxford University Press, 1990.
Norris, Margot. "Darwin, Nietzsche, Kafka, and the Problem of Mimesis." *MLN* 95.5 (December 1980): 1232-53.
Rabinow, Paul, and Nikolas Rose. "Biopower Today." *BioSocieties* 1 (2006): 195-217.
Roberston, Ritchie, ed. *The German-Jewish Dialogue*. Oxford: Oxford University Press, 1999.
Sokel, Walter Herbert. *The Myth of Power and the Self: Essays on Franz Kafka*. Detroit, MI: Wayne State University Press, 2002.
Suleiman, Susan. *Authoritarian Fictions: The Ideological Novel As a Literary Genre*. New York: Columbia University Press, 1983.
Vernant, Jean-Pierre, and Pierre Vidal-Naquet. Translated by Janet Lloyd. *Myth and Tragedy in Ancient Greece*. New York: Zone Books, 1988.
Wahl, Jean. "Kierkegaard and Kafka." Translated by Lienhard Bergel. In *The Kafka Problem*, edited by Angel Flores, 267-90. New York: New Directions, 1946.

CHAPTER 9

# The Calamity of the Rightless: Hannah Arendt and Franz Kafka on Monsters and Members

*Isak Winkel Holm*

"You're not from the castle, you're not from the village, you're nothing. Unfortunately, however, you *are* a stranger, a superfluous person getting in everyone's way, a man who is always causing trouble."[1] K., the protagonist of Franz Kafka's last fragment of a novel, *The Castle*, is a nobody. On the first page, he arrives late at night to a snow-covered village and immediately starts looking for a job as a land surveyor. On the last page Kafka wrote before giving up the novel, K. is still struggling to find a job and a place to be.

In two early essays from 1944, Hannah Arendt writes about the question of rights in *The Castle*. In "The Jew as Pariah," Arendt suggests interpreting K. as an image of the "despised pariah Jew, dismissed by contemporary society as a nobody" (*Jew as Pariah* 83).[2] What interests her is K.'s status as a "nonentity" with no "legal title of residence" in the village (*Jew as Pariah* 82, 88). In "Franz Kafka: A Revaluation," Arendt characterizes K. as a human being that insists on demanding "the unalienable rights of man" ("Franz Kafka" 73).[3] She sums up her reading of *The Castle* by stating her own opinion about a true human life: "A true human life cannot be led by people who feel themselves detached from the basic and simple laws of humanity nor by those who elect to live in a vacuum, even if they be led to do so by persecution" (*Jew as Pariah* 89).

This statement is not just about K. or about Jews in general, but also about Arendt herself. After her escape from Germany in 1937, and up to her naturalization as American citizen in 1951, Arendt was living in a legal and political vacuum. A central challenge she sets for herself in her early works is coming to terms with the life of the stateless person. Before her two early essays on Kafka, in her dissertation on the Romantic writer Rahel Varnhagen, Arendt focused on the Jewish Varnhagen's image of herself as unhappily excluded from society.[4] A few years after the Kafka essays, in *The Origins of Totalitarianism* from 1951, Arendt analyzes the plight of the refugee in the famous chapter on the perplexities of the human rights. The collapse of the multiethnic empires of Russia and Austria-Hungary after World War I was followed by massive denaturalizations of unwanted minorities in the interwar years, turning statelessness into a mass phenomenon. According to Arendt, the masses of allegedly superfluous persons—refugees, expatriates, deported aliens, stateless persons and displaced persons—spelled out the need for a basic human right, namely the right to live as a rights-bearing member of society and not, as K., to live in a normative vacuum outside the bounds of law:

> We became aware of the existence of a right to have rights (and this means to live in a framework where one is judged by one's actions and opinions), as well as the right to belong to some kind of organized community, only when millions of people emerged who had lost and could not regain these rights because of the new global political situation. (*Origins* 296-97)[5]

In her two Kafka essays, Arendt is led astray by some of the philological misunderstandings in the early years of the Kafka reception, first of all by believing that Kafka's first fragment of a novel, *The Man Who Disappeared* (published by Max Brod as *America*), was his last. In the following pages, however, I will show that Arendt has a case. What Arendt dubs "the calamity of the rightless" is indeed a central motif not just in *The Castle,* but in Kafka's entire literary production. Kafka was one generation older and died younger than Arendt, so even if he witnessed the rise of anti-Semitism in Bohemia and some of its early political consequences, he did not live to see his family and friends actually lose their citizenship. Whereas Kafka experienced a normative vacuum opening up in the middle of so-called civilized Europe, Arendt saw it as culminating in the death camps. In this sinister historical situation both authors were not so much interested in the question of specific rights as in the more fundamental question of the right to have rights.

In the first half of the essay, I will identify four key features in Arendt's description of the refugee's normative vacuum in order to show the close affinity between Arendt's (part 2) and Kafka's (part 3) analyses of the calamity of the rightless, the latter exemplified in one of Kafka's lesser-known diary entries (part 1). In the second half of the essay, I will focus on what I see as the most important difference between the two authors, namely that Arendt conceptualizes the calamity of the rightless as a question of rights, whereas Kafka perceives it as a question of injustice (part 4). This may seem a mere matter of vocabulary, and to some degree it is so, but it also entails two different approaches to the vacuum (part 5), and, accordingly, two different conceptions of how works of literature can represent rightlessness (part 6).

## Prague Asbestos Works

Kafka was not only a writer and an insurance man, but also a factory owner. Before the war, he and his brother-in-law, Karl Hermann, were managers of Prague Asbestos Works Hermann & Co. The small factory in the Prague suburb Žižkov consisted of fourteen asbestos machines powered by one diesel motor and maintained by approximately twenty female employees. The plan was that Kafka should function as a legal specialist at the asbestos factory in the afternoon, after his working day at the insurance company ended. Soon, however, his commitment to the factory collided with his commitment to literature. In a diary entry from December 1911, Kafka complains about his father's reproaches,

Karl's silence, and his own sense of guilt (*Tagebücher* 327).[6] Nevertheless, Kafka's longest and most detailed account of the factory—a diary entry from February 7, 1912—is not concerned with the reproaches, silences and guilt-inducements of the Kafkas. Neither does it explain the specifics of the factory's technical functioning, a matter that Kafka confessed he did not bother to understand. The diary-entry deals exclusively with the fact that Kafka himself, in his capacity as manager, is dominating his employees as if they were deprived of any basic moral right:

> Yesterday at the factory. The girls in their absolutely unbearably dirty and untailored clothing, their hair unkempt, as though they had just got out of bed, their facial expressions set by the incessant noise of the transmission belts and by the separate machine that is automatic but unpredictable, stopping and starting; they are not human beings—you don't say hello to them, you don't apologize for bumping into them; when you call them over to do something, they do it but go right back to the machine; with a nod of the head you show them what to do; they stand there in petticoats; they are at the mercy of the pettiest power and do not even have enough calm to acknowledge this power and mollify it with glances and bows. When six o'clock comes, however, and they call it out to one another, they untie their kerchiefs from around their necks and hair, dust themselves off with a brush that is passed around the room and is demanded by the ones who are impatient, they pull their skirts over their heads and clean their hands as well as they can; they are women, after all; they can smile in spite of their pallor and bad teeth, shake their stiff bodies; you can no longer bump into them, stare at them, or ignore them; you squeeze against the greasy crates to make room for them, hold your hat in your hand when they say good night, and you do not know how to react when one of them holds our winter coat for us to put on. (*Tagebücher* 373-74)

The text of the diary entry is made up by two contrasting images of the women working at the factory. In the first half of the text we view the employees with Kafka's eyes during work-time. Here, a verdict is passed about the status of the women: "they are not human beings (*sind nicht Menschen*)." In the second half, however, we see the same women after six o'clock from a slightly different angle. From this perspective, after six o'clock, the harsh verdict is reversed: "they are women, after all (*so sind sie schließlich doch Frauen*)."

The juxtaposition of a dehumanizing and a humanizing perspective on the women can be characterized as stereoscopic. Before World War I, the stereoscope was still a popular visual technology consisting of two different images, representing two perspectives of the same object with a minor deviation of the point of view. Kafka was fascinated by the technologies of communication and perception of his day: the typewriter, the phonograph, the telegraph, the poster, the camera, the movie theatre—and the stereoscope, even if it was at this moment rapidly losing ground to the silent movie.[7] On a business trip a year before the diary entry, Kafka experienced a still functioning "Kaiserpanorama" showing images of the cities of northern Italy, and he wrote about it enthusiastically in his diary and on a postcard to his friend Max Brod.[8] In an optical stereoscope like the "Kaiserpanorama," two juxtaposed images combine to give the illusion of 3-D depth. In Kafka's literary stereoscope, the reader combines two images in a similar way, creating not a perception of depth, but a perception of a moral problem. The bulk of the diary entry about the factory is made up by a meticulous list of social rules that govern polite interactions among equal human beings: you ought to say hello to other human beings, to apologize, to squeeze against a crate to make room for them, to hold your hat in your hand; you ought not to nod your head at them when you want them to do something, to bump into them, to stare at them, ignore them, and so on. The moral shock, made visible by the stereoscopic form of the diary entry, is Kafka's experience of *not* complying with these basic moral rules.

In Arendtian language, the women find themselves in a normative vacuum before six o'clock. In Arendt's case, the refugees have lost each and every of their legal and political rights, whereas in Kafka's case, the employees might seem to have merely lost their right to be treated according to the rules of etiquette. Still, the common plight of the refugees and the employees is not the loss of any specific right, be it political, legal or moral. Rather, it is the loss of a basic right to have rights.

## Arendt on Rightlessness

Arendt's description of the plight of the refugee draws on a classical distinction between private and public, between *oikos* and *polis*, *dominium* and *res publica*. In the Greek city-state, the household (*oikos*)—consisting of the master of the house and his wife, children, slaves and animals—was the economical and familial unit taking care of production and reproduction. According to Aristotle, the relations between citizens in political space (*polis*) are regulated by law, whereas the household is a lacuna in the web of legal rights. Since the laws do not reach into the natural sociability of the household, there is no such thing as injustice here, he asserts in *The Nicomachean Ethics*.[9] As Arendt sums up Aristotle in *The Human Condition*, the aim of the household is to master the necessities of sheer life, and those who toil with these necessities are "by definition outside the realm of the law" (*Human Condition* 37, 34).[10] According to Arendt's analysis of statelessness in *The Origins of Totalitarianism*, the modern refugee, like the Greek slave, is caught in the claustrophobic space of *oikos*:

> The human being who has lost his place in a community, his political status in the struggle of his time, and the legal personality which makes his actions and part of his destiny a consistent whole, is left with those qualities which usually can become articulate only in the sphere of private life and must remain unqualified, mere existence in all matters of public concern. (*Origins* 301)

Arendt highlights four features in the calamity of the rightless which all have their historical background in Aristotle's description of the lawless zone of the household. These four features are contingency, inhumanity, inequality, and speechlessness.

*Contingency*. According to Arendt, the refugee is exposed to the unpredictable contingencies of the private sphere. The quotation above continues:

> This mere existence, that is, all that which is mysteriously given us by birth and which includes the shape of our bodies and the talents of our minds, can be adequately dealt with only by the unpredictable hazards of friendship and sympathy, or by the great and incalculable grace of love, which says with Augustine, "*Volo ut sis* (I want you to be)," without being able to give any particular reason for such supreme and unsurpassable affirmation.

As excluded from regulated political space, the refugee is exposed to the genetic contingencies that have determined her talents and her looks, and is exposed as well to the social contingencies that characterize the kind of social relations that are not based on universal rules but, rather, on the individual human being's inconstant feelings for each other. Arendt describes this groundless sociability by referring to the Augustinian concept of grace: the social relations of the rightless refugee can be seen as so many acts of grace directed toward her since they are a kind of recognition for which nobody is able to give "any particular reason." Therefore, in the quote above, the "I want you to be" of groundless love should be understood as the opposite of the "You have a right to be" of justice. According to Arendt, this is precisely what the villagers living in the shadow of the castle try to explain to K.: "they try to persuade K. that he lacks experience and does not know that the whole of life is constituted and dominated by favor and disfavor, by grace and disgrace, both as inexplicable, as hazardous as good and bad luck" ("Franz Kafka" 73).

*Inhumanity*. According to Arendt's analysis of the calamity of the rightless, the refugee is not only excluded from political space but also from humankind. Caught in a normative vacuum, Arendt writes, the refugee has only "the abstract nakedness of being human and nothing but human" (*Origins* 297). But, as it turns out (and as noted already), this kind of naked humanity is in fact inhumanity. The full members of society regard the rightless person as a "savage," a "beast," a "kind of monster," or a "dog with a name" (*Origins* 300, 287). Once more Arendt is in accordance with Aristotle's description of master and slave as two types of human beings who are as ontologically different as man and beast.[11] However, Arendt views the dehumanization of the refugee as being even worse than that of the slave who, in spite of his serfdom and his rightlessness, still belongs—unlike the refugee—to some sort of human community: "Man, it turns out, can lose all so-called Rights of Man without losing his essential quality as man, his human dignity. Only the loss of a polity itself expels him from humanity" (*Origins* 297).

*Inequality*. According to Arendt, the refugee is caught in the web of unequal power relations of the household sphere. This is the third feature of the calamity of the rightless highlighted in *The Origins of Totalitarianism*:

> This whole sphere of the merely given, relegated to private life in civilized society, is a permanent threat to the public sphere, because the public sphere is as consistently based on the law of equality as the private sphere is based on

> the law of universal difference and differentiation. Equality, in contrast to all that is involved in mere existence, is not given to us, but is the result of human organization insofar as it is guided by the principle of justice. (*Origins* 301)

According to Aristotle, the patriarchal power structure of the *oikos*—the *oikonomia*—is by definition unequal.[12] In Arendt's paraphrase of Aristotle, the household head rules "with uncontested, despotic powers," issuing orders to his wife, children, slaves and animals (*Human Condition* 27). Only when he leaves the household and enters the political realm is he able to live among peers. That is to say, among his fellow household masters who have got the time to participate in political debates (*Human Condition* 32).

*Speechlessness*. To be excluded from the public space is, finally, not only to be deprived of human status but also to be deprived of human voice. In *The Origins of Totalitarianism*, Arendt underlines this feature of rightlessness: "The fundamental deprivation of human rights is manifested first and above all in the deprivation of a place in the world which makes opinions significant and actions effective" (*Origins* 296). Without her political significance, her right to share words and deeds on a public stage, the refugee falls back on the dark background of the household, the immobile "realms in which man cannot change and cannot act" (*Origins* 302). The refugee has no access to the sharing of words and deeds on a public stage and is, therefore, unable to participate in government. This feature, too, is prominent in Aristotle's description of the household. The reason why the slave is no citizen is that he is not furnished with a deliberative faculty and cannot participate in giving judgment (*kritiké*).[13] With the exception of the master, the members of the household only have "voice" (*phone*), which is possessed by other animals as well and can be used to indicate pain and pleasure. They do not possesses "speech" (*logos*), which human beings use to set forth what is just and what is unjust.[14] In "The Jew as Pariah," Arendt echoes this Aristotelian formulation in a comment on Kafka's protagonist K., who, even when the castle officials make him "thoroughly indignant and outraged," is not allowed to make "the simplest inquiry into right and wrong" (*Jew as Pariah* 87).

## Kafka on Rightlessness

Kafka does not write "*I* don't say hello" or "*I* don't apologize," even if the description of the Prague Asbestos Works is found in a diary. Instead, he uses the German impersonal pronoun *man*, which could be translated with "you" or "one." In the institutional machinery of the factory, the pronoun *man* pertains to an anonymous role that could be played by anyone, in this case, hesitatingly, by Kafka himself. Thus, Kafka considers himself to analyze the practice of an institution, not the action of an individual. The same goes for the rest of Kafka's literary production, which is basically about institutions: steamships, underwear factories, brothels, railway agencies, courts of justice, hotels, building projects, and so on.[15]

To Kafka, rightlessness is an institutional fact endemic to the private sphere. Before six o'clock, the women of the Prague Asbestos Works find themselves in a sort of Aristotelian household, in both meanings of the word *oikos*: they are within the confines of the Kafka household as a family *and* as an economic unit. Even if the factory is a workplace, it has the appearance of an intimate space in which usual decorum and dress codes are suspended. In this lacuna in the web of etiquette, the women move around half-naked in petticoats. The intimate character of the atmosphere is more explicit in a parallel diary entry two months earlier about Kafka's erotized interaction with "girls" (*Mädchen*). Before the maids have "become accustomed to the laws of the world," you (in the German text once again an anonymous *man*) can dominate them "with gazes, threats, or with the power of love" (*Tagebücher* 277-78). But when first the maids enter the sphere of laws, they are able to act on their own and even to talk. In the diary entry about the factory, the employees exit private space at six o'clock and dress up like what would be considered decent women that you could meet in the street outside the doors of the factory. In this case, the distinction between private and public is not a matter of different social institutions. It is, rather, a distinction between two modes of human interaction cutting through one institution: on the one hand, a natural sociability in which the social relations are made up by affects and relatively unmediated power; on the other, an organized sociability, in which the social relations are regulated by the social rules of politeness and characterized by respect and distance. On his way out, Kafka, in a demonstrative gesture of respect, squeezes against the greasy crates to make room for the women and holds his hat in his hand when they say good night. This mode of interaction is not public in Arendt's ambitious meaning of the word, which refers strictly to a political space of deliberation; it is public, rather, in a more quotidian meaning referring to a social space regulated by common rules and norms.

The border between *oikos* and *polis* cutting through the factory continues through the multitude of fictional institutions in Kafka's literary works. When Gregor Samsa in "The Metamorphosis" (1912) wakes up one morning and finds himself transformed into a monstrous vermin, people around him basically have two modes of interacting with him: either the private mode of his mother and sister, who take care of his particular bodily needs, or the public mode of the manager from his work, who, in a bureaucratic language, cites abstract rules and standards. As the story unfolds, the border between these two modes of human interaction is continually blurred and transgressed. In the end, it is Gregor's sister, neither his manager nor his father, who ends up passing the verdict that Gregor is not a human being.[16] The fact that the once loving and caring sister passes the dehumanizing verdict is another example of Kafka's skepticism toward the bourgeois family. In a remarkable 1921 letter to his own sister, Elli, Kafka advises her and her husband Karl Hermann (the former co-manager of the Prague Asbestos Works) to send off their ten-year-old son Felix to a boarding school. According to Kafka, a family is a dangerous "*Blutkreislauf*," a "blood circulation," which, step by step, deprives the children of their humanity and their personal rights.[17] In literary works as well as in letters and diaries, Kafka depicts the private space of the family as a claustrophobic and lawless zone in which children are not treated as subjects of justice.

In his analysis of the specific rightlessness created by the institution of the Prague Asbestos Works, we once again find the four features of the private sphere highlighted by Arendt.

*Contingency.* Before six o'clock, the employees at the Prague Asbestos Work are exposed to the unpredictable asbestos machines. It seems as if the mentioning of the women's lack of voluntary control leads directly to the verdict about their non-human status: "their facial expressions [are] set by the incessant noise of the transmission belts and by the separate machine that is automatic but unpredictable, stopping and starting; they are not human beings."

Exposure to contingency and unpredictability is a recurrent theme in Kafka's literary production. In "The Metamorphosis," the manager from Gregor's work simply does not accept contingencies. As he explains, Gregor's performance of late has been very unsatisfactory; this is due to the season which is not the best for doing business, the manager concedes, "but a season for not doing any business, there is no such thing, Mr. Samsa, such a thing cannot be tolerated" (*Metamorphosis* 9). According to his public way of seeing things, the manager is unable to take into account the seasonal fluctuations; he simply cites the universal rule governing what can and what cannot be tolerated. On the other hand, the daily care provided by Gregor's mother and sister takes place in the groundless private sphere. In Arendt's terms, the two women do not say "You have a right to be" but "I want you to be." Unable to raise any claim of justice, Gregor is exposed to the inconstant and unpredictable character of the women's emotions: "If she were not going to do it of her own free will, he would rather starve than call it to her attention, although, really, he felt an enormous urge to shoot out from under the couch, throw himself at his sister's feet, and beg her for something good to eat" (*Metamorphosis* 17).

*Inhumanity.* At six o'clock, Kafka's employees change their status from immature "girls" to grown-up "women" and, more radically, from non-humans to humans. In the first image of the textual stereoscope, the employees are deemed to be outside the bounds of humanity: "they are not human beings"; in the second image, "they are women, after all." This change of status could be termed ontological since the important point is not what the women *do* or what they *say* but, rather, who they *are* within the social order of the factory. This ontological change is reflected in a grammatical change, the "girls" are grammatical objects in the first image, whereas the "women" suddenly develop into active grammatical subjects in the second.

Just like the border between private and public, the border between non-human and human cuts through Kafka's entire literary production. In "The Metamorphosis," the flat of the Samsa family is divided into a human part, in which his family members and their lodgers dwell, and Gregor Samsa's room, which is transformed into some kind of animal dungeon.

*Inequality.* Before six o'clock, the Prague Asbestos Works is a space of hierarchy and domination. Unprotected by the rules of politeness, the half-naked women are "at the mercy of the pettiest power." Which is, of course, Kafka himself, even if he was undoubtedly not a threatening boss. Under these institutional conditions, however, even a meek person like Kafka can exercise uncontested despotic power and issue orders by merely nodding his head. After six o'clock, the social space of the factory is suddenly equalized and—in the last phrase of the diary entry—the hierarchies are even turned upside-down. According to the rules of politeness, a man would have been expected to hold the coat for a woman to put on, but here the gesture of politeness is reversed when one of the women politely holds Kafka's winter coat for him. The sudden inversion of hierarchal power constellations causes a feeling of bewilderment in Kafka when he realizes that he is no longer the master: "you do not know how to react."

The relationship between Gregor Samsa, creeping around on the floor, and the infuriated Mr. Samsa, approaching in his big, threatening boots, could be mentioned as one among innumerable examples of unequal power constellations in Kafka's literary production. Seen from an Arendtian perspective, however, the problem in these scenes is not the inequality in itself but, rather, the normative vacuum which makes even the pettiest imbalance in power relations impossible to oppose and contest.

*Speechlessness*. By dominating the employees' bodies, the unpredictable asbestos machines make them unable to communicate. Hence, before six o'clock, the women's facial expressions are "set" (*festgehalten*), and they do not "have enough calm to acknowledge this power and mollify it with glances and bows." In an overtly literal translation of the German sentence, the women do not have enough "calm reason" (*ruhige[s] Verstand*) to make the power bow toward them with their bowing. To "mollify" the power is in German "*geneigt zu machen*," and "*neigen*" etymologically means to bow, to nod one's head, as the merciful prince nods toward an underling. Such a choreography of mutual bowing would have been a feudal interaction and not a communication among partners on an equal footing—but at least it would have entailed some kind of communication. In the normative vacuum before six o'clock, the women fall out of communication altogether into naked domination. In Aristotelian terms, they do not have any deliberative faculty. At six o'clock, however, the women suddenly turn into discursive agents who are able to smile, to express impatience, to demand the brush, to say good night, and so on.

This border between speechlessness and speech is another recurring figure in Kafka's literary works. Power, in Kafka, is not just exercised through explicit verdicts and arguments, but also through the implicit network of gestures and bodily positions that determine who are entitled to participate in the communication. Gregor Samsa himself believes that he is going to participate in the Samsa family's deliberations on how to organize life in the flat: "In order to make his voice as clear as possible for the crucial discussions that were approaching he cleared his throat a little—taking pains, of course, to do so in a very muffled manner, since this noise, too, might sound different from human coughing" (*Metamorphosis* 11). But of course no one outside the door to Gregor's room understands his voice: "That was the voice of an animal," the manager asserts. In Aristotelian terms, the muffled sounds coming from behind the door can be described as animal *voice* and not as human *speech*.

To sum up, Arendt and Kafka address the same calamity of the rightless that is constituted by the four sub-calamities of the private sphere: contingency, inhumanity, inequality and speechlessness. To be sure, vacuums come in different sizes. In the interwar years, millions of refugees found themselves in a normative vacuum of global dimensions, whereas in the Prague Asbestos Works, the limbo is inhabited by a single manager and less than twenty employees. Moreover, the factory's localized "black hole" in the network of rights does not suspend the whole catalogue of legal and political rights, just the subset of rights consisting in the informal norms of decorum. Seen from another perspective, however, Kafka analyzes a normative vacuum of a wider scope. The calamity of the rightless that Arendt writes about emerged in a specific historical situation. No doubt she is right when she claims that the theme of rightlessness in Kafka's literary works reflects his insecure historical position as a German-speaking Jew squeezed between ethnic Czechs and ethnic Germans in the dissolving Austro-Hungarian empire. But still, rightlessness is not just a problem on the level of citizenship and nationality. In Kafka's letter to Elli about her son Felix, he describes a similar vacuum in the midst of a bourgeois family. And in his diary entry about the factory, the relation between ethnicity and injustice is even turned upside down, so that the two Jewish brothers-in-law, Karl and Franz, are playing the role of rights-bearing managers while the (presumably) ethnic Czechs take up the position of the rightless. As the next section will argue, the important difference between Arendt and Kafka—questions of size and substance of normative vacuums aside—lies in the fact that the former conceives the calamity of the rightless as a question of rights whereas the latter tends to perceive it as a question of injustice.

## Rights or Injustice?

According to Arendt, the right to have rights has little to do with the traditional language of justice:

> The calamity of the rightless is not that they are deprived of life, liberty, and the pursuit of happiness, or of equality before the law and freedom of opinion—formulas which were designed to solve problems *within* given communities—but that they no longer belong to any community whatsoever. Their plight is not that they are not equal before the law, but that no law exists for them; not that they are oppressed but that nobody wants even to oppress them. . . . Something much more fundamental than freedom or justice, which are the rights of citizens, is at stake when belonging to the community into which one is born is no longer a matter of course and not belonging no longer a matter of choice. (*Origins* 295-96)

In Arendt's vocabulary, justice is solely concerned with problems that emerge "*within* given communities." Since the right to have rights is not a right *of* members but a right *to* membership, we have to do with "something much more fundamental than justice." As Arendt writes in an earlier essay on human rights, this right is "the one right without which no other can materialize" ("Rights of Man" 37).[18] When Arendt describes this "something much more fundamental than justice," however, it often sounds as if it was, in fact, a kind of justice. Rahel Varnhagen feels "bitterness" and a "sense of being wronged" by the non-Jewish society (*Rahel Varnhagen* 100). Kafka's heroes are victims of "the greatest injury" when society reduces them to rightless nobodies (*Jew as Pariah* 82). They live in "the world of necessity and injustice and lying" ("Franz Kafka" 71). And the stateless refugees, it is stated in *The Origins of Totalitarianism*, are exposed to arbitrary and unchecked police rule against which there are no lawyers and no appeals: "Privileges in some cases, injustices in most, blessings and doom are meted out to them according to accident and without any relation whatsoever to what they do, did, or may do" (*Origins* 296). But still, in terms of vocabulary, Arendt restricts the concept of justice to disputes between rights-bearing citizens within a bounded polity.

Kafka, on the other hand, tends to analyze the calamity of the rightless as a question of injustice, even if he does not use the concept explicitly in the diary entry about the Prague Asbestos Works. The writing of the diary entry is triggered by Kafka's feeling of shame that he is responsible for—and even enjoying the economical benefits of—an institutional arrangement in which human beings are treated as if they were inhuman. This moral shock, or, in the terms of Judith Shklar, this sense of injustice,[19] is called by name in Kafka's famous letter to his father seven years later, when the asbestos factory had long been disposed of. As a young man, Kafka was ashamed of his father's failure to comply with "normal respectful behavior" in the fancy goods shop that he owned in downtown Prague. In his desire to dominate, Hermann Kafka treated his so-called "paid enemies" with "cries, complaints and storms." "Whatever I could do in my insignificance—even if I licked the soles of their shoes," Kafka writes, "it could not compensate for what you, the master, did to them from above."[20] To Kafka, this is a textbook example of injustice: "There I received the great lesson, that you could be unjust." In the two Kafka companies, regardless of the considerable difference between asbestos and underwear, patriarchal domination generates injustice. This imbalance needs to be compensated, Kafka writes in the letter to his father, the German word "*ausgleichen*" connecting the moral shock of the fancy goods shop with the classical image of the balance of justice.

However, the kind of injustice that Kafka analyzes has little to do with Arendt's narrow concept of justice. What is being weighed on the scales of justice in the two Kafka companies is not material goods but, rather, as Kafka wrote in the letter to his father, the immaterial good of "normal respectful behavior." Approaching the Prague Asbestos Works with the scales of justice, one could indeed have chosen other things to put in its scales. For instance, the economical good represented by the factory's salaries and work hours. After all, this is the historical period in which the workers' unions and the social democratic party were formed in Austria-Hungary. Alternatively, one could have chosen to weigh the good of physical health and security. Seen with contemporary eyes, the most striking injustice of the factory is undoubtedly the fact that the women are protected against the carcinogenic asbestos only by a handkerchief. They are endangering their health for the economic security of the Kafka family. Kafka was a lawyer at a workers' insurance company, and in these years, before World War I, he went on several business trips to the Bohemian province in order to protect workers against the dangers of early industrialization (these trips included the above-mentioned trip to Friedland where he experienced the Kaiserpanorama). In fact, it was his job to rectify precisely this kind of injustice. It is remarkable, however, that Kafka—in his diary account—is uninterested in the rules governing the distribution of material goods such as salary and security. He focuses exclusively on the rules of politeness and, first of all, on the peculiar social mechanism that makes it possible to switch these rules on and off.

According to contemporary theories of justice, the mechanism that is able to switch social rules on and off is an aspect of justice. In *Scales of Justice* (2008), Nancy Fraser gives one of the clearest and most systematic accounts of the contemporary discussion of these issues by distinguishing between two levels of justice. On the first level, we find the distribution of social goods (as well as the procedural principles of this distribution); on the second, we find the taken-for-granted assumptions about justice, i.e. the shared background understandings of *what* can be a matter of justice, *how* justice should be done, *who* can raise claims of justice, and so on. In Fraser's terms, the last of these questions, the basic assumptions about who counts as a legal person, is a question of "misframing": "At issue here is the scope of justice, the frame within which it applies: who counts as a subject of justice in a given matter? Whose interests and needs deserve consideration? Who belongs to the circle of those entitled to equal concern?"[21] At this second level, the issue is not *how* things are distributed but *who* belongs to the circle of those who are relevant for this distribution at all. In the words of Michael Walzer, who opened up the contemporary discussion of the scope of justice in his seminal *Spheres of Justice* (1983), justice, on this level, is not about the distribution of social goods among the members of a society but about the distribution of membership itself.[22] Fraser explicitly refers to Arendt as the thinker who has brought to light the question of the rights of the "politically dead" non-person.[23] Hence, whereas Arendt views the right to have rights as "something more fundamental than justice," contemporary theories of justice tend to conceptualize this "something" as a fundamental aspect of justice, not as something more fundamental than justice.

## Legislation or Imagination?

What is going on in the Prague Asbestos Works, then, is a clear case of second-level injustice. The question of justice raised by Kafka's diary entry is not: "What is just?" Rather, it is the question: "Who is the subject of justice?" This is the way Kafka raises the issue of justice, from the early diary entry about the Prague Asbestos Works through to K.'s struggle for membership in *The Castle* ten years later. To be sure, several of Kafka's fictional characters claim a fair distribution of material goods. Gregor Samsa, for instance, lies in his room making "plans for getting into the pantry to take what was coming to him" (*Metamorphosis* 33). However, these claims of justice most often have a petty and comic appearance. At this stage of the story, Gregor is not even hungry anymore, the vital question being no longer the *substance* of justice, but, exclusively, the *scope* of justice. In Arendtian terms, Gregor's claim of justice is not a vindication of his right to the food but, rather, a vindication of his basic right to have rights.

But even if Arendt and Kafka both analyze the right to have rights, their approaches—and not just their vocabularies—differ. Arendt's theoretical framework is made up by the debate about human rights. In *The Origin of Totalitarianism*, the chapter on human rights was provoked by the Universal Declaration of Human Rights, adopted by the United Nations in 1948, which affirmed the inborn and inalienable rights protecting the human being outside the legal framework of the nation state. According to Arendt, the breakdown of the nation state in the inter-war years spelled out that there are no inborn and inalienable rights of man guaranteed by Nature or by God; there are only the rights of a citizen within the confines of an organized political space. The masses of stateless refugees made clear that "the world found nothing sacred in the abstract nakedness of being human" ("Rights of Man" 31). However, Arendt's ambition can hardly be characterized as a mere deconstruction of human rights. On the contrary, she suggests an alternative construction of the one basic human right that would be robust enough to protect against the calamity of the rightless. In the introduction to *The Origin of Totalitarianism*, Arendt writes that—after anti-Semitism, imperialism and totalitarianism—human dignity "needs a new guarantee which can be found only in a new political principle, in a new law on earth, whose validity this time must comprehend the whole of humanity" (*Origins* xi). This is not the place to delve into the discussion among Arendtians about how to understand a right that is neither guaranteed by the nation state nor by some metaphysical notion of nature, but, instead, by the concept of humanity as a whole.[24] Arendt's formulations are, at best, a little vague in this regard. I will restrict myself to underlining the fact that Arendt describes the calamity of the rightless in the language of rights. To be sure, the right to have rights is a second-order right underlying specific juridical rights—but it still is a kind of right, a quasi-juridical claim guaranteed by "a new law on earth."

In Kafka's analysis, on the other hand, rightlessness is first of all a question of social appearance. In the diary entry, the manager referred to by the impersonal pronoun *man* is characterized not just by the way he behaves toward the women, but also by the way he perceives them. If you look at the women before six o'clock, they will appear to you as though they were mere girls and "as though they had just got out of bed." In Fraser's terms, the women are "misframed," and this misframing takes the form of a metaphorical framing, a series of figural *as-ifs* that make the women appear as non-humans, as minors, as faceless, as demented, as living dead, and as somebody one knows intimately. In this case, the social mechanism, which is able to turn on and off membership in the human community, is, first of all, a system of shared metaphors through which human beings become visible in social space. In the vocabulary of contemporary political philosophy, the manager's perspective on his employees is governed by the factory's social imaginary.[25] The factory is furnished with a pre-conceptual map of social life, a taken-for-granted understanding of human interaction giving the manager a sense of who is entitled to polite treatment and who is not. This focus on imagination rather than on legislation is crucial not just to the diary entry, but to Kafka's analysis of social institutions in his entire literary production. In Kafka, the way human beings are perceived within the confines of an institution is governed by the institution's endemic version of a social imaginary. Most often the framing is a network of metaphors that dress up human beings as Asians, as children, as sexual perverts, as animals, and so on. Kafka demonstrates how human beings' perspectives on one another are not innocent but institutional, entailing an implicit non-verbalized judgment that draws a line between those who are subjects of justice and those who are not. Before the manager of the Prague Asbestos Works has even thought about his employees' entitlement to decent treatment, he perceives their clothing as not just dirty, but "unbearably" dirty.

By approaching the calamity of the rightless as a question of injustice rather than a question of rights, then, Kafka shifts the focus from legislation to imagination. As we have seen, both authors can be said to write about second-level injustice. But to Kafka, this kind of injustice is, first of all, a matter of social images and rhetorical figures governing the public appearance of human beings and, consequently, the distribution of the right to have rights. On the one hand, Arendt, as a philosopher, focuses on the legal or quasi-legal norms that should entitle every subject, even a stateless refugee, to appear in political space; on the other hand Kafka, as a literary writer, analyzes the norms of imagination that determine whether a human being appears to her fellow human beings as a subject at all. In other words, Arendt, by approaching rightlessness as a question of subjective rights, evades the question of the subject itself to whom this basic right is to be attributed. The individual is simply there, like a grown-up refugee who gets off a train on a foreign railway station; the issue is just whether this individual has or has not a right to have rights.[26] In Kafka's analysis of rightlessness, the individual is not a solid fact but, rather, something which is constituted by the imaginary logic of an institution.

## The Literary Representation of Rightlessness

In the essay "The Jew as Pariah," Arendt shows how not only Kafka, but also Heinrich Heine, Bernard Lazare and even Charlie Chaplin were able to "evolve the concept of the pariah as a human type" (*Jew as Pariah* 68). Heine's literary works, for instance, offer a "portrayal" of himself as a pariah poet excluded from formal society, and Kafka, in the same vein, is just "the case of the last and most recent typification of the pariah" (*Jew as Pariah* 71, 82). The notion of "the typical" was conceived as a sociological concept by Max Weber[27] and developed into a tool of literary analysis by Georg Lukács.[28] According to

Lukács' theory of realism, the multitude of bankers, journalists, poets and countesses that inhabit Balzac's fictional Paris are "typical" insofar as they summarize essential features of a given historical situation—elegantly combined with the oddities and peculiarities of individual human beings. By reading Kafka's literary works as a representation of the sociological type of the pariah, Arendt follows a dominating trend in early Kafka research. The well-known idea of the "Kafkaesque," which took shape in these early years of Kafka research, is itself a typological concept describing a specific kind of psychological symptoms in a specific kind of social setting.

Kafka himself was very explicit about his utter dislike for the word "type" (*Tagebücher* 982). And indeed, the sociological concept of the type is useless in the interpretation of "The Metamorphosis" as well as the diary entry on the factory. Human-sized bugs were not typical in Prague bourgeois families at the beginning of the twentieth century. Nor can the manager and the employees of the Prague Asbestos Works be described as types, if by a type we understand a kind of generic human being with a relatively permanent position in the social order. Rather, they take up roles: they fill out a temporary slot in the institutional logic of the factory, and after six o'clock they are able to leave this place and enter into new social constellations. The employees transform into women with dresses and hats; the manager transforms into an author. If the concept of the type has any relevance at all in this context, it is as perceptual type, not as sociological type. The way Kafka the manager behaves toward his employees, and the way he perceives them as half-naked and half-human minors, are governed by the kind of types that, today, we would call stereotypes: a set of fixed cognitive schemes determining the social imagination of fellow human beings.

Literary form is indispensable in the analysis of this type of types. Arendt circumvents the question of literary form in her essays on Kafka, and, for that matter, in her comments on Varnhagen, Heine, Dostoyevsky and Melville. To her, literary form seems to be a transparent medium through which we gain access to sociological types. By contrast, literary form is an indispensable device in Kafka's analysis of social institutions. In the case of the diary entry, literary form is not transparent but stereoscopic. As we have seen, the two juxtaposed representations of the women are seen with Kafka's eyes, but from two slightly different perspectives. Accordingly, the literary form of the diary-text prompts the reader's reflective movement back and forth between these perspectives, comparing the dehumanizing behavior represented in the first half of the text with the respectful behavior depicted in the second. By contrasting an *is* with an *ought*, reality with normativity, the reader's reflective movement creates an awareness of a second-level injustice. It is, in fact, one of the few formal devices with which second-level injustice can be represented in literature. The underlying grammar of justice, in this case the taken-for-granted assumptions about the *who* of justice, cannot be narrated in the same way as the dramatic first level struggles about the fair distribution of social goods. Kafka's stereoscopic form is a literary device that is able to make invisible second-level injustices visible. He does not approach the calamity of the rightless by offering a representation of a typical human being suffering from rightlessness or fighting for her right to have rights. Instead, he frames injustice in stereoscopic texts so that the formal tension between the two perspectives makes palpable the automatized misframings of the social imaginary. My contention is that literary form in Kafka is not just a rhetorical ornament but, rather, a cognitive instrument, a visual prosthesis which is able to expose the inherent injustices in the way social life is perceived.

In Arendtian terms, the reader's reflective movement prompted by the stereoscopic literary form can be characterized as a kind of political thought. In her essay "Truth and Politics," Arendt famously writes:

> Political thought is representative. I form an opinion by considering a given issue from different viewpoints, by making present to my mind the standpoints of those who are absent; that is, I present them. This process of representation does not blindly adopt the actual views of those who stand somewhere else and hence look upon the world from a different perspective; this is a question neither of empathy . . . nor of counting noses and joining a majority, but of being and thinking in my own identity where actually I am not.[29]

The diary entry about the Prague Asbestos Works is representative in Arendt's specific meaning of the word "representation." By considering a given issue—the social status of the women—from different viewpoints, the stereoscopic form offers a representation of these viewpoints and their inherent injustices. In Kafka's case, however, the reflective movement back and forth between *is* and *ought* takes place not in the abstract medium of philosophical concepts or political opinions but, rather, in the concrete medium of literary images. Hence, his literary works are instruments of political thought rather than documents of political injustice: they are cognitive tools opening up a free space in which different perspectives on the social world can be perceived and discussed.

In contemporary Kafka research, Kafka's conception of justice tends to be interpreted as a critique of justice. Today, the majority of Kafka researchers have a vision of justice as a mere cover-up for discipline and domination. Even in the secondary works that confront the clichés of the "Kafkaesque"—the solitary neurotic individual crushed by absurd and unjust institutional powers—justice and law are imagined as cold and dead abstractions destroying any human attempt at freedom.[30] Hannah Arendt challenges this trend of contemporary Kafka research by turning its conception of justice on its head. To Arendt, rights are not just a cover-up for unequal power constellations but, first and foremost, a protection against bare murder (cf. *Jew as Pariah* 90). In this essay, I have been arguing that Arendt is basically right. Experiencing the early rise of twentieth-century anti-Semitism, Kafka conceived of justice not just as a means of oppression but also as a means of protection. To be sure, the specific practices of justice represented in his literary works can be grotesquely unjust and ridiculous. But no less problematic is the total absence of justice experienced by the rightless persons inhabiting the many "black holes" of Kafka's inhomogeneous normative universe. His ambivalent conception of justice can be grasped by distinguishing between first- and second-level justice. Whereas Kafka tends to depict the negotiations of first-level justice (negotiations of how to allocate social goods or mete out punishment) as farcical mock trials, he keeps his focus, throughout his entire literary production, on the second-level question of who counts as a subject of justice and who does not. I have suggested that we interpret Kafka's literary works as instruments of political thought that prompt an exploration of second-level injustice. Of course, such a cognitive tool cannot function without an ideal of justice, be it implicit or explicit. Injustices do not cry to heaven if there is not, at least, a mute idea of justice. The four features of the calamity of the rightless—the contingency, inhumanity, inequality, and speechlessness of the private sphere—give us, as it were, a photo negative of Kafka's implicit conception of justice. It seems to be a kind of democratic justice with four basic conceptual coordinates: predictability, dignity, equality and political participation.

## Notes

1. Franz Kafka, *The Castle*, trans. Anthea Bell (Oxford: Oxford University Press, 2009), 46.

2. Hannah Arendt, *The Jew as Pariah: Jewish Identity and Politics in the Modern Age*, ed. Ron H. Feldman (New York: Grove Press, 1978), 83.

3. Hannah Arendt, "Franz Kafka: A Revaluation," in *Essays in Understanding, 1930-1954*, ed. Jerome Kohn (New York & London: Harcourt, Brace & Co. 1994), 73.

4. Hannah Arendt, *Rahel Varnhagen: The Life of a Jewess*, trans. Richard and Clara Winston, ed. Liliane Weissberg (Baltimore, MD, and London: The Johns Hopkins University Press, 1997), 100.

5. Hannah Arendt, *The Origins of Totalitarianism* (New York: Harcourt Brace, 1979), 296-97.

6. Franz Kafka, *Tagebücher*, eds. Hans-Gerd Koch, Michael Müller, and Malcolm Pasley (Frankfurt a.M.: Fischer, 1990), 327; diary entry from November 28, 1911.

7. For an account of Kafka's fascination with visual technology in general and the "Kaiserpanorama" in particular, see Carolin Duttlinger, *Kafka and Photography* (Oxford: Oxford University Press, 2007), 51.

8. See the entries from Kafka's travel to Friedland in January 1911, *Tagebücher* 936-37, and his letters home, *Briefe 1900–1912*, ed. Hans-Gerd Koch (Frankfurt a.M.: Fischer, 1999), 132.

9. Aristotle, *Nicomachean Ethics*, 1134b10.

10. Hannah Arendt, *The Human Condition*, second edition (Chicago, IL: University of Chicago Press, 1998), 37, 34.

11. Aristotle, *Politics*, 1254b16.

12. Aristotle, *Politics*, 1278b37.

13. Aristotle, *Politics*, 1259b32, 1275a22.

14. Aristotle, *Politics*, 1253a7.

15. For a stimulating discussion of an "institutional" approach to Kafka, see Rüdiger Campe, "Kafkas Institutionenroman. Der Proceß, Das Schloß," in *Gesetz. Ironie*, ed. Rüdiger Campe and Michael Niehaus (Heidelberg: Synchron, 2004), 197-208; and "Kafkas Fürsprache," in *Kafkas Institutionen*, ed. Arne Höcker and Oliver Simons (Bielefeld: Transcript, 2007), 189-212.

16. Franz Kafka, *The Metamorphosis*, ed. and trans. Stanley Corngold (New York: Norton, 1996), 38.

17. Franz Kafka, *Briefe 1902-1924*, ed. Max Brod (New York: Schocken, 1958), 339-47.

18. Hannah Arendt, "'The Rights of Man': What Are They?," *Modern Review* 3:1 (1949): 37.

19. Cf. Judith Shklar, *The Faces of Injustice* (New Haven, CT: Yale University Press, 1990).

20. Franz Kafka, *Letter to my Father*, trans. Howard Colyer (Raleigh, NC: Lulu, 2008), 34-35 (translation modified).

21. Nancy Fraser, "Abnormal Justice," in *Justice, Governance, Cosmopolitanism, and the Politics of Difference*, eds. Kwame Anthony Appiah, Seyla Benhabib, Iris Marion Young and Nancy Fraser (Berlin: Humboldt-Universität, 2007), 123.

22. Michael Walzer, *Spheres of Justice: A Defense of Pluralism and Equality* (New York: Basic Books, 1983), 31.

23. Nancy Fraser, *Scales of Justice: Reimagining Political Space in a Globalizing World* (Cambridge: Polity Press, 2008), 19.

24. See for instance Peg Birmingham, *Hannah Arendt and Human Rights: the Predicament of Common Responsibility* (Bloomington, IN: Indiana University Press, 2006).

25. Here I use a concept recently suggested by Charles Taylor and Arjun Appadurai: see Charles Taylor, *Modern Social Imaginaries* (Durham, NC: Duke University Press, 2004), and Arjun Appadurai, *Modernity at Large: Cultural Dimensions of Globalization* (Minneapolis, MN: University of Minnesota Press, 1996). Parallel concepts are a society's "imaginary institution," its "distribution of the sensible," or its "framing" of public appearance: see Cornelius Castoriadis, *The Imaginary Institution of Society*, trans. Kathleen Blamey (Cambridge: Polity, 1987); Jacques Rancière, *Disagreement: Politics and Philosophy*, trans. Julie Rose (Minneapolis, MN: University of Minnesota Press, 1999); and Judith Butler, *Frames of War: When is Life Grievable?* (London: Verso, 2009).

26. This theme has been developed by Christoph Menke, "The 'Aporias of Human Rights' and the 'One Human Right': Regarding the Coherence of Hannah Arendt's Argument," *Social Research* 74.3 (2007): 739-62.

27. Max Weber, *The Methodology of the Social Sciences*, trans. and ed. Edward A. Shils and Henry A. Finch (New York: Free Press, 1997), 88.

28. Georg Lukács, "Verlorene Illusionen," in *Balzac und der französische Realismus*, *Werke*, vol. 6 (Neuwied: Luchterhand, 1965), 478ff.

29. Hannah Arendt, "Truth and Politics," in *Between Past and Future* (New York: Penguin, 1968), 241.

30. See for instance, Ulf Abraham, *Der verhörte Held: Verhöre, Urteile und die Rede von Recht und Schuld im Werk Franz Kafkas* (München: W. Fink, 1985); Hans Hiebel, *Franz Kafka: Form und Bedeutung* (Würzburg: Königshausen & Neumann, 1999); and, most recently, Susanne Kaul, "Eingriffe im Namen der Gerechtigkeit. Zu Kafkas Erzählung 'In der Strafkolonie,'" in *WestEnd. Neue Zeitschrift für Sozialforschung* 2/2009: 172-78.

## Works Cited

Abraham, Ulf. *Der verhörte Held: Verhöre, Urteile und die Rede von Recht und Schuld im Werk Franz Kafkas*. München: W. Fink, 1985.

Appadurai, Arjun. *Modernity at Large: Cultural Dimensions of Globalization*. Minneapolis, MN: University of Minnesota Press, 1996.

Arendt, Hannah. "Franz Kafka: A Revaluation." In Hannah Arendt, *Essays in Understanding, 1930-1954*, edited by Jerome Kohn, 69-80. New York & London: Harcourt, Brace & Co 1994.

———. *The Human Condition*. Second edition. Chicago, IL: University of Chicago Press, 1998.

———. *The Jew as Pariah: Jewish Identity and Politics in the Modern Age*. Edited by Ron H. Feldman. New York: Grove Press, 1978.

———. *The Origins of Totalitarianism*. New York: Harcourt Brace, 1979.

———. *Rahel Varnhagen: The Life of a Jewess*. Translated by Richard and Clara Winston, edited by Liliane Weissberg. Baltimore, MD, and London: The Johns Hopkins University Press, 1997.

———. "'The Rights of Man': What Are They?" *Modern Review* 3:1 (1949): 24-37.

———. "Truth and Politics." In Hannah Arendt, *Between Past and Future*, 227-64. New York: Penguin, 1968.

Birmingham, Peg. *Hannah Arendt and Human Rights: the Predicament of Common Responsibility*. Bloomington, IN: Indiana University Press, 2006.

Butler, Judith. *Frames of War: When is Life Grievable?* London: Verso, 2009.

Campe, Rüdiger. "Kafkas Fürsprache." In *Kafkas Institutionen*, edited by Arne Höcker and Oliver Simons, 189-212. Bielefeld: Transcript, 2007.

———. "Kafkas Institutionenroman. Der Proceß, Das Schloß." In *Gesetz. Ironie*, edited by Rüdiger Campe and Michael Niehaus, 197-208. Heidelberg: Synchron, 2004.

Castoriadis, Cornelius. *The Imaginary Institution of Society*. Translated by Kathleen Blamey. Cambridge: Polity, 1987.

Duttlinger, Carolin. *Kafka and Photography*. Oxford: Oxford University Press, 2007.

Fraser, Nancy. "Abnormal Justice." In *Justice, Governance, Cosmopolitanism, and the Politics of Difference*, edited by Kwame Anthony Appiah, Seyla Benhabib, Iris Marion Young and Nancy Fraser, 117-46. Berlin: Humboldt-Universität, 2007.

———. *Scales of Justice: Reimagining Political Space in a Globalizing World*. Cambridge: Polity Press, 2008.

Hiebel, Hans. *Franz Kafka: Form und Bedeutung*. Würzburg: Königshausen & Neumann, 1999.

Kafka, Franz. *Briefe 1900–1912*. Edited by Hans-Gerd Koch. Frankfurt a.M.: Fischer, 1999.

———. *Briefe 1902-1924*. Edited by Max Brod. New York: Schocken, 1958.

———. *The Castle*. Translated by Anthea Bell. Oxford: Oxford University Press, 2009.

———. *Letter to my Father*. translated by Howard Colyer. Raleigh, NC: Lulu, 2008.

———. *The Metamorphosis*. Edited and translated by Stanley Corngold. New York: Norton, 1996.

———. *Tagebücher*. Edited by Hans-Gerd Koch, Michael Müller, and Malcolm Pasley. Frankfurt a.M.: Fischer, 1990.

Kaul, Susanne. "Eingriffe im Namen der Gerechtigkeit. Zu Kafkas Erzählung 'In der Strafkolonie.'" *WestEnd. Neue Zeitschrift für Sozialforschung* 2/2009: 172-78.

Lukács, Georg. "Verlorene Illusionen." In Georg Lukács, *Balzac und der französische Realismus*, *Werke*, vol. 6, 474-89. Neuwied: Luchterhand, 1965.

Menke, Christoph. "The 'Aporias of Human Rights' and the 'One Human Right': Regarding the Coherence of Hannah Arendt's Argument." *Social Research* 74.3 (2007): 739-62.

Rancière, Jacques. *Disagreement: Politics and Philosophy*. Translated by Julie Rose. Minneapolis, MN: University of Minnesota Press, 1999.

Shklar, Judith. *The Faces of Injustice*. New Haven, CT: Yale University Press, 1990.
Taylor, Charles. *Modern Social Imaginaries*. Durham, NC: Duke University Press, 2004.
Walzer, Michael. *Spheres of Justice: A Defense of Pluralism and Equality*. New York: Basic Books, 1983.
Weber, Max. *The Methodology of the Social Sciences*. Translated and edited by Edward A. Shils and Henry A. Finch. New York: Free Press, 1997.

CHAPTER 10

# Knowing Life Before the Law: Kafka, Kelsen, Derrida

*Paul Alberts*

## 1.

Kafka interpretation is an industry without foreseeable limits: It has a trajectory of its own—proliferating, propagating in relation to originary texts, each of which anchor further dissemination of critical discourse. Different explanations for this prodigious continuation might be offered, but a common theme in the reception of Kafka has always been the capacity of his texts to instigate, in a positive, intriguing way, doubts and questions in the minds of readers about the proper sense of the texts, or the best way to constitute viable interpretations. Kafka can then be understood as at least implicitly thematizing questions of knowledge—since some part of his art was to tease out readers' desires to know, and produce affects of puzzlement and uncertainty. However, Kafka's literary texts do not suggest a doctrine or a program of delimiting knowledge from ignorance based on such affects. His experiments of writing destabilize different aspects of diegesis, narrative, character, and scene, and many appear to be fragmentary exercises testing readers' expectations for coherency. The very concept of an orderly disclosure of rules or laws of knowledge must be held in sharp contrast to the renowned scenes of Kafkaesque distortion that have made his form of literary innovation canonical in modern literature.

But Kafka was very concerned with a certain epistemological perspective. This essay pursues Kafka's textual treatment of the more specific question of knowing law, since it can be shown that this is at the heart of the knot of writing and life-experience that bound his texts together. Kafka both represented the desire to understand what law is, but wanted to show that knowing law would not of itself provide justice, nor satisfy the perplexities of living together with others, before the law. Such desire for explication, for a rigorous systematization of law, for Kafka, will fail, just as a manic desire can only repeat without end or closure. This thesis begins with a contextualization of Kafka's workplace writings, since his position as a legal official can be weighed now as more significant than some critics had supposed.[1] This then leads to a consideration of Kafka's discursive position at a time of social transformation, and how we can approach his literary writings as concordant with his work demands. Together, these lead to providing an explanatory context for his most developed treatment of law in *The Trial*, and the concentrated "legend" of "Before the Law." In concluding with an analysis of how these renowned texts of Kafka were in cultural discussion with very powerful and particular legal movements of his day, the essay aims to reveal a Kafka whose literary flights were also inextricably bound to a politics of knowledge.

## 2.

As Stanley Corngold argues in an introductory essay to *The Office Writings*, Kafka—although complaining of the conflict between legal work and literary aspirations—undoubtedly lived out his writerly being astride the two territories, inflecting his textual productions with the valences of each; hence, reading the mostly mundane documents written in office hours recalls and echoes some of the structure and tones of *The Trial* or *The Castle*—the bureaucratese of an administrator also capable of fine literary subtlety.[2] Correspondingly, the literary texts can be read more acutely as reflecting Kafka's varied experiences at the Prague Worker's Accident Insurance Institute, sometimes with surprising pathos: for example, the sketched ending of *The Trial*, Josef K.'s execution on a moonlit block of stone is eerily re-contextualized by Kafka's institute report on "Accident Prevention in Quarries" (1914) complete with commissioned photos of stark quarry landscapes.[3] Imagining the photographs supplying Kafka with rich visual material, the reader cannot help but engage in an-almost filmic cross-reference between the photographs Kafka must have pored over during the day, and the novel's scene of Josef K.'s denouement composed around the same time. The sense of dialogical interplay between legal and literary construction, which critical readers of Kafka have already recognized, is strongly reinforced in the many intersections of workplace material with literary texts.

Perhaps more important, *The Office Writings* reveal the impressive range of official responsibilities and personal dexterity required of Kafka in performing his legal duties. Although we know he seriously considered resigning over quite a long period, dreaming of a literary career, those same years also represent much committed work on his part.[4] No minor clerk, Kafka was responsible for implementing major reforms from his Prague bureau, as imperial structures and old European work patterns steadily gave way to the forces of modern management and industrialization.[5] The Prague Worker's Accident Insurance Institute was a relatively new semi-autonomous bureaucracy overseeing the new laws of accident insurance. It had grown tremendously quickly and was disliked by many for its new role in collecting insurance premiums from employers. Kafka had to expand its operations, collating new statistics on accidents and investigating particular cases. He oversaw the drafting of new laws, their promulgation, and much negotiation with various parties coming to terms with the new legal landscape. But new laws and obligations were commonly resisted or avoided, so Kafka's working life was often exposed to many failures of process and contested duties of care. Some of those subjected to new legal requirements sought to avoid their responsibilities, and officials were sometimes then less than properly enthusiastic about enforcing the new laws in established businesses. Kafka wrote articles for local newspapers, carefully supporting the new insurance regimes and smoothing over the conflicts of interest.[6] He visited employers and listened to their complaints, but also represented the Institute in court against those determined to avoid paying their dues.[7] Emerging insurance and risk calculation delivered much-needed protections for workers, but also opened up new and socially divisive discourses on discipline and conformity.[8] Kafka thus saw the advent of one arm of modern biopolitics up close: the new modern statistical subject was born; governments understood their populations as tabulated around norms; disease, death and injury were deemed "acceptable" in certain proportions.[9] As Corngold and Wagner have argued, the biopolitical turn meant that culpability or guilt was successively replaced by risk and provisioning for harm through insurance and compensation schemes.[10] We should add that such "progress" has its corollary in the figure of the bureaucratic technician, who must bifurcate his/her private self from public role—and should administer calmly according to legal duty. Kafka worked from such a difficult position—promulgating a new type of rationalized "care," but dealing with many partialities and failings as new administrative techniques were adopted.

We might suppose in line with many earlier interpretations, that such a position would lead Kafka to a trenchant criticism or unmasking of law's pretensions. Adorno pithily declared that for Kafka the trial is itself on trial; law itself surely stands "convicted."[11] However, since we now can understand in some detail that Kafka clearly also worked actively *with* law to strengthen and improve some of its jurisdictions, and in the light of the close intertextual connections between his workplace writing and literary productions, we should read his literary texts as doing more than simple condemnation. So how can Kafka's approach be characterized?

The Kafkan text can be read then as a sustained meditation on the "believability" of law—the types of trust and confidence in a legal system essential for individuals to feel that it does in fact function "properly" (whatever that might mean), but which can fracture under duress. Of course, all laws require shared meanings and beliefs, but none can guarantee total or absolute confidence in the communication and execution of procedure. The renowned philosopher of law H.L.A. Hart included the vagaries and skeptical attitudes concerning legal operations, such as the "open texture" of language-use, and the possible "rule scepticisms," as integral to legal systems in his seminal work *The Concept of Law*.[12] Even in highly stable societies, such as those Hart basically described, doubts over the interpretation of terms and effectiveness of legal rule can arise. In general, such inconsistencies and problems of understanding are not damaging and are countered by the conformity of participants, but some social conditions produce far greater stresses. When beliefs on which the *integrity* of law depends—such as the beliefs that commands to obey are forceful, that sanctions are guaranteed, that officers of the law are carrying out their duties correctly—are sufficiently strained, then law's principled force is itself called into question.

At one level, Kafka's working life, beginning in fin de siècle Empire conditions, including the years of the First World War and its aftermath, was surely such a disturbed time.[13] In European societies dragging themselves from constitutional monarchies into the modern era of mass production and mass political participation, trust in law, and the very conceptions of what law and justice *should* be, were increasingly open to public contestation. At another level, the introduction of biopolitical principles and bureaucratic rationales signified a commitment to the production of specialized knowledges of the governed subject in order to extend legal rationality across the social order. We know that Kafka's discursive position, both public and private, was oriented to these revolutionary circumstances, and his individual commitment to writing inevitably reflected this.

## 3.

Before turning to a closer examination of *The Trial* and "Before the Law," we can connect this focus on believability with Kafka's literary corpus in general, because the issue of believability implies a concern for epistemic integrity as well. Kafka's literary experimentation was also a sustained working with epistemophilic desires—the desire to know, to explicate, or to satisfy curiosity: the writer's desire to write, and the reader's desire to enjoy knowing through reading. But the unfinished novels and short prose texts testify to the difficulties of finding any *general* rule (or law) of decipherment readily available to readers. As Jonathan Baldo suggests, some of the peculiarity of Kafka's art might be ironically accepted as the "arrest" of readers' standard approaches.[14] Other critics suggest that the particularly fragmentary and open character of the texts implies that avenues of standard interpretive justification had been carefully and deliberately pruned or subtracted through Kafka's writing practice in order to allow the permanent possibility of alternate critical approaches.[15] Therefore, constituting a type of critical rhythm, interpreting the Kafkan text is often to be drawn into a process of installing a likely reference frame, only to uninstall it, as we are alternately satisfied and then unsatisfied with constituting an understanding. Since this instability evades ready explication, different commentators have struggled to characterize it through various analogies and metaphors: Benjamin as an instigated "never-ending series of reflections"; Adorno as a "parabolic system the key to which has been stolen"; Rolleston as a repeatedly experienced "bottomlessness"; Kuna, narrowly, as a superimposition of different planes of reality unreconciled in the protagonist's represented consciousness.[16] The Kafkan text thus modulates epistemic desires and results: What we know, what we want to know, and what we feel we *ought* to know are arranged to tease the reader unsteadily.

That we should want a sense of sufficiency in constituting the text is inscribed in the institutions and practices of literature, even if that desire cannot be unqualified, but Kafka refused to deliver easy pathways. What reader of *The Trial* has not puzzled over their experience, asking something like, "am I understanding this properly, or, am I reading this in the right way?" Kafka elicits the epistemophilic desire to know only to deny its satisfaction, and redeploy its direction. While not a "modern sublime" that *breaks* bounds of reason, Kafka invites the reader to a textual experience of the insecure borders of knowledge, the hinterland between *doxa* and *episteme*. How much do we want to install orderly understanding, and how much do we need to believe, in a way similar to the believability required in law, that order will be apparent, and hopefully shared?

Although we usually read alone, Kafka's epistemic insufficiency has inevitably a social dimension, since reading that is challenged also unsettles the imagined institutions of shared readership. Deinstalling the security of our frames of reference also destabilizes presuppositions of a secure and shared perspective. The very strangeness of the Kafkan text suggests the *Unheimlich*, and an atopic experience for the reader attempting to discern, for example, the shared stability of a represented social world, or the focal point of narration. Standard social-realist conventions are both deployed in many of Kafka's narratives but disavowed by the intrusion of the bizarre or fantastical: the opening scene of "The Metamorphosis," in which the protagonist awakes to his transformed insectival state, or the tale (unpublished in Kafka's lifetime) of Blumfield, an elderly bachelor, who arrives home from work one day to find two striped balls dancing autonomously in the air in his apartment.[17] No comforting adequation of subject and object in such narration is made available. Knowledge for Kafka is not abstractly Cartesian, as if the subject, substantially alone as a constituting point of consciousness, confronts his/her known world of objects, and finds them re-iterated in textual representation—but rather is understood by Kafka as socially inscribed and always moderated in part through the social bond. Alienation, often deduced in reading Kafka, must still suppose, at the very least, the specter of lost community or the need for being-together. Human anxiety, the psychological sign of alienation, is for Kafka often framed through insecurity of understanding—the reader apprehends the unevenly distorted grounds of social relations. In both "The Judgment" and "The Metamorphosis," for example, misapprehension is at the heart of family relations, such that the protagonist's represented self can be read as misrecognizing his reality, and the reader questions the unity of the narrated interactions.

The most poignant Kafkan figure of this crafted insufficiency is of course Josef K. of *The Trial*. The reader must constitute the character of K. obliquely, through pursuing the narrative of his arraignment, as he pursues and is pursued by legal process. Has he possibly forgotten his crime, or is he mistaken in his assumptions, or has he only incomplete knowledge, or is he uncertain when he should be certain, et cetera? The protagonist as conventional guarantee for the coherency of a reading-position is also subverted or "on trial." Questions of what readers know or should know abound. Given its gravity, being before the law *should* be a properly known situation, but this supposition is deferred, fragmented and finally denied. Beginning with the theatrically staged morning of K.'s arraignment, uncomfortably, but inexorably we are drawn along by K.'s partial revelations of a life subsumed in an inexplicable legal process, attempting to supply explananda and explanans at various points in the narrative, but without sure success. We *should* be able to explain the ultimate sense of the trial, which is what exactly: individual freedom, guilt, sexual desire, authority, or existential malaise—some or all of these? *The Trial* discloses none of these possible themes in any detail, and K.'s reported experience often only serves as the teasing metonymic index for the reader's labor of comprehension. On that most central of issues, we are given clues and suggestions that K. may be "guilty" in this or that way—sexual, criminal, familial, social, moral—but denied surety. Although surprised at being arrested, Josef K. quickly confesses to the guards that he is "by no means greatly surprised," but then reverses this again almost immediately under questioning (*Trial* 13).[18] What can we know, and what *should* we believe, if this narration and our protagonist are not readily answerable questions, though generations of scholars have supplied innumerable plausible suggestions? That very "gap" in understanding and our desire to fill it marks the particular experience in reading Kafka, and bears directly on the conception of "believability" and law in crisis found in both the workplace writings and literary texts, since modern law should be a system (we would ordinarily suppose) that provides adjudication based on adequate explanation. The sense of legal process surrounding a trial to which the German title *Der Proceß* also refers, includes investigation, gathering of evidence, preliminary interrogation—the preparations of arranging understanding for relevant parties in order that an actual courtroom trial can then take place. But of course it never arrives for Josef K.—at least not in the way a reader can readily presume it might from reading the earlier parts of the narrative, and the reader is then "suspended in judgment" both in reading practice and within the constructed world of Josef K.

## 4.

We can expand this now in two related directions. One takes us to the historical and intellectual context of Kafka's law, which provides a more detailed view on then contemporary drives to reform law; the second takes us to the more recent deconstruction of "Before the Law," and its focus on the "legend" that Kafka published separately, and also placed in a crucial late chapter of *The Trial*. Together, these directions help conjoin the literary and workplace texts, but more importantly position Kafka texts as critically concerned with the epistemophilic drive to reveal law, and as positioned skeptically against a current of legal thinking which was to become a powerful bureaucratic influence.

Arnold Heidsieck and Theodore Ziolkowski, in separate works, have shown Kafka worked directly with conceptions and mechanisms of law that were either becoming redundant or newly introduced in his day: *The Trial* extensively glosses types of law and legal reform specific to Austro-Hungary of the late nineteenth and early twentieth century.[19] Of course, sources for Kafka's versions of law also include Jewish or Yiddish traditions, his readings of Nietzsche and Dostoyevsky, Kleist and Kierkegaard—a complex of religious, traditional and modern texts.[20] But the direction of legal reform that Kafka worked and wrote within, which generated the bureaucratic and the biopolitical, also inaugurated modern legal positivism—and Kafka's writing is now often regarded as implicitly wrestling with this nascent movement. Legal positivism's place in European history is crucial because its attempted value-free approach to understanding law came to be interpreted as complacent and politically ambivalent to the legalized bureaucratic terrors that were to envelop Germany.[21] Its very "objectivity" appeared to lack the substantive values required for a social order in post-war crisis. Kafka, writing early in the period of positivism's ascendancy, clearly multiplied ironic and deflationary perspectives against law's pretensions to bureaucratic rationality and objective precision. His first-hand experiences of shifting juridical principles, as the biopolitical altered conceptions of legal responsibilities, must have been disorienting. The state's increasing alteration of law, for the sake of its administration of life, was a difficult process demanding legal officials in state bureaucratic command (such as Kafka's position) to juggle the demands of new state regulation with principles of justice that struggled toward reform. By focusing on a particular early contribution to legal positivism contemporaneous with Kafka, that of Hans Kelsen's attempt at a "pure" theory of law, and then specifically his pivotal concept of the *Grundnorm*, we can see further how Kafka dealt with problems of believability, and with the resultant drive to rigorously set the epistemological conditions of law, since we can read him as critically opposed to Kelsen's neo-Kantian approach and the related desire for a rigorous new foundation for understanding law. The fact that Kelsen was also born in Prague, just two years before Kafka, studied law in Vienna, and was already prominent in the Austro-Hungarian legal world, publishing on public law just as Kafka attained his job in the Workman's Accident Insurance Office, while tantalizing, does not point to proof of a specific influence—though his first writings toward the Pure Theory, *Hauptprobleme der Staatsrechtlehre* (1911), must have been available to most working in law throughout the empire.[22] Kelsen will later become instrumental in writing new constitutional documents for Austria, and will disagree with Carl Schmitt over many matters, including his definition of sovereignty.[23] My argument is not that Kafka ostensibly wrote in answer to Kelsen, or had in fact an *explicit* political agenda, but that both, writing from a common cultural experience of law in crisis, occupied contrasting discursive positions that can be held to reveal and resist each other.

Kelsen's legal positivism borrows from Kant of the *Critique of Pure Reason*, renovates earlier legal positivism, and clearly draws methodologically from the emerging epistemological positivism of the Viennese Circle.[24] Kelsen's contribution was to attempt to theorize law in its "purity," as an object of dispassionate "scientific" enquiry—distinct from sociological, psychological, political or ethical motivation. For Kelsen, law is a social fact and can be known objectively: it is a given normative system empowered with its own logic and backed by believable threats of sanctions against contraveners. Law produces a particular class of norms which prescribe, and which derive from and are authorized by, other "higher" norms in the system—not because of any definite content, common or intrinsic good, or universal principle of human conduct. Law is conceptualized as a command system that orders subjects and officials to perform certain acts in response to rule-governed interpretations of behavior. Command and obedience are formal, rational mechanisms. Kelsen thus opposes Natural Law traditions that argue law draws on other exterior-to-law values—moral, traditional, religious—to ground its principles and define its social goals.[25] Kelsen's law is systematic and relies on the existence of interconnected hierarchical institutions (Kelsen refers to a "Stufenbau") and types of obedience, but cannot guarantee that subjects *morally* ought to obey, just that the absence of obedience will invoke sanctions.

Interpreted as setting out from the dream-like (or nightmare) realization of such a type of modern legal positivism, Kafka's *Trial* dramatizes a protagonist responding to the classic indicators of the legal-positivist model of law at work. Josef K. is summarily arrested and inserted forthwith into a legal process. He shows dutiful submission, but cannot discover his crime, nor understand the workings of the law properly and conveniently. Without a necessary moral component, its command is nonetheless insistent, and Kafka's characters are continually compliant and mouth respectful, deferential lines about its proceedings. Law proceeds like a logical automaton commanding all.

The bureaucratic process of *The Trial* reveals its apparent distance from Natural Law traditions that understood law as necessarily tied to some conception of human or common Good: "the court" in *The Trial* can delay, evade, and conceal its workings from subjects, for it has no necessary responsibility for their welfare beyond authorized procedures. No clear program toward a common good seems to stem from its operations; in fact, its apparent efficient arbitrariness might connote an incipient "terror." While many commentators have explored this plausible reading, and its apparent direct anticipation of Nazi bureaucracy to come, such a reading should be supple enough to recognize that Kafka shows this law as also functionally *failing*—as corrupt, permeable in its procedures by all kinds of venality, confusions, illegitimacies, and interceding human desires.[26] Kafka's "law" is also, as Ziolkowski puts it, "a burlesque": arresting officers eat Josef K.'s breakfast, rifle through personal belongings, get whipped in storerooms; officials seduce young women or pass them around like trophies; the law statutes are actually pornographic texts; the places of legal work are attics and slum tenements; the court employs all sorts of suspect extra-legal means, including children, while typically remaining opaque and distant to defendants.[27] *The Trial* becomes a catalogue of parodies of legal procedure, rather than fulfilling a picture of modern rationalized oppression, where domination is calculated and directed by explicit political purpose.

Law's believability, the integrity of its requirements of trust, mutuality and obedience, is fractured and contaminated by extra-legal matters, to the point that law appears bizarrely everywhere, adulterated, carnal and debased. The perspectives of characters, even if obedient, inexplicably turn awry, or private actions that appear to be distinct from the court are revealed as motivated by law's unprincipled commands. Josef K. can be considered something of a Yiddish *schlemiel* (the loser routinely mocked) to find himself in his situation, but law's claims to rational order are also thoroughly mocked as *The Trial* progresses. Further, the parody turns regularly to include the meta-level of jurisprudence. Josef K. increasingly asks questions and enquires about the nature of the courts and legal system, as his arraignment fails to be clarified: the answers often confuse and deny understanding. The glacial detachment that we might ascertain from Kelsen's Pure Theory as the necessary logical comportment to law's procedures is inverted by the carnivalesque dimensions that regularly intercede into "due process." Kafka refuses legal positivist purity of a single objective description—darkly, playfully inmixing a multiplicity of experiences and perspectives, which show human desires and values distorted and discordant, folded into procedure and legal relations.[28] Characters occupy multiple, conflicting positions in the legal system. The logical scaffold that positivism would maintain as the factual basis of law, and which should be transparent, is inverted into characters' whim and personal desire, or never-ending uncertainty about the status of Josef K.'s case or its next stage.

*The Trial*'s legal system is thus a heterogeneous mess, a bundle of dream-like motifs about life under law that subverts logical depiction. The epistemological confidence that we can know law's domain properly from a perspective that can account for "facts of law," as if they are available transparently to consciousness is denied, and the positivist *attitude* in general is refused.

The pivotal concept of the Basic Norm must be understood as the linchpin for Kelsen to secure a positivist theory of law as an ordered unity. Woven together in structure and execution, from particular local laws, grounded then in more general laws, through to constitutional statutes, law ultimately rests on the most fundamental norm, the Basic Norm (*Grundnorm*). The Basic Norm is the concept of a single deep underlying norm that operates as the implicit ground or foundation for all other normative legal statements. It *cannot be articulated*—for any articulation of a "deepest principle" would itself require another deeper norm stating that it should be obeyed or considered binding. In Kelsen's terms, there is a deep basic "ought" to obey that is *implicitly presupposed* beneath all the legal "oughts" that we regularly recognize. Kelsen asserts the Basic Norm is always humanly made, humanly thought, not naturally bequeathed; it is logical-imaginary, transcendental in a Kantian sense—since it conditions the field of normative statements. Empty of determinate content, unsignifiable in essence, the Basic Norm is "centre of a self-referring chain of "ought statements" as one interpretation puts it.[29] Though a "phantom without a sign" and alien to the system of empirical legal norms, it is the authorizing "fiction" internal to law that allows legal reasoning to work, allows for legal knowledge, and grants coherency and authority to the legal system from an a priori position.[30] Although Kelsen gradually developed different versions of the Pure Theory, the epistemological posture was decided early in an attempt to better the positivism that ascribed the final support for law to the will of the state. The Basic Norm does not originate in force or decision. If, in a thought experiment, we were to try to trace it to a point of creation, we could only arrive at the established constitution of a state, and then earlier historical constitutions—but behind those we would still have to presuppose an originating command act or move to natural or supernatural commands. To avoid this infinite regress, and the unwelcome metaphysical implications, Kelsen postulates the Basic Norm as transcendentally presupposed in legal reasoning—a virtual axiom in which our questioning of origins and validity would terminate.[31] Thus, the Basic Norm is chronologically posited as validating law *before* it operates, but this can only be claimed *after* a legal system is in operation—an irresolvable paradox.[32]

This intriguing and influential maneuver remains greatly debated to this day—even if it is now mostly understood as failing to establish the legal field in its logical purity. But its original theoretical motivation in Kantianism and positivism stemmed from recognition in jurisprudence of the rapid breakdown of pre-modern social order in Austro-Hungary, and the need to secure a rationale for legal norms wrenched away from religion and tradition. If modern legal reason was to become established, a self-sufficient science of its knowledge was thought to be required, and legal reasoning itself should supply the principle of its operation.

The Basic Norm forms a strange textual homology with Kafka's use of law, in that the drive to secure the legal network is also viewed by Kafka as a problematic at the heart of law—a problematic worthy of dramatic burlesque. As many commentators discuss, K. suffers the standard pain of not comprehending the specific workings of the legal process, the "veil of mystery" that lawyers can drape before litigants.[33] But K., in the absence of any clarity as to the charge against him, pursues knowledge of the court and law *itself*—which is difficult if not impossible to obtain, even while the court and law are increasingly manifest throughout his experiences. He turns to others who respect and appear to understand the court's authority. But they prove to be unable to elucidate directly the bona fides of proceedings. The painter Titorelli, for example, tells K. of hearing that acquittals, which are considered virtually impossible, have occurred in the dim past. Their formal possibility remains obscure to K.—suggested merely by the personal anecdote of the court painter. Titorelli goes on to discuss the "legends" of past cases, and of power resting finally in a higher court "totally inaccessible to you and me and everyone else" (*Trial* 158). This mythic past, which fictively grounds the court's workings, fits the role of a final legal authorization—but one that is hopelessly vague and cannot be used in the course of a particular trial. If the Basic Norm is best understood as a category of "legal fiction," "the higher court" for K.—in occupying a similar "fictive" position (no-one can ever know it)—promises only an irrational, comical but cruelly never-ending process. Whereas Kelsen's Basic Norm supposedly guaranteed valid legal command, for Kafka such a phantasm collapses into absurdities or admits arbitrary force or violence into the legal system. Kafka's law is likened to a "vast organism" that sometimes responds to perturbations like a life-form under threat (*Trial* 120). Trials mysteriously enter "new stages" wherein nothing more can be known: justification thus does not continue through all steps of the legal process, as if law chooses to ignore its own principles when it so desires (*Trial* 122).

The positivist perspective of law that Kelsen pursued—of a consistent, interlocked and explicable system of norms—is inverted in the surreal inconsistency of K.'s world. For example, scenes of legal drama are rendered inexplicable and abnormalized by veering off-stage to the ob-scene: for example, K.'s sexual dalliances, both with Leni during visits to the lawyer Huld and with the woman in the empty courtroom, suggest that the guilt of unbridled immoral sexual desire is woven into the "evidence" and into the defendant's role in the theatre of legal process. Legal norms are thus interlaced with unpredictable unconscious forces such that the subject of the law does not appear as a neatly responsible agent in a restricted domain of legal action.

Of course, this is one avenue for reading *The Trial*, psychologically, as the process of guilty conscience made manifest: the court is then an interior judgmental agency made exterior. Josef K. puts himself on trial for immorality. The irruption of desire during the "examinations" that he endures then bespeaks the resistances between desire and moral approbation in the self. Along with other readings, Bridgewater's valuable reading in *Kafka and Nietzsche* shows how strongly Kafka might have been working with Nietzsche's *Genealogy of Morals* as a reference while dramatizing the activity of K.'s guilty conscience as a form of enacted juridical theatre.[34] To emphasize the interior struggle of the self is undeniably plausible here, but, as Bridgewater also argues, by the latter sections of *The Trial*, Josef K. is confronted with the issue of his "belief in and obedience to his own rational self."[35]

The figure of K. struggles within himself, but also with social relations, and the rules of interaction, legal and extra-legal, that demand obedience. Human social relations for Kafka are not neatly enframed, regulated or enhanced by the legal system, but appear as too-often insincere, unreliable—threatening or driven by base needs that erupt irregularly. K. cannot ensure his life and happiness by attempting to comprehend law and his trial any better: in fact, he dizzily descends into illness and claustrophobia whenever he attempts to discover more in legal chambers, as if official approaches, perhaps the very fact of officialdom, will strangle the breath from him (*Trial* 78). K.'s uncle even suggests a respite in the countryside, where the powerful reach of law might be weakened, but this is rejected as a maneuver too suggestive of flight and tactically unwise (*Trial* 95). Law for K. thus threatens rather than protects; he is increasingly estranged from the social body, which law should order, and persecuted in proportion to his desires for proper understanding.

After the non-explications of Titorelli, *The Trial* presents what turns out to be K.'s final sustained attempt to understand the court and law; this happens through his dialogue with the priest at the cathedral. The story of "Before the Law," which is told to K. by the priest, forms the concentrated paradox of a fictional "legend" within the fictive world of K. and might finally (we imagine) reveal law's truth. The telling of the legend and the examination of it by K. also foreground problems of legal interpretation, and the question of "laws" of determining meaning in order for law to perform its operations. For Kelsen, as for Kafka, legal norms are carried in discourse, and the legal process inevitably has the character of interpretation, of an engagement with text. But whereas Kelsen's epistemological positivism supposed that problems of interpretation could be ordered neatly and properly into the worlds of facts versus norms,

Kafka clearly doubts such precision. K. is constantly misinterpreting not only the legal processes set upon him, but the ways in which others understand the law and communicate to him its workings. *The Trial* dramatizes the perplexities of legal textual interpretation in order to satirize this most fundamental level of law's process—that of the grasp of law's word.

## 5.

One of the most prominent of more recent readings to open up this site of the question of law's discursive character in *The Trial* has been Derrida's "Before the Law," and it usefully develops in parallel the epistemological opposition shown between Kafka and Kelsen.[36] Derrida reads Kafka's text as (in part) a meditation on the "law of law"—a concept, which would exceed any empirical determination, and which, in Derrida's terms, is aporetic, strictly "impossible" to delineate. Nonetheless we are of course inevitably drawn by the strange attractor of thinking an *arche* for law itself, the principle or rule of its coming into being—and the enormously rich history of the idea of an *arche* or originating event shows a permanence in western philosophy at least since the ancient division of *physis* from *nomos*. Experience of a particular instance of law stimulates the desire to refer back through something that can count as general to something finally ordering or originating. Derrida draws attention to this regress, which shows logical similarities to Kelsen's argument for a Basic Norm (though with crucial differences), that is the imagining of the *arche* of law. The reader is introduced to several explanatory schema—Kantian, Freudian, and Heideggerian, each of which reiterate in Derrida's account various powerful approaches to the "Law of law." In short, these are the fictional character of Kant's Moral Law, the prohibited origins of prohibition in Freud's *Totem and Taboo*, and the Heideggerian withdrawal/non-presence of an essential truth of Law ("Before the Law," 196-206). Each of these philosophical paradigms can only go so far in signifying the mute obscurity of the Law of laws. Each imports rhetoric to speak of a primary principle or ontological condition, which is in itself unavailable for proper representation. Each approach fails in some way, unable to speak purely of the Law of laws without the *impurity* of assumptions and rules, *which must be post-legal*, already established by virtue of the *arche* of law. The deconstructive *aporia* thus reveals the impossible metaphysical object that is the Law of laws beyond the boundaries of legal mechanisms, and which is nonetheless transcendental to law's operations—necessary, but unavailable for proper disclosure. Derrida's insight delineates the organization of the limits of thinking the constructions of law, but it also refers to a dynamic—the *pursuit* of this fictive origin, which is traced in a particular way through Kafka's fable.

In the story told to Josef K., a man from the country comes before the doorkeeper of the portal to the place of Law, and sees that the door, although guarded by the fearsome doorkeeper, is not shut but sits open; however, the initial exchanges between the man and doorkeeper discourage the man from attempting an entry. Respectfully, he camps beside the door, patiently waiting and waiting.

Only at approaching death as physical decline sets in, eyes failing, does he manage to glimpse "a radiance that streams inextinguishably from the gateway of the Law" (*Trial* 216). In Derrida's account, this is "the most religious moment of the writing. . . . There is an analogy with Judaic law here" ("Before the Law" 208). And the "man from the country" could indeed be a transposition by Kafka of the ancient Judaic "*am ha' aretz*" (one from the land)—one who is ignorant, sinful or out of touch with religious law.[37] The light glimpsed is then the sign of the divine, and the man comes to seek re-admission to faith or redemption. But this would be all-too-easy an answer, falsely profound, and would run counter to the whole burlesque tenor of *The Trial* if it remained as a moment of genuine Truth—as if the Law of laws shone forth *simplicitas*. Derrida simply leaves this possibility open and undecided, while developing his reading in other ways. But we should also recall Benjamin argued to Scholem that Kafka failed (a self-defined failure) to find some way toward redemption, and that his novel was *not* a negative theology or religious text.[38] The moment of radiance leads to the dying man's last desperate question to the doorkeeper of why no one else has appeared at the doorway, and the darkly comic truth that the doorway was *his alone*, always open, but *promised* to be closed upon his death by the doorkeeper. Death is thus entwined with the experience of law's origin; it is in fact, on some readings, its necessary counterpart, even a key interpretation of "Before the Law."[39] It is less that a religiosity or divine truth is acknowledged as the "inextinguishable" arriving at the time of death, and more that seeking to know the Law of laws will lead only to the answer of death—the finite closing of the human life that pursues the question. And it is an-other, bonded to the man, to his portal and his questioning, that in fact promises "closure."

The man from the country also *has* his life in the fable: he lives before the law with the doorkeeper, quite dutifully: he *believes* in the law all this time, without having access to it, and without knowing it properly or its origins. He wants to know, but dutifully waits—the rest of his whole life. And the doorkeeper is there *for* the man, waiting in fact to serve him. This is an under-acknowledged side of Kafka's fable: the man from the country lives with another and they are closely bound together by their obedience to law. They share belief, even as they share the drawn-out stalemate of inaccessible understanding of law. They share time; they exchange things and come to know each other well. The man from the country grows old and comes to know even the fleas in the doorkeeper's collar, which, like some of Kafka's other creatures, signify the close intensity of life together with others. The fleas operate as a motif of symbiosis for Kafka, and echo the *Ungeziefer* of *The Metamorphosis*, the jackals, dogs, vultures, rats and mice of other texts, in which living-with merges unsteadily with living-off.

Certainly the man from the country is diminished by his obsession, by his failure to act beyond waiting to be commanded to enter the portal, and that perhaps is his mistake, if we read the story didactically. He declines to a point of infantile communication with the unclean fleas, becoming lowly and creaturely himself (Josef K. of course will die "like a dog"—another creaturely debasement [*Trial*, 231]). But this life close together can be also imagined as the scene or ground for the operation of law, and need not imply a lesson about maintaining composure or distance above others. The man and his companion, the doorkeeper, are "guilty" together in the sense of indebted (*verschuldet*) to each other, thus bonded and belonging symbiotically together in a topos of social life that is *their* particular belonging. Before the generality of law lies the belonging-together of specific lives, their exchanges and finally death.

The radiance experienced by the man from the country in his dying moments—perhaps the light of reason, or the illumination that will unconceal or explain the law—is only glimpsed and changes nothing: it signals that the law does not command you to know—only to believe and live obediently with others. As the priest says at the end of discussion with Josef K., "you don't have to consider everything true, you just have to consider it necessary" (*Trial* 223). Questions torment. In seeking final answers or exhaustive verifications of knowledge, more suffering than necessary can be caused, but life before the law with others is "the necessity" that allows for questions. The reader, like Josef K., who wants to know exhaustively and makes a fetish of understanding, cannot leave law behind and enter into a sanctum beyond the conditional character of law. The "if-then" of law is the moderated bond of human time together, without which not even discourse is possible, nor the iterations of significations that open and re-open interpretive relations.

Derrida's alternate readings from psychoanalysis underline also the physiognomy of the guardian, the masculine force, fear, respect, and the current of sexuality in the setting and the prohibition on entry ("Before the Law," 195). The man from the country is also a "man of nature" before (anterior in time) to law, who arrives at the scene of law, or we might suggest, enters into the social bond with an-other ("Before the Law," 200). If we read this bodily, affective side of the fable against passages from *The Trial* which show Josef K.'s range of desires, it is possible to read the same counterpoised logic: as much as the law demands, structures, shapes and deforms those living before it (the man from the country is gradually lowered in stature), Kafka also underscores the intensity of human relations, of desire, of lives going well and ill, fertile and infertile, happy and threatened in ways *not* reducible to law, even as life with others must be before it. Josef K. pursues his relations with others at times in spite of law's demands. Something of life exceeds law in the place where humans share it. So despite the strength of many readings of Kafka which stress the existential, bureaucratic, religious or political themes of the law, a certain inexhaustible theme recurs and supplements these interpretations, which might be described as life's "relationality" as essential to the life being before (*ante*) the law—relations between humans before the law, relations with non-human life, relations with the non-living—an ensemble or place of being-together. The singular narrative of Josef K. can appear to suggest the fantasy of a single mind, or even solipsism. But, following that reading, the de-formations of normal experience, and the deformation of characters' comportments, show the perversity of solipsistic self-reliance—Josef K. is increasingly estranged by the intensity of his desire to know the court's processes. If the legend told to Josef K. is the condensed scene of this epistemic need, it underscores the importance of the interpretive act and relationship, and then the intense bonds of being-together, the necessity of the other in the place before the law.

## 6.

Kafka worked as an officer of law to reform and impose particular laws, and knew of the struggle to maintain law in the face of its injustices and failings. One dimension of his writing sought to uphold the law's efficacy; another tragicomically dramatized its failures and the poverty beneath its self-assured dignity. Neither side of the Kafkan text offers a "solution" because the very idea of a solution misplaces the character of being before the law. The epistemic task also bears within it the hope for a reaffirmation: that law can be present, meaningful, and effective—that life under its domain is protected and relations properly moderated. Yet, for Kafka, understanding and explicating law *do not* guarantee such reaffirmation. Knowledge of law does not produce stability leading to "the good life" in itself, even if we are inevitably drawn to epistemic tasks as believability fractures. No "answer" to our interrogations of law will guarantee in advance a palliative against the stresses on believability that social bonds inevitably produce. Kafka asserts life before law, which will enter into law's conditions. An ensemble of life-together includes the complex of shared beliefs, which resist complete understanding. The inevitable failures and cruelties of law cannot be solved by a pure explication hoping to present the *arche* or final presupposition for our contemplation.

# Notes

1. Franz Kafka, *The Office Writings*, eds. Stanley Corngold, Jack Greenberg and Benno Wagner, trans. Eric Patton with Ruth Hein (Princeton, NJ: Princeton University Press, 2009).

2. Stanley Corngold, "Kafka and the Ministry of Writing," in *The Office Writings*, 1-18.

3. Kafka, *The Office Writings*, 273-98; Discussed by Jack Greenberg, "From Kafka to Kafkaesque," in *The Office Writings*, 357-58.

4. Benno Wagner, "Kafka's Office Writings: Historical Background and Institutional Setting," in *The Office Writings*, 42.

5. *The Office Writings* and commentaries show the variety of tasks and significant challenges Kafka faced. It puts to rest some of the older views of Kafka as an insignificant assistant inconsequentially "shuffling papers." Although these office writings have been available to scholars (to a limited extent) for some time, the detailed commentaries now make available an accurate social contextual assessment.

6. Kafka, *The Office Writings*, 145-69.

7. Kafka, *The Office Writings*, 225-235.

8. See Stanley Corngold and Benno Wagner, *Franz Kafka: The Ghosts in the Machine* (Evanston, IL: Northwestern University Press, 2011), 207-11.

9. The essential starting point for discussions of "the biopolitical" is Michel Foucault, *The Will to Knowledge: The History of Sexuality vol. 1*, trans. Robert Hurley (London: Penguin, 1998), 133-59; and for the specific issues of the emergence of modern insurance in relation to Foucault's perspective, see contributions by Francois Ewald and others in Graham Burchell, Colin Gordon, Peter Miller, eds., *The Foucault Effect: Studies in Governmentality* (Chicago, IL: University of Chicago Press, 1991).

10. Corngold and Wagner, *Franz Kafka: The Ghosts in the Machine*, 207-8.

11. Theodor W. Adorno, "Notes on Kafka," in *Prisms*, trans. Samuel and Shierry Weber (Cambridge, MA: MIT Press, 1997), 268.

12. H.L.A. Hart, *The Concept of Law*, 2nd Edition. (Oxford: Oxford University Press, 1994), 124-38.

13. See Theodore Ziolkowski, *The Mirror of Justice: Literary Reflections of Legal Crisis* (Princeton, NJ: Princeton University Press, 1997) for one version of Kafka's response to "crisis of law." This essay pursues a related but different interpretation.

14. Jonathan Baldo reads Kafka's reader as "arrested," "on trial" and forced into several roles, none of which "authorize" the status of the literary text, even though we must "adjudicate": Jonathan Baldo, "The Reader on Trial: Or, Is Reading Necessarily an Injudicious Act?," in *Critical Essays on Franz Kafka*, ed. Ruth V. Gross (Boston, MA: G.K. Hall & Co., 1990), 235-59.

15. See Rainer Nägele, "Kafka and the Interpretive Desire," in *Kafka and the Contemporary Critical Performance*, ed. Alan Udoff (Bloomington, IN: Indiana University Press, 1987), 16-29; J.J. White, "Endings and Non-endings in Kafka's Fiction," in *On Kafka: Semi-Centenary Perspectives*, ed. Franz Kuna (London: Elek Books, 1976), 146-66, for analysis of the "fragmentary" in Kafka.

16. Walter Benjamin, "Franz Kafka: On the Tenth Anniversary of his Death," in *Selected Writings*, vol. 2, ed. Michael W. Jennings, trans. Harry Zohn (Cambridge, MA: Belknap, 1999), 802; Theodor Adorno, "Notes on Kafka," 245; James Rolleston, "Introduction: On Interpreting *The Trial*," in *Twentieth Century Interpretations of The Trial: A Collection of Critical Essays*, ed. James Rolleston (Upper Saddle River, NJ: Prentice-Hall, 1976), 4; Franz Kuna, "Rage for Verification: Kafka and Einstein," in *On Kafka: Semi-Centenary Perspectives*, 98. See also Henry Sussman, "Kafka's Aesthetics: A Primer: From the Fragments to the Novels," in *A Companion to the Works of Franz Kafka*, ed. James Rolleston (New York: Camden House, 2003), 135-36, for an insightful view on proliferation of meanings and possible interpretations in the Kafkan text.

17. Franz Kafka, "Blumfeld, an Elderly Bachelor," in *The Complete Stories*, ed. Nahum N. Glatzer (New York: Schocken Books, 1976), 183-205/ "Blumfeld, ein älterer Junggeselle," *Nachgelassene Schriften und Fragmente I*, ed. Malcolm Pasley (Frankfurt a.M., Fischer, 2001), 229-66.

18. Franz Kafka, *The Trial*, trans. Breon Mitchell (New York: Schocken, 1998), 13.

19. Arnold Heidsieck, *The Intellectual Currents of Kafka's Fictions: Philosophy, Law, Religion* (Columbia, SC: Camden House, 1994); Ziolkowski, *The Mirror of Justice*.

20. See Ritchie Robertson, *Kafka: Judaism, Politics and Literature* (Oxford: Clarendon Press, 1985); Iris Bruce, "Kafka and Jewish Folklore," in *The Cambridge Companion to Kafka*, ed. Julian Preece (Cambridge: Cambridge University Press, 2002) 150-68.

21. David Luban, Alan Strudler and David Wasserman in "Moral Responsibility in the Age of Bureaucracy" (*Michigan Law Review* 90.8 [1992], 2348-92) discuss the plausible conceptual linkages between some of the basic tenets of modern legal positivism, and some of the defenses raised during the Nuremberg trials of Nazi officials. They also cite the earlier arguments linking these defenses with classical legal positivism in Stanley L. Paulson, "Classical Legal Positivism at Nuremberg," *Philosophy and Public Affairs* 4.2 (1975), 132-58.

22. Hakan Gustafsson (in "Fiction of Law," in *No Foundations—Journal of Extreme Legal Positivism* 4 [October 2007]: 83-103) discusses various influences on Kelsen and his early development of a "pure theory." Ideas for theorizing an epistemology of law with a fundamental "origin" were shared amongst several German jurists at that time.

23. See David Dyzenhaus, *Legality and Legitimacy: Carl Schmitt, Hans Kelsen and Hermann Heller in Weimar* (Oxford: Oxford University Press, 1997); Stanley L. Paulson, "The Theory of Public Law in Germany: 1914-1945," *Oxford Journal of Legal Studies* 25.3 (2005): 525-45.

24. See Jeffrey Brand-Ballard, "Kelsen's Unstable Alternative to Natural Law: Recent Critiques," *American Journal of Jurisprudence* 41 (1996): 133-64.

25. Hans Kelsen, *Pure Theory of Law*, trans. Max Knight (Berkeley, CA: University of California Press, 1967, 2009), 66-68. This is the translation of Kelsen's second revised edition, which expanded, but didn't fundamentally alter the positivist approach already developing from 1911 through to the first edition of 1934.

26. The reading by J. P. Stern, "The Law of *The Trial*" (in *On Kafka: Semi-Centenary Perspectives*) is amongst several to pursue the interpretation of an insidious authoritarian state pursuing Josef K. without scruple to the point of summary execution. Stern discusses parallels with the Nazis' *Willensstrafrecht*—criminal law that aimed to consider intention behind actions (33-34).

27. Ziolkowski, *The Mirror of Justice*, 226-33.

28. See Margaret Davies, *Delimiting the Law: "Postmodernism" and the Politics of Law* (London: Pluto Press, 1996), 20, for critical discussion of the politics of positivist purity.

29. William E. Conklin, *The Invisible Origins of Legal Positivism: A Re-reading of a Tradition* (Dordrecht: Kluwer, 2001), 197.

30. Conklin, *The Invisible Origins of Legal Positivism*, 199.

31. See Hamish Ross, "Hans Kelsen and the Utopia of Theoretical Purism," *King's College Law Journal* 12 (2001): 174-94.

32. Davies, *Delimiting the Law: "Postmodernism" and the Politics of Law*, 85.

33. Richard A. Posner, *Law and Literature*, 3rd Edition (Cambridge, MA: Harvard University Press, 2009), 180.

34. Patrick Bridgewater, *Kafka and Nietzsche* (Bonn: Bouvier Verlag Herbert Grundmann, 1974), 67-90.

35. Bridgewater, *Kafka and Nietzsche*, 75-76.

36. Jacques Derrida, "Before the Law," trans. Avital Ronell and Christine Roulston in *Acts of Literature*, ed. Derek Attridge (London and New York: Routledge, 1992), 181-220.

37. Ronald Hayman, *K: A Biography of Kafka* (London: Weidenfeld and Nicholson, 1981), 192.

38. Discussed by Bruce K. Ward, "Giving Voice to Isaac: The Sacrificial Victim in Kafka's Trial," *Shofar: An Interdisciplinary Journal of Jewish Studies* 22.2 (2004): 75.

39. Hayman, *K: A Biography of Kafka*, 191; Roberto Calasso, *K.*, trans. Geoffrey Brock (London: Vintage, 2006), 228.

## Works Cited

Adorno, Theodor W. "Notes on Kafka." In Theodor W. Adorno, *Prisms*, translated by Samuel and Shierry Weber, 245-71. Cambridge, MA: MIT Press, 1997.

Baldo, Jonathan. "The Reader on Trial: Or, Is Reading Necessarily an Injudicious Act?" In *Critical Essays on Franz Kafka*, edited by Ruth V. Gross, 235-59. Boston, MA: G.K. Hall & Co., 1990.

Benjamin, Walter. "Franz Kafka: On the Tenth Anniversary of His Death." Translated by Harry Zohn, in Walter Benjamin, *Selected Writings*, edited by Michael W. Jennings, vol. 2, 794-818. Cambridge, MA: Belknap, 1999.

Brand-Ballard, Jeffrey. "Kelsen's Unstable Alternative to Natural Law: Recent Critiques." *American Journal of Jurisprudence* 41 (1996): 133-64.

Bridgewater, Patrick. *Kafka and Nietzsche*. Bonn: Bouvier Verlag Herbert Grundmann, 1974.

Bruce, Iris. "Kafka and Jewish Folklore." In *The Cambridge Companion to Kafka*, edited by Julian Preece, 150-68. Cambridge: Cambridge University Press, 2002.

Burchell, Graham, Colin Gordon, Peter Miller, eds. *The Foucault Effect: Studies in Governmentality*. Chicago, IL: University of Chicago Press, 1991.

Calasso, Roberto. *K.* Translated by Geoffrey Brock. London: Vintage, 2006.

Conklin, William E. *The Invisible Origins of Legal Positivism: A Re-reading of a Tradition*. Dordrecht: Kluwer, 2001.

Corngold, Stanley. "Kafka and the Ministry of Writing." In Franz Kafka, *The Office Writings*, edited by Stanley Corngold, Jack Greenberg and Benno Wagner, translated by Eric Patton with Ruth Hein, 1-18. Princeton, NJ: Princeton University Press, 2009.

Corngold, Stanley, and Benno Wagner. *Franz Kafka: The Ghosts in the Machine*. Evanston, IL: Northwestern University Press, 2011.

Davies, Margaret. *Delimiting the Law: "Postmodernism" and the Politics of Law*. London: Pluto Press, 1996.

Derrida, Jacques. "Before the Law." Translated by Avital Ronell and Christine Roulston in Jacques Derrida, *Acts of Literature*, edited by Derek Attridge, 181-220. London and New York: Routledge, 1992.

Dyzenhaus, David. *Legality and Legitimacy: Carl Schmitt, Hans Kelsen and Hermann Heller in Weimar*. Oxford: Oxford University Press, 1997.

Foucault, Michel. *The Will to Knowledge: The History of Sexuality vol. 1*. Translated by Robert Hurley. London: Penguin, 1998.

Greenberg, Jack. "From Kafka to Kafkaesque." In Franz Kafka, *The Office Writings*, edited by Stanley Corngold, Jack Greenberg and Benno Wagner, translated by Eric Patton with Ruth Hein, 355-71. Princeton, NJ: Princeton University Press, 2009.

Gustafsson, Hakan. "Fiction of Law." *No Foundations—Journal of Extreme Legal Positivism* 4 (October 2007): 83-103.

Hart, H.L.A. *The Concept of Law*. 2nd Edition. Oxford: Oxford University Press, 1994.

Hayman, Ronald. *K: A Biography of Kafka*. London: Weidenfeld and Nicholson, 1981.

Heidsieck, Arnold. *The Intellectual Currents of Kafka's Fictions: Philosophy, Law, Religion*. Columbia, SC: Camden House, 1994.

Kafka, Franz. *The Complete Stories*. Edited by Nahum N. Glatzer. New York: Schocken Books, 1976.

———. *Kritische Asugabe. Nachgelassene Schriften und Fragmente I*. Edited by Malcolm Pasley. Frankfurt a.M., Fischer, 2001.

———. *The Office Writings*. Edited by Stanley Corngold, Jack Greenberg and Benno Wagner, translated by Eric Patton with Ruth Hein. Princeton, NJ: Princeton University Press, 2009.

———. *The Trial*. Translated by Breon Mitchell. New York: Schocken, 1998.

Kelsen, Hans. *Pure Theory of Law*. Translated by Max Knight. Berkeley, CA: University of California Press, 1967, 2009.

Kuna, Franz. "Rage for Verification: Kafka and Einstein." In *On Kafka: Semi-Centenary Perspectives*, edited by Franz Kuna, 83-111. London: Elek Books, 1976.

Luban, David, Alan Strudler and David Wasserman. "Moral Responsibility in the Age of Bureaucracy." *Michigan Law Review* 90.8 (1992): 2348-92.

Nägele, Rainer. "Kafka and the Interpretive Desire." In *Kafka and the Contemporary Critical Performance*, edited by Alan Udoff, 16-29. Bloomington, IN: Indiana University Press, 1987.

Paulson, Stanley L. "Classical Legal Positivism at Nuremberg." *Philosophy and Public Affairs* 4.2 (1975): 132-58.

———. "The Theory of Public Law in Germany: 1914-1945." *Oxford Journal of Legal Studies* 25.3 (2005): 525-45.

Posner, Richard A. *Law and Literature*. 3rd Edition. Cambridge, MA: Harvard University Press, 2009.

Robertson, Ritchie. *Kafka: Judaism, Politics and Literature*. Oxford: Clarendon Press, 1985.

Rolleston, James. "Introduction: On Interpreting *The Trial*." In *Twentieth Century Interpretations of The Trial: A Collection of Critical Essays*, edited by James Rolleston, 1-12. Upper Saddle River, NJ: Prentice-Hall, 1976.

Ross, Hamish. "Hans Kelsen and the Utopia of Theoretical Purism." *King's College Law Journal* 12 (2001): 174-94.

Stern, J. P. "The Law of *The Trial*." In *On Kafka: Semi-Centenary Perspectives*, edited by Franz Kuna, 22-41. London: Elek Books, 1976.

Sussman, Henry. "Kafka's Aesthetics: A Primer: From the Fragments to the Novels." In *A Companion to the Works of Franz Kafka*, edited by James Rolleston, 123-48. New York: Camden House, 2003.

Wagner, Benno. "Kafka's Office Writings: Historical Background and Institutional Setting." In Franz Kafka, *The Office Writings*, edited by Stanley Corngold, Jack Greenberg and Benno Wagner, translated by Eric Patton with Ruth Hein, 19-48. Princeton, NJ: Princeton University Press, 2009.

Ward, Bruce K. "Giving Voice to Isaac: The Sacrificial Victim in Kafka's Trial." *Shofar: An Interdisciplinary Journal of Jewish Studies* 22.2 (2004): 64-84.

White, J.J. "Endings and Non-endings in Kafka's Fiction." In *On Kafka: Semi-Centenary Perspectives*, edited by Franz Kuna, 146-66. London: Elek Books, 1976.

Ziolkowski, Theodore. *The Mirror of Justice: Literary Reflections of Legal Crisis*. Princeton, NJ: Princeton University Press, 1997.

# PART III

# PHILOSOPHICAL READINGS

CHAPTER 11

# Anxiety and Attention: Benjamin and Others

*Brendan Moran*

*Der Mensch ist ja nichts anderes als sein Körper.*
—Heiner Müller, *Gespräche*

*Rien qu'un corps ouvert*
—Jean-Luc Nancy, *L'Adoration*

A colleague and interlocutor of Walter Benjamin, Willy Haas, writes that Franz Kafka begins "from the entirely concrete and, from there . . . sinks into the always more concrete." In a straightforward sense, this could be an exaggeration. If one begins with the *entirely* concrete, it might not be possible that one then sinks into the *always more* concrete. For readers of Kafka, however, it may be easy not to notice that Haas's statement could be an exaggeration. Kafka is often focused on a concreteness that cannot stop drawing his attention further and further. Among the characterizations given by Haas to this "concrete [*Konkrete*]" is that it "is" an "entirely sensate [*sinnlicher*] . . . impression."[1]

Benjamin does not mention these passages of Haas's analysis, but he too considers Kafka's attention to be focused on an inestimable physicality that underlies all and everything. In the following discussion of Benjamin's Kafka-reading, this attention will be examined in relation to anxiety. On behalf of the concretely sensate, the relevant anxiety counters inattentiveness. This anxiety is not just about anything in particular, but is simultaneously an anxiety on behalf of what prevails in the particular. In our very identifications of, and our identifications "with," particulars, what prevails in the particular is neglected. Benjamin and many others call this prevalent force the nothing—*das Nichts*. For Benjamin, Kafka's attention to this nothing is attentiveness to the physicality that is overwhelming. Such attentiveness can be characterized as anxiety on behalf of this physicality that is overwhelming precisely by remaining unidentifiable and thereby making each and every particular insatiably demanding of attention. The following essay will examine how Benjamin's discussion of Kafka's works especially accentuates that experience of the nothing is mediated by particulars: for Benjamin's Kafka, particulars become ever more oblique, and ever more alluring, precisely insofar as anxiety on their behalf lets them into our attention.

Somewhat like Søren Kierkegaard and Martin Heidegger, Benjamin distinguishes this anxiety from fear. For Kierkegaard and Heidegger, fear is about something specific that seems threatening. Anxiety might also arise from a threat, but the threat is *ultimately* nothing particular, and is rather the nothing that is the inexpugnably mysterious condition of the possibility of anything. Although they are very distinct in many respects, Kierkegaard and Heidegger both present anxiety—anxiety with regard to the nothing—as potentially penultimate to resolute regard for the nothing that is the ground of all beings. Emmanuel Levinas's principal objection to both Kierkegaard and Heidegger is that their views entail a disregard for other humans—who, for Levinas, mediate any conception we have of ourselves, others, or anything else: other humans are the very possibility for experience of God, for experience of the ultimate Otherness of existence; if we are to be attentive to such Otherness, we must be above all attentive to other humans. The following essay will be an endeavor to consider this controversy—this "debate" of Kierkegaard, Heidegger, and Levinas—in relation to writings by Benjamin on Kafka.

Benjamin's Kafka will be discussed in terms of an anxiety that is, in certain respects, distinct from Kierkegaardian-Heideggerian anxiety. The latter is supposed potentially to open us to a freedom that is beyond particulars of sense-experience and of social constraint. The anxiety addressed by Benjamin is very much embroiled in sense-experience, particulars, and indeed sociality. Yet Benjamin's Kafka will also be examined in its distinctness from the primacy of ethics that is emphasized by Levinas. Benjamin's Kafka-writings concern an anxiety whose attention is distracted by multifarious diversions into all sorts of things. This distractedness by the intransigent particularity of the diversions will be discussed as a physically felt rejection of much transcendence—be it religious (Kierkegaard), ontological (Heidegger), or ethical (Levinas).

The anxiety detected by Benjamin in Kafka's writings will be formulated as attention impelled by heterogeneous physicality that undermines attempts or presumptions to transcend it. The attention of this anxiety is Heideggerian and indeed Kierkegaardian in at least one sense: it concerns the nothing, which is no particular thing and yet determinate of existence. The nothing determines by continually eliciting beyond containment and control. In many respects, however, the attention of Benjamin's Kafka to this nothing is evoked by intractably heterogeneous physicality, which keeps returning, persisting, registering itself in inextinguishably diverse and concretely impinging entities, events, experiences. The following essay will propose that this intractably heterogeneous physicality cannot be transcended by Kierkegaard's religious dimension, Heidegger's ontological dimension, or Levinas's ethical dimension. The physically heterogeneous is, rather, that in which—or by which—anxiety experiences, and is required to be attentive to, preponderant nothingness.

Although this essay will largely be devoted to distinguishing Benjamin's Kafka from views held by Kierkegaard, Heidegger, and Levinas, the final passages will provide consideration of ways in which Benjamin's analysis of Kafka might itself be inattentive to the potential of anxiety to repel physically any presumption to overcome anxiety.

## A Very Embroiled Anxiety

The anxiety detected by Benjamin in Kafka's writings is more indistinct in its potentials than is the anxiety cultivated by Kierkegaard and Heidegger, who refer to a resolute freedom (however short-lived) that can develop from anxiety. In order to elaborate Benjamin's conception of an embroiled anxiety in Kafka's writings, consideration will be given here to how Benjamin's views on anxiety differ from those of Kierkegaard and Heidegger.

During his student-years, Benjamin was an enthusiastic reader of Kierkegaard (*C*, 20, 44/ *GB* 1, 92, 148; *GB* 1, 168) and specifically notes owning Kierkegaard's *The Concept of Anxiety* (*C*, 44/ *GB* 1, 148; *GB* 1, 168).[2] In subsequent years, Kierkegaard is barely mentioned in letters and only occasionally discussed in writings—and never discussed with reference to anxiety. In his Kafka-writings, therefore, Benjamin does not expressly discuss Kierkegaard on anxiety. Yet his usage of terminology such as "fear" and "anxiety" suggest a Kierkegaardian influence, and it is clear that Kierkegaardian readings of Kafka are an object of his criticism. It may be helpful, therefore, to discuss Kierkegaard, at least briefly.

When urging us to speak with fear and trembling, Kierkegaard distinguishes such fear and trembling from fear of specific harm. Unlike the latter fear, Kierkegaardian anxiety—the aforementioned fear and trembling—is a preliminary opening to the constituter of all existence, the force and the freedom that prevails over and within all beings. Anxiety opens to this freedom, which makes anxiety, and any culture of anxiety, "profound." Anxiety is preliminary to "freedom" that "will come to itself." This profundity of anxiety is its eventual weakness as well, for anxiety has only an inkling of the freedom that is unambiguous, entirely free. The "relation of anxiety to its object, to something that is nothing . . . is altogether ambiguous." Yet this anxiety awakens us to unambiguous freedom, to "freedom's possibility."[3] Anxiety begins, for instance, to confront guilt with freedom from guilt. As long as there is simply a confrontation with guilt, however, the unambiguity of freedom does not emerge: "as freedom with all its passion wishfully stares at itself and would keep guilt at a distance so that not a particle of it might be found in freedom, it cannot refrain from staring at guilt, and this staring is the ambiguous staring of anxiety."[4] Anxiety does not, as unambiguous freedom might, entirely surmount the constraints of physicality, customs, laws and morals. Moving ever so slightly, however, beyond the aesthetic (which is perceptual nature that includes, among other features, dispersal by the senses) and the ethical (which is morality), anxiety may be a catalyst for rising into the religious (into the spiritual that would be freedom beyond either the aesthetic or the ethical).[5] Anxiety can be a catalyst into what Kierkegaard eventually formulates as "absolutely nothing but the individual, without connections and complications."[6] "[S]piritlessness" has no anxiety that could facilitate such a break. The transcendent potential for such a break inheres in anxiety.[7]

In most respects, there is not such a transcendent potential in Benjamin's Kafka-writings. There is instead a tendency for a kind of indistinctness—perhaps even a kind of ambiguity—to prevail. Anxiety opens to this condition—

even if anxiety is also an inkling of freedom in relation to guilt and in relation to human order generally. Not surprisingly, therefore, Benjamin opposes the "theological" view that Kafka is a sort of descendent of Kierkegaard (*SW* 2, 806-7/ II:2, 426-27). For Benjamin, the principal representative of this theological view is the aforementioned Willy Haas, who contends that Kafka's writings are fundamentally religious, and that works such as *The Castle* deal with God's "awful" playing with the human being. For Haas, the latter motif is a Kierkegaardian-Pascalian one in which the human is somehow generically "always wrong" before an ultimately benign "God."[8] Expressly against Haas's theological reading, however, Benjamin stresses that *The Castle* provides no indication of a forgiving, omnipotent authority; it suggests, rather, the lack of such authority (*SW* 2, 807/ II:1, 426). Benjamin is also critical of Max Brod's religious reading of Kafka. Brod does claim that there are Kierkegaardian tensions in Kafka: "The world of God's justice and the world of human ethics gape wide asunder—the space for Kierkegaard's *Fear and Trembling* emerges."[9] Brod considers Kafka's work (and person) *largely* incompatible, however, with Kierkegaard's "theology of crisis," and claims there is no Kierkegaardian "heteronomy between God and human" for Kafka.[10] Yet Brod suggests there is an affinity of Kafka and Kierkegaard concerning what Brod calls the human's "good ethical strength and possibility of effectiveness."[11] This seems to be what Brod means by Kafka's "holiness," Kafka's path toward becoming a saint.[12] Although Benjamin does not discuss Brod's remarks on Kafka and Kierkegaard, he does criticize Brod's biography as bad hagiography, which crassly subsumes Kafka's creative work under his supposed life-path toward "holiness." This removal of tension strikes Benjamin as irrelevant to consideration of Kafka (*SW* 3, 317-18, 322/ III, 526-27, *GB* 6, 106). For Benjamin, God is not a powerful force in Kafka's writings (II:3, 1192); there is, rather, a shamelessness in theological readings (1210 Ms. 261).[13] Perhaps in the vein of such a critique of religiosity, Benjamin objects elsewhere that Kierkegaard advances a mythic inwardness—ultimately, an attempt at a consoling escape from the historical world (*SW* 2, 703-5/ III, 380-83).[14] This reading of Kierkegaard (however debatable) seems a significant factor both in Benjamin's dissociation of Kafka from Kierkegaard and in the potential for dissociating Benjamin's notion of anxiety from Kierkegaard's notion that anxiety can be a catalyst to transcendent freedom.

The anti-transcendentalism permeating Benjamin's reading of Kafka (and Kierkegaard), and Benjamin's attendant notion—to be elaborated in later sections of this essay—of anxiety as a physical and heterogeneous development, could be read as a response (whether intended or not) to Heidegger's treatment of anxiety as potentially catalytic for Dasein's resolutely ontological transcendence of the ontic (the dimension of beings, which is distinct from that of being as such).

For Heidegger in *Being and Time* as well as in other writings, fear is about a specific being (*Seiendes*), whereas that before which there is anxiety "*is being-in-the-world as such.*" In its very indefiniteness and its daunting, even stifling, character, being-in-the-world as such induces anxiety. Whereas—as will be discussed later—Benjamin stresses the mediation of anxiety by specific objects, Heidegger remarks: "Nothing which is at hand and present within the world functions as that before which anxiety is anxious about. . . . / Thus neither does anxiety 'see' a definite 'here' and 'there' from which what is threatening approaches." Yet, as will be elaborated later, Benjamin is apparently in agreement with Heidegger's view that anxiety, however inundated and compromised by mediation, is ultimately about nothing, which cannot be thoroughly specified. Heidegger says: "That what is threatening is *nowhere* characterizes what anxiety is about. Anxiety 'does not know' what it is anxious about."[15] Heidegger adds: "In what anxiety is about, the 'it is nothing and nowhere' becomes manifest." *Being-in-the-world as such* is nowhere, but—as mentioned above—it is daunting, even stifling, which is the feeling of anxiety about this nothing-and-nowhere. "What stifles [*beengt*] is not this or that, also not everything objectively present as sum, but the possibility of things at hand as such, that is, the world itself." The daunting character of this nowhere registers, as outlined above, in anxiety.[16]

Benjamin will be shown to place greater emphasis on the relationship of this anxiety with what Heidegger might call *beings*. This emphasis might not be incompatible with the following comment by Heidegger: "So if what anxiety is about exposes nothing, that is, the world as such, this means that *that about which anxiety is anxious is being-in-the-world itself*."[17] Beyond this, however, Heidegger proposes: anxious about being-in-the-world as such, anxiety "makes manifest the nothing" *and* "induces the slipping away of beings as a whole."[18] This slipping away of beings is not so readily recognized by Benjamin, for whom beings are what impose themselves to occasion a feeling for preponderant nothing.

Heidegger, in contrast, says simply: what is threatening for anxiety is nowhere—this threat "is so near that it is oppressive and stifles one's breath—and yet it is nowhere."[19] That the threat is nowhere and is, therefore, the threat of being-in-the-world as such, makes it ontological, in Heidegger's sense of fundamental ontology. This ontology includes (among other points): Dasein's ontological status as the existence that experiences existence *as such* to be determinative; Dasein's ontological status whereby Dasein has "—as constitutive for its understanding of existence—an understanding of the being of all beings."[20] This gives Dasein a unique relationship with the being of all beings. "The world . . . ontologically belongs essentially to the being of Dasein as being-in-the-world."[21] Heidegger's privileging of Dasein will be of further concern in the closing section of this article (on "Distractedly Attentive Attention"), but is noteworthy here for its association with anxiety that can potentially lead to ontologically transcending mere beings.

Whereas this potential for ontological transcendence will be shown below to be not clearly conceded in Benjamin's remarks on anxiety in Kafka's works, Heidegger not only stresses that the nothing is open potentiality, but specifies that anxiety is ontological potential.

Heidegger does not, of course, consider this potential for ontological transcendence to be without concreteness. There is in anxiety, he says, a *primor-*

*dial, elemental concretion* of being-free for potential authenticity: "Being-free for its ownmost potentiality-for-being, and thus for the possibility of authenticity and inauthenticity, shows itself in a primordial, elemental concretion in anxiety."[22] This concretion is potential for authentic choosing and comprehending of self, for authentic being-in-the-world—in other words, for the authentic experience of self (as something that is amidst the all-pervasive nowhere, amidst the all-pervasive nothing): anxiety "reveals in Da-sein its *being toward* its ownmost potentiality of being, that is, *being free for* the freedom of choosing and grasping [*-ergreifens*] itself. Anxiety brings Da-sein *before its being free for* . . . the authenticity of its being as possibility which it always already is."[23] This "always already is" is the primordial elemental concretion to which Heidegger refers. It is the primordial elemental concretion into which Dasein is always already thrown. Anxiety takes this thrownness seriously—as a constant to which Dasein can open: that before which anxiety arises, and toward which it is oriented, "is thrown being-in-the-world"; anxiety is, therefore, on behalf of "potentiality-for-being-in-the-world."[24] In its attention to this primordially concrete potentiality, anxiety is regarded by Heidegger as important in the development of what he describes at the outset of *Being and Time* as Dasein's possibility of transcending beings and entering an ontological approach to being as such.[25]

Benjamin's previously discussed anti-Kierkegaardian tendency might even indicate his critical impression of Heidegger's *Being and Time*. In a note commenting on editorial remarks made by Brod and Hans Joachim Schoeps in the collection of Kafka's writings published in 1931 as *Beim Bau der Chinesischen Mauer* (*Building the Wall of China*), Benjamin objects that "Sometimes the language of the editors comes into dubious proximity to the language of the *Existentialphilosophie*" (II:3, 1219). In Benjamin's time, the term *Existentialphilosophie* was applied to Kierkegaard (Benjamin critically refers elsewhere to "the mythic . . . in the existential philosophy [*Existentialphilosophie*] of Kierkegaard" [*SW* 2, 703/ III, *381*]) but was also applied to Heidegger (as well as to others, such as Karl Jaspers).[26] In his objection to Brod and Schoeps's proximity to "the language of *Existentialphilosophie*," Benjamin cites their conceptions of the "'possibility of salvation'" (*Heilsmöglichkeit*) and of "'mythic divination of the fatefulness of historical contexts'" (*mythischen Ahnungswissen um die Schicksalhaftigkeit der geschichtlichen Zusammenhänge*) (II:3, 1219). Brod and Schoeps actually make these comments while contrasting Kierkegaard with Kafka's emphasis on "the historical character of existence [*die Geschichtlichkeit des Daseins*]."[27] Yet they provide the aforementioned references to a possibility of salvation and to mythic divination of fatefulness, and do so as though these are transcendent potentials recognized in Kafka's writings. These references to such a transcendent element in Kafka's writing evidently disturb Benjamin, and are associated by him with *Existentialphilosophie*. If the aside about *Existentialphilosophie* indicates Benjamin's anti-transcendentalist objection to Heidegger, Adorno's attacks on Heidegger's conception of authentic being-in-the-world might seem not entirely un-Benjaminian. In his highly polemical *The Jargon of Authenticity*, Adorno opposes what he considers to be Heidegger's "hypostasis of the ontological sphere."[28] Whether or not it is directed at Heidegger, Benjamin's view of anxiety may be taken to counter would-be registrations of anxiety as penultimate to Dasein's ontological transcendence. For Benjamin, anxiety is precisely an opening to the dynamic in which beings (the ontic) and being as such (the ontological) intermingle to the extent that their very distinction is (almost, if not entirely) annulled.

Benjamin's (usually declarative) expressions of hostility to Heidegger's views are well-known, and Heidegger may, as noted above, accordingly be an implicit antagonist for Benjamin's writings on Kafka.[29] Benjamin's writings on Kafka mark, however, a slight divergence from his earlier formulations (in the 1921-22 study, *Goethe's Elective Affinities*) that associate the term "*Angst*" (anxiety) only with fretful attachment to, and fear of, mythic moral-legal order (*SW* 1, 316-17/ I:1, 150-51).[30] In contrast with this earlier notion of anxiety as mythic, Benjamin's Kafka-writings distinguish the terms "fear" and "anxiety" in a manner that is close to aspects of the usages of these terms by Kierkegaard and Heidegger. In what could seem a somewhat Kierkegaardian and Heideggerian formulation, for instance, one of Benjamin's rough notes on Kafka characterizes "fear [*Furcht*]" as "a reaction [*Reaktion*]" and stresses that "anxiety" (*Angst*) is not a reaction. Benjamin refers to anxiety as an "organ [*Organ*]"; anxiety is "*Organ*" in the sense that it is an initiating, rather than just a reactive, agent (II:3, 1196).[31] Benjamin also refers, however, to the "*Doppelgesichtigkeit*," the two-sidedness, of "the Kafkan anxiety"; he does not really clarify, but he might be suggesting that anxiety is not entirely free of fear (II:3, 1196).[32] In any case, it will be proposed below that Benjamin regards anxiety and fear as intermingled in Kafka. In the *extent* of this ambiguity and of a correlative resistance to transcendence, the anxiety detected by Benjamin in Kafka is distinct from the potential attributed to anxiety by Kierkegaard and Heidegger.

In 1927, Benjamin sent Gershom Scholem a note, which Scholem claims is "the first evidence of the influence of Kafka's 'The Trial' on Benjamin."[33] The note accompanies a letter indicating that Benjamin is reading Kafka's *The Trial* (*GB* III, 303), which had first been published in 1925. Benjamin had probably been reading other writings by Kafka for some time (*GB* III, 64). The note ascribed by Scholem to the influence of *The Trial* is titled "Idea of a Mystery" (*Idee eines Mysteriums*). In this note, Benjamin sketches a scenario in which there will eventually be no credible arbiters (much as is indeed the case in *The Trial*). An ensuing anxiety, although fleeting, dissociates people momentarily from orders that they otherwise thoroughly perpetuate. This anxiety could be construed as wariness of the illusory character of human orders. It is, above all, a feeling for experience that somehow eludes such orders and yet does not have the pretense of transcending all attachment to such orders. This is, of course, the prevailing condition in *The Trial*.

In Benjamin's Mystery-note, would-be jurors experience dissociation from their juror-positions. The positions are perhaps inherently dissociative; these are positions from which the jurors have "mistrust" for "the human prosecutor" (*Mensch-Ankläger*) and for "witnesses" (*Zeugen*) alike. Such dissociation is accompanied, however, by apparent attachment to those very positions: the jurors eventually develop "anxiety" that they might be driven from their juror-places. As a feeling for displacement, the anxiety (in this scenario) is a feeling for what dissociates from human orders, but could also be anxiety (as a kind of fear) about losing place in such orders. In the latter respect, the jurors are pointedly untranscendent.

Even if it is a compromised feeling, however, the anxiety of jurors is soon vindicated: there is no longer place for their feeling or for their position. "In the end, all jury-members have fled; only the prosecutor [*Kläger*] and the witnesses remain." Although Benjamin's note is not very clear, it seems to be saying that there remain only those exacting the "torture" (*Folter*) and those giving witness to their own "martyrdom" (*Martyrium*) (*SW* 2, 68/ II:3, *1153-54*). There is ultimately not even pretense to independent adjudication; with the flight of the jurors, we have a motif in which there are only accusers, who administer and apply systems of judgment, and witnesses, who lament such judgment as it applies to them. If there are no jurors, however, it would seem possible (although Benjamin does not expressly say so) that many—if not all—of us are to be considered torturers and martyrs, prosecutors and witnesses. We live in, and enact, systems of judgment or articulation (we are *torturers* and *prosecutors*), and yet somehow experience the resistance of "mute nature" and of "the future" to such systems (we are *martyrs* and *witnesses*). We continue to exploit and suffer those systems, but those systems cannot entirely contain the resistance of nature and of the future to them(*SW* 2, 68/ II:3, *1153*).[34]

Such embroilment of anxiety in societal participation is a striking trait of Benjamin's texts on Kafka. The anxiety on behalf of the nothing that eludes orders is compromised, and rendered ambiguous, by attachment to those orders—or at least by the wish to survive and advance in some variation of such orders.

## An Obscure Physicality of Anxiety

The term "*Organ*" has many possible meanings in German, and at least two of these are likely relevant to Benjamin's usage as he refers to anxiety as an "organ." "Organ" can refer to the aforementioned initiating function of anxiety, the function of not just being reactive. As should become clear below, however, it refers simultaneously to a bodily *organ* of anxiety that might undermine, rather than nurture, aspirations for a religiously, ontologically, or even ethically transcending element.

Such diminishment of transcending potential may initially be illustrated by a contrast of Kierkegaard's Abraham and Kafka's Abraham, which Benjamin admires.[35]

Benjamin does not mention Kierkegaard's reading of the Abraham story. In Kierkegaard's account of the biblical tale, however, Abraham is ready, willing, and able to follow God's wish that Abraham execute his own son Isaac: "it was God, the unchangeable and inscrutable will of the Almighty. . . . [A]long with the knife the fate of Isaac was put into Abraham's own hand. . . . He knew it was God the Almighty that tried him; but he also knew that no sacrifice was too hard when God demanded it—and he drew the knife."[36] This bond with God can open one to an eternity where killing your beloved son is conceivably legitimate; as Kierkegaard tells us, "my eternal consciousness is my love of God."[37] In his speech in praise of Abraham, Kierkegaard summarizes: "he who loved himself became great in himself, and he who loved others became great through his devotion, but he who loved God became greater than all."[38]

Benjamin is drawn toward Kafka's retelling in which Abraham does not have such a transcending capacity. Kafka's Abraham is impeded by his sense of physical constraints that are intermingled with social constraints. Abraham is "willing as a waiter" to serve God.[39] How willing might a waiter be? Not as willing, presumably, as Kierkegaard's Abraham. As Jean-Paul Sartre suggests, a waiter has a project of being waiter whereby he plays at being—in his waiter-role—a waiter, which—other than in this occupational role—he is not.[40] This kind of compromising by socio-economic life emerges in Kafka's reading and is part of what Benjamin seems to appreciate so much: Abraham is impeded by his economic responsibilities from serving God, and is anyway so impressed by the social that he even "fears" the divine assignment will mean he'll become a laughing stock before the world.[41] The intermingling of these societal constraints (of economy and social fear) with an overwhelming physicality is, moreover, noted in Kafka's consideration of the possibility that Abraham cannot quite believe God means this mission for him and his son, a "disgusting old man" and "a dirty youth."[42] A feeling of non-transcendence is associated with intrusive physical forces: age (agedness, youth) and dirt. With apparent approbation, Benjamin takes note of all that has been mentioned above regarding Kafka's Abraham and the role of societal-physical constraints in his demeanor (II: 3, 1268-69; *SW* 2, 807-8/ II:2, 427).

In reading Kafka's account, Benjamin seems to recognize that Abraham's sense of impediments to God's mission combines the societal judgment (entailed in the appellations "disgusting" and "dirty") with a judgment about creeping physical forces (age and dirtiness). The physical forces intermingle with the societal impediments and impose themselves as part of the difficulty for Abraham to take God's command quite seriously. Albeit in a different context, Jean Wahl contrasts Kierkegaard's distinction of the communicable "general" (from the divine) with Kafka's view that the general itself becomes a "mysterious driving force."[43] In Benjamin's view, the force of the bodily and that of societal judgment combine to intrude upon any possible aura of religious transcendence, much as it could be taken to prevail over attempted ontological transcendence. There is not the abyss of religious freedom into which Kierkegaard's Abraham leaps (in passages not quoted by Benjamin, Kafka insists he can recognize no "leap" [*Sprung*] even in "the real Abraham"—evidently the biblical Abraham[44]). Nor is there the Heideggerian freedom for an ontologically transcending and authentic experience. God's mission for Abraham is just one representation among others. For Benjamin, Kafka's Abraham has a life inundated by mundane household obligations and social fears, which converge with a physicality that has a heteronomous power unto itself (II:3, 1269). In remarks not published by Brod until long after Benjamin's lifetime, Kafka himself suggests that the biblical Abraham suffers from "an insufficiently profound mingling with the manifold nature of the world."[45] For Kafka's Abraham and for Benjamin's account, any impetus to religious or ontological transcendence is stifled by what could be called a physically impelled anxiety that dissociates from the supposedly transcendent claims of the biblical Abraham, or the Kierkegaardian Abraham, upon us. Kafka himself remarks further that Kierkegaard "does not see the ordinary human being . . . and paints this monstrous Abraham in the clouds."[46]

Even if its physicality gives the organ of anxiety a heteronomous power unto itself, Benjamin's reference to Abraham's economic responsibilities and social fears might seem to show Benjamin and Kafka abandoning anxiety for fear. Benjamin and Kafka might seem to be abandoning the kind of anxiety that is anxious on behalf of the nothing, the kind of anxiety possibly suggested as Benjamin mentions instances of study devoted to nothing: the young Karl Rossmann in *The Missing Person* (*Amerika*), the horse Bucephalus in the "The New Lawyer," and Kafka's Sancho Panza (*SW* 2, 813/ II:2, 434-35, II:3, 1243).[47] Do Kafka and Benjamin submit themselves to an Abraham who surrenders himself entirely to household obligations, societal judgments, and fatalistic associations with bodily conditions such as agedness and youth? Although Benjamin does not quite say so, it seems clear that Kafka's lightly ironic treatment of Abraham's sense of obligation and fear is already a slight distancing from the imperatives recognized by such obligation and fear.[48] Albeit in a different context, Günther Anders refers to a tendency of Kafka to present customs and morals from the perspective of someone not belonging to their world.[49] Kafka's Abraham belongs to this world, and yet Kafka treats this world with a slight irony. The slight irony emerges as Kafka discusses Abraham's involute quandary. Abraham believes in God, and would like to oblige God—yet his fear includes not simply that others will laugh at him but also that he might join in the laughing and that his laughable state might make him (and his son) more repelling: "It is not the laughableness [*Lächerlichkeit*] in itself that he fears—though he fears that too, above all his laughing along [*Mitlachen*]—but mainly he fears that this laughableness will make him even older and more repelling, and his son even dirtier, even more undignified." Under these conditions, he—they—really could not "be called" by God.[50] Perhaps there is something humorous as well as horrific in the portrayal of the seemingly exaggerated association of social deviation (ridiculousness, *Lächerlichkeit*) with allegedly ensuing physical intrusions (aging and dirtiness).[51] With his humor, Kafka does not rise above these specific societal-physical hindrances (to transcendence) but also does not quite identify with them. Benjamin says Kafka simply tries to hide behind the "hindrances": Kafka "piles up hindrances. In order to overcome them? Not at all; but rather to hide himself behind them," just as "his most distinguished gesture, shame, compels him" to do (II:3, 1269).[52]

This is *not* ultimately shame before others, as is partly the case for Kafka's Abraham. The shame is also *not* an anxiety so before God that it proffers resolute transcendence. Kafka's anxiety cannot bear the idea of such a relationship with God. Benjamin comments: "To be seen by God on this earth is not bearable [*erträglich*] and a God that inspects the earth, not to be invented [*nicht auszusinnen*]" (II:3, 1269). Kafka's shame involves an anxiety that reminds us of hindrances to such an idea of God but also avoids turning those hindrances into something divine. Kafka renders the hindrances with a gently distancing irony. After all, they too are not an ultimate answer to life's oblique forcefulness. In relation to the latter forcefulness, the anxiety of Benjamin's Kafka emerges as a feeling for life, which has no ultimate answer.

## Anxiety as Inhuman Irresoluteness

As indicated above, this feeling for life includes a physical dimension that especially contributes to anxiety having an inhuman element, an element eluding the human. Anxiety in Benjamin's Kafka might challenge, therefore, the interhuman priorities of Levinas's outlook. In Levinas's early career, he was of course Heideggerian, and his expositions of Heidegger's theory of anxiety are correlatively sympathetic.[53] This early Levinas is very Heideggerian in describing anxiety as an incomparable "comprehension" that "grasps" and "accomplishes" "Dasein as deed par excellence."[54] Even considerably later, in *Otherwise than Being*, the much less Heideggerian Levinas does not follow, but at least adapts, Heidegger's notion of anxiety in order to accentuate a "movement" of the "self" in its opposition to "constriction."[55] Yet this later Levinas's critique of Kierkegaard and Heidegger could be extended to their conceptions of anxiety, which in their respectively religious and ontological priorities could seem inhuman, and potentially inhumane, from a Levinasian perspective. Benjamin's previously discussed incompatibility with Kierkegaardian religiosity and Heideggerian ontology could accordingly make him somewhat Levinasian *avant la lettre*. Benjamin's conception of anxiety is based, however, on an inhuman physicality that eludes what seem to be Levinas's interhuman parameters or emphases.

As is well-known, Levinas presents his own alternative to Kierkegaard's Abraham. His reading of Kierkegaard's Abraham, and of Kierkegaard generally, has been the focus of much, sometimes indignant, discussion among Kierkegaard scholars.[56] Most aspects of these debates cannot be dealt with even superficially here. Yet even among these critics of Levinas, it has been conceded that Levinas is correct in noting one fundamental difference between his views and those of Kierkegaard. According to Merold Westphal, for instance, Kierkegaard considers God to be the precondition of "properly" recognizing "either myself or my neighbor," whereas Levinas reverses "this order and insists that I relate first to my neighbor."[57] Kierkegaard gives priority to God; Levinas suggests the radically Other is always another human being.[58] Whereas Kierkegaard—on behalf of "the religious"—suspends the ethical, Levinas suspends one kind of "ethical" (state, custom, morality) in favor of another kind of "ethical" (my infinite obligation to the other human); for Levinas, Kierkegaard's relative neglect of the latter ethical "opens the door to a violence that cannot be accepted."[59] In his own remarks, Levinas criticizes the forced—the violent—character of what he takes to be Kierkegaard's dissociation of the religious self from the ethical. With regard to Abraham, therefore, Levinas simply stresses that the biblical story continues, after all, beyond Abraham's willingness to follow God's command about killing Isaac; the story shows Abraham remaining open to the divine voice that tells him *not* to kill Isaac. In disagreement with what Levinas takes to be Kierkegaard's notion that the religious takes Abraham beyond the ethical, Levinas concludes that "[p]erhaps Abraham's ear for hearing the voice that brought him back to the ethical order was the highest moment in this drama."[60] For Levinas, there is "transcendence" whereby Abraham recognizes "an infinite responsibility for the other."[61]

This ethical transcendence is not evident in Kafka's Abraham or in Benjamin's account of Kafka's Abraham. If there is anxiety in Kafka's Abraham and in Benjamin's account, it includes Abraham's unwillingness or inability to identify with any transcendent image that would be bestowed upon him—be it religious, ontological, or ethical. Without reference to Kafka's Abraham, Jacques Derrida adapts Nietzsche to question the "sacrificial *hubris*" of the biblical story of Abraham, as well as of Kierkegaard's rendering of it.[62] Suggesting something other than an ethical transcendence (as detected by Levinas in the Abraham story), moreover, Derrida wonders about the possible trauma to Isaac: Abraham is concerned with God's pardon, and "does not ask forgiveness of Isaac, somewhat in the way that the French Conference of Bishops does not ask forgiveness of the Jews, but of God."[63] This concern about the aftereffect on Isaac could seem, however, at least somewhat Levinasian—more Levinasian than Levinas perhaps.[64] Yet Kafka's priority is somehow pre-ethical and thereby undermines any even potentially authoritative role for Abraham. In the biblical portrayal of Abraham as patriarch, there may be a religious chauvinism concerning Abraham and his descendants (who are promised possession of their enemies' cities).[65] Kafka seems to reject this possible element of the story, and thus has an Abraham who would not cut it as "patriarch" (*Erzvater*)—indeed, would not even make it as an "old-clothes dealer."[66] Benjamin notes this aspect of Kafka's Abraham, along with the aforementioned doubt of Kafka's Abraham that this sacrificial mission is meant for him—a supposedly repelling, aged man—and his filthy son (*SW* 2, 807-8/ II:2, 427, II:3, 1269).[67] More than religious, ontological, or ethical transcendence, there is simply a freedom to treat such notions of transcendence as suspect.

For Benjamin's Kafka, anxiety is *this* freedom, this feeling of a relentlessly physical, heterogeneous life that rebuffs religious, ontological, or ethical accounts. On the basis of this feeling of pervasively heterogeneous physicality, there emerges "a secret solidarity of anxiety" between the beings of all levels of hierarchy (II:3, 1197). The solidarity is secret, for mythic, ostensibly closed, hierarchies almost always prevent it from being indulged. Neither our speech nor our deeds can, it seems, deviate too much from some variation of such hierarchies. Yet hope—as the term "solidarity" might suggest—could emerge as the shared anxiety that recognizes, and is concerned with, existence in its inhuman, non-human, elusion of hierarchies. This hope would be complemented, rather than mitigated, by the dissociation of anxiety from religious, ontological, or ethical transcendence.

In its very diffuse and heterogeneous physicality, after all, Benjamin's Kafkan anxiety is significantly based on Kafka's attention to the "strangeness" that is "one's own body [*der eigene Körper*]" (*SW* 2, 810/ II:2, 431). Whereas Heidegger refers to both "care" (*Sorge*) and "anxiety" (*Angst*) as potentially enabling a resolutely ontological relationship of Dasein with being (*Sein*),[68] terms such as "*Sorge*" and "*Angst*" in Benjamin's writings on Kafka pertain to an irresoluteness: anxiety even turns into dispersed anxieties (*Ängste*). "Irresolutely," the thinking of Kafka's non-human animals, for instance, "swings from one worry [*Sorge*] to another; it nibbles at all anxieties [*Ängten*] and has . . . fickleness." There is "something very distracted" in the thinking (*SW* 2, 810/ II:2, *430*). Much as exposure of corruption can remove facades of sanctity from law, anxiety dissociates somewhat from ostensibly closed orders and claims; it does so by feeling a continual distractedness, by *feeling* a thinking—for it is a bodily thinking—that such orders and claims cannot absorb or subsume (*SW* 2, 810/ II:2, 431).[69]

The physical, heterogeneous distractedness of this anxiety—intractable for aspirations of religious, ontological, or ethical transcendence—might, as noted, be hopeful in its potential for unsettling hierarchies and other forms of would-be subsumption. Anxiety—the organ of heterogeneous physicality—"messes up the course of events [*den Vorgang*] and yet is the sole hopeful element [*Hoffnungsvolle*] in that course of events" (*SW* 2, 810/ II:2, *431*).[70] This anxiety is hopeful in freeing thinking for messy, intractable living. This messy, inhuman elusiveness of life might seem especially suggested by "Before the Law" (which gives rise to so much interpretative speculation in the story itself, in the reception, and in the relevant chapter of *The Trial*), and by K.'s desperate attempts (in the fifth chapter of *The Castle*) to understand Klamm's letter to K.[71] With regard to these texts, Benjamin refers to Kafka's "'*Folie d'interpretation*,'" and notes that "interpretation of the law, interpretation of files, constitute the whole content of *The Trial* and *The Castle*." Even Kafka's testament, which insisted to Brod that Kafka's unpublished writings be burned, is considered by Benjamin to strain the ability to interpret (II:3, 1229 Ms. 297). In Kafka's writings, freed thinking is resonant with the inhuman that cannot be entirely rendered in hierarchies or other forms of interpretative closure.

## Distractedly Attentive Attention

For Benjamin, Kafka's anxiety is simply a thinking that feels it cannot stop being attentive to heterogeneous physicality, which is too messily and intractably imposing to be ordered or transcended. In these closing pages, an attempt will be made to further elucidate this attention. The inhuman physicality is so intrusive that it is incompatible with any claim of preeminence for human attention. In this respect, it is distinct from Heidegger's view of the human being as *the* uniquely ontological being. Levinas considers Heidegger's ontological human to be inattentive to human relations. Although Benjamin's writings on Kafka do not conceive of the human as ontologically advantaged, they do conceive of attentiveness as a level of distraction and physical waywardness that Levinas might also consider irresponsible toward humans.

Benjamin does not mention Kafka's Prometheus legend, but that short text is suggestive of the relationship of anxiety with attention (although it does not specifically refer to either anxiety or attention). Whereas some portray the ancient Prometheus legend as a victory of Zeus over humanity and others treat it as a heroic show of humanity's importance, Kafka's account of the Prometheus legend concentrates on the rock to which Prometheus, the Titan who has incurred Zeus's wrath by aiding humanity, is bound: "There remained the inexplicable mass of rock." This inexplicability of the rock somehow suspends hierarchies of humans and of the gods that humans have imagined. "Legend attempts to explain the inexplicable; because it comes out of a basis of truth [*Wahrheitsgrund*]," however, legend "must again end in the inexplicable."[72] Benjamin must have been aware of Kafka's Prometheus text: it first appeared in 1931 in *Beim Bau der Chinesischen Mauer: Ungedruckte Erzählungen und Prosa aus dem Nachlaß* that was edited by Brod and Schoeps and was reviewed on radio by Benjamin in 1931 (*SW* 2, 494-500/ II:2, 676-83).[73] Although Benjamin does not mention Kafka's Prometheus legend with its focus on the rock, one of Benjamin's Brecht commentaries does refer to a "rock of astonishment" that breaks human word and deed (*UB*, 13/ II:2, 531). Rock is associated here with astonishment that dissociates from whatever is considered human. Such astonishment dissociating from the human is also mentioned in Benjamin's Kafka commentaries (e.g., *SW* 2, 814/ II:2, 435-36).[74] For Kafka, as noted, the rock is taken as an occasion for attention to the very materially non-human that ultimately defies human comprehension. It may often seem that humans are sovereign over rocks, but rocks also elude complete comprehension. Even in their manipulations of rocks, humans find themselves confronted with unmanageable consequences of those manipulations. In the context of his Kafka writings, Benjamin's rock of astonishment emerges as astonishment on behalf of the inexplicable and intrusive nothing that resonates in all *somethings* and thereby makes them ultimately unmalleable for human hierarchies and indeed for human aspirations of dominance or independence (*SW* 2, 813-14/ II:2, 434-36, II:3, 1243).[75] Anxiety—as elaborated above—is attentive to the nothing in which *somethings* are wrenched from any would-be transcendence that humans might consider themselves, or their imagined gods, to have as unique accomplishment, development, or endowment.[76]

This non-hierarchical attention is distinct from the tendency in some of Heidegger's works to identify an ontological being somehow apart from non-ontological beings. In this respect, some texts by Heidegger specifically articulate what could seem an anthropocentric conception of the human in relation to the rock and other entities. For instance, in the 1949 introduction to "What is Metaphysics" (1929) there is the now-famous remark: "The being that exists is the human being. The human being alone exists. Rocks are, but they do not exist."[77] In the same introduction, Heidegger specifies that the human being is unique in its ontological opening to the being of beings: an openness in which being as such "announces and conceals itself, grants itself and withdraws."[78] For Heidegger in this text, "[t]he proposition 'the human being exists' means: the human being . . . is distinguished by an open standing that stands in the unconcealedness of being" as such, and the human being proceeds from—and in—this being as such.[79] Correlatively, Heidegger remarks in the "The Origin of the Work of Art" (1935-36) that the artwork is not about "the reproduction [*Wiedergabe*]" of a "particular being" but rather "the reproduction of the general essence of things."[80] The general essence of things is the being of beings, the being as such to which the human is uniquely open. In the Postscript (1943), as in the Introduction, to "What Is Metaphysics?," Heidegger refers specifically to the human being. On the basis of thinking "out of an attentiveness [*Achtsamkeit*] to the voice [*Stimme*] of being" as such "and into the attunement [*Stimmen*] coming from this voice," "the human being" in its "essence" is taken by "the claim" of being as such, "so that in the nothing the human being may learn to experience" being as such.[81] In its capacity for experiencing the nothing of being as such, the human emerges as the ontological being.

To Heidegger's ontological priorities, Levinas takes exception—less to the privileging of the human than to an inattentiveness that Levinas considers inherent in Heidegger's conception of attentiveness to being as such. The latter attentiveness, Levinas contends, gives rise to an inattentive human. In lectures of the mid-1970s that often refer or allude to Heidegger, Levinas retorts: "Life is not measured by being"; rather, "the other affects us despite ourselves."[82] In the earlier *Totality and Infinity* (1961), Levinas evidently counters Heidegger (among others) with a formulation of "the primacy of the ethical"—the "relationship" on which "all the other structures rest (and in particular all those which seem to put us primordially in contact with an impersonal sublimity, aesthetic or ontological)."[83]

In accordance with Levinas's primacy of the ethical, it might be thought that Benjamin and Kafka are neglectful of the preeminence and the potential of interhuman relations. In such an extension of Levinas's critique of Heidegger, Benjamin and Kafka might be accused of trying to decontaminate their work of the primacy, and the ethical potential, of every human's predominance by other humans.

Benjamin's Kafkan anxious attention is not, however, the Heideggerian attention in which, according to Levinas's worry, other humans are ultimately depreciated by would-be attunement to ontological being. While it strains interhuman relations, Benjamin's Kafkan attention involves a strange bodily force that is also inextricable from other humans, as well as from other creatures and indeed from all entities (*SW* 2, 810-12/ II:2, 430-32). All of these are bound in inexplicable nature. In a somewhat similar manner, Jean-Luc Nancy remarks that "[o]ur bodies are . . . quite entirely . . . openings of the world," as are "the other open bodies, those of the animals, the plants."[84] Nancy emphasizes immersion of "the 'with'"—the with-others—in *physis* that "presents itself and . . . accomplishes itself by itself." The "'with,'" he proposes, is thereby "unachieved and unachievable."[85] This being-together/being-apart in *physis* keeps everyone and everything together and apart: shared strangeness in *physis* is what everyone and everything has most inextinguishably in common. Benjamin's Kafka stresses this commonality and its potential for enhancing attention to all and everything.

In the available English translation, Benjamin's 1934 Kafka essay refers to "attentiveness," which is a translation of the German word "*Aufmerksamkeit*" that is used by Benjamin as a translation of Nicolas de Malebranche's French word "*attention*."[86] Although these words could be rendered in English by the term "attention," "attentiveness" may indeed be the more suitable translation for Benjamin's context, not least given his accompanying characterization of "*Aufmerksamkeit*" as what Malebranche calls "'the natural prayer of the soul'" (*SW* 2, 812/ II:2, 432).[87]

Benjamin's account of this attentiveness is no straightforward theologizing of Kafka. Benjamin claims that the word "God" does not appear in Kafka's writings—an exaggeration, of course, even if one only includes texts of which Benjamin was aware, such as the letter that deals with Abraham. For Benjamin, nonetheless, to interpret Kafka's writings in a seamlessly theological way is not much more credible than putting Heinrich von Kleist's novellas into catchy rhyme in order to appeal more to readers (II:3, 1214). There is a "depth" whereby "Kafka touches the ground" that, contrary to the previously discussed theological readings, is not given to him by "'mythic divination'" or "'existential theology'" (*SW* 2, 812/ II:2, *432*).[88] This ground will be formulated below as an insatiable demand on attention. For Benjamin, Kafka's depth of ground is, however, not only his anxious attention to what cannot be absorbed by attention. Kafka's attention simultaneously concerns people, other creatures, and things that must often have an adverse relationship with, and must distract from, most—if not all—claims to religious, ontological, or ethical transcendence.

In an essay-section titled "Transcendence," and on the basis of a citation of Benjamin in Paul Celan's *Der Meridian*, Levinas in 1972 briefly elaborates Benjamin's remarks on Kafka's attentiveness.[89] Levinas refers to "extreme receptivity, but extreme donation." Both Celan and Benjamin's Kafka are indeed interested in an extreme receptiveness that involves giving extreme attention. Yet Levinas continues: "attentiveness—a mode of consciousness without distraction, that is to say, without the power of escape [*evasion*] through dark [*obscurs*] underground passages." "[I]n order to prohibit evasion [*la dérobade*]," there is a responsibility that includes the ability "to transcend against nature."[90] This transcendent responsibility is also suggested in an earlier work, *From Existence to the Existent*, where Levinas uses the term "attention" quite differently, contrasting it unfavorably with "vigilance." A difference with Benjamin may already be noted perhaps as Levinas distinguishes attention, which turns toward objects ("whether . . . internal or external"), from vigilance, as a concern with the "*il y a*" (there is, there are) that is independent of objects. The vigilance is here advanced as a corrective to the prevalence of nothingness in Heidegger's notion of anxiety: anxiety for the nothing is replaced by what can be "horror" of the "*il y a*."[91] This horror might seem quite Kafkan, but the transcending element of vigilance—the transcending element of the "*il y a*"—already seems distinct from the attention or attentiveness that Benjamin detects in Kafka, which is an attention always already mediated by objects—be they human or otherwise. For Levinas, moreover, it is in the human that the "*il y a*" transpires. The human could thus seem—in a certain sense and admittedly in very unLevinasian terms—the being of beings. Although largely with respect to *Totality and Infinity*, Derrida refers to Levinas's "[e]thico-metaphysical transcendence" that "presupposes ontological transcendence."[92] Even if the ethical exigency becomes—in later texts such as *Otherwise than Being*—a kind of deliverance from the "there is,"[93] Levinas's transcending human, or his conceptions of a transcending relation of human and human, could seem an ontological transcendence whereby there is a being of beings: the human. In any case, vigilance with regard to the "*il y a*" is treated as a unique potential of humans. Additionally, the transcendent relation of human and human is suggested in Levinas's aforementioned conceptions of ethical transcendence against nature and against distraction into underground passages.

For Benjamin's Kafka, in contrast, attentiveness and its anxiety require distraction, and this distraction might require escape or evasion into obscure dimensions of a nature that—in its heterogeneous, powerful physicality—does not entirely release us and cannot, therefore, be transcended (religiously, ontologically, or ethically): "the age in which Kafka lived" was considered by Kafka to be "no progress beyond the primal beginnings" (*keinen Fortschritt über die Uranfänge*) (*SW* 2, 808–9/ II:2, *428*). There can be anxiety against the presumption of religion, ontology, or ethics to transcend those beginnings. The powerful, and ultimately indeterminate, play of those beginnings distracts the attentive by demanding of their attention that it go into what Levinas might consider obscure underground passages. "Distraction" (*Zerstreuung*), Benjamin contends, is a "physiological" phenomenon (*SW* 3, 141/ VII, 678).

To what, however, is devoted the distraction into, attention to, those primal beginnings? It has been proposed above that this distracted attention or attentive distraction emerges as an anxiety on behalf of what eludes orders in which humans otherwise endeavor to control and to organize their lives. This anxiety, it has also been suggested, is so embroiled in those controls and organizations that it does not proffer the possibility of completely transcending them. As a bodily *organ*, however, it cannot be limited by those controls and organization, even if it is often subject to controls and organization. In physical distractedness, attention cannot indulge notions of transcending the sensate, oblique nature from which there emerges anxiety's sense of the nothing—anxiety's sense of the determinate, yet ultimately indeterminable, physical force underlying all identified and identifiable particulars.

This physicality might seem betrayed in aspects of the messianism in Benjamin's reading of Kafka. The mockingly laughing "little hunchbacked man," drawn by Benjamin from an old German folk song and regarded by him as the prototype of the distortion pervading Kafka's work, will—Benjamin claims—"disappear with the coming of the Messiah, who . . . will not wish to change the world by force but will merely make a slight adjustment in it" (*SW* 2, 811/ II:2, 432). It is to this messianic change that Benjamin apparently thinks Kafka's aforementioned alleged *prayer* is ultimately oriented.

The prayer is an attentiveness that opens to all creatures: "If Kafka did not pray—which we do not know—he still possessed in the highest degree what Malebranche calls 'the natural prayer of the soul'—attentiveness. And in this attentiveness he included all creatures, as saints include them in their prayers" (*SW* 2, 812/ II:2, *432*). It could be that Benjamin considers this attentiveness to take these creatures, as saints' prayers are supposed to do, into a dimension where the creatures have an enhanced rapport with the messiah. It might be asked, however, what happens to that inexplicable and intrusive materiality to which Kafka's Prometheus legend refers in its remarks on the rock? After all, the messianic attention is supposed to lead to the disappearance of irritants (represented by the mockingly laughing little hunchbacked man), or at least to a slight adjustment whereby they would no longer be what they once were: irritants, distractions (SW 2, 811/ II:2, 432).

Such an outlook may indicate a more belittling attitude toward the distractions, and toward the attendant lack of control, than is often evident in Benjamin's writings. The messianic effect in the distractions is supposed ultimately to overcome them. The messianic effect is presumably also to overcome the orders in relation to which there is dismissal of distractions. Simply by virtue of the elimination of those orders, the distractions would themselves—at least in some way—disappear with the coming of the messiah: they would be overcome as distractions, as would the orders disregarding them. Yet Benjamin's apparent envisioning of a loss of anxiety concerning the disregard in such orders might itself entail inattentiveness. There may be a lapse in his anxiety, and thus in his attention, as he pronounces not simply the coming of the messiah but also the disappearance of the distractions. The would-be transcendent messianism might have neglected its own anxious attention to the physicality that eludes, and somehow defies, many claims to transcendence. As a lapsed attention, the loss of such anxiety is a lapse in the ability to get distracted by whatever takes us down underground passages where our concern with transcendence—our fear of anxiety—might not want to go.

## Notes

1. See Willy Haas, *Gestalten der Zeit* (Berlin: Gustav Kiepenheuer Verlag, 1930), 181.

2. *AP* = *The Arcades Project*, trans. H. Eiland and K. McLaughlin (Cambridge, MA: Harvard University Press, 1999); *C* = *The Correspondence of Walter Benjamin*, ed. Gershom Scholem and Theodor Adorno, trans. Manfred R. Jacobson and Evelyn M. Jacobson (Chicago, IL: University Chicago Press, 1994); *GB* = Benjamin, *Gesammelte Briefe*, eds. C. Gödde and H. Lonitz (Frankfurt a.M.: Suhrkamp, 1995-2000). Roman numerals, usually followed by Arabic numerals, indicate volume numbers of Benjamin, *Gesammelte Schriften*, Vols. I–VII, ed. R. Tiedemann and H. Schweppenhäuser et al. (Frankfurt a.M.: Suhrkamp, 1974–99). The following abbreviations are also used for

works by Benjamin: *UB* = *Understanding Brecht*, trans. Anna Bostock (London: Verso, 1998); *SW* (followed by a volume number) = *Selected Writings*, Vols. 1–4, ed. Michael W. Jennings et al. (Cambridge, MA: The Belknap Press of Harvard University Press, 1996, 1999, 2002, 2003). If an existing English-translation has been modified, the pagination for the German (or French) text will be italicized.

3. Søren Kierkegaard, *The Concept of Anxiety*, trans. and ed. Reider Thomte with Albert B. Anderson (Princeton, NJ: Princeton University Press, 1981), 42-43.

4. Kierkegaard, *The Concept of Anxiety*, 109.

5. Søren Kierkegaard, *Fear and Trembling*, trans. Alistair Hannay (London: Penguin Books, 1986), *passim*.

6. Kierkegaard, *Fear and Trembling*, 107.

7. Kierkegaard, *The Concept of Anxiety*, 95.

8. See Haas, *Gestalten der Zeit*, 176-77.

9. Max Brod, *Franz Kafka: A Biography*, trans. G. Humphreys Roberts and Richard Winston (New York: Schocken Books, 1963), 181/ *Über Franz Kafka* (Frankfurt a.M.: Fischer, 1989), *159*.

10. Brod, *Franz Kafka* , 184, 198/ *Über Franz Kafka*, 162, 172-73.

11. Brod, *Franz Kafka*, 170/ *Über Franz Kafka*, *150*. For other remarks on Kierkegaard, see too 144, 164 / 129, 145.

12. Brod, *Franz Kafka:* 49/ *Über Franz Kafka*, 50.

13. Here and once below, for purposes of enabling the reader to find more quickly the relevant passage in the cited text, "Ms." refers to the manuscript number (these numbers are the same as those in the *Walter Benjamin-Archiv* at the *Akademie der Künste*, Berlin).

14. The text cited here is Benjamin's review (published in 1933) of Adorno's book, *Kierkegaard: Konstruktion des Ästhetischen* (first published in 1932). The assessment of Kierkegaard (in this review) echoes (often on the basis of Adorno's book) in some of Benjamin's references in the Arcades study to Kierkegaard. See, for instance, *AP*, 219-20, 542/ V:1, 290-91, 672.

15. Martin Heidegger, *Being and Time*, trans. Joan Stambaugh, revised by Dennis Schmidt (Albany, NY: SUNY Press, 2010), 180/ *Sein und Zeit* (Tübingen: Niemeyer, 1986), *186*.

16. Heidegger, *Being and Time*, 181-82/ *Sein und Zeit*, 186-87.

17. Heidegger, *Being and Time*, 181/ *Sein und Zeit*, 187.

18. Martin Heidegger, "What is Metaphysics?," *Pathmarks*, ed. William McNeill (Cambridge: Cambridge University Press, 1999), 88/ "Was ist Metaphysik?," *Wegmarken*, (Frankfurt a.M.: Vittorio Klostermann, 2004), *112*.

19. Heidegger, *Being and Time*, 231/ *Sein und Zeit*, 186.

20. Heidegger, *Being and Time*, 12/ *Sein und Zeit*, *13*.

21. Heidegger, *Being and Time*, 181/ *Sein und Zeit*, 187.

22. Heidegger, *Being and Time*, 185 / *Sein und Zeit*, 191.

23. Heidegger, *Being and Time*, 182/ *Sein und Zeit*, 188.

24. Heidegger, *Being and Time*, 185/ *Sein und Zeit*, 191.

25. Heidegger, *Being and Time*, 35-36/ *Sein und Zeit*, 37-38.

26. See Herbert Schnädelbach, *Philosophy in Germany 1831-1933*, trans. Eric Matthews (Cambridge: Cambridge University Press, 1984), 200.

27. Max Brod and Hans Joachim Schoeps, "Nachwort," in Franz Kafka, *Beim Bau der Chinesischen Mauer. Ungedruckte Erzählungen und Prosa aus dem Nachlaß* (Berlin: Gustav Kiepenheuer Verlag, 1931), 255.

28. Theodor W. Adorno, *Jargon of Authenticity*, trans. Knut Tarnowski and Frederic Will (Evanston, IL: Northwestern University Press, 1973), 120 / *Jargon der Eigentlich-*

*keit. Zur deutschen Ideologie* (Frankfurt a.M: Suhrkamp, 1964), *100*. See too: *Negative Dialectics*, trans. E.B. Ashton (New York: Continuum, 1973), 61-131, especially 129/ *Negative Dialektik* (Frankfurt a.M.: Suhrkamp, 1975), 67-136, especially, 134.

29. For instances of anti-Heideggerian remarks by Benjamin, see *GB* 1, 344, *C*, 168/ *GB* 2, 108, *C*, 172/ *GB* 2, *127*, *C*, 372/ *GB*, Vol. 4, 19.

30. In a special issue of *Les Cahiers du Sud* on "German Romanticism," a very small part of Benjamin's *Elective Affinities* study appeared in French with the appropriate title "L'angoisse mythique chez Goethe." In a commentary in the 1938 issue of the Moscow German-language journal *Internationale Literatur* (1930-1945), Alfred Kurella contends Benjamin's piece is indicative of something "dangerous"; it attempts to make "a metaphysical anxiety in Goethe's life the actual source of his greatness"—an attempt that Kurella claims would do credit to Heidegger. This characterization irritates Benjamin considerably (*GB* 6, 138). See: Benjamin, "L'angoisse mythique chez Goethe," trans. Pierre Klossowski, *Les Cahiers du Sud* 24/194 (May-June 1937): 342-48; Alfred Kurella, "Deutsche Romantik. Zum gleichnamigen Sonderheft der 'Cahiers du Sud,'" *Internationale Literatur* 6 (1938): 113-28, especially 127.

31. On faith as an "organ" in Kierkegaard, see Peter Fenves, *"Chatter," Language and History in Kierkegaard* (Stanford, CA: Stanford University Press, 1993), 130-35.

32. For this view of the two-sidedness of anxiety, Benjamin claims to be following Willy Haas's interpretation of Kafkan anxiety. Benjamin wrote for *Die Literarische Welt*, which Haas edited, so perhaps he is referring to an exchange with Haas. There is, however, no such characterization of Kafka's *Angst* in Haas's *Gestalten der Zeit*, which is the only work by Haas that is referred to in Benjamin's writings and notes on Kafka. See Willy Haas, *Gestalten der Zeit* (172-99), which interprets Kafka through Kierkegaard.

33. Gershom Scholem, *Walter Benjamin: The Story of a Friendship*, trans. Harry Zohn (Philadelphia, PA: The Jewish Publication Society of America, 1981), 145/ *Walter Benjamin—die Geschichte einer Freundschaft* (Frankfurt a.M.: Suhrkamp, 1975), 181.

34. My reading leaves out important aspects of Benjamin's note, some of which I am addressing more extensively in a larger work. For instance, there is a multidisciplinary theme as witnesses for the future include poets, sculptors, musicians, and philosophers whose witnessing does not converge.

35. For further discussion of Kafka's Abraham, see Chris Danta, "Sarah's Laughter: Kafka's Abraham," *Modernism/modernity* 15.2 (April 2008): 343-59; Gesine Palmer, "Geheimnisse eines bereitwilligen Kellners: Abraham bei Derrida, Benjamin und Kafka," *Zeitschrift für Religions-und Geistesgeschichte* 51.1 (1999): 48-63. In a broader context, see too: Danta, "The Poetics of Distance: Kierkegaard's Abraham," *Literature and Theology* 21.2 (June 2007): 160-77 and "'The Absolutely Dark Moment of the Plot.' Blanchot's Abraham," in *After Blanchot: Literature, Criticism, and Philosophy*, eds. Leslie Hill, Brian Nelson, and Dimitris Vardoulakis (Newark, DE: University of Delaware Press, 2005), 205-20.

36. See especially "Speech in Praise of Abraham," *Fear and Trembling*, 55; see too: 49-56.

37. Kierkegaard, *Fear and Trembling*, 77.

38. Kierkegaard, *Fear and Trembling*, 50.

39. Kafka, letter of June 1921 to his friend Robert Klopstock, *Briefe. 1902-1924*, ed. Max Brod (Frankfurt a.M.: Fischer Verlag, 1983), 333.

40. Jean-Paul Sartre, *Being and Nothingness*, trans. Hazel Barnes (New York: Washington Square Press, 1992), 102-3/ *L'être et le néant* (Paris: Gallimard, 1943), 94-95. If the article at hand were to be more extensive, it could include consideration of Sartre's reworking of the conceptions of anxiety in Kierkegaard and Heidegger (65-85/ 64-80).

41. Kafka, letter of June 1921, *Briefe. 1902-1924*, 333.

42. Kafka, letter of June 1921, *Briefe. 1902-1924*, 333-34.

43. Jean Wahl, "Kierkegaard and Kafka," trans. Lienhard Bergel in *The Kafka Problem*, ed. Angel Flores (New York: Octagon Books, 1963), 265/ "Kafka et Kierkegaard," in Wahl, *Petite histoire de l'existentialisme* (Paris: Éditions Club Maintenant, 1947), 102.

44. Kafka, letter of June 1921, *Briefe. 1902-1924*, 333.

45. Franz Kafka, *The Blue Octavo Notebooks*, trans. Ernst Kaiser and Eithne Wilkins (Cambridge, MA: Exact Change, 1991), 55/ *Nachgelassene Schriften und Fragmente* II, ed. Jost Schillemeit, *Kritische Ausgabe* (Frankfurt a.M.: Fischer Verlag, 2002), 105.

46. Kafka, letter of March 1918 to Max Brod, *Briefe. 1902-1924*, 235-36. Kafka did read Kierkegaard, occasionally recording very strong impressions, not entirely favorably (*Briefe* 190, 224-25, 235-36, 237-40).

47. Concerning Karl Rossmann, see Kafka, *The Missing Person*, trans. Mark Harman (New York: Schocken Books, 2008), 233/ Kafka, *Der Verschollene*, ed. Jost Schillemeit, *Kritische Ausgabe* (Frankfurt a.M.: Fischer, 2002), 342-43. Concerning Bucephalus, see Kafka "The New Lawyer," in Stanley Corngold ed. and trans., *Kafka's Selected Stories* (New York: Norton: 2007), 59-60/ "Der neue Advokat," *Drucke zu Lebzeiten*, eds. Wolf Kittler, Hans-Gerd Koch und Gerhard Neumann, *Kritische Ausgabe* (Frankfurt a.M.: Fischer Verlag, 2002), 251-52. And with regard to Sancho Panza, see Kafka, *Nachgelassene Schriften und Fragmente* II, ed. Jost Schillemeit, *Kritische Ausgabe*, 38.

48. Walter Sokel provides suggestive readings of Kafka's ironic treatment of Kierkegaardain motifs (*Franz Kafka. Tragik und Ironie* [Frankfurt a.M.: Fischer, 1976], 520-24). With regard to the "Abraham parody" in the letter to Klopstock, see 624-25 n. 5.

49. Günther Anders, *Kafka. Pro and Contra. Die Prozeß-Unterlagen* (Munich: Verlag C.H. Beck, 1984), 25-28.

50. Kafka, letter of June 1921, *Briefe*, 333-34.

51. On the combination of horror and humor in Kafka—or at least in Benjamin's Kafka—see Brendan Moran, "Foolish Wisdom in Benjamin's Kafka," in *Laughter—Eastern and Western Philosophies*, eds. Hans-Georg Möller and Günter Wohlfart (Freiburg/Munich: Verlag Karl Alber, 2010), 175-92, especially 179-83.

52. For more detailed remarks on shame in Benjamin's Kafka, see Moran, "An Inhumanly Wise Shame," *The European Legacy* 14.5 (2009): 573-85.

53. Emmanuel Levinas, *En découvrant l'existence avec Husserl et Heidegger* (Paris: Librarie philosophique J. Vrin, 2001), 100-1, 105-8, 122, 124, 132, 141, 144.

54. Levinas, *En découvrant*, 105.

55. Emmanuel Levinas, *Otherwise than Being, or Beyond Essence*, trans. Alphonso Lingis (Pittsburgh, PA: Duquesne University Press, 2000), 108/ *Autrement qu'être ou au-delà de l'essence* (Paris: Livre de Poche, n.d.), 70-71. Also see pp. 194-95 for an interpretation of Heidegger's notion of anxiety, as well as *God, Death, and Time*, trans. Bettina Bergo (Stanford, CA: Stanford University Press, 2000), 46-49/ *Dieu, la Mort et le Temps*, ed. Jacques Rolland (Paris: Bernard Grasset, 1993), 57-60.

56. See, for instance, Merold Westphal, *Levinas and Kierkegaard in Dialogue* (Bloomington and Indianapolis, IN: Indiana University Press, 2008) and J. Aaron Simmons and David Wood eds., *Kierkegaard and Levinas. Ethics, Politics, and Religion* (Bloomington and Indianapolis, IN: Indiana University Press, 2008)—in view of the concerns of this chapter, see perhaps especially the essays by Westphal (21-40) and John J. Davenport (169-96).

57. Merold Westphal, "The Many Faces of Levinas as a Reader of Kierkegaard," in *Kierkegaard and Levinas*, eds. Simmons and Wood, 23-24.

58. Westphal, "The Many Faces," 30-31.

59. Westphal, "The Many Faces," 33. Also see 34. At this point, Westphal defends Kierkegaard somewhat (34-36), as does Davenport even more emphatically ("What Kierkegaardian Faith Adds to Alterity Ethics: How Levinas and Derrida Miss the Eschatological Dimension," 169-96, especially 176-80).

60. Emmanuel Levinas, *Proper Names*, trans. Michael Smith (Stanford, CA: Stanford University Press, 1997), 72-74/ *Noms Propres* (Paris: Livres de Poche, 1987), 84-87. See too 68, 76/79-80, 89.

61. Levinas, *Proper Names*, 78, 77/ *Noms Propres*, 91, 90.

62. Jacques Derrida, *"The Gift of Death" (second edition) and "Literature in Secret,"* trans. David Wills (Chicago, IL: Chicago University Press), 82-116, especially 115-16/ *Donner la mort* (Paris: Éditions Galilée, 1999), 79-157, especially 156. It seems that Derrida's writings do not discuss Kafka's Abraham more than very briefly, although—having become aware of it "a few weeks" beforehand—Derrida uses Kafka's formulation "another Abraham" as a kind of leitmotif for a lecture on his—Derrida's—"Jewish thought," his thought about calling himself Jewish, a thought that would retain something undecidable. See Jacques Derrida, "Abraham, the Other," trans. Gil Anidjar in *Religion: Beyond a Concept*, ed. Hent de Vries (New York: Fordham University Press, 2008), 311-38, especially 311-12, 321, 335, 336, 337-338/ "Abraham, l'autre," in *Judéités. Questions pour Jacques Derrida*, eds. Joseph Cohen and Raphael Zagury-Orly (Paris: Galilée, 2003), 11-42, especially 11-12, 22, 38, 40, 41-42.

63. Derrida, *"The Gift of Death" (second edition) and "Literature in Secret,"* 127/ *Donner la mort*, 169-70.

64. In other criticisms of Levinas, Derrida contends that Levinas is prone to stay "within" Kierkegaard's premises by distinguishing the "infinitely other as God and the infinitely other as another human." Derrida thinks this is a problem that is insufficiently recognized by Levinas, but concedes that the tendency of Levinas amidst this confusion is as follows: "in taking into account . . . the absolute alterity obtaining in relations between one human and another, Levinas is no longer able to distinguish between the infinite alterity of God and that of every human" (*"The Gift of Death" [second edition] and "Literature in Secret,"* 83-84/ *Donner la mort*, 116-17).

65. *Genesis*, 22:17. 18, *The New English Bible with the Apocrypha (Oxford Study Edition)* (New York: Oxford University Press, 1976), 21.

66. Kafka, letter of June 1921, *Briefe*, 333.

67. See Kafka, letter of June 1921, *Briefe*, 333-34.

68. See Heidegger, *Being and Time/ Sein und Zeit*, part one: sixth chapter and part two: second and third chapters.

69. On corruption, see too: II:3, 1200-1. Benjamin refers specifically to Kafka's *The Trial*.

70. See this statement too in II:3, 1238.

71. Franz Kafka, "Before the Law," in Stanley Corngold ed. and trans., *Kafka's Selected Stories* (New York: Norton: 2007), 68-69/ *Drucke zu Lebzeiten*, eds. Wolf Kittler, Hans-Gerd Koch, and Gerhard Neumann, *Kritische Ausgabe* (Frankfurt a.M.: Fischer, 2002), 267-69; *The Trial*, trans. Breon Mitchell (New York: Schocken Books, 1998), 215-23/ *Der Proceß*, ed. Malcolm Pasley *Kritische Ausgabe* (Frankfurt a.M.: Fischer, 2002), 292-303; *The Castle*, trans. Mark Harman (New York: Schocken Books, 1998), especially 69-71/ *Das Schloß*, ed. Malcolm Pasley, *Kritische Ausgabe* (Frankfurt a.M.: Fischer, 2002), 112-115.

72. Franz Kafka, "Prometheus," *Kafka's Selected Stories*, 129/ *Kritische Ausgabe, Nachgelassene Schriften und Fragmente* II, ed. Jost Schillemeit (Frankfurt a.M.: Fischer Verlag, 2002), *69-70*. Although without mention of Kafka's Prometheus text, Derrida's

Abraham musings include a reference to the "rock" of Kafka's "fictional writing" whereby there emerges a "truth" of vigilant "doubt" ("Abraham, the Other," 337/ "Abraham, l'autre," 41).

73. Kafka, *Beim Bau der Chinesischen Mauer. Ungedruckte Erzählungen und Prosa aus dem Nachlaß*, 42.

74. For elaboration of this astonishment, see Moran, "An Inhumanly Wise Shame," 579-80.

75. Concerning the role of "the nothing" in Benjamin's Kafka writings, see the section on "Use of nothing" in Moran, "Foolish Wisdom in Benjamin's Kafka," 183-87.

76. This reading of Kafka's Prometheus text is different from that of Hans Blumenberg, who reads the text as itself "myth," and thereby as an exercise in the diminishment of anxiety about the "absolutism of reality." On Kafka's text, see Hans Blumenberg, *Work on Myth*, trans. Robert M. Wallace (Cambridge, MA: The MIT Press, 1985), 633-36/ *Arbeit am Mythos* (Frankfurt a.M.: Suhrkamp, 2006), 685-89. On myth as diminishment of anxiety, see 4, 48, 550/ 10, 56, 597.

77. Martin Heidegger, "Introduction to 'What is Metaphysics?,'" *Pathmarks*, 284/ "Einleitung zu: 'Was ist Metaphysik?,'" *Wegmarken*, 374-75.

78. Heidegger, "Introduction," 283/ "Einleitung," 373.

79. Heidegger, "Introduction," 284/ "Einleitung," *375*.

80. Martin Heidegger, "The Origin of the Work of Art," *Off the Beaten Track*, trans. Julian Young and Kenneth Haynes (Cambridge: Cambridge University Press, 2002), 16/ "Der Ursprung des Kunstwerkes," *Holzwege, Gesamtausgabe*, vol. 5 (Frankfurt a.M.: Vittorio Klostermann, 2003), *22*.

81. Martin Heidegger, "Postscript to 'What is Metaphysics?,'" *Pathways*, 234/ "Nachwort zu: 'Was ist Metaphysik?,'" *Wegmarken, 307*.

82. Levinas, *God, Death, and Time*, 184/ *Dieu, la Mort et le Temps*, 212.

83. Emmanuel Levinas, *Totality and Infinity. An Essay on Exteriority*, trans. Alphonso Lingis (Pittsburgh, PA: Duquesne University Press, 1969), 79/ *Totalité et Infini. Essai sur l'extériorité* (The Hague: Martinus Nijhoff, 1961), 78.

84. Jean-Luc Nancy, *L'Adoration (Déconstruction du christianisme, 2)* (Paris: Éditions Galilée, 2010), 43.

85. Jean-Luc Nancy, *Being Singular Plural*, trans. Robert Robertson and Anne O'Byrne (Stanford, CA: Stanford University Press, 2000), 70, 202 n. 61/ *Être singulier pluriel* (Paris: Éditions Galilée, 1996), 93.

86. For a discussion of the topic of "Aufmerksamkeit," see the contributions in *Aufmerksamkeiten. Archäologie der literarischen Kommunikation VII*, eds. Aleida and Jan Assmann (Munich: Wilhelm Fink Verlag, 2001) and in *Aufmerksamkeit*, eds. Norbert Haas, Rainer Nägele, Hans-Jörg Rheinberger (Eggingen: Isele, 1998).

87. Unless something has been overlooked in preparation of the essay at hand, there is no statement in Malebranche's works that matches Benjamin's quotation exactly, although there are statements very close to it. See: Nicolas Malebranche, *Recherche de la Vérité, Oeuvres* Vol. II (Paris: J. Vrin, 1963), 453; *Conversations Chrétiennes, Oeuvres* Vol. IV (Paris: J. Vrin, 1959), 11-12; *Traité de la Nature et de la Grace, Oeuvres* Vol. V (Paris: J. Vrin, 1958), 25-26, 102, 103; *Recueil de toutes les réponses a Monsieur Arnauld, Oeuvres* Vols. VI-VII (Paris: J. Vrin, 1966), 126, 130; *Recueil de toutes les réponses a Monsieur Arnauld, Oeuvres* Vols. VIII-IX (Paris: J. Vrin, 1966), 633; *Méditations Chrétiennes et Métaphysiques, Oeuvres* Vol. X (Paris: J. Vrin, 1959), 144, 148, 168; *Réflexions sur la Prémotion Physique, Oeuvres* Vol. XVI (Paris: J. Vrin, 1958), 48.

88. See too II:3, 1214, 1219.

89. Levinas, *Proper Names*, 42-43/ *Noms propres*, 51-52. See Paul Celan, "Der Meridian. Rede anläßlich der Verleihung des Georg-Büchner-Preises," *Der Meridian.*

*Endfassung—Entwürfe—Materialien*, eds. Bernhard Böschenstein and Heino Schmull with Michael Schwarzkopf and Christine Wittkopp, *Werke. Tübinger Ausgabe*, ed. Jürgen Wertheimer (Frankfurt a.M.: Suhrkamp, 1999), 9.

90. Levinas, *Proper Names* 43/ *Noms propres*, 52-53.

91. Emmanuel Levinas, *Existence and Existents*, trans. Alphonso Lingis (Pittsburgh: Duquesne University Press, 2001), 4-5, 57-62/ *De l'existence à l'existant* (Paris: Vrin, 2004), 19-21, 102-11.

92. Jacques Derrida, "Violence and Metaphysics," *Writing and Difference*, trans. Alan Bass (Chicago, IL: Chicago University Press, 1978), 141/ *L'écriture et la difference* (Paris: Éditions du Seuil, 1967), 208.

93. This could be suggested in *Otherwise than Being*, 164/*Autrement qu'être ou au-delà de l'essence*, 256.

## Works Cited

Adorno, Theodor W. *Jargon der Eigentlichkeit. Zur deutschen Ideologie*. Frankfurt a.M: Suhrkamp, 1964. / *Jargon of Authenticity*. Translated by Knut Tarnowski and Frederic Will. Evanston, IL: Northwestern University Press, 1973.

———. *Negative Dialektik*. Frankfurt a.M.: Suhrkamp, 1975. / *Negative Dialectics*. Translated by E.B. Ashton. New York: Continuum, 1973.

Anders, Günther. *Kafka. Pro and Contra. Die Prozeß-Unterlagen*. Munich: Verlag C.H. Beck, 1984.

Assmann, Aleida and Jan, eds. *Aufmerksamkeiten. Archäologie der literarischen Kommunikation VII*. Munich: Wilhelm Fink Verlag, 2001.

Benjamin, Walter. "L'angoisse mythique chez Goethe." Translated by Pierre Klossowski. *Les Cahiers du Sud* 24/194 (May-June 1937): 342-48.

———. *The Arcades Project*. Translated by H. Eiland and K. McLaughlin. Cambridge, MA: Harvard University Press, 1999.

———. *The Correspondence of Walter Benjamin*. Edited by Gershom Scholem and Theodor Adorno, translated by Manfred R. Jacobson and Evelyn M. Jacobson. Chicago, IL: University Chicago Press, 1994.

———. *Gesammelte Briefe*. Edited by C. Gödde and H. Lonitz. Frankfurt a.M.: Suhrkamp, 1995-2000.

———. *Gesammelte Schriften*, VII volumes. Edited by R. Tiedemann and H. Schweppenhäuser et al. Frankfurt a.M.: Suhrkamp, 1974-99.

———. *Selected Writings*, 4 volumes. Edited by Michael W. Jennings et al. Cambridge, MA: The Belknap Press of Harvard University Press, 1996-2003.

———. *Understanding Brecht*. Translated by Anna Bostock. London: Verso, 1998.

Blumenberg, Hans. *Arbeit am Mythos*. Frankfurt a.M.: Suhrkamp, 2006. / *Work on Myth*. Translated by Robert M. Wallace. Cambridge, MA: The MIT Press, 1985.

Brod, Max. *Über Franz Kafka*. Frankfurt a.M.: Fischer, 1989. / *Franz Kafka: A Biography*. Translated by G. Humphreys Roberts and Richard Winston. New York: Schocken Books, 1963.

Brod, Max, and Hans Joachim Schoeps. "Nachwort." In Franz Kafka, *Beim Bau der Chinesischen Mauer. Ungedruckte Erzählungen und Prosa aus dem Nachlaß*, 250-266. Berlin: Gustav Kiepenheuer Verlag, 1931.

Celan, Paul. *Der Meridian. Endfassung—Entwürfe—Materialien*. Edited by Bernhard Böschenstein and Heino Schmull with Michael Schwarzkopf and Christine

Wittkopp. *Werke. Tübinger Ausgabe*. Edited by Jürgen Wertheimer. Frankfurt a.M.: Suhrkamp, 1999.

Danta, Chris. "'The Absolutely Dark Moment of the Plot.' Blanchot's Abraham." In *After Blanchot: Literature, Criticism, and Philosophy*, edited by Leslie Hill, Brian Nelson, and Dimitris Vardoulakis, 205-20. Newark, DE: University of Delaware Press, 2005.

———. "The Poetics of Distance: Kierkegaard's Abraham." *Literature and Theology* 21.2 (June 2007): 160-77.

———. "Sarah's Laughter: Kafka's Abraham." *Modernism/modernity* 15.2 (April 2008): 343-59.

Davenport, John J. "What Kierkegaardian Faith Adds to Alterity Ethics: How Levinas and Derrida Miss the Eschatological Dimension." In *Kierkegaard and Levinas. Ethics, Politics, and Religion*, edited by J. Aaron Simmons and David Wood, 169-96. Bloomington and Indianapolis, IN: Indiana University Press, 2008.

Derrida, Jacques. "Abraham, l'autre." In *Judéités. Questions pour Jacques Derrida*, edited by Joseph Cohen and Raphael Zagury-Orly, 11-42. Paris: Galilée, 2003. / "Abraham, the Other." Translated by Gil Anidjar. In *Religion: Beyond a Concept*, edited by Hent de Vries, 311-38. New Yourk: Fordham University Press, 2008.

———. *Donner la mort*. Paris: Éditions Galilée, 1999. / *"The Gift of Death" (second edition) and "Literature in Secret."* Translated by David Wills. Chicago, IL: Chicago University Press.

———. *L'écriture et la difference*. Paris: Éditions du Seuil, 1967. / *Writing and Difference*. Translated by Alan Bass. Chicago, IL: Chicago University Press, 1978.

Fenves, Peter. *"Chatter," Language and History in Kierkegaard*. Stanford, CA: Stanford University Press, 1993.

Haas, Norbert, Rainer Nägele and Hans-Jörg Rheinberger, eds. *Aufmerksamkeit*. Eggingen: Isele, 1998.

Haas, Willy. *Gestalten der Zeit*. Berlin: Gustav Kiepenheuer Verlag, 1930.

Heidegger, Martin. *Holzwege. Gesamtausgabe*, vol. 5. Frankfurt a.M.: Vittorio Klostermann, 2003. / *Off the Beaten Track*. Translated by Julian Young and Kenneth Haynes. Cambridge: Cambridge University Press, 2002.

———. *Sein und Zeit*. Tübingen: Niemeyer, 1986. / *Being and Time*. Translated by Joan Stambaugh, revised by Dennis Schmidt. Albany, NY: SUNY Press, 2010.

———. *Wegmarken*. Frankfurt a.M.: Vittorio Klostermann, 2004. / *Pathmarks*. Edited by William McNeill. Cambridge: Cambridge University Press, 1999.

Kafka, Franz. *The Blue Octavo Notebooks*. Translated by Ernst Kaiser and Eithne Wilkins. Cambridge, MA: Exact Change, 1991.

———. *Briefe. 1902-1924*. Edited by Max Brod. Frankfurt a.M.: Fischer Verlag, 1983.

———. *The Castle*. Translated by Mark Harman. New York: Schocken Books, 1998.

———. *Kafka's Selected Stories*. Edited and translated by Stanley Corngold. New York: Norton: 2007.

———. *Kritische Ausgabe. Drucke zu Lebzeiten*. Edited by Wolf Kittler, Hans-Gerd Koch and Gerhard Neumann. Frankfurt a.M.: Fischer Verlag, 2002.

———. *Kritische Ausgabe. Nachgelassene Schriften und Fragmente* II. Edited by Jost Schillemeit. Frankfurt a.M.: Fischer Verlag, 2002.

———. *Kritische Ausgabe. Der Proceß*. Edited by Malcolm Pasley. Frankfurt a.M.: Fischer, 2002.

———. *Kritische Ausgabe. Das Schloß*. Edited by Malcolm Pasley. Frankfurt a.M.: Fischer, 2002.

———. *Kritische Ausgabe. Der Verschollene*. Edited by Jost Schillemeit. Frankfurt a.M.: Fischer, 2002.

———. *The Missing Person*. Translated by Mark Harman. New York: Schocken Books, 2008.

———. *The Trial*. Translated by Breon Mitchell. New York: Schocken Books, 1998.

Kierkegaard, Søren. *The Concept of Anxiety*. Translated and edited by Reider Thomte with Albert B. Anderson. Princeton, NJ: Princeton University Press, 1981.

———. *Fear and Trembling*. Translated by Alistair Hannay. London: Penguin Books, 1986.

Kurella, Alfred. "Deutsche Romantik. Zum gleichnamigen Sonderheft der 'Cahiers du Sud.'" *Internationale Literatur* 6 (1938): 113-28.

Levinas, Emmanuel. *Autrement qu'être ou au-delà de l'essence*. Paris: Livre de Poche, n.d. / *Otherwise than Being, or Beyond Essence*. Translated by Alphonso Lingis. Pittsburgh, PA: Duquesne University Press, 2000.

———. *De l'existence à l'existant*. Paris: Vrin, 2004. / *Existence and Existents*. Translated by Alphonso Lingis. Pittsburgh, PA: Duquesne University Press, 2001.

———. *Dieu, la Mort et le Temps*. Edited by Jacques Rolland. Paris: Bernard Grasset, 1993. / *God, Death, and Time*. Translated by Bettina Bergo. Stanford, CA: Stanford University Press, 2000.

———. *En découvrant l'existence avec Husserl et Heidegger*. Paris: Librarie philosophique J. Vrin, 2001.

———. *Noms Propres*. Paris: Livres de Poche, 1987. / *Proper Names*. Translated by Michael Smith. Stanford, CA: Stanford University Press, 1997.

———. *Totalité et Infini. Essai sur l'extériorité*. The Hague: Martinus Nijhoff, 1961. / *Totality and Infinity. An Essay on Exteriority*. Translated by Alphonso Lingis. Pittsburgh, PA: Duquesne University Press, 1969.

Malebranche, Nicolas. *Conversations Chrétiennes. Oeuvres* Vol. IV. Paris: J. Vrin, 1959.

———. *Méditations Chrétiennes et Métaphysiques. Oeuvres* Vol. X. Paris: J. Vrin, 1959.

———. *Recherche de la Vérité. Oeuvres* Vol. II. Paris: J. Vrin, 1963.

———. *Recueil de toutes les réponses a Monsieur Arnauld. Oeuvres* Vols. VI-VII. Paris: J. Vrin, 1966.

———. *Recueil de toutes les réponses a Monsieur Arnauld. Oeuvres* Vols. VIII-IX. Paris: J. Vrin, 1966.

———. *Réflexions sur la Prémotion Physique. Oeuvres* Vol. XVI. Paris: J. Vrin, 1958.

———. *Traité de la Nature et de la Grace. Oeuvres* Vol. V. Paris: J. Vrin, 1958.

Moran, Brendan. "An Inhumanly Wise Shame." *The European Legacy* 14.5 (2009): 573-85.

———. "Foolish Wisdom in Benjamin's Kafka." In *Laughter—Eastern and Western Philosophies*, edited by Hans-Georg Möller and Günter Wohlfart, 175-92. Freiburg/Munich: Verlag Karl Alber, 2010.

Nancy, Jean-Luc. *L'Adoration (Déconstruction du christianisme, 2)*. Paris: Éditions Galilée, 2010.

———. *Être singulier pluriel*. Paris: Éditions Galilée, 1996. / *Being Singular Plural*. Translated by Robert Robertson and Anne O'Byrne. Stanford, CA: Stanford University Press, 2000.

*The New English Bible with the Apocrypha (Oxford Study Edition)*. New York: Oxford University Press, 1976.

Palmer, Gesine. "Geheimnisse eines bereitwilligen Kellners: Abraham bei Derrida, Benjamin und Kafka." *Zeitschrift für Religions-und Geistesgeschichte* 51.1 (1999): 48-63.

Sartre, Jean-Paul. *L'être et le néant*. Paris: Gallimard, 1943. / *Being and Nothingness*. Translated by Hazel Barnes. New York: Washington Square Press, 1992.

Schnädelbach, Herbert. *Philosophy in Germany 1831-1933*. Translated by Eric Matthews. Cambridge: Cambridge University Press, 1984.

Scholem, Gershom. *Walter Benjamin—die Geschichte einer Freundschaft*. Frankfurt a.M.: Suhrkamp, 1975. / *Walter Benjamin: The Story of a Friendship*. Translated by Harry Zohn. Philadelphia, PA: The Jewish Publication Society of America, 1981.

Simmons, J. Aaron, and David Wood, eds. *Kierkegaard and Levinas. Ethics, Politics, and Religion*. Bloomington and Indianapolis, IN: Indiana University Press, 2008.

Sokel, Walter. *Franz Kafka. Tragik und Ironie*. Frankfurt a.M.: Fischer, 1976.

Wahl, Jean. "Kafka et Kierkegaard," in Jean Wahl, *Petite histoire de l'existentialisme*, 93-131. Paris: Éditions Club Maintenant, 1947. / "Kierkegaard and Kafka." Translated by Lienhard Bergel. In *The Kafka Problem*, edited by Angel Flores, 262-75. New York: Octagon Books, 1963.

Westphal, Merold. *Levinas and Kierkegaard in Dialogue*. Bloomington and Indianapolis, IN: Indiana University Press, 2008.

———. "The Many Faces of Levinas as a Reader of Kierkegaard." In *Kierkegaard and Levinas. Ethics, Politics, and Religion*, edited by J. Aaron Simmons and David Wood, 21-40. Bloomington and Indianapolis, IN: Indiana University Press, 2008.

CHAPTER 12

# On the Mimesis of Reification: Adorno's Critical Theoretical Interpretation of Kafka*

*Brian O'Connor*

One of the most central concepts of Adorno's aesthetic theory is that of mimesis. It is, perhaps, surprising to find this concept—so deeply associated with a debate in ancient philosophy—employed in the context of a new theory of aesthetic modernism, one conceived within the intellectual space of critical theory. And it is not only its archaic associations that appear to make it an unlikely way of capturing the specific properties of modernism. Mimesis carries with it connotations of imitation and representation. It has something to do with art's supposed mission, that of copying reality. Yet these are the traditional norms of aesthetic production that modernism self-consciously and often polemically repudiated. Mimesis, however, is an evolving concept. As Jacques Derrida notes: "The whole history of the interpretation of the arts of letters has moved and been transformed within the diverse logical possibilities opened up by the concept of *mimesis*."[1]

Adorno argues that art has a continuing engagement with reality, and he radically reconceives the notion of mimesis in order to explain the distinctive nature of that engagement. His new conception of mimesis provides an explanation of the kind of *expression* of reality of which modernist artworks are capable. Modernist expression is not, according to Adorno, imitation. His claim is that expression, in this context, consists in giving *aesthetic form* to the form of social reality itself. As we shall see, for Adorno form—not content, image or representations—is the key property of what constitutes the specifically *aesthetic* construction—the mimesis—of that reality. As Peter Uwe Hohendahl explains: for Adorno "modern works articulate, more poignantly than do historical narratives or philosophical systems (such as existentialism), the horrors of the twentieth century. Only through their extreme formal construction do the works of Kafka or Joyce or Beckett become legitimate witnesses to this horror."[2]

The case of Kafka stands at the very center of Adorno's articulation of modernist mimesis. His main study of Kafka is the long and complex essay "Notes on Kafka" (1953), which he republished in the collection *Prisms* (1955). But numerous references to Kafka are found throughout his unfinished master-

* Part of this chapter appeared in Brian O'Connor, *Adorno* (New York: Routledge, 2012).

piece *Aesthetic Theory* (first published in 1970) and in the four-part collection of essays, *Notes to Literature*. From his correspondence with Walter Benjamin (on the subject of Benjamin's essay, "Franz Kafka"), we can also see how deeply Adorno had been considering Kafka's work from the very beginning of his professional career.[3] Adorno claims that historical "processes" are found as "ciphers" in Kafka's work (*P* 252).[4] This might seem to say that Adorno takes Kafka to be a social commentator who sought to say something about history. Although Adorno is aware of Kafka's political standpoints, he does not take them to be determinative of the content of Kafka's fiction. Kafka qua writer was engaged in a purely aesthetic activity which nevertheless unintentionally but necessarily achieves a mimesis of social reality. As Adorno writes, "Kafka's works protected themselves against the deadly aesthetic error of equating the philosophy that an author pumps into a work with its metaphysical substance. Were this so, the work of art would be stillborn; it would exhaust itself in what it says and would not unfold itself in time" (*P* 247). Adorno's reading of Kafka, then, is not an effort to find an implicit theory or illustrated examples of philosophical insights in the texts. As Walter H. Sokel puts it, "Kafka's reader, Adorno maintained, should not rush to look for the 'meaning' of over-arching images by translating them into cultural concepts ready at hand but external to the text."[5] Adorno does not "read off" a Kafkaesque philosophy from the literary work. He adopts Benjamin's description of Kafka's works as "damaged parables" (*AT* 126)[6]: damaged in that they constantly suggest complexes of metaphors, metaphors that cannot be unlocked. The key to the interpretation of Kafka's work, Adorno says, "has been stolen" (*P* 246). Each work invites decoding yet "none will permit it" (*P* 246). When Adorno speaks about Kafka he is not attempting, then, to tell us what the works are really all about: the hidden meanings that he can bring to our attention. He treats them as works of art with their own irreducible integrity. The philosophical claims he makes about Kafka's work, as we shall see, relate to the forms they distinctively bear within the historical conditions of modernity. The interpretative claims about Kafka's works that Adorno develops emerge through an examination of their aesthetic dimensions. The aesthetic dimensions are primarily, for Adorno, a work's formal properties. Adorno thinks of the artist as placed within an ever changing historical context in which form must constantly be reinvented. This appears to be self-evident from the perspective of the history of art. Where the interest of critical theory enters, however, is through Adorno's contention that art is the expression of social reality. The development of form is a response to societal evolution. The expression that art achieves cannot be translated into purely theoretical terms. Because, then, art provides us with a distinctive view of social reality, considerations of the aesthetic dimension turn out to be significant in directing critical theory to the very phenomenon of social reality. It is important to note—as the analysis to be offered here cannot do justice to it—that Adorno's conclusions about the general mimetic qualities of Kafka's work are rooted in a broad range of specific details in the texts of Kafka (principally the three novels and several of the longer stories).

There are two distinguishable senses of mimesis in Adorno's discussions of Kafka (they may already be apparent). The first relates to the mimetic content of artworks: what they express ("ciphers"). The second is what Adorno calls the "mimetic comportment" of the artist: the process of creativity. Both of these dimensions will be examined below. The concept of mimesis sits within an inter-dependent network of ideas in Adorno's aesthetic theory, and it is intelligible only within that network. So before looking at the details of Adorno's enthusiastic appraisal of Kafka we need to appreciate, even briefly, what Adorno means by the autonomy of art, aesthetic authenticity, mimesis and the relationship between art and social criticism.

## Art and Autonomy

Adorno holds that authentic works of art in modernity are characterized by their *autonomy* from the life-processes of society. To ascribe autonomy to art is not to claim that it has some kind of existence outside history or society. The matter of autonomy is not a metaphysical one. The complexity of Adorno's thesis consists in its claim for a very specific relationship of art to society: art is autonomous from the processes of reification that, according to the critical tradition to which he belongs, disfigures the social world. A corollary of a work's autonomy is, for Adorno, its authenticity. An autonomous work is authentic because it has been formed without regard to the requirements of society: the social norms of communication or of purpose and usefulness. "The more authentic the works, the more they follow what is objectively required, the object's consistency, and this is always universal," Adorno writes (*AT* 201). They are guided by an aesthetic necessity—"objectivity"—rather than by the purposes imposed on social production generally. A work of art that is oriented toward a social purpose is therefore inauthentic: it has, according to Adorno's theory, constrained itself—thereby losing its autonomy—in order to give that purpose aesthetic form. It is characterized, Adorno contends, by heteronomy in that its meaning must conform to an idea antecedently established outside the work.

Adorno, as we shall see, valorizes Kafka's works as mimetic expressions of reified life, as "a cryptogram of a decaying capitalist social order."[7] We need to be clear about what the concept of reification means to him. Adorno holds that individuals become reified by living within the conditions of contemporary capitalism. Two essential features of that form of society are instrumental rationality and capitalism. Both of these, it seems, mutually sustain each other. In order to be an efficient agent of capitalism one must have internalized the "rules of exchange," and these rules shape the general consciousness of the individual. By exchange Adorno means the system in which all phenomena—things, labor, time—become translatable into a pecuniary value. He calls this "equivalence." Once made equivalent in this sense phenomena can be bought or sold for the universal token, money. The manipulative rationality which is required for the effective operation of exchange—the capacity to translate the diverse objects of the world into fiscally equivalent phenomena—informs rationality as a whole, since it is the prevailing social rationality. The everyday belief in this exchange system is not voluntaristic. Individuals are inducted, from their earliest experiences, into the distinctive form of social behavior characteristic of an exchange society. A growing capacity to translate everything into abstract value—what it is "worth"—comes to determine individuals' perceptions of wider reality. Adorno writes: "Bourgeois society is ruled by equivalence. It makes the dissimilar comparable by reducing it to abstract quantities."[8]

A common personality is generated by the total system of exchange. Together, individuals form a network which sustains the system that determines them. As Adorno writes: "What really makes society a social entity, what constitutes it both conceptually and in reality, is the relationship of exchange which binds together virtually all the people participating in this kind of society."[9] The exchange principle, then, is not a pragmatic option, but one with quasi-natural compellingness. It becomes a piece of second nature to us, as the way in which self-preservation is to be pursued. As Adorno puts it: "The form of the total system requires everyone to respect the law of exchange if he does not wish to be destroyed, irrespective of whether profit is his subjective motivation or not."[10] Society is a *totality* in that it integrates all individual moments of life into it: each moment bears the determinations of the totality. A world so organized can sustain and reproduce itself because of the acquiescence of those within it: they accede to the imperatives of exchange, though they do not seek justifications for those imperatives. These imperatives govern life, they must be followed, yet they are antagonistic to human flourishing. Robert W. Witkin describes the pertinence of Kafka to Adorno for the diagnosis of this kind of society: "On a literary plane, Franz Kafka conveyed, with chilling effect, in *The Castle* and *The Trial*, the nightmare of a legal-rational existence bereft of spiritual life, of a subjectivity that filled out empty forms as its historical core."[11] It is for this reason that Adorno thinks of the social totality as irrational: it constantly acts against individuals who, at the same time, seek no explanation for its apparent necessity and its demanding norms. Kafka—and Proust—perceived this "necessity," Adorno writes, "in something that is wholly contingent, a necessity that can be perceived only negatively."[12]

Given that Adorno holds that the social totality pervasively influences consciousness, it might seem that art can be autonomous only when it is detached from history. That is, if the phenomena of exchange and reified life are everywhere, art—if it is at all possible—must operate outside the space of everywhere. And that looks like a metaphysical conception of art, after all. Adorno does indeed see art as free of the forms of determination that characterize reified life. At the same time, though, autonomous art draws its content from society: from *this* society in which "damaged life," as he famously calls it in *Minima Moralia*, prevails. In that respect artworks are, he believes, socio-historical phenomena. They are not, at the same time, typical social products. Adorno understands aesthetic experience—from creativity, to performance and experience—to operate in a space that it not yet inhabited by reification. It expresses history, but is not, because it is free, reducible to historical processes. Its form of expression—its mimetic property—has somehow eluded the reach of reification. Adorno offers no account of art's special capacity to resist reification.

Art's autonomous position is frequently explained contrastively by Adorno: in conventional non-aesthetic expression, reified life is represented in reified ways. Social processes are reproduced through reified forms of communication. We might see this in the rather extreme case of TV "soap opera" dramas. These dramas imitate the apparently everyday events of society. They seek to engage their consumers with the would-be slice of life of society that they present, and consumers will enjoy the dramas only insofar as they identify with their plots and characters. These dramas are intensifications of experiences already known to and thematized by the audiences: they are not unsettling and the consumer is drawn passively into their narratives. They are "realistic" insofar as they meet their consumers' expectations of what reality essentially looks like. Modernist work, by contrast, endeavors to break the pattern of identification between the work and expectations. Adorno addresses this specific accomplishment in Kafka: "Among Kafka's presuppositions," he writes, "not the least is that the contemplative relation between text and reader is shaken to its very roots" (*P* 246). And again, in radical contrast to the passive consumption which sustains heteronomous work, Adorno sees Kafka's works as breaking down the "distance between themselves and their victim" (*P* 246), the victim being the reader. The experience of the reader—Adorno speaks of the agitation of "feelings" (*P* 246)—is that of ceasing simply to observe what happens to the characters as the dreadful worlds they inhabit begin to become the reader's own.

The critique of heteronomous art geared toward mass consumption applies equally, for Adorno, to political art. In political art the consumer is to be led in a particular direction. Adorno rejects the very idea that art remains authentically aesthetic when it endeavors to represent empirical social reality as it thinks it actually is in order to educate its audiences in politics. Adorno regards social realism, for instance, as "crude propaganda" (*AT* 243). Social realism subverts art by turning it into an ideological vehicle. In that case the aesthetic process is heteronomous, not self-determining (autonomous).

Autonomous artworks, then, are artifactual forms that do not generate familiar patterns of experiences. And this is because they are produced outside the space of familiarity. The autonomous quality is indeed more apparent the greater the difference between society and the aesthetic. Within an all-encompassing social totality authentic art appears to be radically at odds with society. The forms of experience enabled by the autonomous work are not a matter of novelty. Rather, autonomous works enable experiences of social reality as it really is: i.e. a commodified reality, filled with useless junk. Kafka, Adorno claims, expresses in his work, the "waste-products" (*P* 251) of society. His work is autonomous as it builds itself upon a reality in decay. It reproduces society *negatively* by expressing irrational social norms in a way that gives heightened perception to them. "Kafka's power," Adorno writes, "is that of a negative feel for reality" (*AT* 19). Non-autonomous art, by contrast, *positively* reproduces the norms of society: it takes society at face value, that is, as being the rational, freedom-enabling entity it claims to be.

## Mimetic Comportment

The various theses of Adorno that we have already discussed—autonomy and authenticity—have been met with considerable criticism.[13] The essence of the various criticisms—an answer to which is important in the context of Adorno's assessment of Kafka—is that Adorno offers a stipulative theory of art. He specifies, as we have seen, that art must be autonomous if it is to be authentic. It will be constituted by forms that separate it radically from conventional modalities of expression. Furthermore, he directly excludes realism as a genuine aesthetic form. Realism takes "reality" as its standard of aesthetic quality and it thereby places the criterion of art outside of art itself. But what is the basis of Adorno's claim that art is compromised when guided by external considerations? Without a principle to support his exclusions (of realism, of political art, of popular art) Adorno's position may indeed be vulnerable to the "stipulation" criticism. An answer is to be found, however, in his conception of mimetic comportment as a characteristic of autonomous art.

The mimetic comportment of the artist means for Adorno unconstrained creativity. Adorno has a complex account of how the natural mimetic capacities of human beings have been damaged by the development of instrumental reason (the history of reification). Ideally mimesis is a capacity in which the individual gives herself over to a process of uninhibited interaction with another. In that process experiences of what cannot be anticipated emerge. This capacity, however, is now found only in aesthetic activity (*AT* 331). It is not mimesis in its original form—interaction with another—but an attenuated variety which nevertheless involves a relinquishment of subjective control. Relinquishment does not mean passivity, however. The subject is involved in a series of decisions thrown up within the creative process itself as the problematic legacies of her recent tradition. The flow of creativity is a series of judgments about what—if anything—is required as the next step in the process. The norms of those judgments are aesthetic: they bear upon the history of art, though they are not guided by that history. And the act of judgment is mimetic: it is the act of a self not seeking to control or categorize, unlike the acts of non-aesthetic (reified) judgment. Rather, the subject, through mimetic comportment, adopts a behavior toward her task in which she frees herself from any sense of what is expected of her. In *Aesthetic Theory* Adorno writes: "Only the autonomous self is able to turn critically against itself and break through its illusory imprisonment. This is not conceivable as long as the mimetic element is repressed by a rigid aesthetic superego" (*AT* 117). This is no demand for randomness or wild spirits. It is a process of evolving aesthetic judgments. We can see, therefore, how Adorno can speak of Arnold Schoenberg's expressionistic work as "untrammelled, mimetic creation" (*P* 151). It is mimetic in that it refers to the surrendering of the decisionistic ego to the creative process, regardless of where the process goes. When art is controlled it loses its autonomy. If art is the activity of "the mimetic impulse" (*AT* 54) it follows, what Adorno refers frequently to as, a law of form. The law does not, he claims, "predominate" in artworks; "they are seldom planned" (*AT* 64). But a procedure that attempted to make randomness the form would be non-mimetic production in its abstention from the effort to develop the inner coherence of the work. That is, it would be guided by a principle that lay outside the aesthetic process. Mimetic comportment alone is, Adorno holds, fidelity to the aesthetic process itself.

Through the mimetic process Kafka, Adorno claims, develops his distinctive form. Kafka's works are "determined by their inner form" (*P* 265). This is evident by their inner coherence in which their narratives unfold "in time" (*P* 247). It develops according to its immanent logic, thereby gaining its own specific integrity. Crucially, Kafka's narratives do not follow any sequence the reader can anticipate, yet they are not randomly constructed. Haphazardness could generate no coherence. Adorno, however (as we have seen), ascribes inner coherence to Kafka's work. Mimetic productivity generates coherent works because it involves developing work through a process and unfolding sequence. A work designed with randomness as a principle would be heteronomous: its meaning would lie outside the work. Adorno's claim here reflects the hierarchical place of expressionist works of art in his evaluation of contemporary art forms. This is the very quality he praises in Kafka. The expressionist path—Kafka's "authentic horizon" (*P* 261) as it is Schoenberg's, according to Adorno—is mimetic. It is a committed process of creativity in which the artist seeks to produce a determinable whole (which does not mean constructing a narrative that follows the classical rule about wholes). The notion of mimetic creativity, then, turns out to be the basis for what might otherwise appear to be stipulations within Adorno's theory. If there is such a capacity and it bears the features Adorno describes—principally, the artistic individual relinquishing control—then the notion of authenticity as that which is produced without an agenda gains some ground. Needless to say, a deeper investigation of the concept of mimetic comportment than can be given here is required if Adorno's conception of authenticity is to have more than prima facie plausibility.

## Realism

In view of the connection Adorno draws between authenticity and autonomy, his claim that authentic work mimetically expresses social reality looks quite mysterious. How is it that free, uninhibited creation, pursuing purely aesthetic objectives just so happens to be a mimesis of social reality? Why should it have that content and somehow encipher social reality? Adorno does not provide a sketched-out theory of this relationship. The key to understanding this, though, it seems to me, lies in a claim we have already seen. Namely, that art is a historical, non-metaphysical practice. The materials that it must use—social ideas, forms of life that influence experience—are historical in nature. But handling these materials aesthetically means presenting them aesthetically. As Adorno says of Kafka's work: "Kafka sins against an ancient rule of the game by constructing art out of nothing but the refuse of reality" (*P* 251). His work expresses only experiences given by the social totality. When these experiences or materials are taken up by conventional forms of expression—mass entertainment, political art, social realism—they are simply reproduced. They are mirrored, not illuminated. When they are the materials of authentic works of art, however, they are expressed in ways in which the truth of what they are is no longer occluded by the vehicle of their expressions. In this respect Kafka's work, Adorno claims, stands against "an age when sound common sense only reinforces universal blindness" (*P* 254). His work opens up the possibility that we might actually experience the truth of what we take to be natural. The artwork, in this context, really does become a cipher of falsity (as we shall see in more detail below). As Adorno writes: "it may be said of Kafka that not *verum* but *falsum* is *index sui*" (*P* 247).

Adorno's position, then, is that, in spite of the apparent indifference of the artwork to social reality, its form—its logic—reveals the form of social reality. And it does so without any recourse to realism. If "social realists," Adorno notes, "took reality seriously enough they would eventually realize what Lukács condemned when during the days of his imprisonment in Romania he is reported to have said that he had finally realized that Kafka was a realist writer" (*AT* 322). The "realism" of Kafka's work, then, is its effective expression of the distinctive conditions of late capitalism, the period of the irrational social totality. In this period society is not only geared toward the production of commodities, but social life bears the characteristics of commodification.[14] Hence, the aesthetic expression of this is, as Simon Jarvis writes, "a realism of the loss of experience."[15] Kafka never names the social totality, yet, as Adorno writes, no "world could be more homogeneous than the stifling one which [Kafka] compresses to a totality by means of petty-bourgeois dread; it is logically air-tight and empty of meaning like every system" (*P* 256). The totality encompasses all behavior and all interaction. It operates without justification since individuals who are constituted through it do not conceive it as unreasonable, unnecessary or unnatural. For them, it is the space within which they exercise their freedom. Kafka's work is set within this totality, and it mimetically adopts the form of that totalized world. The logic of the totality, however, is false, as are the conventions of the worlds set out in Kafka's novels. What gives those worlds their coherence is not their truth, but their sustained falseness. Adorno writes: "Kafka, in whose work monopoly capitalism appears only distantly, codifies in the dregs of the administered world what becomes of people under the total social spell more faithfully and powerfully than do any novels about corrupt industrial trusts" (*AT* 230). And he does so simply by expressing society's form: closed, unjustifiable, yet determining the lives of everyone within it.

Mimesis, then, consists in expressing a world without reproducing it. It is not mirroring, but aesthetic expression. To express the world aesthetically is to imitate it *aesthetically*. Outside the space of the aesthetic, Adorno effectively says, there is simply the damaged experience of individuals adhering spontaneously to the imperatives of the social totality. But authentic art provides us with an entirely different relation to that experience: it is no longer undergone without a sense that there is something wrong. In the "mimesis" of social processes "a universal which has been repressed by sound common sense" becomes apparent (*P* 249): the universal and all pervasive social totality.

Kafka's works are negative not in any explicit "negation" of sociality reality, but rather in the sense that they express patterns of irrationality and unsettle the unthinking relationship we have with societal norms. Through these artworks we gain a heightened experiential appreciation of a reified world in which we are normally uncritically immersed. As a "mimesis of reification" (*AT* 230) Kafka's work, according to Adorno, achieves this experiential expression of the problematic social totality.

Adorno appraises the work of Baudelaire and of Beckett in similar terms. He says of Baudelaire that he "neither railed against nor portrayed reification; he protested against it in the experience of its archetypes, and the medium of this experience is the poetic form" (*AT* 21). And of Beckett: "This shabby, damaged world of images is the negative imprint of the administered world. To this extent Beckett is realistic" (*AT* 31). However, he accords specifically to Kafka the capacity to expose what he sees as the *mythic* structure of society: its indefensible norms and conventions that are, nevertheless, uncritically lived. The myth of society, that it is a collection of free individuals voluntarily committed to it because it is consonant with their freedom and based on some kind of rational principles, is a powerful one. It is the narrative that bourgeois society gives to itself, and it frames the self-understanding of bourgeois individuals. Hence it is not just one myth among others: it is the foundational myth of capitalist society. But Kafka, Adorno writes, "convicts civilization and bourgeois individuation of their illusoriness" (*P* 251). Kafka's mimetic presentation exposes the mythic nature of its binding yet arbitrary character. He presents us with reified characters working within "the myth" in which we see "blind force endlessly reproducing itself" (*P* 260). Adorno maintains that Kafka's narratives express the truth behind the self-understanding of modern individuality. Individuals are "the bare material existence that emerges in the subjective sphere through the total collapse of a submissive consciousness, divest of all self-assertion" (*P* 252). In reality the individual is not an agent. The social totality reproduces itself only when human beings have ceased to be its agents. Hence individuals have become the means by which the social totality reproduces itself: "The crucial moment, however, toward which everything in Kafka is directed, is that in which men become aware that they are not themselves—that they themselves are things" (*P* 255). They are the material of the system, not its masters.

## Immanence

Adorno considers the form of experience enabled by Kafka's works as significant to the business of illuminating the essential character of society. His works puncture the illusion of a neutral social totality with no determinative power that is supposedly merely a form of social organization which pragmatically facilitates self-preservation. Kafka demystifies social experience in a purely negative way, that is, he does not indicate anything about a new world, free of reification. No utopia is offered in image. Adorno identifies this approach as Kafka's literalness. His works "take everything literally; cover up nothing with concepts invoked from above" (*P* 247). However, this literalness has a productive negativity. It is what Adorno generally refers to as determinate negation. Kafka, Adorno claims, can define society "all the more precisely in its negative" (*P* 256). A determinate negation is knowledge bearing. This knowledge—in this context—has emancipatory potential in that it gives us a view of what our deepest beliefs (about society and our selves as individuals in it) actually commit us to doing. Conceiving of our impulsive identification with society as a neurosis, Adorno says of Kafka: "Instead of curing neurosis, he seeks in it itself the healing force, that of knowledge: the wounds with which society brands the individual are seen by the latter as ciphers of the social untruth, as the negative of truth" (*P* 252).

By admitting no concepts "from above" Kafka's engagement with society is immanent. His consistent immanence gives exact—literal—expression to the nature of the social totality. Kafka's work, according to Adorno, "must renounce any claim to transcending myth, it makes the social web of delusion knowable in myth through the how, through language. In his writing, absurdity is as self-evident as it has actually become in society" (*AT* 230-31). Kafka's works confirm that there are no normative sources beyond the institutions and conventions of the totality. The existing conventions predominate and, in the absence of any consciousness of alternatives take on the character of inevitability. Adorno writes: "The closed complex of immanence becomes concrete in the form of a flight from prisons. In the absence of contrast, the monstrous becomes the entire world, as in Sade, the norm, whereas the unreflective adventure novel, by concentrating on extraordinary events thus confirms the rule of the ordinary" (*P* 265). The purely immanent approach, then, disturbs the settled experiences of everydayness.

Adorno confronts and criticizes rather generally the existentialist reading of Kafka with his own immanentist interpretation (*P* 244). Adorno presents existentialism as the recommendation that in an absurd universe human beings can do little but accommodate themselves to it. This accommodation means surrendering the notion that the world in which we live can be altered by our actions: we must therefore resign ourselves to the given rather than rail at our conditions. Faced with absurdity of our situation—our desire for agency and freedom on the one side and the non-responsiveness of the universe on the other—"the only alternative" left to the individual by existentialism, according to Adorno, is that he does "his duty, humbly and without great aspirations, and to integrate himself into a collective which expects just this" (*P* 245). The existentialist reading, then, like Adorno's interpretation, identifies Kafka's immanentism: the notion that there is nothing outside the plane of given experience. Adorno argues, however, that existentialism entirely misunderstands the significance of immanence. Whereas the existentialist reading suggests that Kafka's work is a protest against the yearning for happiness—he claims—it is for Adorno a revelation of—and implicitly a protest against—the conditions which constantly deny happiness. Adorno, we might say, ascribes a negative immanentism to Kafka: pure immanence implicitly speaks against a closed world. Existentialism, by contrast, frames Kafka's worlds as positive immanence: they supposedly provide us with reasons to act in ways that ultimately embrace the world.

This negative immanentism interpretation also informs Adorno's reading of the status of hope in Kafka's work. He cites Kafka's comment "that there is infinite hope except for us" (*P* 230-31). Adorno does not see this as metaphysical pessimism, as a statement about the intrinsic order of the universe (*pace* existentialism). It is not an effort to produce hopelessness. Adorno sees it, rather, as extinguishing false hope, i.e. the hope that our current arrangements are not irredeemable. A determinate negation of false hope, however, is the beginning of a way beyond those arrangements. As Adorno puts it: "If there is hope in Kafka's work, it is in those extremes rather than in the milder phases: in the capacity to stand up to the worst by making it into language" (*P* 254). Although Adorno, as we have seen, holds that Kafka does not impose a personal philosophical conception of the world on his narratives, he finds a valuable interpretative aide in a comment from Kafka's notebooks (*Blue Octavo*). He cites it to support the notion of a rejection of false hope in Kafka: "To believe in progress is to believe that there has not yet been any" (*P* 257). Adorno articulates the same idea as follows: "the name of history may not be spoken since what would truly be history, the other, has not yet begun" (*P* 257). Again, hope cannot be considered until we realize that there is now no basis for hope. This thesis resonates powerfully with Adorno's own notion of history and progress: "no progress is to be assumed that would imply that humanity in general already existed and therefore could progress."[16] The liberal faith in the progress of the West masks the deformation of human life and the ever-closing systematization of our social arrangements.

The immanentism of Kafka's narratives is of particular significance to Adorno as it coincides with his own epistemological vantage point. Adorno advocates social criticism in the form of "immanent critique." For criticism to be immanent means, according to Adorno, working to show the inherent contradictions of society without introducing standards of a good or better society from outside. There is, in any case, no "Archimedean position above culture and the blindness of society" (*P* 31). The social critic does not occupy a normative space that is somehow independent of existing society. In order then to avoid utopian irrelevancies or the delusion of purity, social criticism becomes immanent critique. Kafka achieves this in the great novels. Joseph K. and the land surveyor K. appear at first to be normal people thrown into unusual circumstances. The decisions they take in order to negotiate those circumstances, however, end up integrating them within the very systems that seem at first to have no authority or justification. In this process the protagonists, in their attempts to reason their way within the system, actually give it an authority that eventually defeats them. As Adorno writes: "The heroes of the *Trial* and the *Castle* become guilty not through their guilt—they have none—but because they try to get justice on their side. . . . [T]heir sound reasoning strengthens the delusion against which it protests" (*P* 270). Their actions—perfectly consistent with the irrational norms of the system—are the actions of non-agents. Kafka's narratives express the fall of the subject. As Adorno continues: "Through reification of the subject, demanded by the world in any event, Kafka seeks to beat the world at its own game" (*P* 270). Beating the world at its own game requires pressing the implications of what is required of the social actor to its limits. In this way, Adorno claims, Kafka's writing works against "the untruth of the abstract utopia" (*P* 270). It is, in effect, social criticism that succeeds by an insistent immanence.

## Conclusion

In *Negative Dialectics* Adorno suggests that Kafka may be the "apotheosis" of the self-reflection of philosophy that Adorno himself had attempted to stimulate and develop.[17] Self-reflection is thought "thinking against itself," guarding against its tendencies to construct, at the expense of the particularities of reality, abstractions and utopias. Those tendencies obscure what Kafka recognized as "the disturbed and damaged course of the world."[18] We have seen, from looking at "Notes on Kafka" and *Aesthetic Theory*, why Adorno finds in Kafka a deep affinity with his own philosophical project. Although Kafka does not engage in social criticism, his work is, for Adorno, a mimetic expression of society. It is historical and engaged with the materials of society. The immanence of Kafka's mimeticism shatters our complacency about the everyday by expressing its essential form. Kafka demonstrates, according to Adorno, that "form is the locus of social content" (*AT* 230). This principle transcends its aesthetic context and function. And it is the reason why Adorno does not conceive of Kafka's work as a literary version of the philosophical program of critical theory, but as providing vital foundational support for its deepest theoretical endeavors: that of elucidating the formal conditions of reified society.

## Notes

1. Jacques Derrida, *Dissemination*, trans. Barbara Johnson (Chicago, IL: University of Chicago Press, 1981), 187. Quoted in Matthew Potolsky, *Mimesis: The New Critical Idiom* (London and New York: Routledge, 2006), 2.

2. Peter Uwe Hohendahl, *Prismatic Thought: Theodor W. Adorno* (Lincoln, NE: University of Nebraska Press, 1995), 87.

3. See Adorno's letter to Benjamin, 17 December, 1934, in Theodor W. Adorno and Walter Benjamin, *The Complete Correspondence 1928-1940*, ed. Henri Lonitz, trans. Nicholas Walker (Cambridge, MA: Harvard University Press, 2001), 66-71. For an analysis of this letter see Shierry Weber Nicholsen, *Exact Imagination, Late Work* (Cambridge, MA, and London: MIT Press, 1997), 183ff. Benjamin's essay appeared as "Franz Kafka: On the Tenth Anniversary of his Death," trans. Harry Zohn, in Walter Benjamin, *Selected Writings*, ed. Michael W. Jennings (Cambridge, MA: Belknap, 1999), vol. 2, 794-818.

4. Theodor W. Adorno, "Notes on Kafka," in *Prisms*, trans. Samuel and Shierry Weber (London and Cambridge, MA: MIT Press, 1981), 243-71. Hereafter as *P*.

5. Walter H. Sokel, "Beyond Self-Assertion: A Life of Reading Kafka," in *A Companion to the Works of Franz Kafka*, ed. James Rolleston (Rochester, NY: Camden House, 2003), 40.

6. Theodor W. Adorno, *Aesthetic Theory*, trans. Robert Hullot-Kentor (Minneapolis, MN: University of Minnesota Press, 1997). Hereafter as *AT*.

7. Stanley Corngold, "Adorno's 'Notes on Kafka': A Critical Reconstruction," *Monatshefte* 94.1 (Spring, 2002): 27.

8. Theodor W. Adorno, *Negative Dialectics*, trans. E. B. Ashton (London: Routledge and Kegan Paul, 1973), 7.

9. Theodor W. Adorno, *Introduction to Sociology*, trans. Edmund Jephcott (Stanford, CA: Stanford University Press, 2000), 31.

10. Theodor W. Adorno, "Society," trans. Fredric Jameson, *Salmagundi* 10-11 (1969-1970): 149.

11. Robert W. Witkin, "Philosophy of Culture," in *Theodor Adorno: Key Concepts*, ed. Deborah Cook (Stocksfield: Acumen, 2008), 168.

12. Theodor W. Adorno, *Notes to Literature*, Vol. 1, trans. Shierry Weber Nicholsen (New York: Columbia University Press, 1991), 181.

13. See Lambert Zuidervaart, *Adorno's Aesthetic Theory* (Cambridge, MA, and London: MIT Press 1991), 217-47, for a summary of these criticisms, especially Peter Bürger's influential objection to Adorno's characterization of the avant-garde.

14. See Theodor W. Adorno, "Late Capitalism or Industrial Society?" in *Can One Live After Auschwitz? A Philosophical Reader*, ed. Rolf Tiedemann (Stanford, CA: Stanford University Press, 2003).

15. Simon Jarvis, *Adorno: A Critical Introduction* (Cambridge: Polity, 1998), 123.

16. Theodor W. Adorno "Progress," trans. Henry W. Pickford, in Adorno, *Critical Models: Interventions and Catchwords* (New York: Columbia University Press, 1998), 145.

17. Adorno, *Negative Dialectics*, 365.

18. Adorno, *Negative Dialectics*, 403.

## Works Cited

Adorno, Theodor W. *Aesthetic Theory*. Translated by Robert Hullot-Kentor. Minneapolis, MN: University of Minnesota Press, 1997.

———. *Introduction to Sociology*. Translated by Edmund Jephcott. Stanford, CA: Stanford University Press, 2000.

———. "Late Capitalism or Industrial Society?" Translated by Rodney Livingstone. In *Can One Live After Auschwitz? A Philosophical Reader*, edited by Rolf Tiedemann, 111-25. Stanford, CA: Stanford University Press, 2003.

———. *Negative Dialectics*. Translated by E. B. Ashton. London: Routledge and Kegan Paul, 1973.

———. "Notes on Kafka." In Theodor W. Adorno, *Prisms*, translated by Samuel and Shierry Weber, 243-71. London and Cambridge, MA: MIT Press, 1981.

———. *Notes to Literature*. Vol. 1. Translated by Shierry Weber Nicholsen. New York: Columbia University Press, 1991.

———. "Progress." In Theodor W. Adorno, *Critical Models: Interventions and Catchwords*, translated by Henry W. Pickford, 143-60. New York: Columbia University Press, 1998.

———. "Society." Translated by Fredric Jameson. *Salmagundi* 10-11 (1969-1970): 144-53.

Adorno, Theodor W., and Walter Benjamin. *The Complete Correspondence 1928-1940*. Edited by Henri Lonitz, translated by Nicholas Walker. Cambridge, MA: Harvard University Press, 2001.

Benjamin, Walter. "Franz Kafka: On the Tenth Anniversary of His Death." Translated by Harry Zohn. In Walter Benjamin, *Selected Writings*, edited by Michael W. Jennings, vol. 2, 794-818. Cambridge, MA: Belknap, 1999.

Corngold, Stanley. "Adorno's 'Notes on Kafka': A Critical Reconstruction." *Monatshefte* 94.1 (Spring, 2002): 24-42.

Derrida, Jacques. *Dissemination*. Translated by Barbara Johnson. Chicago, IL: University of Chicago Press, 1981.

Hohendahl, Peter Uwe. *Prismatic Thought: Theodor W. Adorno*. Lincoln, NE: University of Nebraska Press, 1995.

Jarvis, Simon. *Adorno: A Critical Introduction*. Cambridge: Polity, 1998.

Potolsky, Matthew. *Mimesis: The New Critical Idiom*. London and New York: Routledge, 2006.

Sokel, Walter H. "Beyond Self-Assertion: A Life of Reading Kafka." In *A Companion to the Works of Franz Kafka*, edited by James Rolleston, 33-60. Rochester, NY: Camden House, 2003.

Weber Nicholsen, Shierry. *Exact Imagination, Late Work*. Cambridge, MA, and London: MIT Press, 1997.

Witkin, Robert W. "Philosophy of Culture." In *Theodor Adorno: Key Concepts*, edited by Deborah Cook, 161-78. Stocksfield: Acumen, 2008.

Zuidervaart, Lambert. *Adorno's Aesthetic Theory*. Cambridge, MA, and London: MIT Press 1991.

CHAPTER 13

# "In the Penal Colony" in the Philosophy of Gilles Deleuze

*Ronald Bogue*

As Raymond Bellour and François Ewald rightly observed in a 1988 interview with Gilles Deleuze, "Literature is everywhere present in your work, running parallel, almost, to the philosophy."[1] Of the 279 writers Deleuze references in his work,[2] far and away the two most frequently cited and most extensively investigated are Proust and Kafka, the former the subject of Deleuze's monograph *Proust and Signs* (1964; 2nd ed. rev. and aug. 1970; 3rd ed. rev. and aug. 1976), the latter the focus of Deleuze and Félix Guattari's jointly authored *Kafka: Toward a Minor Literature* (1975).[3] Deleuze's fascination with Proust appears to have been longstanding, whereas his interest in Kafka, although evident as early as 1965, seems to have grown exponentially after 1970 when he began his collaborative efforts with Guattari, who himself had a lifelong passion for Kafka above all other writers.[4] In *Kafka: Toward a Minor Literature* Deleuze and Guattari cover a number of topics, but of those the two that Deleuze returns to most often in his other writings are Kafka's "deterritorialization" of language (a topic I will not address in this essay) and Kafka's treatment of the law. If one were to choose a single Kafka text as most central to Deleuze's thought about the law, it would be *The Trial*, but other works, most notably "Building the Great Wall of China" and "In the Penal Colony," play an important role as well. The role of the former is relatively clear: it generally stands as a figure for the despotic regime of law, in which the despot (in this case, the emperor) is the unifying principle that brings together the fragmented pieces of the law (represented here by the disconnected blocks of the great wall that are scattered across China). The role played by "In the Penal Colony," by contrast, is much less evident and hence worth exploring in some detail.

## Carrouges, Kafka and Duchamp

Deleuze first mentions "In the Penal Colony" in his initial collaborative project with Guattari, *Anti-Oedipus: Capitalism and Schizophrenia I* (1972).[5] There Deleuze and Guattari cite the story in connection with what they call the "celibate machine" (*machine célibataire*, translated as "bachelor machine" in *Kafka:*

*Toward a Minor Literature* [98]—both translations are acceptable, since *célibataire* can mean either celibate or bachelor) (*Anti-Oedipus* 17). They appropriate the term from Michel Carrouges, who in his 1954 book *Les machines célibataires* draws analogies among several twentieth-century works of art to disclose the emergence of a new myth symptomatic of the modern condition. That myth, which he calls "the myth of the celibate machine," bears on "the quadruple tragedy of our times: the Gordian knot of the interferences of machinism, terror, eroticism, and religion or anti-religion."[6] All four elements are not patent in every artwork, but through a juxtaposition of several works Carrouges discerns the latent presence of all.

Carrouges says that his inspiration for the study came from startling parallels he noted between Kafka's penal colony machine and the structure of Marcel Duchamp's *magnum opus*, *The Bride Stripped Bare by her Bachelors, Even (The Large Glass)* (*La Mariée mise à nu par ces célibataires, même [Le grande verre]*) (1912-1923).[7] We will recall that Kafka's execution machine, as the officer explains to the traveler, has three parts for which "people have developed various nicknames. . . . The lower one is called the bed (*das Bett*), the upper one is called the scriber (*der Zeichner*), and, here, the middle part, the free-hanging one, is called the harrow (*die Egge*)" ("Penal Colony" 37).[8] The scriber and bed, of equal size, resemble two dark chests, the scriber six feet above the bed, the two connected at the corners by four brass poles. The harrow hangs from the scriber on a steel band. The harrow consists of an array of needles embedded in glass, which inscribe on the prisoner's body the specific commandment the prisoner has disobeyed (in this case, "Honor thy superiors!"). The prisoner to be executed is stripped naked and placed facedown on the bed, which is lined with absorbent cotton. As the harrow inscribes the commandment, the bed quivers with tiny vibrations that are "painstakingly attuned to the movements of the harrow" ("Penal Colony" 39). The movements of the harrow are controlled by the scriber, whose cogwheels translate the elaborate designs of the Old Commandant, the machine's inventor, into the pattern of wounds in the victim's flesh. The execution takes place over twelve hours. Until the sixth hour, the victim suffers only excruciating pain, but thereafter he begins to decipher the commandment through his wounds, and "understanding dawns even on the dumbest. It begins around the eyes. From there it spreads. A sight that could seduce one to lie down alongside him under the harrow" ("Penal Colony" 44-45). As the victim attains this understanding, witnesses can observe in the victim an "expression of transfiguration from his martyred face" ("Penal Colony" 48).

Carrouges notes that the execution apparatus combines man and machine in a single construction, whose purpose is to visit a harsh law from on high upon a naked body below. The story's multiple religious allusions suggest to Carrouges that a once efficacious means of delivering divine commandments has given way to a meaningless ritual of terror and pain, as is made clear upon the death of the officer following his voluntary submission to the machine's operation. As the traveler tries to remove the officer's body from the machine, "he saw, almost against his will, the face of the corpse. It was as it had been in life; no sign of the promised deliverance could be detected" ("Penal Colony" 58). Hence Carrouges reads the story as an allegory of "the tragedy of the death of God" (Carrouges 48) coupled to a myth of technological terror. He also discerns a latent eroticism in the officer's passion for the machine and a voyeuristic element in the glass casing of the harrow that allows spectators to enjoy the victim's suffering throughout the process.

If eroticism is only latent in Kafka, in Duchamp's *Bride* it is all-pervasive. Duchamp's composition is made up of various media (paint, varnish, lead wire, lead foil and dust) on two glass panels, one above the other, each measuring roughly four and a half feet by three and a half feet. The *Bride* has two basic components: the bride panel above and the bachelor panel below. Duchamp provided elaborate and complex commentary on the composition in three collections of documents, which he viewed as constituent elements of the artwork: a box of 15 documents assembled in 1915, *The Green Box* (1934) and *The White Box* (1967). In these collections, Duchamp labeled the upper panel the Bride's Domain, and the lower the Bachelor Machine (*machine célibataire*) (or Bachelor Apparatus [*appareil célibataire*], or simply the Bachelor [*célibataire*]). The central elements of the upper panel are the vertical figure of the Bride on the left and a horizontal cloud surrounding three empty squares that runs from the Bride's head across the top quarter of the panel. Duchamp describes the Bride variously as a "steam engine," a "skeleton," a "female hanged person" (*pendu femelle*), and "the apotheosis of virginity." The Bride has a reservoir of "love gasoline" that is fed to her "motor with quite feeble cylinders" where it is ignited by the "desire magneto," which in turn is controlled by the "wasp," or "sex cylinder." Duchamp calls the horizontal cloud "the milky way," "the halo of the Bride," the Bride's "cinematic blossoming," "the title," and "the top inscription." The three boxes within the cloud are labeled "draft pistons," "nets," and the "triple cipher."

The lower glass panel contains on the left side the nine bachelors atop a metal framework called the "chariot," "sleigh," "slide" or "glider." In the center are two horizontal rotor-like bars called "the scissors," supported by a pole fixed to the "chocolate grinder" below, with an arc of seven conic "sieves" passing up from the bachelors through the cross-point of the scissor and down to the point where the spiraling line of the "splashings" commences its movement to the right. On the right side, the final loop of the spiraling "splashings" ends at the bottom of the panel. Above the spiral are situated three stacked oval discs, "the ocular witnesses," and atop them the "Kodak magnifying glass lens." The nine Bachelors, which roughly resemble chess pieces, are "malic moulds" that together constitute a "cemetery of uniforms and liveries" as well as "Eros' matrix." The Bachelors emit a gas that is solidified and then converted into sparks as it passes from left to right through the elaborate machinery of the lower panel. The Bachelors' Eros is one of "onanism" and a "vicious circle" of desire enforced by the barrier between the upper and lower glass panels against which their desires continually rebound.

In the *Bride*, Duchamp combines humans and machines in improbable circuits of desire, whose Eros is pervaded with death and frustration (the Bride an "apotheosis of virginity" and the Bachelors the "matrix" of onanistic celibacy).

Carrouges has no difficulty identifying the themes of mechanism and eroticism in the *Bride*, but the remaining two motifs of the "myth of the celibate machine," terror and anti-religion, are less evident, and only revealed, he claims, through a comparison of the *Bride* and Kafka's torture machine. Carrouges likens the *Bride*'s cloud to the "scriber" in Kafka's story, arguing that the cloud's designations of "inscription" and "milky way," and its inclusion of three draft pistons called "ciphers," suggest that the cloud is a celestial, quasi-religious source of mysterious messages communicated to the Bride and Bachelors below. He speculates further that the thin long tube running diagonally from the base of the Bride to the bottom of her panel is the counterpart of the needles of the torture machine's "harrow," and hence that the tube is the instrument which inscribes the cloud's "inscription" on the Bachelors in the lower panel. Given the designation of the Bride as the "skeleton" and "female hanged person," Carrouges claims that the Bride is an agent of death and that her inscription of the celestial ciphers is part of a dehumanizing circuit of erotic terror.

## Machines and *la machine célibataire*

Deleuze and Guattari have little use for Carrouges' claim that Kafka's torture machine and Duchamp's *Bride* reveal a tragic myth of modernity, but they are taken by the juxtaposition of Kafka and Duchamp in particular, and by the notion of "machines," and especially that of "desiring machines" in general. That Deleuze and Guattari find Carrouges's association of Kafka and Duchamp fruitful is evident in their initial description of the celibate machine, with "its cogs, its sliding carriage, its shears, needles, magnets, rays" (*Anti-Oedipus* 18)—a clear amalgam of the penal colony machine (cogs, needles) and the *Bride* machine (sliding carriage, shears, magnets, rays). This association, I would argue, suggests that whenever one confronts Kafka's execution machine in a text of Deleuze or Deleuze and Guattari, one should have Duchamp's *Bride* machine in the back of one's mind as well.

As regards the term "machine," Carrouges's use of the word in his concept of "celibate machines" resonates with interests that for Guattari date at least to 1961, when he wrote an essay proposing a reformulation of the psychoanalytic concept of "partial objects" as machines.[9] The first sign of Deleuze's interaction with Guattari appears in the 1970 second edition of Deleuze's *Proust and Signs*, which includes a new section analyzing Proust's treatment of time in terms of three machines. There Deleuze argues not only that Proust's *Recherche* should be seen as a collection of machines, but also that the modern artwork in general is a machine, in that it does not communicate any particular hidden meaning but simply functions (see *Proust and Signs*, 145-46). In *Anti-Oedipus*, the machine is a dominant concept, central to Deleuze and Guattari's argument for a "schizoanalysis" with which to replace psychoanalysis. Psychoanalysis seeks to interpret the manifestations of desire, whereas schizoanalysis merely maps their functioning.

In Deleuze and Guattari's parlance, "machine" has a very broad meaning. Indeed, everything is a machine, and since desire is a positive force immanent within the world, all machines are engaged in a process of desiring-production. At one level of analysis, individual humans are made up of multiple machines, each connected to the next in an open-ended, additive structure (A and C and X and . . .), with a flow of some kind (liquid, solid, gas, electricity, information, or whatever) passing through the sequence. A simple example of a connective sequence of desiring-machines is that of a nursing infant: a breast machine hooked to a mouth machine, to the machines of the infant's digestive tract through which passes a flow of milk (and of course, the breast machine for its part is connected to the diverse machines involved in lactation, digestion of nutrients, hormone excretion, and so on). Although individual machines are connected one-to-one, machines may also participate in multiple circuits fulfilling different functions (the mouth as eating machine, breathing machine, singing machine, and so on).

On a macroscopic level, however, machines are made up of multiple elements that may include individual humans among their working parts. Deleuze and Guattari cite as an example of such a machine one offered by Lewis Mumford, who argues that the collective enterprise involved in the construction of the Egyptian pyramids was the first "megamachine." "If, more or less in agreement with Rouleaux's classic definition, one can consider the machine to be the combination of solid elements, each having its specialized function and operating under human control in order to transmit a movement and perform a task, then the human machine was indeed a true machine" (Mumford, cited in *Anti-Oedipus* 141). The components of the pyramid machine were: the pharaoh, his ministers, architects, engineers, managers, artists, workers and slaves; the tools used to quarry the stones, transport them to the site, move them into place, and then decorate the pyramid interiors; and the material elements with which the pyramids and all the tools were constructed—stone, wood, reeds, metal and so on.

Although one may, for the sake of analysis, distinguish a microscopic, subindividual level from a macroscopic, supraindividual level, in truth the two levels are seamlessly interconnected. For Deleuze and Guattari, this point is crucial, since in their critique of psychoanalysis they insist that all psychological investments of desire are immediately social and political, and in no way restricted to the individual psyche or the limited milieu of the family. Indeed, such a restriction of desire is the fundamental ideological mistake of the psychoanalytic enterprise. The infant at the mother's breast is not simply an assemblage of multiple machines connected to a single maternal assemblage of machines, but also a component with the mother in multiple circuits of production involving various people, materials, tools, and institutions that reach into the larger sociopolitical world.

## Desiring Production

Deleuze and Guattari subdivide the general process of "desiring production" into the production of production, the production of recording (*enregistrement*, also referred to as the production of inscription), and the production of consumption/consummation (*consummation*). (Clearly, Deleuze and Guattari are here adopting a modified version of Marx's terminology of production, exchange, distribution and consumption, simply collapsing exchange and distribution into a single process of recording/inscription.) The production of production operates through a connective synthesis of "desiring-machines"; the production of recording through a disjunctive synthesis of those desiring-machines upon a "body without organs" (a term borrowed from Antonin Artaud); and the production of consumption through a conjunctive synthesis that gives rise to the "nomadic subject." Deleuze and Guattari associate Carrouges's *machine célibataire* with the conjunctive synthesis of the nomadic subject.

With the terms desiring-machines, the body without organs and the nomadic subject, Deleuze and Guattari are offering a somewhat whimsical alternative to the Freudian psychological model of id, ego and superego, their triad being founded not in neurosis but in psychosis. Desiring-machines correspond to the dissociative experience of psychotics who perceive their body parts as alien entities, or feel their fragmented bodies connected to external energy sources (invading rays, electrical circuits) or to various objects, machines, and so on. The body without organs is the catatonic body, an unmoving, viscous substance gelled into an amorphous solid. And the nomadic subject is the psychotic exclaiming in succession, "I'm Joan of Arc," "I'm Jesus Christ," "I'm Napoleon," and so on. Desiring-machines in one sense produce the body without organs, yet paradoxically the body without organs also functions as the precondition of the desiring-machines. As the desiring-machines engage in their connective production of production, the body without organs senses the desiring-machines as persecutory invasions, and in this interaction between desiring-machines and the body without organs a "repulsion machine" begins to operate as the body without organs attempts to expel the alien attackers. But soon an attracting, "miraculating machine" emerges, whereby the body without organs is restored to its state of glorious equanimity, the desiring-machines now seeming to emanate from the body without organs, as if they had been "miraculated" (a term used by the psychotic Schreber to describe the way in which his body was transformed by the rays of God). At this point of miraculation, the body without organs is like a giant, embryonic egg, whose surface is crisscrossed by a grid of interconnecting desiring-machines, the entire grid marking the production of recording or inscription. Each line of interconnected desiring-machines is a gradient or zone of intensity of a given quantity, whereas the body without organs is a body at zero intensity (not a negative state, simply the base line from which all positive degrees of intensity may be measured). As zero intensity, the body without organs is a force of "anti-production," since it momentarily interrupts the desiring-machines's incessant production; such anti-production is extracted from production and then re-injected into the production process, thereby ensuring that production and anti-production are part of a single process during which the desiring-machines only function while simultaneously breaking down. In the operation of the repulsion machine and miraculating machine, intensities pass from one level to another. In that passage, a process of "becoming-other" takes place. That passage, that "becoming," *is* the nomadic subject, a moment of consumption/consummation, an ecstatic, orgasmic excess of libido saying, now here, now there, "that's me!" Hence, across the egg traversed by a grid of lines, intermittent flashes of a nomadic subject are scattered, or rather, flashes of multiple nomadic subjects are scattered. In this third phase of desiring-production, the production of consumption/consummation, the repulsion machine and the miraculating machine are brought into relation with yet another machine, the celibate machine, which is responsible for the emergence of the nomadic subject.

Although Deleuze and Guattari introduce the triad of desiring-machines, body without organs and nomadic subject via a psychological model, the model also applies at a broad social level. Every social body, or *socius*, has a body without organs, upon which desiring-machines are recorded and nomadic subjects made manifest. In *Anti-Oedipus*'s sweeping history of social formations, Deleuze and Guattari identify three modes of production, or social machines, each with its own body without organs: the primitive machine, whose body without organs is the body of the earth; the despotic machine, with the body of the despot functioning as a body without organs; and the capitalist machine, whose body without organs is capital itself. In traditional societies, typically the people see themselves as autochthonous emanations of an undivided earth; in despotic regimes, the body of the despot (or king or State) usurps the function of the earth, uncoding or deterritorializing primitive codes and then "over-coding" or reterritorializing them on the centralizing despotic corpus; and in capitalist societies, capital functions as a miraculating body without organs, a fetishized magical element from which all social and natural relationships seem to emanate, one that undoes previous codings and over-codings and reterritorializes them in shifting commodity and labor relations and provisional appropriations of the State apparatus. The body without organs as anti-production is the outside limit of each socius, the point of absolute deterritorialization immanent within the relatively deterritorialized body of the earth, body of the despot or body of capital. In this regard, all social machines, like all psychological machines, are inherently unstable and metamorphic, always in the process of breaking down even as they function.

## Desiring Production and the Penal Colony

Clearly, Kafka's penal colony machine and Duchamp's Bride/Bachelor machine are exemplary instances of social desiring-machines. In the Kafka story, initially the components of the machine include the execution machine itself, the officer, the traveler, the soldier, and the condemned man. By the story's end, the components are reduced to the machine, the officer/victim and the traveler. And yet the entire assemblage of machine and human beings is a penal colony machine, and hence connected to the colony prison, which in turn is merely a tropical outpost of the home country's entire legal/juridical system, which itself is a component of the complex machinery of the social, cultural and economic production of an imperial power. When the execution machine begins operating, its immediate constituent desiring-machines are the scriber and its complex of cogs, gears and design protocol, the harrow, the bed, the executioner and the victim. The body without organs is the miraculating aura produced through the machine's operation and enveloping the entire apparatus (or at least an aura envisioned in the officer's ecstatic descriptions of the machine as it functioned in former times). The nomadic subject, of course, is the officer, even if he himself does not experience the mystical transformation of former victims. The officer's erotic attachment to the machine is self-evident, and for Deleuze and Guattari, representative of the kind of libidinal investments humans have in systems of oppression: "Oh how beautiful the machine is! The officer of 'In the Penal Colony' demonstrates what an intense libidinal investment of a machine can be, a machine that is not only technical but social, and through which desire desires its own repression" (*Anti-Oedipus* 346). One of the questions Deleuze and Guattari pose often in *Anti-Oedipus* is, why do people accept and even acquiesce in their own oppression? And their answer is provided by the penal colony officer: at some level, people have formed a libidinal attachment to the social machine within which they find themselves, however perverse and warped that desire may be. That the penal colony machine comes apart at the conclusion of the tale is an apt representation of desiring-production in general, with its integration of production and anti-production within its functioning. As Deleuze and Guattari remark in *Kafka*, "In the 'Penal Colony,' the machine seems to have a strong degree of unity and the man enters completely into it. Maybe this is what leads to the final explosion and the crumbling of the machine" (*Kafka* 8).

For Deleuze and Guattari, then, the breakdown of the torture machine reveals the truth of desiring-production beneath the veneer of the dominant order's view of itself as a unified, efficient apparatus. The manifestation of that truth, however, puts an end to the machine. Duchamp's *Bride*, by contrast, seems to remain intact as an operational machine, but its preposterous design and improbable functioning suggest that its workings are rife with breakdowns—starts and stutters, interruptions, hesitations, catatonic seizures. As Deleuze and Guattari remark, desiring-machines "continually break down as they run, and in fact run only when they are not functioning properly. . . . Art often takes advantage of this property of desiring-machines by creating veritable group fantasies in which desiring-production is used to short-circuit social production, and to interfere with the reproduction function of technical machines by introduction an element of dysfunction. Arman's charred violins, for instance, or César's compressed car bodies" (*Anti-Oedipus* 31). The desiring-machines of Duchamp's Rube Goldberg contraption display very clearly Deleuze and Guattari's conception of desiring-machines as entities that cut across standard taxonomies of bodies, machines and natural substances. The Bride is a wasp/skeleton/steam engine with gas tank, cylinders and magneto, and the

Bachelors are malic molds, a cemetery and erotic matrix that emit combustible gases. The ludicrous assemblage of Bride, cloud, pistons, Bachelor, sleigh, scissors, chocolate grinder, splashings, optical witnesses and lens is perhaps an ideal model of the nature of desiring-production as Deleuze and Guattari see it: a process that combines heterogeneous elements in arational circuits of multiple flows and fluxes. In Duchamp's *Bride*, the various components are the desiring-machines, the entire artwork is the body without organs, and the Bride and Bachelors are the machine's nomadic subjects (although one might conjecture that the other components of the composition are also nonhuman nomadic subjects).

Carrouges labels Kafka's machine and the *Bride* "*machines célibataires*" to indicate their connection to frustrated sexuality, but one might ask why Deleuze and Guattari should choose to adopt the term *célibataire*. Since for Deleuze and Guattari desire is not a yearning for something missing (as it is for Carrouges and for psychoanalysis in general) but a positive dimension of all processes of production, "celibate desire" does not denote frustration. Rather, it poses in an apparently oxymoronic fashion two fundamental aspects of all desiring-production. First, the moment of consumption/consummation is always onanistic, but only in the sense that it is a moment of ecstatic self-enjoyment (with no sense of "self" in its standard meaning), and in that regard it is "celibate." "A genuine consummation is achieved by the new machine, a pleasure that can rightly be called autoerotic, or rather automatic: the nuptial celebration of a new alliance, a new birth, a radiant ecstasy, as though the eroticism of the machine liberated unlimited forces" (*Anti-Oedipus* 18). Second, desire is impersonal, or rather "pre-personal" and "pre-individual," and definitely not maternal, paternal or filial, as psychoanalysis would have it. For this reason Deleuze and Guattari often say in *Anti-Oedipus* that desire is an anonymous orphan, unattached to any family, Oedipal or otherwise. They make the same point in *Kafka*, where they discuss the "*machine célibataire*" in a commentary on Kafka's 1910 diary fragment about a bachelor (*Junggeselle*) who feels displaced from the ordinary world of families and the extended bonds of the human community.[10] In Deleuze and Guattari's appropriation of the fragment, the bachelor is the outsider who ultimately is only an impersonal function, a deterritorialized and deterritorializing force at play in the social body. The bachelor "doesn't flee the world; he grasps it and makes it take flight on a continuous and artistic line: 'I must just take my walks and that must be sufficient, but in compensation there is no place in all the world where I could not take my walks.' With no family, no conjugality, the bachelor is all the more social, social-dangerous, social-traitor, a collective in himself ('We are outside the law, no one knows it and yet everyone treats us accordingly.')" (*Kafka* 71). The artist is a bachelor, and Kafka's writing machine is a *machine célibataire*: "If we are to sum up the nature of the artistic machine for Kafka, we must say that it is a bachelor machine, the only bachelor machine, and, as such, plugged all the more into a social field with multiple connections. Machinic definition and not an aesthetic one. The bachelor is a state of desire much larger and more intense than incestuous desire and homosexual desire" (*Kafka* 70).

## Desiring Machines and the Penal Colony Torture Machine

In Chapter One of *Anti-Oedipus*, Kafka's penal colony machine is associated with the celibate machine of the production of consumption/consummation (the third stage of desiring-production), but as I have shown, one can also see clearly in the execution machine the presence of the "production of production" of desiring-machines and the "production of recording" of the body without organs. In *Anti-Oedipus*'s lengthy third chapter, Deleuze and Guattari detail their universal history of social formations, which they identify as the primitive machine, the despotic machine and the capitalist machine. (The "primitive machine" corresponds roughly to what are often designated "traditional societies," such as hunter-gatherers, sedentary tribes, and all the other small human communities which are the most frequent subjects of anthropological ethnographies; the "despotic machine" is a very broad designation for all social formations in which a central authority controls a populace, such as empires, fiefdoms, kingdoms, and states of various sorts; the "capitalist machine" refers to the specific social and political structures of capitalism, which are manifest across diverse governmental systems.) They cite "In the Penal Colony" during their exposition of the "Barbarian or Imperial Representation" of the despotic machine, arguing that the story's presentation of the law and its inscription aptly characterizes the despotic machine's production of recording. But there are also distinct, though unstated, echoes of "In the Penal Colony" in Deleuze and Guattari's description of the production of recording in the primitive machine, and those echoes connect Kafka's story to Nietzsche's *Genealogy of Morals*.

The primitive machine's production of recording is a "graphism," but not a writing: "a dance on the earth, a drawing on a wall, a mark on the body are a graphic system, a geo-graphism, a geography." Such recording is oral rather than written because the marks of this "geographism" form "a graphic system that is independent of the voice, a system that is not aligned on the voice and not subordinate to it, but connected to it, co-ordinated 'in an organization that is radiating, as it were,' and multidimensional" (*Anti-Oedipus* 188). Primitive signs are interrelated, but only as a loosely connected, non-totalized network of relays from one sign to another. Marks on human bodies—tattoos, scarification, piercings, and so on—are constitutive elements of primitive societies. If exchangists like Lévi-Strauss regard the exchange of women as foundational in traditional societies, Deleuze and Guattari see the marking of bodies and the extraction of debt as the true basis of such societies. They argue that Nietzsche's account in *On the Genealogy of Morals* of the origin of the human capacity to make and honor promises is the proper guide to understanding debt in the primitive social machine (*Anti-Oedipus* 144-45).

In Nietzsche's analysis humans must develop a faculty of memory in order to make and keep promises, and such a faculty is formed through a mnemotechnics of pain: "Man could never do without blood, torture, and sacrifices when he felt the need to create a memory for himself; the most dreadful sacrifices and pledges (sacrifices of the first-born among them), the most repulsive mutilations (castration, for example), the cruelest rites of all the religious cults (and all religions are at the deepest level systems of cruelties)—all this has its origin in the instinct that realized that pain is the most powerful aid to mnemonics."[11] Once humans develop a memory, they can make meaningful promises. In this early stage of human development, Nietzsche conjectures, if person A promises something to person B, and then breaks the promise, person B is allowed to inflict pain on person A. Inflicting pain on A, then, is the compensation offered B for the unfulfilled promise. Nietzsche reasons that inflicting pain on another individual only makes sense as a form of compensation if B gains something by inflicting pain on A—and Nietzsche concludes that what B gains is the intense pleasure of making another individual suffer. In this compensation we see the ancient "contractual relationship between *creditor* and *debtor*" (*Genealogy* 63), and that extracted pain is the debt repaid to the creditor.

According to Deleuze and Guattari, the primitive social machine operates through the interaction of alliance (marriage relations) and filiation (blood relations), and it is the extraction of debt that brings alliance and filiation together and assigns individual society members their position in the group. The primitive production of recording that takes place in ritual scarification simultaneously situates the initiate within the network of alliances and filiations and produces the debt of the initiate to the collectivity. The primitive machine's "savage inscription process or territorial representation" (*Anti-Oedipus* 188) operates through a triad of "voice-audition," "hand-graphics" and "eye-pain." The voice "is like a voice of alliance to which, on the side of the extended filiation, a graphics is coordinated that bears no resemblance" (*Anti-Oedipus* 188). Between the voice-audition and hand-graphics,

> pain is like the surplus value that the eye extracts, taking hold of the effect of active speech on the body, but also of the reaction of the body as it is acted upon. This is indeed what must be called a debt system, or territorial representation: a voice that speaks or intones, a sign marked in bare flesh, an eye that extracts enjoyment from the pain; these are the three sides of a savage triangle forming a territory of resonance and retention, a *theater of cruelty* that implies the triple independence of the articulated voice, the graphic hand, and the appreciative eye. (*Anti-Oedipus* 189)

The resemblances are unmistakable between this primitive "theater of cruelty" and the Penal Colony's execution ceremonies as they took place during the reign of the Old Commandant. In the primitive machine, punishment is "a festive occasion" (*Anti-Oedipus* 212), and according to the officer, former executions were definitely festive communal rituals. As in ritual scarification, the Penal Colony punishment is inscribed in the body, and the appreciative eyes of the onlookers, gazing through the glass structure of the harrow, extract an excess of pleasure as they await the sixth-hour transfiguration of the victim. The parallel between the primitive theater of cruelty and the Penal Colony executions is only strengthened when Deleuze and Guattari, in their presentation of the primitive recording machine, cite the anthropologist Michel Cartry's description of an

African ritual of scarification in which young women are incised with a calabash shard. According to Cartry,

> In order for the young woman's transformation to be fully effective, a direct contact must take place between her stomach, on the one hand, and the calabash and the signs inscribed on her, on the other hand. The young woman must become physically saturated with the signs of procreation and she must incorporate them. The young women are never taught the meaning of the ideograms during their initiation. The sign acts through its inscription in the body. (qtd. in *Anti-Oedipus* 189)

Like this young woman, the Penal Colony victim is not informed of his infraction or punishment, but he eventually "deciphers it with his wounds" ("Penal Colony" 45).

Despite such resonances, Deleuze and Guattari associate "In the Penal Colony" with the production of recording in the despotic rather than the primitive machine. The despot deterritorializes the plurivocal, decentered primitive signs and codes, and then recodes them as univocal, unified signs emanating from a totalitarian center. With the despot comes the invention of writing, which entails as well the alignment of the voice-audition and hand-graphic in what Saussure will call the signifier. Law now is recorded "on stones, parchments, pieces of currency, and lists" (*Anti-Oedipus* 211), leading one to surmise that in this regard the despotic machine is milder than the primitive. But this is not the case. "In point of fact the regime is not milder; the system of terror has replaced the system of cruelty" (*Anti-Oedipus* 211). The notion that the state through its laws might restrain the ruler is a very late development. Rather, despotic law is originally simply an expression of despotic power, and according to Deleuze and Guattari, it is Kafka who best characterizes that law. Making use of Melanie Klein's psychoanalytic terminology of the "paranoid-schizoid position" (the infant's first four months, during which the infant perceives only partial objects in a primal world of ingestion, ejection and excretion) and the "depressive position" (months four to twelve, during which the infant gradually pieces partial objects together and forms a sense of the mother as a whole body), Deleuze and Guattari identify two characteristics of despotic law,

> the two features that Kafka so forcefully developed: first, the paranoiac-schizoid trait of the law (metonymy) according to which the law governs nontotalizable and nontotalized parts, partitioning them off, organizing them as bricks, measuring their distance and forbidding their communication, henceforth acting in the name of a formidable but formal and empty Unity, eminent, distributive, and not collective; and second, the maniacal depressive trait (metaphor) according to which the law reveals nothing and has no knowable object, the verdict having no existence prior to the penalty, and the statement of the law having no existence prior to the verdict. (*Anti-Oedipus* 212)

Although Deleuze and Guattari do not say so, their reference to the paranoiac-schizoid law in Kafka is to "Building the Great Wall of China." In that story, the isolated fragments of the great wall are only unified by an infinitely distant

Emperor, this architectural model serving as an apt figure for the relationship between the laws and the despot. (We might note as well that the Imperial wall construction enterprise as "megamachine" parallels nicely Mumford's pharaonic pyramid megamachine.) As regards the maniacal depressive trait of despotic law, Deleuze and Guattari identify their Kafka source directly: "As in the machine of 'In the Penal Colony,' it is the penalty that writes both the verdict and the rule that has been broken" (*Anti-Oedipus* 212).

Any illusion that the body has escaped suffering in the shift from the primitive theater of cruelty to the despotic reign of terror must be dispelled:

> In vain did the body liberate itself from its characteristic graphism in the system of connotation, for it now becomes the stone and the paper, the tablet and the currency on which the new writing is able to mark its figures, its phonetism, and its alphabet. Overcoding is the essence of the law and the origin of the new sufferings of the body. Punishment has ceased to be a festive occasion, from which the eye extracts a surplus value in the magic triangle of alliance and filiations. *Punishment becomes a vengeance.* (*Anti-Oedipus* 212)

## "In the Penal Colony" and Deleuze's Concept of Law

If "In the Penal Colony" is approached via a general theory of desiring production and a universal history of social machines in *Anti-Oedipus,* the story is assigned a different role in Deleuze and Guattari's next collaborative work, *Kafka: Toward a Minor Literature* (1975). In this study, Deleuze and Guattari's primary concern is to characterize Kafka's "writing machine," with its three components of the letters, short stories and novels, and chart its functioning (while avoiding any interpretation of its deeper meaning—including the Oedipal, oneiric and mystical readings that dominate Kafka criticism). In Deleuze and Guattari's anti-interpretive, functional analysis, the problem for Kafka is to keep the writing machine running and avoid any premature closure. In the letters, there is always the threat of conjugality, and Kafka's effort is to postpone as long as possible his marriage to Felice, which he recognizes as incompatible with his vocation as a writer. The letters represent at best only a makeshift solution for keeping the writing machine running. The short stories are essentially stories of "becoming-animal" and the search for a means of escape, a "line of flight." (Deleuze and Guattari bring "In the Penal Colony" within this taxonomy by pointing out that in 1917 diary drafts of alternative endings to the story, Kafka toys in one with the appearance of a snake-woman, and in another with the explorer running around on all fours like a dog.)[12] As the ape says in "A Report to an Academy," when he was placed in a cage, "it was not freedom I wanted. Just a way out; to the right, to the left, wherever. . . . To move on, to move on!" ("A Report" 80).[13] Unfortunately, processes of becoming-animal generally do not succeed. Paradigmatic in this regard is "The Metamorphosis," in which Gregor's becoming-insect provides only a temporary line of flight, which is closed each time he is driven back into his bedroom, where he eventually dies from the wounds inflicted by his father. Only in the novels does the writing machine succeed in operating indefinitely, the unfinished, fragmentary nature of *Amerika*, *The Trial* and *The Castle* representing not Kafka's failure to complete his works but his ability to invent constitutively uncompletable, open-ended fiction-machines that form multiple connections with the outside world.

In Deleuze and Guattari's analysis, "In the Penal Colony" is an instance of a particular impasse in the writing machine: the invention of an "abstract machine" (*Kafka* 40), one that is fully functional, but isolated and unconnected to other machines, and hence incapable of continuing indefinitely. In this story, "the seed of a novel exists, connected this time to an explicit machine. But this machine, which is too mechanical, still too connected to overly Oedipal coordinates (the commandant-officer = father-son), doesn't develop at all" (*Kafka* 39). *The Trial*, by contrast, is a machine connected to various "assemblages" (Deleuze and Guattari's term for any collection of heterogeneous entities that somehow function together). In this novel, the law machine is a dispersed, proliferating network of connections that passes through Josef K.'s bedroom, the bank, the provisional court in the tenements, the lawyers' quarters, the endless hallways of bureaucratic offices, Titorelli's art loft and the city cathedral, and that involves characters of diverse classes and professions. The law represents itself as a transcendent, unknowable power (a paranoid despotic machine in the language of *Anti-Oedipus*). Yet "if the machine of the Penal Colony, as representative of the law, appears to be archaic and outmoded, it is not because, as people have often claimed, there is a new law that is much more modern but because the form of the law in general is inseparable from an abstract, self-destructive machine and cannot develop in a concrete way" (*Kafka* 47-48). The truth uncovered by K. is that the law is permeated by desire and open to a justice that is a kind of anti-law. There is no way one can escape law entirely, any more than one can escape society as a whole, but one can induce a schizophrenic undoing of the hierarchical structure. Titorelli outlines three theoretical possibilities in the disposition of K.'s case: definite acquittal, ostensible or superficial acquittal, and unlimited postponement.[14] The first is impossible, given that in the eyes of the law everyone is always and already guilty. The second is a means of securing a temporary illusion of freedom, but one that may be revoked at any time. Only the third, "unlimited postponement," allows a schizophrenic dismantling of the law by keeping the individual in constant contact with the components of the law machine, but only to facilitate the individual's endless movement from one component to another, thereby creating a destabilizing line of flight within the machine.

As one can see, there is an intimate relationship between Kafka's writing machine and the question of law in general. Deleuze's philosophy of law is partially revealed in *Kafka*, but it receives its first and fullest articulation in *Masochism: Coldness and Cruelty* (1967).[15] In this study of the fiction of Leopold von Sacher-Masoch, Deleuze distinguishes two conceptions of the law, one classical, the other modern. The classical, Platonic conception sees law as subservient to the Idea of the Good. The law "is only a representative of the Good in a world that the Good has more or less forsaken" (*Masochism* 81). The modern, Kantian conception reverses the relationship between the Good and the law: "In the *Critique of Practical Reason* Kant gave a rigorous formulation of a radically new conception, in which the law is no longer regarded as dependent on the Good, but on the contrary, the Good itself is made to depend on the law. This means that the law no longer has its foundation in some higher principle from which it would derive its authority, but that it is self-grounded and valid solely by virtue of its own form" (*Masochism* 82). The Kantian law is "totally undetermined," "a pure form," and hence "by definition unknowable and elusive" (*Masochism* 83). Both the classical and modern conceptions of the law are open to critique through irony and humor. Indeed, "the comic is the only possible mode of conceiving the law, in a peculiar combination of irony and humor" (*Masochism* 86). Kafka's critique of Kant is simply to take Kant at his word, and to present the law as a pure form, unknowable by definition: "Kafka gives to humor and irony their full modern significance in agreement with the transformed character of the law. Max Brod recalls that when Kafka gave a reading of *The Trial*, everyone present, including Kafka himself, was overcome by laughter" (*Masochism* 85).

Deleuze summarizes this analysis of law and the Kafka-Kant connection in the 1970 edition of *Proust and Signs*, in *Kafka* and in his 1986 essay "On Four Poetic Formulas That Might Summarize the Kantian Philosophy."[16] In *Proust and Signs*, "Building the Great Wall of China" serves as the illustrative model of Kafka's humorous critique of Kant. In *Kafka*, the critique of the law as pure form is said to be found in "the famous passages of *The Trial* (as well as in 'The Penal Colony' and 'The Great Wall of China')" (*Kafka* 43), with "In the Penal Colony" representing a negative critique of the law and *The Trial* providing both a negative critique and a positive assessment of the law's potential for transformation through the strategy of "unlimited postponement." This positive valorization of *The Trial* is also found in the "Four Poetic Formulas" essay, where Kant's *Critique of Practical Reason* is compared to *The Trial*, and the strategy of "unlimited postponement" is cited as a means of uncovering in Kant's *Critique* a latent possibility of transcending the very law the text articulates. In Deleuze's 1991 essay "To Have Done with Judgment,"[17] however, an interesting reversal takes place: "In the Penal Colony" is considered a relatively positive presentation of the law, whereas *The Trial* is seen negatively. In this essay Deleuze explicitly compares Nietzsche's analysis of law in *On the Genealogy of Morals* to Kafka's treatment of the law in "In the Penal Colony" and *The Trial*. After sketching Nietzsche's understanding of debt and its relationship to the theater of cruelty, Deleuze summarizes *The Genealogy*'s analysis of debt's metamorphosis into the guilt of a guilty conscience, a process whereby the finite debt between creditor and debtor is transformed into an infinite debt owed to the gods, and in Christianity rendered an oppressive, unpayable debt of original sin. Deleuze then asks whether this same opposition of an archaic, cruel justice and a modern system of infinite guilt and judgment is not present in Kafka:

> Is this not also the case with Kafka, when to the great book of *The Trial* he opposes the machine of "The Penal Colony"—a writing in bodies that testifies

> both to an ancient order and to a justice in which obligation, accusation, defense, and verdict all merge together. The system of cruelty expresses the finite relations of the existing body with the forces that affect it, whereas the doctrine of infinite debt determines the relationships of the immortal soul with judgments. The system of cruelty is everywhere opposed to the doctrine of judgment. ("To Have Done with Judgment" 128)

It might seem that Deleuze's philosophy of law, while attributing greater integrity to the ancient theater of cruelty than the modern regime of terror, ultimately advocates nothing more than anarchic resistance to law through the activation of deterritorializing lines of flight. There is, however, another dimension to Deleuze's philosophy of law, beyond critique, that of a clinical practice of jurisprudence, in which law is viewed as a salubrious and life-affirming force capable of fashioning new communal relations.[18] Kafka plays no role in this clinical line of thought, but in the domain of critique, his works are of central importance, and "In the Penal Colony" is an essential component of that critique. The Penal Colony machine is a literal machine of law, but it is also a condensed figure of the relationship between human bodies and the pure form of law (that is, law as a general principle with no details specifying its nature, and hence nothing but a "form" without any "contents"). An instrument of both ancient cruelty and modern terror, the machine is a parody of the institutions of law, and hence an instance of the darkest form of humorous critique (and I concur with Deleuze and Guattari that the story is ultimately not tragic but comic). In *Kafka*, *The Trial* takes center stage and "In the Penal Colony" plays a minor role, but when properly situated in *Anti-Oedipus*, "In the Penal Colony" proves to be as vital an element in Deleuze's thought as *The Trial*. As Bellour and Ewald aptly note, literature is everywhere present in Deleuze's work, running parallel to the philosophy, and this is nowhere more evident than in Deleuze's treatment of Kafka.

## Notes

1. Gilles Deleuze, *Negotiations: 1972-1990*, trans. Martin Joughin (New York: Columbia University Press, 1990), 142.

2. See Dominique Drouet, "Index des références littéraires dans l'œuvre de Gilles Deleuze," in *Deleuze et les écrivains: littérature et philosophie*, ed. Bruno Gelas and Hervé Micolet (Nantes: Cécile Defaut, 2007), 551-81.

3. Gilles Deleuze, *Proust and Signs: The Complete Text*, trans. Richard Howard (London: Athlone, 2000); Gilles Deleuze and Félix Guattari, *Kafka: Toward a Minor Literature*, trans. Dana Polan (Minneapolis, MN: University of Minnesota Press, 1986).

4. In *The Anti-Oedipus Papers*, ed. Stéphane Nadaud, trans. Kélina Gotman (New York: Semiotext(e), 2006), Guattari recalls the following event from early in his career: "The case of R. A., my first schizo, took up at least four to five hours a day. It took over everything. Including my friends and even my girlfriends. Likening him in spite of myself to my favorite author, I made him copy out *The Castle*. He even got into dressing up quite amazingly like Kafka himself" (146). See also François Dosse, *Gilles Deleuze & Félix Guattari: Intersecting Lives*, trans. Deborah Glassman (New York: Columbia

University Press, 2007), 246, for details about what Dosse call's Guattari's "passion" for Kafka; and Gary Genosko, "Introduction to Félix Guattari's 'Project for a Film *by* Kafka,'" *Deleuze Studies* 3.2 (2009): 145-49.

5. Gilles Deleuze and Félix Guattari, *Anti-Oedipus: Capitalism and Schizophrenia I*, trans. Robert Hurley, Mark Seem and Helen R. Lane (Minneapolis, MN: University of Minnesota Press, 1977).

6. Michel Carrouges, *Les Machines célibataires*, rev. and aug. (Paris: Chêne, 1972), 24.

7. For a detailed description of Duchamp's *Bride*, see John Golding, *Marcel Duchamp: The Bride Stripped Bare by her Bachelors, Even* (New York: Viking, 1972). My discussion of the work and the names of the elements of the visual composition, all offered by Duchamp in his commentaries, are taken from Golding's study. Golding also scrupulously traces the appearance of the "boxes" of documents assembled by Duchamp to which I make reference. Duchamp viewed all of those documents as constituent components of *The Bride*.

8. Franz Kafka, "In the Penal Colony," *Kafka's Selected Stories*, ed. and trans. Stanley Corngold (New York: Norton, 2007), 39.

9. Félix Guattari, "D'un signe à l'autre," in Félix Guattari, *Pychanalyse et transversalité* (Paris: Maspero, 1972), 131-50.

10. Franz Kafka, *The Diaries of Franz Kafka: 1910-1913*, ed. Max Brod, trans. Joseph Kresh (New York: Schocken, 1948), 22-29.

11. Friedrich Nietzsche, *On the Genealogy of Morals and Ecce Homo*, trans. Walter Kaufman and R. Hollingdale (New York: Vintage, 1967), 61.

12. See Franz Kafka, *The Diaries of Franz Kafka: 1914-1917*, ed. Max Brod, trans. Martin Greenberg (New York: Schocken, 1949), 178-79.

13. Franz Kafka, "A Report to an Academy," *Kafka's Selected Stories*, 80.

14. The terms "definite acquittal, ostensible or superficial acquittal, and unlimited postponement" are those used by Edwin and Willa Muir in their translation of *The Trial* (New York: Modern Library, 1956), and the English translator of Deleuze and Guattari's *Kafka* adopts the Muirs' terminology when referring to these processes. In Breon Mitchell's more reliable translation of *The Trial* (New York: Schocken, 1998), the pertinent passage is rendered as "actual acquittal, apparent acquittal, and protraction" (152). Since my focus here is on Deleuze and Guattari, I have retained the Muirs' translation of the three terms.

15. Gilles Deleuze, *Masochism: Coldness and Cruelty*, trans. Jean McNeil (New York: Zone Books, 1989).

16. Gilles Deleuze, "On Four Poetics Formulas That Might Summarize the Kantian Philosophy," *Essays Critical and Clinical*, trans. Daniel W. Smith and Michael A. Greco (Minneapolis, MN: University of Minnesota Press, 1997), 27-35.

17. "To Have Done with Judgment," *Essays Critical and Clinical*, 126-35.

18. For an outstanding analysis of Deleuze's philosophy of law, see Laurent de Sutter, *Deleuze: La pratique du droit* (Paris: Michalon, 2009).

## Works Cited

Carrouges, Michel. *Les Machines célibataires*. Revised and augmented edition. Paris: Chêne, 1972.

Deleuze, Gilles. *Essays Critical and Clinical*. Translated by Daniel W. Smith and Michael A. Greco. Minneapolis, MN: University of Minnesota Press, 1997.

———. *Masochism: Coldness and Cruelty*. Translated by Jean McNeil. New York: Zone Books, 1989.

———. *Negotiations: 1972-1990*. Translated by Martin Joughin. New York: Columbia University Press, 1990.

———. *Proust and Signs: The Complete Text*. Translated by Richard Howard. London: Athlone, 2000.

Deleuze, Gilles, and Félix Guattari. *Anti-Oedipus: Capitalism and Schizophrenia I*. Translated by Robert Hurley, Mark Seem and Helen R. Lane. Minneapolis, MN: University of Minnesota Press, 1977.

———. *Kafka: Toward a Minor Literature*. Translated by Dana Polan. Minneapolis, MN: University of Minnesota Press, 1986.

Dosse, François. *Gilles Deleuze & Félix Guattari: Intersecting Lives*. Translated by Deborah Glassman. New York: Columbia University Press, 2007.

Drouet, Dominique. "Index des références littéraires dans l'œuvre de Gilles Deleuze." In *Deleuze et les écrivains: littérature et philosophie*, edited by Bruno Gelas and Hervé Micolet, 551-81. Nantes: Cécile Defaut, 2007.

Genosko, Gary. "Introduction to Félix Guattari's 'Project for a Film *by* Kafka'." *Deleuze Studies* 3.2 (2009): 145-49.

Golding, John. *Marcel Duchamp: The Bride Stripped Bare by her Bachelors, Even*. New York: Viking, 1972.

Guattari, Félix. *The Anti-Oedipus Papers*. Edited by Stéphane Nadaud, translated by Kélina Gotman. New York: Semiotext(e), 2006.

———. "D'un signe à l'autre." In Félix Guattari, *Pychanalyse et transversalité*, 131-50. Paris: Maspero, 1972.

Kafka, Franz. *The Diaries of Franz Kafka: 1910-1913*. Edited by Max Brod, translated by Joseph Kresh. New York: Schocken, 1948.

———. *The Diaries of Franz Kafka: 1914-1917*. Edited by Max Brod, translated by Martin Greenberg. New York: Schocken, 1949.

———. *Kafka's Selected Stories*. Edited and translated by Stanley Corngold. New York: Norton, 2007.

———. *The Trial*. Translated by Edwin and Willa Muir. New York: Modern Library, 1956.

———. *The Trial*. Translated by Breon Mitchell. New York: Schocken, 1998.

Nietzsche, Friedrich. *On the Genealogy of Morals and Ecce Homo*. Translated by Walter Kaufman and R. Hollingdale. New York: Vintage, 1967.

Sutter, Laurent de. *Deleuze: La pratique du droit*. Paris: Michalon, 2009.

CHAPTER 14

# In a Messianic Gesture: Agamben's Kafka

*Carlo Salzani*

"The greatest theologian of the twentieth century":[1] with these words Giorgio Agamben describes, in a recent essay, Franz Kafka, thereby stressing anew the importance and centrality that the writer from Prague holds in his work. Though Agamben, in his productive career, has devoted only two essays to Kafka—"Four Glosses on Kafka" (1986), and, more recently, "K." (2009)[2]—Kafka casts, as William Watkin notes, a long shadow over his work.[3] Agamben's thought, I would more strongly argue, is thoroughly immersed in Kafka. Not merely in the sense that, starting from his very first book, *The Man Without Content* (1970), his work is adorned with quotations and suggestions from, as well as analyses and exegeses of, Kafka's oeuvre; but neither simply in the sense that these Kafka-exegeses very often constitute the theoretical kernel and key point of his argumentation. If these two aspects highlight and emphasize Kafka's importance and centrality for Agamben's thought, they do not exhaust the significance and influence the Prague writer exerts on him. Rather, and perhaps more important, Kafka *also* informs Agamben's work with a philosophical "mode," with an intellectual strategy, which is grounded in a profane messianism and crystallizes into tactical *gestures*.

Kafka's (and Benjamin's) messianism constitutes the philosophical and strategic perspective from which and through which Agamben approaches his object of analysis. The unfolding of argument, moreover, very often proceeds in a series of gestures, those same gestures that Benjamin identified as the decisive mode of Kafka's understanding. This means that Agamben's philosophy, like Kafka's writings, eludes traditional classifications and "attempts to convert poetry into teaching,"[4] or, better, proposes a "creative criticism" (as he calls it in *Stanzas*, xii/xv)[5] which, merging poetry and philosophy, seeks its *topos outopos* in "the impossible task of appropriating what must, in any case, remain unappropriable" (*St* xv/viii). Agamben's Kafkan gestures favor a poetic, paradoxical prose which hardly explains, but rather seeks a messianic reversal in the paradox itself, in the usage of sense to convey prevailing or preponderant non-sense. Hence the convergence of poetic and philosophic.

## The Inexplicable

The last chapter or "threshold" of Agamben's *Idea of Prose* (1985) is entitled "Kafka defended against his interpreters." As in many other chapters or small treatises of this dense and unorthodox book, the text does not present an evident and unambiguous relation to its title: it does not deal in fact explicitly with Kafka, who is never mentioned, but rather presents, in a Kafkan language and fashion, a "parable" about the "inexplicable." Among the many legends on the inexplicable, Agamben writes, the most ingenious explains that, as such, it remains inexplicable in all possible explanations, and that precisely these explanations guarantee its inexplicability. The only content of the inexplicable is the command—truly inexplicable—"explain!" This does not presuppose anything to explain, but is in itself the only presupposition, and whatever the answer—even silence—will contain an explanation. The patriarchs, the parable continues, decided that the best way to explain that there is nothing to explain is to give explanations. However, a codicil of this doctrine, left ignored by the actual "guardians of the Temple," specifies that the explanations will not be eternal, but will finally cease in the "day of Glory." Explanations, Agamben concludes, constitute only a moment in the tradition of the inexplicable, in which the inexplicable is preserved insofar as it is left unexplained. Inexplicable are only the explanations, and in order to explain them the legend was invented: "what was not to be explained is perfectly contained in what does not explain anything anymore" (*IP* 128/137).[6]

The text deals not so much with Kafka as with his interpreters, or, better, with the act of interpretation itself. Vivian Liska links this text to Agamben's representation of the state of exception and to another text of *Idea of Prose*, "Idea of Language II," which in fact discusses Kafka's story "In the Penal Colony" as exemplifying the intimate connection between *logos* and judgment.[7] Agamben states here that the torture machine of the Kafkan legend is, in reality, language: that is, language is, on earth, an instrument of justice and punishment, and the secret of the legend is revealed in a sentence he quotes from *Malina* by Ingeborg Bachmann (to whom "Idea of Language II" is dedicated): "language is the punishment" (*IP* 105/115).[8] Language *as* signification, for Agamben, is inherently bound to "judgment": "logic finds its exclusive ambit in judgment: the logical judgment is, in reality, immediately penal judgment, *sentence*" (*IP* 106/116). This is the true meaning of language, which eludes comprehension until for everyone there comes "the sixth hour," in which we measure and understand our guilt, and justice is done. The twist in the interpretation comes however with the second part of the legend, when the Officer, since he understands he cannot convince the Traveller to support his cause (the conservation of the old punishment system), frees the Convict and takes his place in the machine. The text that the machine should now write on the Officer's flesh has not, Agamben notes, the form of a precise commandment ("honor your superior," for example, as in the case of the Convict), but rather consists of the pure and simple injunction "be just." This injunction not only destroys the machine, but also reneges on the task of the machine: "The harrow did not write, it only stabbed. . . . [I]t was no torture, . . . it was downright murder."[9] The precept "be just," Agamben argues, is the instruction meant to destroy the machine; this means, for Agamben, that the utmost meaning of language is the injunction "be just," but precisely the sense of this injunction is what language—in its signifying function—is not able to transmit. In order to do it, it must cease to perform its "penal"—that is, signifying—task. That for the Officer, at the end, "there was, in language, nothing more to understand" (*IP* 107/117), means for Agamben that the "justice" of language resides only in its messianic destruction—or, better, deposition, *désoeuvrement* –, in the messianic overcoming of its signifying/penal structure.[10]

"Idea of Language II" is reproduced word for word, under the title "In the Penal Colony," as the second of the "Four Glosses on Kafka," published the following year. The first "gloss," "On Apparent Death," also deals with the same subject: language. Agamben takes here inspiration from Kafka's homonymous legend[11] to argue that language is like an apparent death. As in Plato's myth of the cave, in the Kafkan legend, he writes, the decisive moment is that of return. Death is in fact the impossibility of return, and in it there is no place for us. Only the one who has come back from an apparent death knows that from a true death he could not have returned. Thus he has derived the idea of a true death precisely from an apparent death; that is: that there is something from which one cannot return, he discovered only by pretending to have returned from it. Likewise, speech (*la parola*) has never been outside language, in non-language; non-language, the "inexpressible" (*l'indicibile*), are only inventions of language itself, and only in language could we conceive such ideas. Therefore Agamben concludes:

> When we comprehend language as language, we cease to imagine a beyond of language, we cease to pretend to have been in true death. Returned from where we have never been, we are finally here, where we will not be able to return. The non-language, untold by language, is now perfectly speakable. (*QGK* 38)

The idea of language which underlies these texts is derived from Walter Benjamin's early essays on language.[12] Agamben posits, with Benjamin, the necessary intertwining of signification and judgment, and this is the core idea that also sustains—though it remains often unperceived—his more recent project on biopolitics. In *Homo Sacer* (1995), in fact, this similarity is used precisely to explain the paradox of sovereignty: just as a word acquires its denotative power only insofar as it subsists independently from its concrete use in the discourse, so the norm can refer to the concrete case only insofar as it is in force, as pure potency, in the suspension of any actual reference, in the sovereign exception; just as language presupposes the non-linguistic as that with which it must maintain itself in a virtual relation so that it may later denote it in actual speech, so the law presupposes the nonjuridical as that with which it maintains itself in a potential relation in the state of exception.[13] This necessary structure can only be suspended in the messianic de-position, in the "day of Glory," of any signification and thus of any commandment and of any law. In *The Time that Remains* (2000) and *The Kingdom and the Glory* (2007), poetry, or, better, the poem, is taken as an example of that messianic operation that de-activates language in its communicative and informative functions, and in which language finally contemplates its potentiality and opens itself to a new, possible use.[14]

If the texts of *Idea of Prose* and "Four Glosses on Kafka" are indebted to Benjamin's theory for their content, their "form" is however peculiarly "Kafkan": they do not present a "theory" in the customary, academic form; they do not "explain," but propose instead, in a rather evocative fashion, a figure and a paradox. The paradox not only questions the possibility of interpretation, but also pushes philosophy to its limits. These texts epitomize, therefore, I will argue, Agamben's most intimate relation to Kafka's oeuvre: as Liska and others have noted, Agamben, like Benjamin, finds in Kafka's works both a critical diagnosis of the state of the world—be it language, as in *Idea of Prose* and "Four Glosses," or, more often, the cultural and political stalemate of modernity—and the traces of a messianic reversal.[15] I will add a third layer: Agamben almost mimics what Benjamin called Kafka's "gestures" and pushes the philosophical analysis to a poetic, quasi-paradoxical edge in which the argument is never exhausted by what is explainable; rather, the paradox itself contains the possibility of a sudden and salvific reversal.

## The Diagnostician of Modernity

Kafka marks Agamben's oeuvre from his very first book, *The Man Without Content*, published in 1970 when he was only 28. The last chapter, "The Melancholic Angel," focuses on the crises of tradition and transmissibility, whereby between old and new there is no longer any possible link besides an infinite accumulation into a monstrous archive, in which the very organ—culture—that should assure the transmission of the past guarantees its alienation. In Kafka's *The Castle*, the castle which "lies heavy on the village with the obscurity of its decrees and the multiplicity of its offices" (*UsC* 163/108),[16] exemplifies a culture that has lost its significance to us and hovers upon us as a menace. Only the work of art, in its present form of aesthetic alienation, guarantees a phantasmagorical survival of our culture, "just like the indefatigable demystifying action of the land-surveyor K. guarantees the only semblance of reality to which the castle of count West-West can aspire" (*UsC* 167/111). But the castle of our culture, like Kafka's castle, is by now a museum, in which, on the one hand, the past is accumulated and offered to mere aesthetic contemplation, and, on the other, aesthetic enjoyment is possible only through the alienation that deprives it of the poetic capacity of opening a space for action and knowledge. This situation is exemplified by another Kafkan image: modern men cannot find their own space in the tension between past and future, just like Kafka's train travellers, who "had an accident in a long tunnel and find themselves in a spot from which they cannot see the light of the entry anymore, and perceive the light of the exit so feebly, that they must continuously seek it and they continuously lose it, whereby one is no longer sure whether it is the light from the entry or that from the exit."[17]

From these early pages on, Agamben finds in Kafka's works an unparalleled diagnosis of the West's cultural and political crisis. And right from this brilliant incipit, his assessment is strongly indebted to Benjamin's reading of Kafka. In a letter to Scholem on June 12, 1938, concerning his essay on Kafka—and this correspondence will be a fundamental text for Agamben, especially in his later analysis of the structure of law—Benjamin writes: "Kafka's work is an ellipsis, whose distant foci are on the one hand the mystic experience (which is primarily the experience of tradition) and, on the other, the experience of modern inhabitants of big cities."[18] A later passage of the same letter, a passage that must have inspired Agamben's analysis in *The Man Without Content*, reads: "Kafka's work represents a sickness of tradition."[19] Benjamin's interpretation thus constitutes a sort of lens through which Agamben reads Kafka reading modernity.

Kafka's centrality is confirmed—though obliquely—in Agamben's second book, *Stanzas* (1979), the second part of which is entitled "In Odradek's World": Kafka's work is not discussed here and is hardly mentioned, but Kafka's figure Odradek is taken to symbolize the whole problem of commodity and commodification in modernity.[20] Agamben quotes Kafka here in an authoritative and evocative mode, as in the discussion of *acedia* (sloth): what Agamben calls the paradox of the accidious is illustrated by the following Zürau aphorism: "there is a destination, but no path; what we call path is our hesitation."[21] The same oblique mode characterizes the sparse references to Kafka in *Infancy and History* (1979),[22] but his presence returns dominant, as we have seen, in *Idea of Prose*.

It is in the philosophical-political project begun with *Homo Sacer* that Kafka's diagnosis becomes one of the cornerstones of Agamben's analysis of modernity. Kafka's legal world unveils in fact, for Agamben, the true nature of law, and is epitomized by the legend "Before the Law," which "represented the structure of the sovereign ban in an exemplary abbreviation" (*HS* 57/49). The Kafkan legend exposes the pure form of law, in which it affirms itself with the greatest force precisely at the point in which it no longer prescribes anything. The door of the law is open and nothing prevents the man from the country passing through it; however, it is precisely this openness that keeps him in the ban: "the man from the country is delivered over to the power of law, because law demands nothing of him and commands nothing other than its own openness" (*HS* 57-58/50). The open door destined only for him includes the man by excluding him, and excludes him in including him; the words of the prison chaplain which conclude the chapter "In the Cathedral" of Kafka's *Trial* enounce the original structure of the *nomos*: "the court wants nothing from you. It receives you when you come, it lets you go when you go."[23]

From a letter by Scholem to Benjamin, dated September 20, 1934, and concerning the Kafka essay, Agamben derives the definition of this structure as "*Being in force without significance*."[24] Scholem intended, with this definition, to counter Benjamin's account of the law in Kafka: a law reduced to the zero point of its own content, he wrote, does not disappear, is not absent, but rather appears in the form of its unrealizability.[25] Without knowing it, Agamben argues, Scholem provides thereby the definition of the originary structure of the sovereign relation, which is today revealed by the contemporary crisis of all traditions.

Kafka's novels also provide a figure for Agamben's notion of "bare life," the life of the *homo sacer* that can be killed yet not sacrificed, that is, the life in the grip of sovereign power. Life under a law that is in force without signifying is the life in the state of exception, in which law is all the more pervasive insofar as it lacks of any content, and comes finally to coincide with life. This is the life Kafka describes in his novels: in the village at the foot of *The Castle*, the empty potentiality of law is "so much in force as to become indistinguishable from life"; in the same way, in the *Trial*, the "existence and the very body of Joseph K. ultimately coincide with the Trial; they *are* the trial" (*HS* 61/53). This Kafkan representation of the law remains the cornerstone of Agamben's later work: in *State of Exception* he rehearses the argument: the Scripture (the Torah) without its key, he writes, is the cipher of the law in the state of exception, which "is in force but is not applied or is applied without being in force"; according to Benjamin, this law is no longer law, but life, that life described by Kafka. "Kafka's most proper gesture," Agamben concludes (following Benjamin), "consists not (as Scholem believes) in having maintained a law that no longer has any meaning, but in having shown that it ceases to be law and blurs at all points with life" (*SE* 81-82/63).[26]

This conception of law is taken a step further in *Remnants of Auschwitz* (1998): Kafka's *Trial*, Agamben writes here, unveils the deepest nature of law insofar as it represents it only in the form of the trial: the law (*diritto*) "is not so much here—according to the common opinion—norm, but rather judgment, and thus trial" (*QRA* 16/18).[27] And he continues:

> But if the essence of law (*legge*)—of any law—is the trial, if all law (*diritto*) (and morality contaminated by it) are only prosecutorial law (and prosecutorial morality), then enforcement and transgression, innocence and guilt, obedience and disobedience mix up and lose importance. . . . The ultimate goal of the norm is to produce the judgment; but the judgment does aim neither at punishing nor at rewarding, neither at doing justice nor at ascertaining the truth. The judgment is in itself the goal, and this—it has been said—constitutes its mystery, the mystery of the trial. (*QRA* 16-17/18-19)

The mystery of law and of the trial reappears in *The Time that Remains*, in which the law is defined as "only the knowledge of guilt, trial in the Kafkaesque sense of the term, a perpetual self-accusation without a precept" (*TR* 102/108). And in the recent essay "K.," Agamben again states with regard to Kafka's *Trial*:

> What defines the trial is neither guilt . . . nor punishment, but rather the accusation. Indeed, accusation is perhaps the juridical "category" *par excellence* (*kategoria* means in Greek "accusation"), that part without which the whole structure of law would collapse: the inclusion of the being into the law. That is, law is, in its essence, accusation, "category." (*K* 37/23)

This structure entails that, as the prison chaplain tells Josef K., there is no sentence, but rather "the trial itself gradually becomes the sentence."[28] The mystery of the trial, Agamben glosses, lies in the fact that the principle *nulla poena sine iudicio* means that there is no judgment without punishment, because all punishment is the judgment. "To be in such a trial," the uncle tells Josef K., "means to have lost it already."[29]

In "K.," Agamben also proposes a new interpretation of the parable "Before the Law." "The door of the law is the accusation," he writes, "through which the individual becomes implicated into the legal system (*nel diritto*)" (*K* 47/30). The strategy of the law consists of making the accused believe that the accusation (the door) is destined (perhaps) for him, that the court demands (perhaps) something from him, that there is (perhaps) a trial which concerns him. "In reality," Agamben concludes, "there is no accusation and no trial, at least until the moment in which he who believes he is accused has not accused himself" (*K* 47/30). The legal system, therefore, is based on a deception, which consists precisely in the existence of "keepers," "from the lowest clerk to the lawyers and to the highest judge—whose goal is to induce the others to accuse themselves, to make them pass through the door that leads nowhere except to the trial" (*K* 48/30-31).

Kafka's legal world remains the dominant case in Agamben's analysis of modernity, but it is also accompanied, in a minor tone, by two other references. Kafka portrayed his functionaries and clerks as angels and thus understood, more than anyone else, the strict connection between angelology and bureaucracy in the development of Western political *oikonomia*, which Agamben analyses in *The Kingdom and The Glory* (2007) and in the recent collection *The Angels*.[30] A final example of the incomparable "diagnosis" Agamben finds in Kafka appears in *Means Without End* (1996), where he recalls Kafka's story "The Burrow":[31] like the animal-protagonist of the story, which obsessively builds an unconquerable burrow as defense and finally finds himself trapped in it, so the "houses" or "homelands" that the Western nation-states have built "revealed themselves in the end to be only lethal traps for the very 'peoples' that were supposed to inhabit them" (*MSF* 108/140).[32] In a conference paper of the same year, "Heidegger and Nazism," he rehearses the same argument, adding that Kafka is "certainly the author who described with outmost clarity the end of the Western political space, and the absolute indeterminacy between public space and private space, 'castle' and bedroom, tribunal and garret, derived from this event."[33]

## Messianism and Reversal

Kafka's centrality for Agamben is not limited, however, to the level of the diagnosis, but rather takes its full significance in its messianic intention, which offers a way out from the dire straits of contemporary political and cultural crisis. "One of the peculiar traits of the Kafkan allegories," Agamben writes in *Homo Sacer*, "is that they contain right at the end a possibility of reversal which overturns completely their meaning" (*HS* 67/58). This is again an insight that Agamben derives from Benjamin, who emphasizes the "*Umkehr*" (reversal) of Kafka's parables and writes to Scholem: "Kafka's messianic category is the 'reversal' or the 'study.'"[34]

This reversal constitutes the kernel of Agamben's readings, right from *The Man Without Content*. Kafka, Agamben argues here, is the author that more than anyone else undertook the task of conciliating, in our age, the conflict between old and new, and the precariousness of human action in the interval they constitute: "facing the impossibility of appropriating his own historical presuppositions," Agamben writes, "[Kafka] tried to make this impossibility the very ground on which man could find himself again" (*UsC* 169/112). The Kafkan reversal is grounded on a messianic understanding of time, one that will remain at the core both of Agamben's interpretation of Kafka and of his later philosophical-political project. He refers here to two of the Zürau aphorisms: 1) "there is a destination, but no path; what we call path is our hesitation"; and 2) "It is only our conception of time that makes us call the Last Judgment by this name. It is, in fact, a kind of martial law."[35] We are always already in the Last Judgment, Agamben glosses; the Last Judgment is our normal historical condition. Kafka, that is, replaces a notion of history as an empty linear time (the one criticized by Benjamin in "On the Concept of History") with the paradoxical image of a *condition of history* in which the fundamental event is always already happening. This involves that the goal is inaccessible precisely because it is here present before us, and this presence constitutes human historicity, which is inherently characterized, therefore, by the inability to appropriate the human historical situation. Kafka's solution to the question about the task of art vis-à-vis this situation was to resolve the problem of cultural transmission by transforming art itself in the transmission of the act of transmission, by making the content of art the very task of transmission, independently of what is being transmitted:

> Since the goal is already present and thus no path exists that could lead there, only the perennially late stubbornness of a messenger whose message is nothing other that the task of transmission can give back to man, who has lost his ability to appropriate his historical space, the concrete space of his action and knowledge. (*UsC* 171/114)[36]

Again, as Agamben acknowledges, this intuition is taken from Benjamin, who wrote to Scholem: "he [Kafka] relinquished truth, in order to secure transmissibility."[37]

This messianic notion of time returns in *Infancy and History*, where Kafka briefly accompanies Benjamin in the chapter on "Time and History."[38] It is, however, in *Idea of Prose* that Agamben explores at length the possibilities of the Kafkan messianic paradoxes. As we have already seen, in the story on "The Penal Colony," the torture machine, which represents language, breaks down when the commandment/punishment it should write on the body of the Officer is "be just": the justice of language is thus revealed as the breakdown of its connection to judgment, and thus to signification; the justice of language is the—messianic—overcoming of language as judgment and signification (cf. *IP* 105-7/115-17). *Idea of Prose* contains, however, two other—Kafkan—"ideas" which will be integrated as a constant reference in Agamben's later work. The first is the idea of "study" and the question of redemption that it involves. Every study is inherently endless, Agamben writes, and as such it is like Aristotle's "potentiality," both in the sense of *potentia passiva* and in that of *potentia activa*, because, despite its intrinsic unfinalizability, it always tends toward a messianic fulfillment or completion. Kafka's students—like Melville's Bartleby—prefigure the messianic fulfillment of *studium* insofar as they study "like, after the end of times, unbaptized children or the pagan philosophers could study in limbo, where they have nothing to hope for, neither from the future nor from the past" (*IP* 45/65). Study, that is, returns the world to its potentiality and thus, to use a term that in Agamben's later work will accompany that of study, renders it "inoperative." This notion of study will become, as we will see, a fundamental component of Agamben's proposal for a messianic overcoming of law.[39]

The second Kafkan "idea" is that of "shame." Vis-à-vis the failure of theodicy and the "banality of evil" which characterize our age, Agamben writes, Kafka decided to renounce theodicy and to leave aside the question of guilt and innocence, and the question of freedom and destiny, in order to focus only on shame. Shame is in fact the "index of the outmost, frightful proximity of human beings with themselves" (*IP* 68/84). In shame is thus contemplated the problem of subjectivity and subjectivation, since shame is the "pure, empty form of the most intimate sense of the self" (*IP* 69/85). Kafka described a humanity reduced to a planetary petty bourgeoisie, expropriated from any experience but its own shame, and tried to identify in this very shame a possibility of redemption: he "tries to teach the use of the only reality left to human beings: not to free oneself from shame, but rather to free shame itself" (*IP* 69/85). The central reference here is the last thought of Josef K. at the very end of the *Trial*: "it was as if the shame would outlive him."[40] It is in order to save his shame, not his innocence, that Josef K. submits to his destiny, and in this task—to preserve at least human shame—Kafka found, according to Agamben, "something like an old bliss" (*IP* 69/85). Shame as a privileged—and revolutionary—opening to subjectivization and to the inner self, and thus as a possibility for a new, post-biopolitical ethics, will briefly reappear, together with the quotation from the *Trial*, in *Means Without End* and *Remnants of Auschwitz*.[41]

These Kafkan notions of subjectivity, evil, time and redemption constitute a fundamental pillar in the construction of the political soteriology proposed in *The Coming Community* (1990). The apodictic, "essayistic" structure of the book allows only for sparse mentions of, and quotations from, Kafka, but his profane messianism constitutes the invisible structure that sustains the whole project. The torture machine of "The Penal Colony" epitomizes here the politico-theological apparatus, the destruction of which gives way, in the day after the last day, to a life only and properly human that is liberated from the constrictions of this apparatus. This is the life described in Kafka's (and Robert Walser's) stories, indifferent to redemption because devoid of expectations and thus restored to its potentialities.[42] Perhaps the most "Kafkan" statement is, however, the aphorism contained in the section "The Irreparable," which summarizes the idea that redemption must be sought in the irreparable facticity of the world:

> We can have hope only in what has no remedy. That things are so and so—this is still in the world. Yet, that this is irreparable, that this *so* (*così*) has no remedy, that we can contemplate it as such—this is the only opening out of the world. (The innermost character of salvation: that we are saved only when we no longer want to be saved. Because of this, in this moment, there is salvation—but not for us). (*CV* 85/102)[43]

Like *Idea of Prose*, *The Coming Community* eschews the discursive, academic style, and proceeds instead through a series of strategic and fragmented images that compress the argument into a messianic quasi-paradox. From *Homo Sacer* onward, Agamben will return to a more "traditional" style, but his use of Kafkan images will retain the power of the paradox.

The strategy of the reversal is thus also central to Agamben's interpretation of law. In *Homo Sacer*, he famously reads the legend "Before the Law" not as the tale of a defeat, of the irremediable failure of the man from the country before the impossible task imposed upon him by the law. The last sentence of the parable presents in fact the messianic reversal: the doorkeeper tells the man from the country that that door was open only for him and concludes: "Now I go and close it."[44] So, if the invincible power of law, its "force," consists in its openness, then, Agamben argues, the conduct of the man from the country can be read as nothing but a complicated and patient strategy to obtain the closure of the door, to interrupt the force of law.[45] At the end, he succeeds, the door of the law is closed forever, since, Agamben notes, it was open "only for him." Following a suggestion from Kurt Weinberg, Agamben interprets the figure of the man from the country as a messianic figure, remarking that the Messiah is the figure with which the monotheist religions attempt to master the problem of law. The coming of the Messiah signifies the fulfillment and complete consummation of the law, and the consummation of a law that is in force without signifying, is, perhaps, the provocative strategy of the Kafkan man: "the messianic task of the man from the country . . . might then be precisely that of making the virtual state of exception real, of compelling the doorkeeper to close the door of the Law" (*HS* 66/56-57). "The Messiah," Agamben quotes from Kafka's notebooks, "will only come when he is no longer necessary, he will only come after his arrival, he will come not on the last day, but on the very last day."[46] The Messiah will be able to enter only after the door is closed, only after the end of a law which is in force without signifying. The messianic aporias of the Kafkan man from the land, Agamben concludes, perfectly express the difficulty of our age in coming to terms with the sovereign ban.

With Benjamin, Agamben interprets the sense of the reversal to be found in many Kafkan allegories as the attempt to rescue life from the ban in which the law holds it. Benjamin wrote to Scholem: "in the attempt to transform life into Scripture I see the sense of the reversal to which tend many Kafkan allegories

(*Gleichnisse*)."[47] Agamben quotes this passage in *Homo Sacer* and comments: "A life that resolves itself completely into writing corresponds, for Benjamin, to a Torah whose key has been lost" (*HS* 63/54). In the same way, Benjamin's thesis VIII of "On the Concept of History" counterpoises to the state of exception that has become the rule, a "real" and "effective" (*wirklich*) state of exception, in which law that becomes indistinguishable from life is confronted by a life that, in a symmetrical but inverse gesture, is entirely transformed into law:

> The absolute intelligibility of a life wholly resolved into writing corresponds to the impenetrability of a writing that, having become indecipherable, now appears as life. Only at this point do the two terms, distinguished and kept united by the relation of ban (bare life and the form of law), abolish each other and enter into a new dimension. (*HS* 64/55)

The same reversal identified in the obstinacy of the man from the country is found by Agamben in other characters from Kafka: just as in the legend "Before the Law" the law is insuperable precisely because it does not prescribe anything, so in "The Silence of the Sirens" the sirens' most terrible weapon is not their singing, but their silence, and Ulysses' cunning consists in realizing this and in opposing his "comedy" to it.[48]

In *State of Exception* (2003), Agamben refines this interpretation and confers on the Kafkan "reversal" the name of *désoeuvrement*, de-activation. At the end of the chapter on Schmitt and Benjamin, Agamben quotes Benjamin's interpretation of Kafka's "The New Advocate"[49]: Bucephalus, the "new advocate," does not practice the law anymore, but merely studies it; "the law which is studied but no longer practiced," Benjamin argues, "is the gate to justice"; thus "The gate to justice is study."[50] The Benjaminian interpretation expresses for Agamben the possible figure of law after its nexus with violence and power has been deposed: a law which no longer has force or application. This new law, Agamben notes, is not already justice, but only the "gate" that leads to justice. What opens a passage toward justice is not the destruction of law, but rather its deactivation and *inoperosity*, that is, another use of the law. "Kafka's characters," he concludes, "have to do with this spectral figure of the law in the state of exception; they seek, each one following his or her own strategy, to 'study' and deactivate it, to 'play' with it" (*SE* 83/64).[51]

In *The Time that Remains*, Kafka's work is again used to describe exemplarily the messianic vocation and messianic time. The sense of the Kafkan parable "On Parables,"[52] Agamben writes, is that the messianic is simultaneously the abolition and realization of the syntagm "as if" of any parable. The one who keeps within the messianic vocation (*klesis*) knows no similes, knows no "as if"; the messianic vocation transforms language into life, and thus consists, as we have seen, in the overcoming of language itself (cf. *TR* 45-46/42-43). In describing, in the following chapter, messianic time, Agamben recalls Kafka's above quoted aphorism about the coming of the Messiah to argue that the messianic event is always already completed, but "his presence contains within it another time, which outstretches its *parousia*, not in order to defer it, but, on the contrary, in order to allow us to seize it" (*TR* 71/71). For this reason, he quotes from

Benjamin, every instant can be "the small gateway in time through which the Messiah might enter"[53]; "The Messiah makes always already his own time," Agamben glosses, "that is, he simultaneously seizes time and consummates it" (*TR* 71/71).

The Kafkan strategy of messianic reversal is illustrated at length in the essay "K.," which analyses the figures of Josef K. and the land-surveyor K. The "K" of Josef K., Agamben argues, does not stand for "Kafka," as has been assumed since Max Brod, but rather for "*kalumniator*," slanderer. The incipit of the *Trial* in fact reads: "Someone must have been slandering Josef K., for one morning, without having done anything wrong, he was arrested."[54] The slanderer, Agamben states, is Josef K. himself, and he slanders himself in order to question the very principle of the trial: the accusation, and thus the principle that there is no punishment without guilt. This constitutes for Agamben a strategy aimed at deactivating and rendering inoperative the accusation, and as such law (*il diritto*) itself. If the accusation is false, and if, on the other hand, accuser and accused coincide, then it is the very fundamental implication of human beings in the law that is revoked: "the only way to affirm one's innocence before the law . . . is, in this sense, to falsely accuse oneself" (*K* 39/24). K. thus slanders himself in order to elude the law, to elude the invariable accusation of the law from which it is not possible to escape. It is a strategy that is ultimately insufficient and doomed to fail; but the *Trial* also contains, in the chapter "In the Cathedral," the parable "Before the Law," which presents, as we have seen, another strategy: in "K.," unlike in *Homo Sacer*, Agamben emphasizes not the final closure of the door of the law, but rather the "long study"[55] of the doorkeeper by the man from the country: "thanks to this study, to this new Talmud, the man from the country, unlike Josef K., succeeded in living until the end outside the trial" (*K* 48/31).

The same strategy of messianic deactivation and inoperativity characterizes the land-surveyor K. of *The Castle*. Here, Agamben argues, "K." stands for "*kardo*," the line that divided in direction North-South the Roman *castrum* and city, and that constituted, with the *decumanus* (East-West), the fundamental axes of the inhabited area. The conflict that opposes K. and the castle, Agamben proposes, is thus a conflict about the determination or transgression of the lines and limits which separate the castle from the village, the high from the low: "since life in the village is, in fact, entirely determined by the boundaries that, simultaneously, separate it from, and keep it bound to, the castle, it is these boundaries that the coming of the land-surveyor questions" (*K* 54-55/35). We have seen that the life of the village represents, in *Homo Sacer*, the life in the state of exception, life caught in that relation of inclusionary exclusion or exclusionary inclusion in which the law keeps life in its power by excluding life from law's domain. K.'s strategy aims at deactivating these boundaries and limits—that is, law itself—and is thus a messianic figure: if Bucephalus is the "new advocate" who studies the law without applying it, "K. is the 'new land-surveyor', who renders inoperative the limits and boundaries that separate (and simultaneously bind) high and low, castle and village, temple and house, divine and human" (*K* 56/36).[56]

## Philosophy and/as Gesture

The third of Agamben's "Four Glosses on Kafka" is entitled "On Gravity" and is dedicated to Italo Calvino, whose first "American Lesson" was devoted to "Lightness."[57] Here Agamben compares the lightness of Kafka's "The Bucket Rider"[58] with Paul Celan's rewriting of the same story and Nietzsche's discussion of gravity in *Zarathustra*'s chapters "The Vision and the Enigma" and "The Spirit of Gravity." Contrary to Zarathustra, who takes upon himself the "heaviest burden" and wants to transform it into supreme lightness (the acceptance of the eternal return), the bucket rider would want to find some gravity and return to earth. His destiny is not the eternal return, but rather the lightness of a feather spirited away by the wind. "True lightness," Agamben enigmatically explains, "is not the eternal return, but a never coming back." In the kingdom of the Ice Mountains, where he has ended up, the bucket rider finds perhaps his peace, as a projected epilogue seems to imply by depicting him with his mount now on his shoulder. Agamben's conclusion hermetically reads: "So up in the air, lightness is of no use: one might as well take it on one's back. 'The legends, which leave the earth, turn toward humanity'" (*QGK* 42).[59]

This "gloss" or "apologue" epitomizes, once again and more than others, how Kafkan images work in and with Agamben's texts. These images, that is, do not merely stand as simple substitutes for thoughts, which could otherwise be conceptually formulated. They cannot be fully paraphrased, unfolded or explained. They retain instead their intrinsic and unsolvable paradoxical character, which is precisely what confers on them a messianic potential. In Kafka's as in Agamben's texts, I argue, the force of the paradox lies in its working simultaneously as poetic and philosophical *gesture*.

It is again Benjamin who identified "gesture" as the most characteristic trait of Kafka's prose. Kafka's legends, Benjamin writes, are "fairy tales for dialecticians,"[60] but tales that are seen in their full light only when they are "put on as acts" (*als Akte . . . versetzt*) on a theatre stage. Theatre dissolves events into their gestural components, and thus Benjamin argues that:

> Kafka's entire work constitutes a code of gestures which surely had no definite symbolic meaning for the author from the outset; rather, the author tried to derive such meaning from them in ever-changing contexts and experimental groupings. The theatre is the logical place for such groupings.[61]

Far from metaphorizing a clear and univocal content, Kafka's theatrical gesture is what the author himself "could fathom least of all" (*am unabsehbarsten*). "Each gesture is an event," Benjamin writes, "one might even say a drama—in itself";[62] but a drama in which Kafka tears open the sky behind the action. "The gesture remains the decisive thing, the center of the event," but unfolds "the way a bud turns into a blossom."[63] Kafka's writings are not really parables. They do not want to be taken at face value, yet they do not offer any clear and distinct "teaching" (*Lehre*); rather, "his parables are never exhausted by what is explainable; on the contrary, he took all conceivable precautions against the interpretation of his writings."[64] He could understand things only in the form of a gesture, but he himself did not understand the gesture: "he did fail in his grandiose attempt to convert poetry into teaching."[65]

The notion of gesture is central both to Agamben's idea of philosophy and to his political soteriology. And it is a notion, again, heavily indebted to Benjamin. In the essay "Notes on Gesture," first published in 1992 and then included in *Means Without End* (1996), Agamben defines gesture as the "*exhibition of a mediality: it is a process of making a means visible as such*" (*MSF* 52/58, emphasis in the original). Insofar as it allows the emergence of the being-in-a-medium of human beings, the gesture opens the ethical dimension. Moreover, if language is the medium of communication, then the linguistic gesture exposes language without transcendence in its pure mediality: "gesture is, in this sense, communication of a communicability. It has properly nothing to say, because what it shows is the being-in-language of the human beings as pure mediality" (*MSF* 52/59). This mediality is in itself not something that can be phrased, and thus gesture is always the exposition of a lack; it is *gag*, and this makes, according to Agamben, for its proximity to philosophy: if philosophy is in fact the exposition of the being-in-language of humanity, "pure gestuality," then every great philosophical text is "the *gag* that exhibits language itself, the very being-in-language as a gigantic loss of memory, as an incurable speech defect" (*MSF* 53/60).[66]

This definition of philosophy is a sort of Agambian *discours de la méthode*, which rephrases in Benjaminian terms a practice that dates from Agamben's early works and was conceptualized as early as the preface to *Stanzas* (1979). Here, to a poetry which "possesses its object without knowing it" and a philosophy which "knows it without possessing it" (*St* xiii/xvii), Agamben counterpoises a notion of criticism which neither represents nor knows, but knows the representation:

> To appropriation without consciousness and to consciousness without enjoyment, criticism opposes the enjoyment of what cannot be possessed and the possession of what cannot be enjoyed. . . . What is secluded in the "stanza" of criticism is nothing, but this nothing guards inappropriability as its most precious possession. (*St* xiv/xvii)

Kafka is not mentioned in the preface—the reference is rather Hölderlin—and Kafka's presence in the book is that of an invisible authority hardly hinted at. I am not claiming, moreover, that Kafka is the only influence on Agamben philosophical "mode"; what I'm trying to argue is that Kafka's messianic paradoxology, congealed into gestures which "attempt to convert poetry into teaching,"[67] endows Agamben's philosophy with a "mode" that becomes increasingly central. If Agamben's engagement in the early 1980s with Hegel and Heidegger on the question of language leaves Kafka aside, at least from the publication of *Idea of Prose* (1985)—a veritable collection of philosophical gestures—this Kafkan modality becomes central, and the increasing emphasis on messianism from the publication of *The Coming Community* (1990) onward unfolds its full potentiality.

This "philosophical topology," grounded in *gaudium*, in *jouissance*, and focused on "the impossible task of appropriating what must, in any case, remain inappropriable" (*St* xv/xviii), can certainly be accused of aesthetization, and correctly so, when this inappropriable object becomes life itself, or violence, the camp, and the horrors of modern biopolitics.[68] These—Kafkan—messianic gestures as critical events, however, constitute an original and important proposal that pushes philosophy to its limit: the inexplicable.

# Notes

1. Giorgio Agamben, "Introduzione," in *Angeli: Ebraismo Cristianesimo Islam*, eds. Giorgio Agamben and Emanuele Coccia (Vicenza: Neri Pozza, 2009; hereafter as *A*), 12. In what follows, I will use my own translation of all Agamben's texts; when English translations are available, I will point them out, giving reference to both the Italian and English editions.

2. Cf. "Quattro glosse a Kafka," in *Rivista di estetica* 26 (1986): 37-44, hereafter as *QGK*; and "K.," in *Nudità* (Rome: Nottetempo, 2009), 33-57 / "K.," in *Nudities*, trans. David Kishik and Stefan Pedatella (Stanford, CA: Stanford University Press, 2011), 20-36. Hereafter as *K*.

3. William Watkin, *The Literary Agamben: Adventures in Logopoiesis* (London: Continuum, 2010), 170.

4. Walter Benjamin, "Franz Kafka: Zur zehnten Wiederkehr seines Todestages," in *Gesammelte Schriften*, ed. Rolf Tiedemann and Hermann Schweppenhäuser (Frankfurt a.M: Suhrkamp, 1974ff.), vol. 2.2, 427 / "Franz Kafka: On the Tenth Anniversary of His Death," in *Selected Writings*, ed. Michael W. Jennings (Cambridge, MA: Belknap, 1997-2003), vol. 2, 808.

5. Giorgio Agamben, *Stanze. La parola e il fantasma nella cultura occidentale* (Turin: Einaudi, 1979), xii / *Stanzas: Word and Phantasm in Western Culture*, trans. Ronald L. Martinez, (Minneapolis, MN: University of Minnesota Press, 1993), xv. Hereafter as *St*.

6. Giorgio Agamben, *Idea della prosa* (Milan: Feltrinelli, 1985; then Macerata: Quodlibet, 2002), 128 / *Idea of Prose*, trans. Sam Whitsitt and Michael Sullivan (Albany, NY: SUNY Press, 1995). Hereafter as *IP*. This text can be read as Agamben's rewriting of Kafka's brief text "Prometheus", which begins: "The legend (*Sage*) attempts to explain the inexplicable; because it arises from a ground of truth, it must end again in the inexplicable," Franz Kafka, ["Prometheus"], in *Kritische Ausgabe. Nachgelassene Schriften und Fragmente II*, ed. Jost Schillemeit (Frankfurt a.M.: Fischer, 2002), 69-70. I will hereafter always refer to the text of the *Kritische Ausgabe* and will specify only the volume title. All translations from German are my own. (I thank an anonymous reader for the suggestion about "Prometheus".)

7. Cf. "Idea del linguaggio II," in *IP* 105-7/115-17; cf. Vivian Liska, *Giorgio Agambens leerer Messianismus: Hannah Arendt, Walter Benjamin, Franz Kafka* (Vienna: Schlebrügge, 2008), 58-60. For a discussion of "Idea del linguaggio II" in its relation to Agamben's later work, cf. Jessica Whyte, "Its Silent Working Was a Delusion," in *The Work of Giorgio Agamben: Law, Literature, Life*, eds. Justin Clemens, Nicholas Heron and Alex Murray (Edinburgh: Edinburgh University Press, 2008), 66-81.

8. The German sentence reads: "*die Sprache ist die Strafe*," (Ingeborg Bachmann, *Malina* [Frankfurt a.M: Suhrkamp, 2004], 96). Liska notes that Agamben distorts the meaning of Bachmann's text, where language as revelation of the crimes of the past in post-Nazi Austria becomes the punishment of the guilt of silence, and as such is the medium of justice. Cf. Liska, *Giorgio Agambens leerer Messianismus*, 56.

9. Franz Kafka, "In der Strafkolonie," in *Drucke zu Lebzeiten*, eds. Wolf Kittler, Hans-Gerd Koch and Gerhard Neumann, 244-45.

10. Cf. Liska, *Giorgio Agambens leerer Messianismus*, 57.

11. Franz Kafka, ["Vom Scheintod"], in *Nachgelassene Schriften und Fragmente II*, 141-42.

12. Cf. Walter Benjamin, "Über Sprache überhaupt und über die Sprache des Menschen" (1916), in *Gesammelte Schriften*, vol. 2.1, 140-56 / "On Language as Such and on the Language of Man," in *Selected Writings*, vol. 1, 62-74; and "Die Aufgabe des Übersetzers" (1921), in *Gesammelte Schriften*, vol. 4.1, 9-22 / "The Task of the Translator," in *Selected Writings*, vol. 1, 253-63.

13. He concludes: "Only language as the pure potentiality to signify, withdrawing itself from every concrete instance of speech, divides the linguistic from the non-linguistic and allows for the opening of areas of meaningful speech in which certain terms correspond to certain denotations. Language is the sovereign who, in a permanent state of exception, declares that there is nothing outside language and that language is always beyond itself. The particular structure of law has its foundation in this presuppositional structure of human language. It expresses the bond of inclusive exclusion to which a thing is subject because of the fact of being in language, of being named. To speak (*dire*) is, in that sense, always to 'speak the law,' *ius dicere*," Giorgio Agamben, *Homo sacer. Il potere sovrano e la nuda vita* (Turin: Einaudi, 1995), 26 / *Homo Sacer: Sovereign Power and Bare Life*, trans. Daniel Heller-Roazen (Stanford, CA: Stanford University Press, 1998], 21. Hereafter as *HS*.

14. Cf. Giorgio Agamben, *Il tempo che resta. Un commento alla «Lettera ai romani»* (Turin: Bollati Boringhieri, 2000), 77-84 / *The Time that Remains: a Commentary on the Letter to the Romans*, trans. Patricia Dailey (Stanford, CA: Stanford University Press, 2005), 81-87; hereafter as *TR*; and *Il regno e la gloria. Per una genealogia teologica dell'economia e del governo*. Homo sacer. Vol. 2/2 (Vicenza: Neri Pozza, 2007), 258-62, 274-75 / *The Kingdom and the Glory: For a Theological Genealogy of Economy and Government*, trans. Lorenzo Chiesa and Matteo Mandarini (Stanford, CA: Stanford University Press, 2011), 234-39, 251-52. Hereafter as *RG*.

15. Cf. Liska, *Giorgio Agambens leerer Messianismus*, 51.

16. Giorgio Agamben, *L'uomo senza contenuto* (Milan: Rizzoli, 1970, then Macerata: Quodlibet, 1994), 163 / *The Man Without Content*, trans. Georgia Albert, Stanford, CA: Stanford University Press, 1999), 108. Herafter as *UsC*.

17. Franz Kafka, ["Eisenbahnreisende"], *Nachgelassene Schriften und Fragmente II*, 33. Cf. *UsC*, 168/112.

18. Walter Benjamin and Gerschom Scholem, *Briefwechsel 1933-1940* (Frankfurt a.M: Suhrkamp, 1980), 269.

19. Benjamin and Scholem, *Briefwechsel*, 272.

20. Cf. *St* 37-70/31-61. Odradek is the central character of Kafka's brief apologue "The Cares of a Family Man" ("Die Sorge des Hausvaters," in *Drucke zu Lebzeiten*, 282-84) and is actually—and hastily—mentioned in Agamben's book only at pp. 60/50 and 171/144.

21. Kafka, *Nachgelassene Schriften und Frangmente II*, 118. Cf. *St* 12/6.

22. Cf. Giorgio Agamben, *Infanzia e storia. Distruzione dell'esperienza e origine della storia* (Turin: Einaudi, 1979) / *Infancy and History: On the Destruction of Experience*, trans. Liz Heron (London: Verso, 1996), 108/102, 136/128.

23. Franz Kafka, *Der Proceß*, eds. Jürgen Born, Gerhard Neumann, Malcom Pasley and Jost Schillemeit (Frankfurt a.M: Fischer, 2007), 304. Cf. *HS* 58/50.

24. Cf. Benjamin and Scholem, *Briefwechsel*, 175; cf. *HS* 59/51. The Benjamin-Scholem correspondence is also thoroughly analyzed in the 1992 essay "Il messia e il sovrano: Il problema della legge in Walter Benjamin," in *La potenza del pensiero. Saggi e conferenze* (Vicenza: Neri Pozza, 2005), 251-70 / "The Messiah and the Sovereign: The Problem of Law in Walter Benjamin," in *Potentialities: Collected Essays in Philosophy*, trans. Daniel Heller-Roazen (Stanford, CA: Stanford University Press, 1999), 160-74.

25. Cf. Benjamin, "Franz Kafka," 420/803. A discussion of this Benjaminian interpretation appears also in Agamben's 1982 essay "Walter Benjamin e il demonico," in *La potenza del pensiero*, 227 / "Walter Benjamin and the Demonic," in *Potentialities*, 138-59.

26. Giorgio Agamben, *Stato di Eccezione*. Homo sacer, Vol 2/1 (Turin: Bollati Boringhieri, 2003), 81-82 / *State of Exception*, trans. Kevin Attell (Chicago, IL: University of Chicago Press, 2005), 63. Hereafter as *SE*.

27. Giorgio Agamben, *Quel che resta di Auschwitz. L'archivio e il testimone*. Homo sacer. Vol 3 (Turin: Bollati Boringhieri, 1998), 16 / *Remnants of Auschwitz*, trans. Daniel Heller-Roazen (New York: Zone, 1999), 18. Hereafter as *QRA*.

28. Kafka, *Der Proceß*, 289.

29. Kafka, *Der Proceß*, 126. Agamben quotes the last two sentences in "K.," 38/24.

30. Cf. *RG*, 57/43, 175/157, 185/166, and *A*, 12, 21.

31. Cf. Kafka, ["Der Bau"], in *Nachgelassene Schriften und Fragmente II*, 576-632.

32. Giorgio Agamben, *Mezzi senza fine. Note sulla politica* (Turin: Bollati Boringhieri, 1996), 108 / *Means without End: Notes on Politics*, trans. Vincenzo Binetti and Cesare Casarino (Minneapolis, MN: University of Minnesota Press, 2000), 140. Hereafter as *MSF*. Cf. also 95/122.

33. Agamben, "Heidegger e il nazismo," in *La poteza del pensiero*, 327 (not included in *Potentialities*). Cf. also *MSF* 95/122.

34. Benjamin and Scholem, *Briefwechsel*, 167.

35. Kafka, *Nachgelassene Schriften und Fragmente II*, 122 (the first aphorism is at p. 118). Cf. *UsC* 169/113.

36. For a brief analysis of Agamben's text, cf. Daniel Morris, "Life, or Something Like It: The Philosophical Chiaroscuro of Giorgio Agamben," *Bookforum* (Summer 2004), http://www.bookforum.com/archive/sum_04/morris.html (accessed December 2011); and Vivian Liska, "Die Tradierbarkeit der Lücke in der Zeit: Arendt, Agamben und Kafka," in *Hannah Arendt und Giorgio Agamben. Parallelen, Perspektiven, Kontroversen*, eds. Eva Geulen, Kai Kauffmann and Georg Mein (Munich: Wilhelm Fink, 2008), 191-206.

37. Benjamin and Scholem, *Briefwechsel*, 272. Cf. *UsC* 171/114.

38. Cf. Agamben, *Infanzia e storia*, 108/102, 136/128. On the same topic, cf. also the 1985 essay "Tradizione dell'immemorabile," in *La potenza del pensiero*, 148 / "Tradition of the Immemorial," in *Potentialities*, 104-15.

39. "Idea of Study" is reproduced word for word as the fourth of "Four Glosses on Kafka," under the title "The Students," cf. *QGK* 42-44. For other examples, cf. *SE* 81-83/63-64, and "K.," 48/31. For the messianic connections between Kafka's students and potentiality, cf. Agamben, *Bartleby, la formula della creazione* (Macerata: Quodlibet, 1993), 49, 70, 91 / "Bartleby, or On Contingency," in *Potentialities*, 243-74. With the messianic figure of the students it is possible to associate that of the "assistants"

(*Gehilfe*); cf. Agamben "Gli aiutanti," in *Profanazioni* (Rome: Nottetempo, 2005), 31-38 / "The Assistants," in *Profanations*, trans. Jeff Fort (New York: Zone Books, 2007), 29-36.

40. Kafka, *Der Proceß*, 312.

41. Cf. *MSF* 102/132, and *QRA* 96/104.

42. Cf. Giorgio Agamben, *La comunità che viene* (Turin: Einaudi, 1990), 12, 31, 32 / *The Coming Community*, trans. Michael Hardt (Minneapolis, MN: University of Minnesota Press, 1993) 10, 30, 31. Hereafter as *CV*.

43. The Kafkan statement "there is hope, but not for us" recurs also in *Profanazioni*, 21 (*Profanations*, 21).

44. Kafka, "Vor dem Gesetz," in *Drucke zu Lebzeiten*, 269.

45. Cf. *HS*, 64-65/55. Cf. also Catherine Mills, "Agamben's Messianic Politics: Biopolitics, Abandonment and Happy Life," *Contretemps* 5 (December 2004): 42-62.

46. Kafka, *Nachgelassene Schriften und Fragmente II*, 56-57. Quoted in *HS* 66/57.

47. Benjamin and Scholem, *Briefwechsel*, 167. Cf. *HS* 63-64/54-55.

48. Cf. Franz Kafka, ["Das Schweigen der Sirenen"], in *Nachgelassene Schriften und Frangmente II*, 40-42. Cf. *HS* 67/58. "The Silence of the Sirens" is also evoked in a discussion of language in the 1999 essay "Sull'impossibilità di dire Io: Paradigmi epistemologici e paradigmi poetici in Furio Jesi," in *La potenza del pensiero*, 117 (not included in *Potentialities*).

49. Cf. Franz Kafka, "Der neue Advokat," in *Drucke zu Lebzeiten*, 251-52; cf. *SE* 83/64.

50. Benjamin, "Franz Kafka," 437/815.

51. Cf. also *RG*, 185/166, and "Walter Benjamin e il demonico," 227/153-54.

52. Franz Kafka, ["Von den Gleichnissen"], in *Nachgelassene Schriften und Fragmente II*, 531-32.

53. Benjamin, "Über den Begriff der Geschichte," *Gesammelte Schriften*, vol. 1.2., 704 / "On the Concept of History," in *Selected Writings*, vol. 4, 397.

54. Kafka, *Der Proceß*, 7.

55. "*in dem jahrelangen Studium des Türhüters*," Kafka, *Der Proceß*, 294.

56. Cf. also Justin Clemens, Nicholas Heron and Alex Murray, "The Enigma of Giorgio Agamben," in *The Work of Giorgio Agamben: Law, Literature, Life*, 1-12.

57. Cf. Italo Calvino, *Lezioni americane: Sei proposte per il prossimo millennio* (Milan: Garzanti, 1988 / *Six Memos for the Next Millennium. The Charles Eliot Norton Lectures 1985-86*, trans. Patrick Creagh (New York, Vintage, 1993).

58. Cf. Franz Kafka, "Der Kübelreiter," in *Drucke zu Lebzeiten*, 444-47.

59. The last sentence is a loose translation of part of the first stanza of Hölderlin's "Der Herbst" (Autumn), which reads: "*Die Sagen, die der Erde sich entfernen, / Vom Geiste, der gewesen ist und wiederkehret, / Sie kehren zu der Menschheit sich, und vieles lernen / Wir aus der Zeit, die eilends sich verzehret*" (The fleeing legends, which the Earth narrated / [of spirit that once was and is returning], / are turning toward humanity, so increased learning / can grow from times that long since dissipated), Friedrich Hölderlin, *Sämtliche Werke*, kleine stuttgarter Ausgabe, ed. Friedrich Beissner (Stuttgart: W. Kohlhammer, 1953), vol. 2, 290.

60. Benjamin, "Franz Kafka," 415/799.

61. Benjamin, "Franz Kafka," 418/801.

62. Benjamin, "Franz Kafka," 419/802.

63. Benjamin, "Franz Kafka," 420/802.

64. Benjamin, "Franz Kafka," 422/804.

65. Benjamin, "Franz Kafka," 427/808.

66. The emphases on "means without end" and the mediality of language are, of course, strongly Benjaminian and proceed, respectively, from "Zur Kritik der Gewalt" (1921) (*Gesammelte Schriften*, vol. 2.1, 179-203 [trans. "Critique of Violence," in *Selected Writings*, vol. 1, 236-52]) and the already cited "Über Sprache überhaupt und über die Sprache des Menschen" (1916).

67. Benjamin, "Franz Kafka," 427/808.

68. This accusation is directed mostly, but not only, against Agamben's book on Auschwitz; cf., for example, Philippe Mesnard and Claudine Kahan, *Giorgio Agamben à l'épreuve d'Auschwitz* (Paris: Kimé, 2001).

# Works Cited

Agamben, Giorgio. *Bartleby, la formula della creazione*. Macerata: Quodlibet, 1993.

———. *La comunità che viene*. Turin: Einaudi, 1990. / *The Coming Community*. Translated by Michael Hardt. Minneapolis, MN: University of Minnesota Press, 1993.

———. *Homo sacer. Il potere sovrano e la nuda vita*. Turin: Einaudi, 1995. / *Homo Sacer: Sovereign Power and Bare Life*. Translated by Daniel Heller-Roazen. Stanford, CA: Stanford University Press, 1998.

———. *Idea della prosa*. Milan: Feltrinelli, 1985. / *Idea of Prose*. Translated by Sam Whitsitt and Michael Sullivan. Albany, NY: SUNY Press, 1995.

———. *Infanzia e storia. Distruzione dell'esperienza e origine della storia*. Turin: Einaudi, 1979. / *Infancy and History: On the Destruction of Experience*. Translated by Liz Heron. London: Verso, 1996.

———. "Introduzione." In *Angeli: Ebraismo Cristianesimo Islam*, edited by Giorgio Agamben and Emanuele Coccia, 11-21. Vicenza: Neri Pozza, 2009.

———. *Mezzi senza fine. Note sulla politica*. Turin: Bollati Boringhieri, 1996. / *Means without End: Notes on Politics*. Translated by Vincenzo Binetti and Cesare Casarino. Minneapolis, MN: University of Minnesota Press, 2000.

———. *Nudità*. Rome: Nottetempo, 2009 / *Nudities*. Translated by David Kishik and Stefan Pedatella. Stanford, CA: Stanford University Press, 2011.

———. *La potenza del pensiero. Saggi e conferenze*. Vicenza: Neri Pozza, 2005. / *Potentialities: Collected Essays in Philosophy*. Translated by Daniel Heller-Roazen. Stanford, CA: Stanford University Press, 1999.

———. "Quattro glosse a Kafka," in *Rivista di estetica* 26 (1986): 37-44.

———. *Quel che resta di Auschwitz. L'archivio e il testimone*. Homo sacer. Vol 3. Turin: Bollati Boringhieri, 1998. / *Remnants of Auschwitz*. Translated by Daniel Heller-Roazen. New York: Zone, 1999.

———. *Il regno e la gloria. Per una genealogia teologica dell'economia e del governo*. Homo sacer. Vol. 2/2. Vicenza: Neri Pozza, 2007. / *The Kingdom and the Glory: For a Theological Genealogy of Economy and Government*. Translated by Lorenzo Chiesa and Matteo Mandarini. Stanford, CA: Stanford University Press, 2011.

———. *Stanze. La parola e il fantasma nella cultura occidentale*. Turin: Einaudi, 1979. / *Stanzas: Word and Phantasm in Western Culture*. Translated by Ronald L. Martinez. Minneapolis, MN: University of Minnesota Press, 1993.

———. *Stato di Eccezione*. Homo sacer, Vol 2/1. Turin: Bollati Boringhieri, 2003. / *State of Exception*. Translated by Kevin Attell. Chicago, IL: University of Chicago Press, 2005.

———. *Il tempo che resta. Un commento alla "Lettera ai romani."* Turin: Bollati Boringhieri, 2000. / *The Time that Remains: a Commentary on the Letter to the Romans*. Translated by Patricia Dailey. Stanford, CA: Stanford University Press, 2005.

———. *L'uomo senza contenuto*. Milan: Rizzoli, 1970. / *The Man Without Content*. Translated by Georgia Albert. Stanford, CA: Stanford University Press, 1999.

Bachmann, Ingeborg. *Malina*. Frankfurt a.M: Suhrkamp, 2004.

Benjamin, Walter. "Die Aufgabe des Übersetzers." In Walter Benjamin, *Gesammelte Schriften*, edited by Rolf Tiedemann and Hermann Schweppenhäuser, vol. 4.1, 9-22. Frankfurt a.M: Suhrkamp, 1974ff. / "The Task of the Translator." Translated by Harry Zohn in Walter Benjamin, *Selected Writings*, edited by Michael W. Jennings, vol. 1, 253-63. Cambridge, MA: Belknap, 1997-2003.

———. "Franz Kafka: Zur zehnten Wiederkehr seines Todestages." In *Gesammelte Schriften*, vol. 2.2, 409-37. / "Franz Kafka: On the Tenth Anniversary of His Death." Translated by Harry Zohn in *Selected Writings*, vol. 2, 794-818.

———. "Über den Begriff der Geschichte." In *Gesammelte Schriften*, vol. 1.2, 691-704 / "On the Concept of History." Translated by Harry Zohn in *Selected Writings*, vol. 4, 389-400.

———."Über Sprache überhaupt und über die Sprache des Menschen." In *Gesammelte Schriften*, vol. 2.1, 140-56. / "On Language as Such and on the Language of Man." Translated by Edmond Jephcott in *Selected Writings*, vol. 1, 62-74.

———. "Zur Kritik der Gewalt." In *Gesammelte Schriften*, vol. 2.1, 179-203. / "Critique of Violence." Translated by Edmond Jephcott in *Selected Writings*, vol. 1, 236-52.

Benjamin, Walter, and Gerschom Scholem. *Briefwechsel 1933-1940*. Frankfurt a.M: Suhrkamp, 1980.

Calvino, Italo. *Lezioni americane: Sei proposte per il prossimo millennio*. Milan: Garzanti, 1988. / *Six Memos for the Next Millennium. The Charles Eliot Norton Lectures 1985-86*. Translated by Patrick Creagh. New York, Vintage, 1993.

Clemens, Justin, Nicholas Heron and Alex Murray. "The Enigma of Giorgio Agamben." In *The Work of Giorgio Agamben: Law, Literature, Life*, edited by Justin Clemens, Nicholas Heron and Alex Murray, 1-12. Edinburgh: Edinburgh University Press, 2008.

Hölderlin, Friedrich. *Sämtliche Werke*, kleine stuttgarter Ausgabe, vol. 2. Edited by Friedrich Beissner. Stuttgart: W. Kohlhammer, 1953.

Kafka, Franz. *Kritische Ausgabe. Drucke zu Lebzeiten*. Edited by Wolf Kittler, Hans-Gerd Koch and Gerhard Neumann. Frankfurt a.M.: Fischer, 2002.

———. *Kritische Ausgabe. Nachgelassene Schriften und Fragmente II*. Edited by Jost Schillemeit. Frankfurt a.M.: Fischer, 2002.

———. *Kritische Ausgabe. Der Proceß*. Edited by Jürgen Born, Gerhard Neumann, Malcom Pasley and Jost Schillemeit. Frankfurt a.M: Fischer, 2007.

Liska, Vivian. *Giorgio Agambens leerer Messianismus: Hannah Arendt, Walter Benjamin, Franz Kafka*. Vienna: Schlebrügge, 2008.

———. "Die Tradierbarkeit der Lücke in der Zeit: Arendt, Agamben und Kafka." In *Hannah Arendt und Giorgio Agamben. Parallelen, Perspektiven, Kontroversen*, edited by Eva Geulen, Kai Kauffmann and Georg Mein, 191-206. Munich: Wilhelm Fink, 2008.

Mesnard, Philippe, and Claudine Kahan. *Giorgio Agamben à l'épreuve d'Auschwitz*. Paris: Kimé, 2001.

Mills, Catherine. "Agamben's Messianic Politics: Biopolitics, Abandonment and Happy Life." *Contretemps* 5 (December 2004): 42-62.

Morris, Daniel. "Life, or Something Like It: The Philosophical Chiaroscuro of Giorgio Agamben." *Bookforum*. Summer 2004. http://www.bookforum.com/archive/sum_-04/morris.html (accessed December 2011).

Watkin, William. *The Literary Agamben: Adventures in Logopoiesis*. London: Continuum, 2010.

Whyte, Jessica. "Its Silent Working Was a Delusion." In *The Work of Giorgio Agamben: Law, Literature, Life*, edited by Justin Clemens, Nicholas Heron and Alex Murray, 66-81. Edinburgh: Edinburgh University Press, 2008.

# Index

# About the Contributors

**Paul Alberts** teaches in the areas of ethics, communications and history of political thought in the School of Humanities and Languages at the University of Western Sydney, Australia. He is currently researching and writing on philosophical responses to climate change and environmental issues, in particular how Continental philosophy can contribute to better understanding of the emerging climate change challenges.

**Ronald Bogue** is distinguished research professor and Josiah Meigs Distinguished Teaching Professor in the department of comparative literature at the University of Georgia, USA. His books include *Deleuze and Guattari* (Routledge, 1989), *Deleuze on Literature* (London: Routledge, 2003), *Deleuze on Cinema* (Routledge, 2003), *Deleuze on Music, Painting, and the Arts* (Routledge, 2003), and *Deleuze's Wake* (SUNY Press, 2004).

**Chris Danta** teaches English literature in the School of English, Media and Performing Arts at the University of New South Wales, Australia. His book *Literature Suspends Death: Sacrifice and Storytelling in Kierkegaard, Kafka and Blanchot* has recently appeared (Continuum, 2011); he has co-edited *The Political Animal*, Special Issue of *SubStance* 37.3 (2008).

**Paul Haacke** received his PhD in comparative literature from the University of California, Berkeley, and is currently teaching in the media, culture and communication department at New York University. His work has appeared or is forthcoming in *diacritics*, *French Forum*, *The Review of Contemporary Literature*, *American Book Review*, and *In These Times*, among other publications.

**Brendan Moran** is currently research scholar at the Calgary Institute for the Humanities, and adjunct associate professor at the University of Calgary, Canada, where he has taught in the department of philosophy, the Faculty of Humanities, and the Faculty of Arts. Under the anagrammatic pseudonym Monad Rrenban, he has published *Wild, Unforgettable Philosophy*, a book on Walter Benjamin's early writings. He has also published essays on Benjamin,

Agamben, and Salomo Friedlaender, and is completing a book on Benjamin's Kafkan politics.

**Rainer Nägele** teaches in the department of German studies at Yale University, USA. He has taught and written on German literature from the Baroque to the twentieth century and has written as well on French and classical Greek literature. His many books include: *Heinrich Böll: Einführung in das Werk und die Forschung*; *Peter Handke*; *Literatur und Utopie: Versuche zu Hölderlin*; *Text, Geschichte und Subjektivität in Hölderlins Dichtung: Uneßbarer Schrift gleich*; *Reading after Freud. Essays on Goethe, Hölderlin, Habermas, Nietzsche, Brecht, Celan, and Freud*; *Theater, Theory, Speculation: Walter Benjamin and the Scenes of Modernity*; *Echoes of Translation: Reading Between Texts*; *Lesarten der Moderne: Essays*; *Literarische Vexierbilder: Drei Versuche zu einer Figur*; *Echos: Übersetzen. Lesen zwischen Texten*; *Hölderlins Kritik der poetischen Vernunft*.

**Brian O'Connor** teaches in the school of philosophy at the University College Dublin, Ireland. He has published *Adorno's Negative Dialectic: Philosophy and the Possibility of Critical Rationality* (MIT Press, 2004) and *Adorno: The Routledge Philosophers* (Routledge, 2010), and edited or co-edited *The Adorno Reader* (Blackwells, 2000), *German Idealism: An Anthology and Guide* (Edinburgh University Press, 2006), and *The Routledge Companion to German Idealism* (Routledge, 2010).

**Andrew R. Russ** taught as a tutor and associate lecturer in European studies at the University of Adelaide, Australia, for five years, teaching the literature, philosophy, visual art, politics and history of modern Europe. He is now teaching casually at the University of Sydney in international and global studies and European studies, and the University of Notre Dame (Sydney) in philosophy. Along with this teaching, Andrew Russ has been active in experimental theatre as a founding member of *The Border Project*.

**Carlo Salzani** holds a degree in philosophy from the University of Verona (Italy) and a PhD in comparative literature from Monash University (Australia). He has published *Crisi e possibilità: Robert Musil e il tramonto dell'Occidente* (Peter Lang, 2010), *Constellations of Readings: Walter Benjamin in Figures of Actuality* (Peter Lang, 2009) and co-edited *Essays on Boredom and Modernity* (Rodopi, 2009). He has translated into Italian some of Slavoj Žižek's books.

**Peter Schwenger** is resident fellow at the Centre for the Study of Theory and Criticism, University of Western Ontario, Canada. His most recent book is *The Tears of Things: Melancholy and Physical Objects* (University of Minnesota Press, 2006). Forthcoming is his *At the Borders of Sleep: On Liminal Literature* (University of Minnesota Press, 2012).

**Kevin W. Sweeney** teaches philosophy at the University of Tampa, USA. His research interests center on philosophical aesthetics, ethics, and the history of modern philosophy. In aesthetics, he has published essays on film theory and Hollywood silent comedy, particularly on the silent films of Buster Keaton. He has also published articles analyzing philosophical themes in literary works, including essays on Kafka, Sartre, and Harold Pinter. A previous article on Kafka's *The Metamorphosis* was selected for inclusion in the Norton Critical Edition of *The Metamorphosis* (1996) and republished in Harold Bloom's *Franz Kafka's The Metamorphosis*, New Edition (2008).

**Dimitris Vardoulakis** teaches in the department of writing and society at the University of Western Sydney, Australia. He has published *The Doppelgänger: Literature's Philosophy* (Fordham University Press, 2010) and co-edited the collections *After Blanchot: Literature, Criticism, Philosophy* (University of Delaware Press, 2005), *Spinoza Now* (University of Minnesota Press, 2010), *"Sparks will Fly": Martin Heidegger and Walter Benjamin* (SUNY, forthcoming) and *Freedom and Confinement in Modernity: Kafka's Cages* (Palgrave Macmillan, 2011). He is currently writing a book on sovereignty and another book on prison writings.

**Isak Winkel Holm** is associate professor in the department for arts and cultural studies at the University of Copenhagen. His research field is the interregnum between philosophy and literature: Rousseau, Schlegel, Hegel, Nietzsche, Dostoevsky, Musil, Kafka, Kundera, DeLillo, Sebald, McCarthy. He is presently working on a monograph on Kafka (*Kafka's Justice. An Introduction*, Gyldendal 2012). He has translated the first complete Danish edition of Kafka's stories in two volumes (Franz Kafka, *Fortællinger* and *Efterladte fortællinger*, Gyldendal 2008).

**Karen Zumhagen-Yekplé** is Harvard College Fellow in Comparative Literature at Harvard. Previously, she was a postdoctoral fellow in the Andrew W. Mellon Fellowship of Scholars in the humanities and in the English department at Stanford. She has written articles on Joyce, Kafka, Woolf, Wittgenstein and Piglia. Her current book project, *A Different Order of Difficulty: Question, Quest and Transformative Yearning in Modernism*, examines the ethics of enigma and the unorthodox modern narratives of quest and conversion that resonate in the high-modernist puzzle text. Her next project deals with the legacy of modernism's absorption in riddles and transformative longing in the work of J. M. Coetzee.

Lightning Source UK Ltd.
Milton Keynes UK
UKOW041312100613

212028UK00002B/5/P

9 780739 180891